CHEVY & GMC
ASTRO & SAFARI
COMPACT VANS
1985-1988

By
KALTON C. LAHUE

ALAN AHLSTRAND
Editor

CLYMER PUBLICATIONS

*World's largest publisher of books
devoted exclusively to automobiles and motorcycles*

A division of INTERTEC PUBLISHING CORPORATION
P.O. Box 12901, Overland Park, Kansas 66212

Copyright ©1989 Intertec Publishing Corporation

FIRST EDITION
First Printing March, 1989

Printed in U.S.A.

ISBN: 0-89287-457-0

COVER: *Photographed by Mark Clifford.*

W5P

CONTENTS

QUICK REFERENCE DATA

ENGINE OIL VISCOSITY

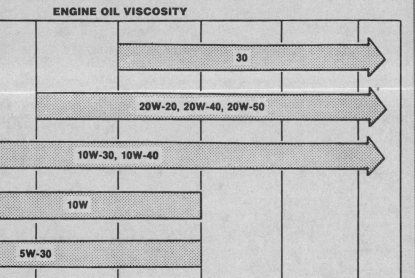

30
20W-20, 20W-40, 20W-50
10W-30, 10W-40
10W
5W-30
5W-20

°F −20   0   20   40   60   80   100

°C −30   −20   −10   0   10   20   30   40

Temperature range anticipated before next oil change

NOTE: Do not use SAE 5W-20 oils for continuous high-speed driving.

APPROXIMATE REFILL CAPACITIES

	qt.	pt.
Engine crankcase		
I4 (with or without filter)	3	
V6		
With filter	5.0	
Without filter	4.0	
Automatic transmission**		
After rebuild		23.0
After fluid change		10.0
Manual transmission		
4-speed	1.3	
5-speed	2.2	
Differential		
7 1/2 in.		3.5
Cooling system*		
I4	10	
V6	13.5	

* If equipped with rear heater, add 2.84 qt.

AUTOMATIC TRANSMISSION FLUID OXIDATION

Temperature (degrees F)	Life expectancy (in miles)
175	100,000
195	50,000
212	25,000
235	12,000
255	6,250
275	3,000
295	1,500
315	750
335	325
355	160
375	80
390	40
415	Less than 30 minutes

STANDARD DRIVE BELT TENSION

Belt	Tension in lbs. New	Used*
I4		
Air conditioning	169	90
Power steering	146	67
V6		
Alternator	135	67
Air conditioning	169	90
AIR pump	146	67
Power steering	146	67

* A belt is considered used after one complete revolution on the engine pulleys.

RECOMMENDED LUBRICANTS

Engine crankcase	API Service SF, SF/CC or SF/CD oil
Engine coolant	Prestone II or equivalent
Brake fluid	Delco Supreme 11 or other DOT 3 or DOT 4 fluid
Power steering pump	GM power steering fluid or equivalent
Manual steering gear	GM lubricant part No. 1051052 or equivalent
Manual transmission	SAE 80W or SAE 80W/90 GL-5 gear lubricant
Rear axle (standard)	SAE 80W or SAE 80W/90 GL-5 gear lubricant
Rear axle (limited slip)	GM part No. 1052271 or equivalent plus 4 oz. GM part No. 1052358 additive or equivalent
Automatic transmission	DEXRON II automatic transmission fluid
Shift linkage	Engine oil
Front wheel bearings	GM lubricant part No. 1051344 or equivalent
Chassis lubrication	GM chassis grease meeting 6031-M specification
Hood latch, all hinges	Engine oil
Windshield washer	GM Optikleen washer solvent or equivalent
Key lock cylinders	WD-40 or equivalent

CHEVY & GMC
ASTRO & SAFARI
COMPACT VANS
1985-1988

INTRODUCTION

This detailed, comprehensive manual covers the 1985-1988 Chevrolet Astro and GMC Safari rear wheel drive M-van. The expert text gives complete information on maintenance, repair and overhaul. Step-by-step instructions and hundreds of illustrations guide you through jobs ranging from simple maintenance to complete overhaul.

This manual can be used by anyone from a first-time do-it-yourselfer to a professional mechanic. Easy to read type, detailed drawings and clear photographs give you all the information you need to do the work right and guide you through every step. The book includes all you need to know to keep your Astro or Safari running right.

Where repairs are practical for the owner/mechanic, complete procedures are given. Equally important, difficult jobs are pointed out. Such operations are usually more economically performed by a dealer or independent garage.

Where special tools are required or recommended, the tool numbers are provided. These tools can often be rented from rental dealers, but they can also be purchased from Kent-Moore Tool Division, 28635 Mound Road, Warren, MI 48092.

A shop manual is a reference. You want to be able to find information fast. As in all Clymer books, this one is designed with such use in mind. All chapters are thumb tabbed. Important frequently used specifications and capacities are summarized on the *Quick Reference Data* pages at the front of the book.

Keep this shop manual handy in your tool box and use it often. It can save you hundreds of dollars in maintenance and repair bills and keep your vehicle reliable and performing well.

CHAPTER ONE

GENERAL INFORMATION

The troubleshooting, tune-up, maintenance, and step-by-step repair procedures in this book are written for the owner and home mechanic. The text is accompanied by useful photos and diagrams to make the job as clear and correct as possible.

Troubleshooting, tune-up, maintenance, and repair are not difficult if you know what tools and equipment to use and what to do. Anyone not afraid to get their hands dirty, of average intelligence, and with some mechanical ability can perform most of the procedures in this book.

In some cases, a repair job may require tools or skills not reasonably expected of the home mechanic. These procedures are noted in each chapter and it is recommended that you take the job to your dealer, a competent mechanic, or machine shop.

MANUAL ORGANIZATION

This chapter provides general information and safety and service hints. Also included are lists of recommended shop and emergency tools as well as a brief description of troubleshooting and tune-up equipment.

Chapter Two provides methods and suggestions for quick and accurate diagnosis and repair of problems. Troubleshooting procedures discuss typical symptoms and logical methods to pinpoint the trouble.

Chapter Three explains all periodic lubrication and routine maintenance necessary to keep your vehicle running well. Chapter Three also includes recommended tune-up procedures, eliminating the need to constantly consult chapters on the various subassemblies.

Subsequent chapters cover specific systems such as the engine, transmission, and electrical systems. Each of these chapters provides disassembly, repair, and assembly procedures in a simple step-by-step format. If a repair requires special skills or tools, or is otherwise impractical for the home mechanic, it is so indicated. In these cases it is usually faster and less expensive to have the repairs made by a dealer or competent repair shop. Necessary specifications concerning a particular system are included at the end of the appropriate chapter.

When special tools are required to perform a procedure included in this manual, the tool is illustrated either in actual use or alone. It may be possible to rent or borrow these tools. The inventive mechanic may also be able to find a suitable substitute in his tool box, or to fabricate one.

The terms NOTE, CAUTION, and WARNING have specific meanings in this manual. A NOTE provides additional or explanatory information. A CAUTION is used to emphasize areas where equipment damage could result if proper precautions are not taken. A WARNING is used to stress those areas where personal injury or death could result from negligence, in addition to possible mechanical damage.

SERVICE HINTS

Observing the following practices will save time, effort, and frustration, as well as prevent possible injury.

Throughout this manual keep in mind two conventions. "Front" refers to the front of the vehicle. The front of any component, such as the transmission, is that end which faces toward the front of the vehicle. The "left" and "right" sides of the vehicle refer to the orientation of a person sitting in the vehicle facing forward. For example, the steering wheel is on the left side. These rules are simple, but even experienced mechanics occasionally become disoriented.

Most of the service procedures covered are straightforward and can be performed by anyone reasonably handy with tools. It is suggested, however, that you consider your own capabilities carefully before attempting any operation involving major disassembly of the engine.

Some operations, for example, require the use of a press. It would be wiser to have these performed by a shop equipped for such work, rather than to try to do the job yourself with makeshift equipment. Other procedures require precision measurements. Unless you have the skills and equipment required, it would be better to have a qualified repair shop make the measurements for you.

Repairs go much faster and easier if the parts that will be worked on are clean before you begin. There are special cleaners for washing the engine and related parts. Brush or spray on the cleaning solution, let it stand, then rinse it away with a garden hose. Clean all oily or greasy parts with cleaning solvent as you remove them.

WARNING
Never use gasoline as a cleaning agent. It presents an extreme fire hazard. Be sure to work in a well-ventilated area when using cleaning solvent. Keep a fire extinguisher, rated for gasoline fires, handy in any case.

Much of the labor charge for repairs made by dealers is for the removal and disassembly of other parts to reach the defective unit. It is frequently possible to perform the preliminary operations yourself and then take the defective unit in to the dealer for repair, at considerable savings.

Once you have decided to tackle the job yourself, make sure you locate the appropriate section in this manual, and read it entirely. Study the illustrations and text until you have a good idea of what is involved in completing the job satisfactorily. If special tools are required, make arrangements to get them before you start. Also, purchase any known defective parts prior to starting on the procedure. It is frustrating and time-consuming to get partially into a job and then be unable to complete it.

Simple wiring checks can be easily made at home, but knowledge of electronics is almost a necessity for performing tests with complicated electronic testing gear.

During disassembly of parts keep a few general cautions in mind. Force is rarely needed to get things apart. If parts are a tight fit, like a bearing in a case, there is usually a tool designed to separate them. Never use a screwdriver to pry apart parts with machined surfaces such as cylinder head and valve cover. You will mar the surfaces and end up with leaks.

Make diagrams wherever similar-appearing parts are found. You may think you can remember where everything came from — but mistakes are costly. There is also the possibility you may get sidetracked and not return to work for days or even weeks — in which interval, carefully laid out parts may have become disturbed.

Tag all similar internal parts for location, and mark all mating parts for position. Record number and thickness of any shims as they are removed. Small parts such as bolts can be iden-

1

tified by placing them in plastic sandwich bags that are sealed and labeled with masking tape.

Wiring should be tagged with masking tape and marked as each wire is removed. Again, do not rely on memory alone.

When working under the vehicle, do not trust a hydraulic or mechanical jack to hold the vehicle up by itself. Always use jackstands. See **Figure 1**.

Disconnect battery ground cable before working near electrical connections and before disconnecting wires. Never run the engine with the battery disconnected; the alternator could be seriously damaged.

Protect finished surfaces from physical damage or corrosion. Keep gasoline and brake fluid off painted surfaces.

Frozen or very tight bolts and screws can often be loosened by soaking with penetrating oil like Liquid Wrench or WD-40, then sharply striking the bolt head a few times with a hammer and punch (or screwdriver for screws). Avoid heat unless absolutely necessary, since it may melt, warp, or remove the temper from many parts.

Avoid flames or sparks when working near a charging battery or flammable liquids, such as brake fluid or gasoline.

No parts, except those assembled with a press fit, require unusual force during assembly. If a part is hard to remove or install, find out why before proceeding.

Cover all openings after removing parts to keep dirt, small tools, etc., from falling in.

When assembling two parts, start all fasteners, then tighten evenly.

The clutch plate, wiring connections, brake shoes, drums, pads, and discs should be kept clean and free of grease and oil.

When assembling parts, be sure all shims and washers are replaced exactly as they came out.

Whenever a rotating part butts against a stationary part, look for a shim or washer. Use new gaskets if there is any doubt about the condition of old ones. Generally, you should apply gasket cement to one mating surface only, so the parts may be easily disassembled in the future. A thin coat of oil on gaskets helps them seal effectively.

Heavy grease can be used to hold small parts in place if they tend to fall out during assembly. However, keep grease and oil away from electrical, clutch, and brake components.

High spots may be sanded off a piston with sandpaper, but emery cloth and oil do a much more professional job.

Carburetors are best cleaned by disassembling them and soaking the parts in a commercial carburetor cleaner. Never soak gaskets and rubber parts in these cleaners. Never use wire to clean out jets and air passages; they are easily damaged. Use compressed air to blow out the carburetor, but only if the float has been removed first.

Take your time and do the job right. Do not forget that a newly rebuilt engine must be broken in the same as a new one. Refer to your owner's manual for the proper break-in procedures.

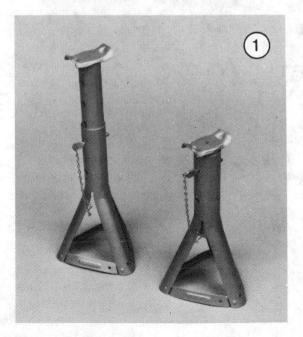

SAFETY FIRST

Professional mechanics can work for years and never sustain a serious injury. If you observe a few rules of common sense and safety, you can enjoy many safe hours servicing your vehicle. You could hurt yourself or damage the vehicle if you ignore these rules.

1. Never use gasoline as a cleaning solvent.

2. Never smoke or use a torch in the vicinity of flammable liquids such as cleaning solvent in open containers.

3. Never smoke or use a torch in an area where batteries are being charged. Highly explosive hydrogen gas is formed during the charging process.

4. Use the proper sized wrenches to avoid damage to nuts and injury to yourself.

5. When loosening a tight or stuck nut, be guided by what would happen if the wrench should slip. Protect yourself accordingly.

6. Keep your work area clean and uncluttered.

7. Wear safety goggles during all operations involving drilling, grinding, or use of a cold chisel.

8. Never use worn tools.

9. Keep a fire extinguisher handy and be sure it is rated for gasoline (Class B) and electrical (Class C) fires.

EXPENDABLE SUPPLIES

Certain expendable supplies are necessary. These include grease, oil, gasket cement, wiping rags, cleaning solvent, and distilled water.

Also, special locking compounds, silicone lubricants, and engine cleaners may be useful. Cleaning solvent is available at most service stations and distilled water for the battery is available at most supermarkets.

SHOP TOOLS

For proper servicing, you will need an assortment of ordinary hand tools (**Figure 2**).

As a minimum, these include:

  a. Combination wrenches
  b. Sockets
  c. Plastic mallet
  d. Small hammer
  e. Snap ring pliers
  f. Gas pliers
  g. Phillips screwdrivers
  h. Slot (common) screwdrivers
  i. Feeler gauges
  j. Spark plug gauge
  k. Spark plug wrench

Special tools necessary are shown in the chapters covering the particular repair in which they are used.

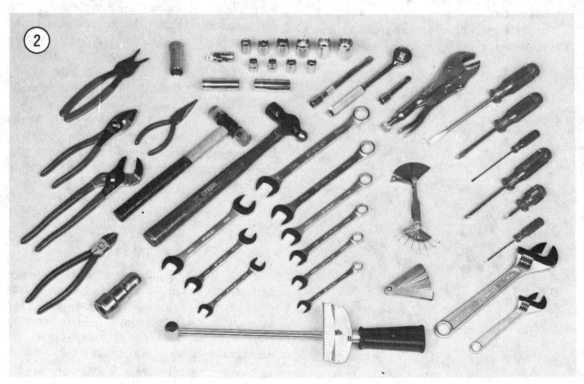

Engine tune-up and troubleshooting procedures require other special tools and equipment. These are described in detail in the following sections.

EMERGENCY TOOL KIT

A small emergency tool kit kept in the trunk is handy for road emergencies which otherwise could leave you stranded. The tools listed below and shown in **Figure 3** will let you handle most roadside repairs.

a. Combination wrenches

b. Crescent (adjustable) wrench

c. Screwdrivers — common and Phillips

d. Pliers — conventional (gas) and needle nose

e. Vise Grips

f. Hammer — plastic and metal

g. Small container of waterless hand cleaner

h. Rags for clean up

i. Silver waterproof sealing tape (duct tape)

j. Flashlight

k. Emergency road flares — at least four

l. Spare drive belts (water pump, alternator. etc.)

TROUBLESHOOTING AND TUNE-UP EQUIPMENT

Voltmeter, Ohmmeter, and Ammeter

For testing the ignition or electrical system, a good voltmeter is required. For automotive use, an instrument covering 0-20 volts is satisfac-

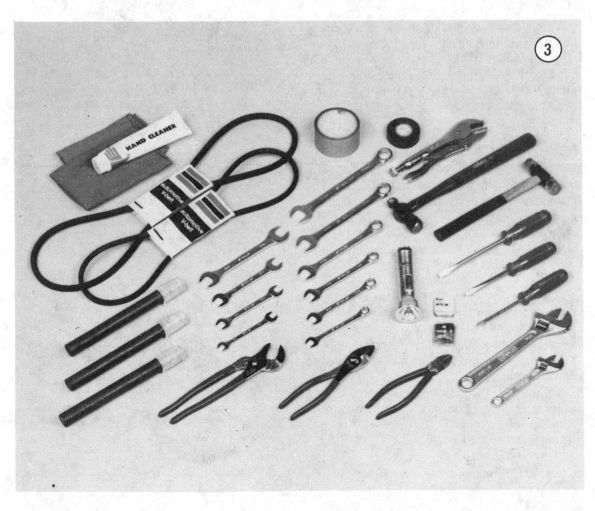

tory. One which also has a 0-2 volt scale is necessary for testing relays, points, or individual contacts where voltage drops are much smaller. Accuracy should be ± ½ volt.

An ohmmeter measures electrical resistance. This instrument is useful for checking continuity (open and short circuits), and testing fuses and lights.

The ammeter measures electrical current. Ammeters for automotive use should cover 0-50 amperes and 0-250 amperes. These are useful for checking battery charging and starting current.

Several inexpensive VOM's (volt-ohm-milliammeter) combine all three instruments into one which fits easily in any tool box. See **Figure 4**. However, the ammeter ranges are usually too small for automotive work.

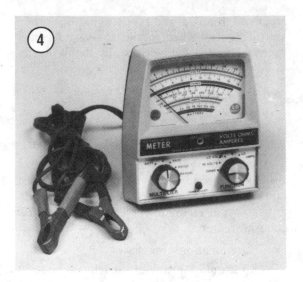

Hydrometer

The hydrometer gives a useful indication of battery condition and charge by measuring the specific gravity of the electrolyte in each cell. See **Figure 5**. Complete details on use and interpretation of readings are provided in the electrical chapter.

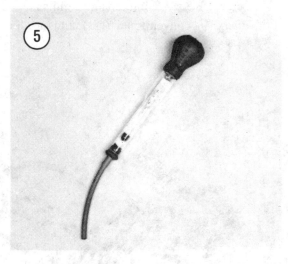

Compression Tester

The compression tester measures the compression pressure built up in each cylinder. The results, when properly interpreted, can indicate general cylinder and valve condition. See **Figure 6**.

Vacuum Gauge

The vacuum gauge (**Figure 7**) is one of the easiest instruments to use, but one of the most difficult for the inexperienced mechanic to interpret. The results, when interpreted with other findings, can provide valuable clues to possible trouble.

To use the vacuum gauge, connect it to a vacuum hose that goes to the intake manifold. Attach it either directly to the hose or to a T-fitting installed into the hose.

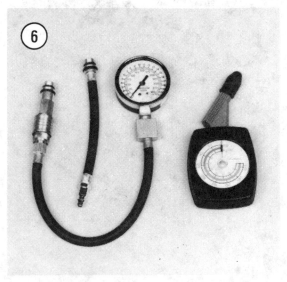

NOTE: *Subtract one inch from the reading for every 1,000 ft. elevation.*

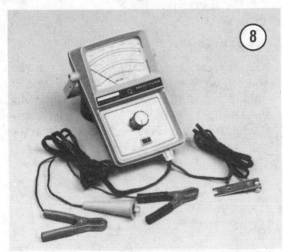

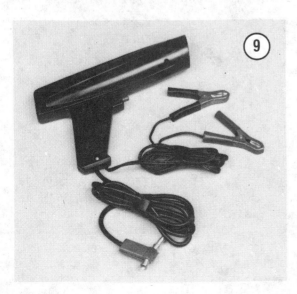

Fuel Pressure Gauge

This instrument is invaluable for evaluating fuel pump performance. Fuel system trouble-shooting procedures in this manual use a fuel pressure gauge. Usually a vacuum gauge and fuel pressure gauge are combined.

Dwell Meter (Contact Breaker Point Ignition Only)

A dwell meter measures the distance in degrees of cam rotation that the breaker points remain closed while the engine is running. Since this angle is determined by breaker point gap, dwell angle is an accurate indication of breaker point gap.

Many tachometers intended for tuning and testing incorporate a dwell meter as well. See **Figure 8**. Follow the manufacturer's instructions to measure dwell.

Tachometer

A tachometer is necessary for tuning. See **Figure 8**. Ignition timing and carburetor adjustments must be performed at the specified idle speed. The best instrument for this purpose is one with a low range of 0-1,000 or 0-2,000 rpm for setting idle, and a high range of 0-4,000 or more for setting ignition timing at 3,000 rpm. Extended range (0-6,000 or 0-8,000 rpm) instruments lack accuracy at lower speeds. The instrument should be capable of detecting changes of 25 rpm on the low range.

Strobe Timing Light

This instrument is necessary for tuning, as it permits very accurate ignition timing. The light flashes at precisely the same instant that No. 1 cylinder fires, at which time the timing marks on the engine should align. Refer to Chapter Three for exact location of the timing marks for your engine.

Suitable lights range from inexpensive neon bulb types ($2-3) to powerful xenon strobe lights ($20-40). See **Figure 9**. Neon timing lights are difficult to see and must be used in dimly lit areas. Xenon strobe timing lights can be used outside in bright sunlight. Both types work on this vehicle; use according to the manufacturer's instructions.

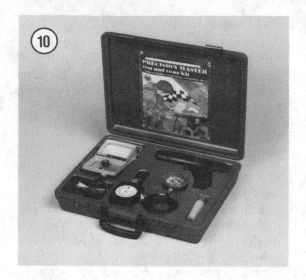

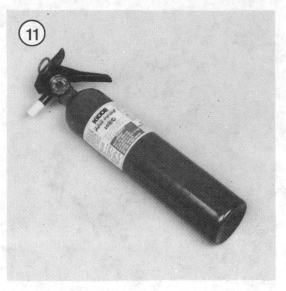

Tune-up Kits

Many manufacturer's offer kits that combine several useful instruments. Some come in a convenient carry case and are usally less expensive than purchasing one instrument at a time. **Figure 10** shows one of the kits that is available. The prices vary with the number of instruments included in the kit.

Fire Extinguisher

A fire extinguisher is a necessity when working on a vehicle. It should be rated for both *Class B* (flammable liquids—gasoline, oil, paint, etc.) and *Class C* (electrical—wiring, etc.) type fires. It should always be kept within reach. See **Figure 11**.

CHAPTER TWO

TROUBLESHOOTING

Troubleshooting can be a relatively simple matter if it is done logically. The first step in any troubleshooting procedure must be defining the symptoms as closely as possible. Subsequent steps involve testing and analyzing areas which could cause the symptoms. A haphazard approach may eventually find the trouble, but in terms of wasted time and unnecessary parts replacement, it can be very costly.

The troubleshooting procedures in this chapter analyze typical symptoms and show logical methods of isolation. These are not the only methods. There may be several approaches to a problem, but all methods must have one thing in common — a logical, systematic approach.

STARTING SYSTEM

The starting system consists of the starter motor and the starter solenoid. The ignition key controls the starter solenoid, which mechanically engages the starter with the engine flywheel, and supplies electrical current to turn the starter motor.

Starting system troubles are relatively easy to find. In most cases, the trouble is a loose or dirty electrical connection. **Figures 1 and 2** provide routines for finding the trouble.

CHARGING SYSTEM

The charging system consists of the alternator (or generator on older vehicles), voltage regulator, and battery. A drive belt driven by the engine crankshaft turns the alternator which produces electrical energy to charge the battery. As engine speed varies, the voltage from the alternator varies. A voltage regulator controls the charging current to the battery and maintains the voltage to the vehicle's electrical system at safe levels. A warning light or gauge on the instrument panel signals the driver when charging is not taking place. Refer to **Figure 3** for a typical charging system.

Complete troubleshooting of the charging system requires test equipment and skills which the average home mechanic does not possess. However, there are a few tests which can be done to pinpoint most troubles.

Charging system trouble may stem from a defective alternator (or generator), voltage regulator, battery, or drive belt. It may also be caused by something as simple as incorrect drive belt tension. The following are symptoms of typical problems you may encounter.

1. *Battery dies frequently, even though the warning lamp indicates no discharge* — This can be caused by a drive belt that is slightly too

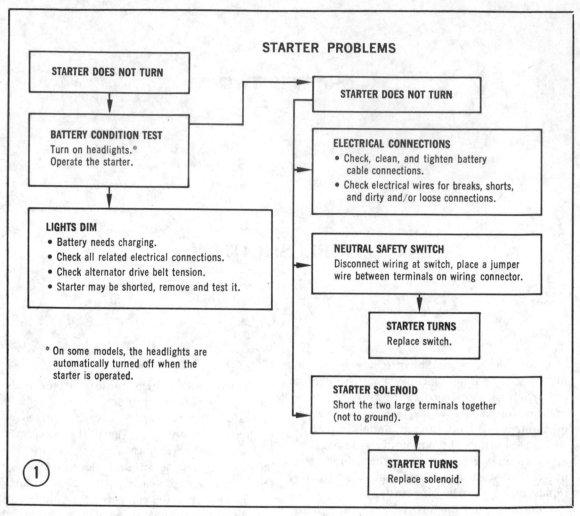

STARTER PROBLEMS

STARTER DOES NOT TURN

BATTERY CONDITION TEST
Turn on headlights.*
Operate the starter.

LIGHTS DIM
• Battery needs charging.
• Check all related electrical connections.
• Check alternator drive belt tension.
• Starter may be shorted, remove and test it.

* On some models, the headlights are
automatically turned off when the
starter is operated.

STARTER DOES NOT TURN

ELECTRICAL CONNECTIONS
• Check, clean, and tighten battery
cable connections.
• Check electrical wires for breaks, shorts,
and dirty and/or loose connections.

NEUTRAL SAFETY SWITCH
Disconnect wiring at switch, place a jumper
wire between terminals on wiring connector.

STARTER TURNS
Replace switch.

STARTER SOLENOID
Short the two large terminals together
(not to ground).

STARTER TURNS
Replace solenoid.

①

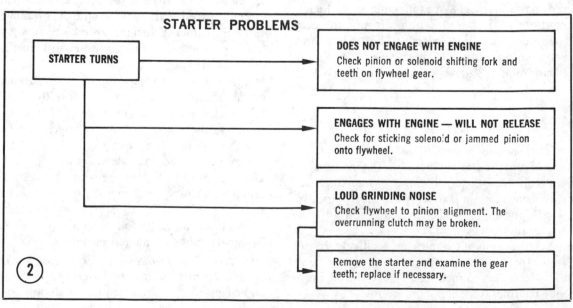

STARTER PROBLEMS

STARTER TURNS

DOES NOT ENGAGE WITH ENGINE
Check pinion or solenoid shifting fork and
teeth on flywheel gear.

ENGAGES WITH ENGINE — WILL NOT RELEASE
Check for sticking solenoid or jammed pinion
onto flywheel.

LOUD GRINDING NOISE
Check flywheel to pinion alignment. The
overrunning clutch may be broken.

Remove the starter and examine the gear
teeth; replace if necessary.

②

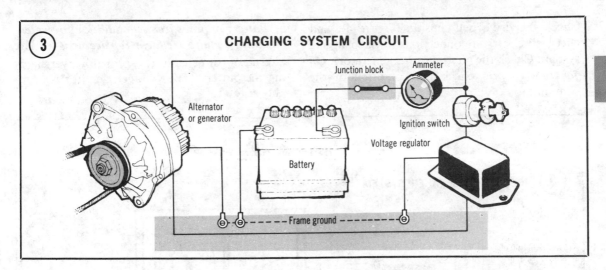

③ **CHARGING SYSTEM CIRCUIT**

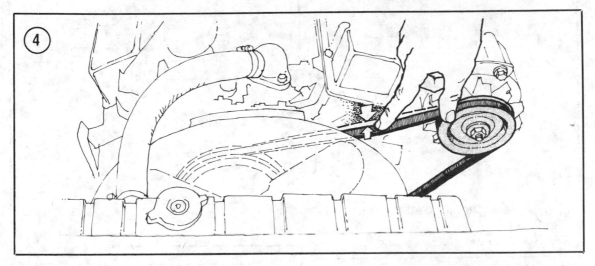

④

loose. Grasp the alternator (or generator) pulley and try to turn it. If the pulley can be turned without moving the belt, the drive belt is too loose. As a rule, keep the belt tight enough that it can be deflected about ½ in. under moderate thumb pressure between the pulleys (**Figure 4**). The battery may also be at fault; test the battery condition.

2. *Charging system warning lamp does not come on when ignition switch is turned on* — This may indicate a defective ignition switch, battery, voltage regulator, or lamp. First try to start the vehicle. If it doesn't start, check the ignition switch and battery. If the car starts, remove the warning lamp; test it for continuity with an ohmmeter or substitute a new lamp. If the lamp is good, locate the voltage regulator

and make sure it is properly grounded (try tightening the mounting screws). Also the alternator (or generator) brushes may not be making contact. Test the alternator (or generator) and voltage regulator.

3. *Alternator (or generator) warning lamp comes on and stays on* — This usually indicates that no charging is taking place. First check drive belt tension (**Figure 4**). Then check battery condition, and check all wiring connections in the charging system. If this does not locate the trouble, check the alternator (or generator) and voltage regulator.

4. *Charging system warning lamp flashes on and off intermittently* — This usually indicates the charging system is working intermittently.

Check the drive belt tension (**Figure 4**), and check all electrical connections in the charging system. Check the alternator (or generator). *On generators only*, check the condition of the commutator.

5. *Battery requires frequent additions of water, or lamps require frequent replacement* — The alternator (or generator) is probably overcharging the battery. The voltage regulator is probably at fault.

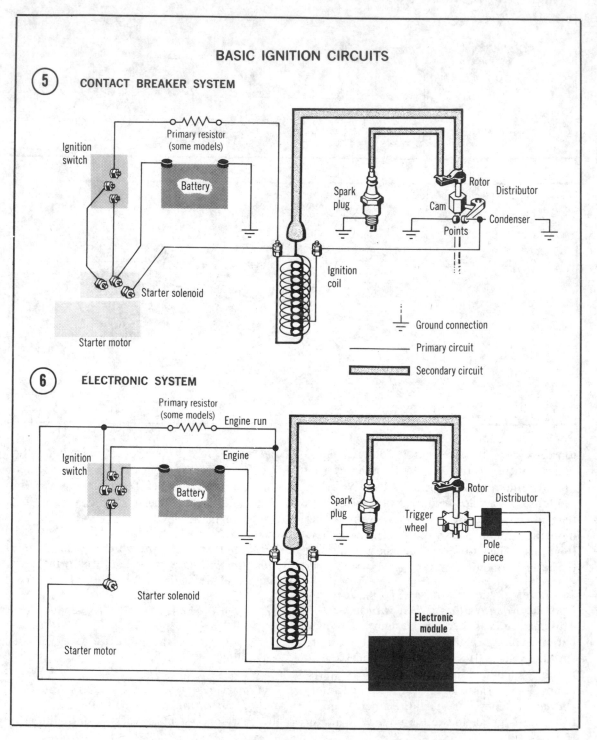

BASIC IGNITION CIRCUITS

⑤ CONTACT BREAKER SYSTEM

Primary resistor (some models)
Ignition switch
Battery
Spark plug
Rotor
Distributor
Cam
Condenser
Points
Ignition coil
Starter solenoid
Starter motor

⏚ Ground connection
—— Primary circuit
▭ Secondary circuit

⑥ ELECTRONIC SYSTEM

Primary resistor (some models)
Engine run
Ignition switch
Engine
Battery
Spark plug
Rotor
Distributor
Trigger wheel
Pole piece
Starter solenoid
Electronic module
Starter motor

6. *Excessive noise from the alternator (or generator)* — Check for loose mounting brackets and bolts. The problem may also be worn bearings or the need of lubrication in some cases. If an alternator whines, a shorted diode may be indicated.

IGNITION SYSTEM

The ignition system may be either a conventional contact breaker type or an electronic ignition. See electrical chapter to determine which type you have. **Figures 5 and 6** show simplified diagrams of each type.

Most problems involving failure to start, poor performance, or rough running stem from trouble in the ignition system, particularly in contact breaker systems. Many novice troubleshooters get into trouble when they assume that these symptoms point to the fuel system instead of the ignition system.

Ignition system troubles may be roughly divided between those affecting only one cylinder and those affecting all cylinders. If the trouble affects only one cylinder, it can only be in the spark plug, spark plug wire, or portion of the distributor associated with that cylinder. If the trouble affects all cylinders (weak spark or no spark), then the trouble is in the ignition coil, rotor, distributor, or associated wiring.

The troubleshooting procedures outlined in **Figure 7** (breaker point ignition) or **Figure 8**

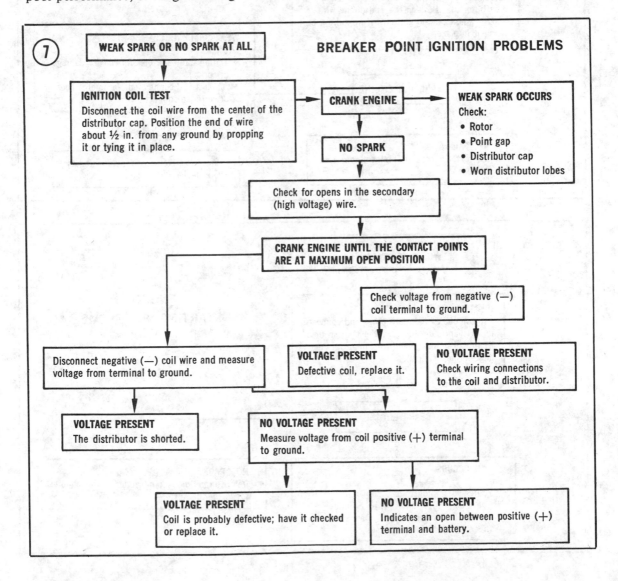

(electronic ignition) will help you isolate ignition problems fast. Of course, they assume that the battery is in good enough condition to crank the engine over at its normal rate.

ENGINE PERFORMANCE

A number of factors can make the engine difficult or impossible to start, or cause rough running, poor performance and so on. The majority of novice troubleshooters immediately suspect the carburetor or fuel injection system. In the majority of cases, though, the trouble exists in the ignition system.

The troubleshooting procedures outlined in **Figures 9 through 14** will help you solve the majority of engine starting troubles in a systematic manner.

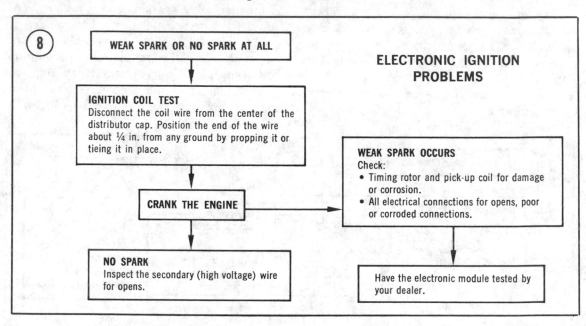

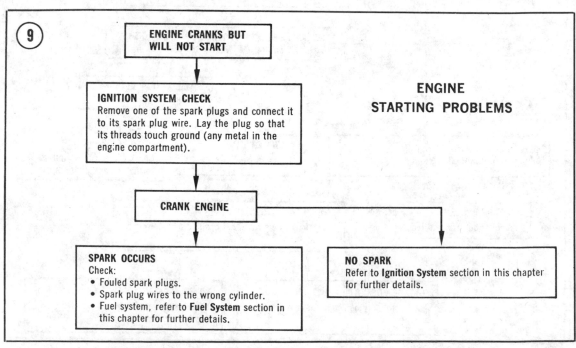

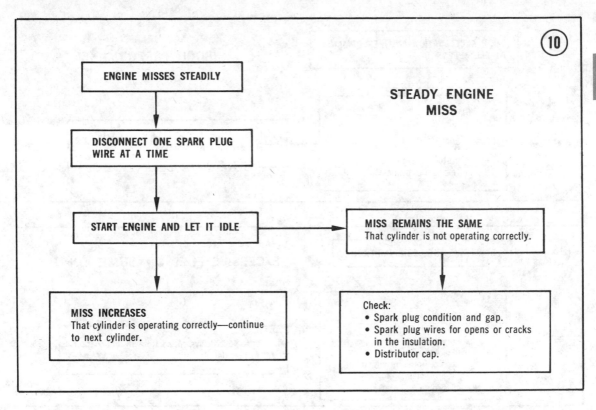

⑩

ENGINE MISSES STEADILY

↓

DISCONNECT ONE SPARK PLUG
WIRE AT A TIME

↓

START ENGINE AND LET IT IDLE → MISS REMAINS THE SAME
                                  That cylinder is not operating correctly.

↓   ↓

MISS INCREASES   Check:
That cylinder is operating correctly—continue   • Spark plug condition and gap.
to next cylinder.   • Spark plug wires for opens or cracks
                                    in the insulation.
                                  • Distributor cap.

STEADY ENGINE
MISS

2

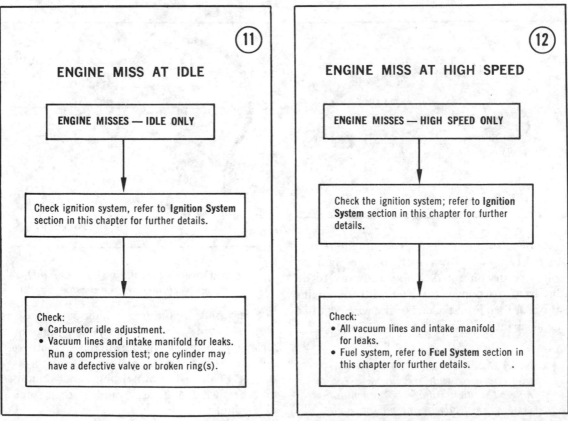

⑪

ENGINE MISS AT IDLE

ENGINE MISSES — IDLE ONLY

↓

Check ignition system, refer to **Ignition System**
section in this chapter for further details.

↓

Check:
• Carburetor idle adjustment.
• Vacuum lines and intake manifold for leaks.
  Run a compression test; one cylinder may
  have a defective valve or broken ring(s).

⑫

ENGINE MISS AT HIGH SPEED

ENGINE MISSES — HIGH SPEED ONLY

↓

Check the ignition system; refer to **Ignition
System** section in this chapter for further
details.

↓

Check:
• All vacuum lines and intake manifold
  for leaks.
• Fuel system, refer to **Fuel System** section in
  this chapter for further details.

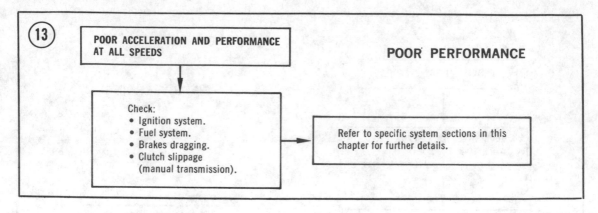

⑬ POOR ACCELERATION AND PERFORMANCE AT ALL SPEEDS

POOR PERFORMANCE

Check:
• Ignition system.
• Fuel system.
• Brakes dragging.
• Clutch slippage (manual transmission).

Refer to specific system sections in this chapter for further details.

⑭ EXCESSIVE FUEL CONSUMPTION

EXCESSIVE FUEL CONSUMPTION

Check:
• Brakes dragging.
• Clutch slippage (manual transmission).
• Wheel bearings.
• Incorrect front end alignment.
• Ignition system.
• Fuel system.

Refer to specific system sections in this chapter for further details.

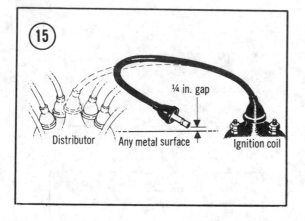

⑮ ¼ in. gap

Distributor   Any metal surface   Ignition coil

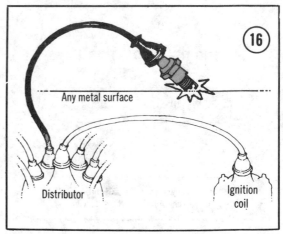

⑯ Any metal surface

Distributor   Ignition coil

Some tests of the ignition system require running the engine with a spark plug or ignition coil wire disconnected. The safest way to do this is to disconnect the wire with the engine stopped, then prop the end of the wire next to a metal surface as shown in **Figures 15 and 16**.

WARNING
Never disconnect a spark plug or ignition coil wire while the engine is running. The high voltage in an ignition system, particularly the newer high-energy electronic ignition systems could cause serious injury or even death.

Spark plug condition is an important indication of engine performance. Spark plugs in a properly operating engine will have slightly pitted electrodes, and a light tan insulator tip. **Figure 17** shows a normal plug, and a number of others which indicate trouble in their respective cylinders.

2

- Appearance—Firing tip has deposits of light gray to light tan.
- Can be cleaned, regapped and reused.

- Appearance—Glazed yellow deposits with a slight brownish tint on the insulator tip and ground electrode.
- Replace with new plugs.

- Appearance—Dull, dry black with fluffy carbon deposits on the insulator tip, electrode and exposed shell.
- Caused by—Fuel/air mixture too rich, plug heat range too cold, weak ignition system, dirty air cleaner, faulty automatic choke or excessive idling.
- Can be cleaned, regapped and reused.

- Appearance — Brown colored hardened ash deposits on the insulator tip and ground electrode.
- Caused by—Fuel and/or oil additives.
- Replace with new plugs.

- Appearance — Severely worn or eroded electrodes.
- Caused by—Normal wear or unusual oil and/or fuel additives.
- Replace with new plugs.

- Appearance—Wet black deposits on insulator and exposed shell.
- Caused by—Excessive oil entering the combustion chamber through worn rings, pistons, valve guides or bearings.
- Replace with new plugs (use a hotter plug if engine is not repaired).

- Appearance — Melted ground electrode.
- Caused by—Overadvanced ignition timing, inoperative ignition advance mechanism, too low of a fuel octane rating, lean fuel/air mixture or carbon deposits in combustion chamber.

- Appearance — Yellow insulator deposits (may sometimes be dark gray, black or tan in color) on the insulator tip.
- Caused by—Highly leaded gasoline.
- Replace with new plugs.

- Appearance—Melted center electrode.
- Caused by—Abnormal combustion due to overadvanced ignition timing or incorrect advance, too low of a fuel octane rating, lean fuel/air mixture, or carbon deposits in combustion chamber.
- Correct engine problem and replace with new plugs.

- Appearance—Yellow glazed deposits indicating melted lead deposits due to hard acceleration.
- Caused by—Highly leaded gasoline.
- Replace with new plugs.

- Appearance—Melted center electrode and white blistered insulator tip.
- Caused by—Incorrect plug heat range selection.
- Replace with new plugs.

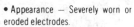

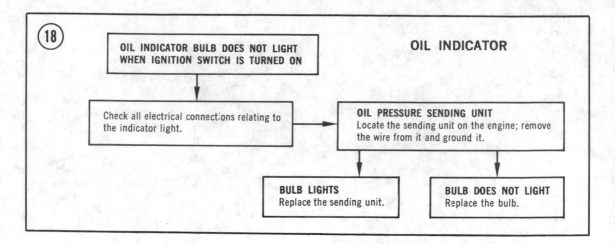

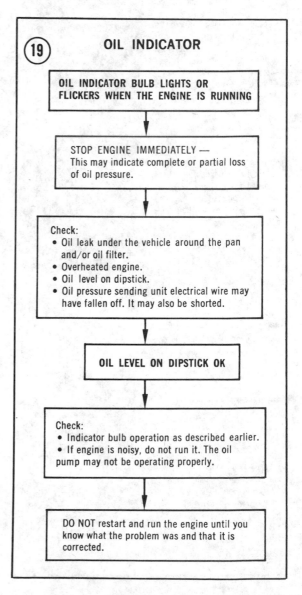

ENGINE OIL PRESSURE LIGHT

Proper oil pressure to the engine is vital. If oil pressure is insufficient, the engine can destroy itself in a comparatively short time.

The oil pressure warning circuit monitors oil pressure constantly. If pressure drops below a predetermined level, the light comes on.

Obviously, it is vital for the warning circuit to be working to signal low oil pressure. Each time you turn on the ignition, but before you start the car, the warning light should come on. If it doesn't, there is trouble in the warning circuit, not the oil pressure system. See **Figure 18** to troubleshoot the warning circuit.

Once the engine is running, the warning light should stay off. If the warning light comes on or acts erratically while the engine is running there is trouble with the engine oil pressure system. *Stop the engine immediately*. Refer to **Figure 19** for possible causes of the problem.

FUEL SYSTEM (CARBURETTED)

Fuel system problems must be isolated to the fuel pump (mechanical or electric), fuel lines, fuel filter, or carburetor. These procedures assume the ignition system is working properly and is correctly adjusted.

1. *Engine will not start* — First make sure that fuel is being delivered to the carburetor. Remove the air cleaner, look into the carburetor throat, and operate the accelerator

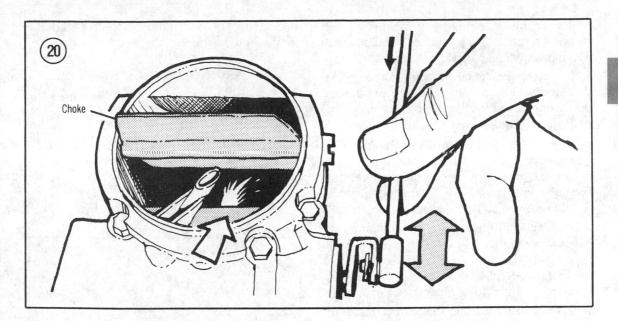

Choke

linkage several times. There should be a stream of fuel from the accelerator pump discharge tube each time the accelerator linkage is depressed **(Figure 20)**. If not, check fuel pump delivery (described later), float valve, and float adjustment. If the engine will not start, check the automatic choke parts for sticking or damage. If necessary, rebuild or replace the carburetor.

2. *Engine runs at fast idle* — Check the choke setting. Check the idle speed, idle mixture, and decel valve (if equipped) adjustment.

3. *Rough idle or engine miss with frequent stalling* — Check idle mixture and idle speed adjustments.

4. *Engine "diesels" (continues to run) when ignition is switched off* — Check idle mixture (probably too rich), ignition timing, and idle speed (probably too fast). Check the throttle solenoid (if equipped) for proper operation. Check for overheated engine.

5. *Stumbling when accelerating from idle* — Check the idle speed and mixture adjustments. Check the accelerator pump.

6. *Engine misses at high speed or lacks power* — This indicates possible fuel starvation. Check fuel pump pressure and capacity as described in this chapter. Check float needle valves. Check for a clogged fuel filter or air cleaner.

7. *Black exhaust smoke* — This indicates a badly overrich mixture. Check idle mixture and idle speed adjustment. Check choke setting. Check for excessive fuel pump pressure, leaky floats, or worn needle valves.

8. *Excessive fuel consumption* — Check for overrich mixture. Make sure choke mechanism works properly. Check idle mixture and idle speed. Check for excessive fuel pump pressure, leaky floats, or worn float needle valves.

FUEL SYSTEM (FUEL INJECTED)

Troubleshooting a fuel injection system requires more thought, experience, and knowhow than any other part of the vehicle. A logical approach and proper test equipment are essential in order to successfully find and fix these troubles.

It is best to leave fuel injection troubles to your dealer. In order to isolate a problem to the injection system make sure that the fuel pump is operating properly. Check its performance as described later in this section. Also make sure that fuel filter and air cleaner are not clogged.

FUEL PUMP TEST (MECHANICAL AND ELECTRIC)

1. Disconnect the fuel inlet line where it enters the carburetor or fuel injection system.

2. Fit a rubber hose over the fuel line so fuel can be directed into a graduated container with about one quart capacity. See **Figure 21**.

3. To avoid accidental starting of the engine, disconnect the secondary coil wire from the coil or disconnect and insulate the coil primary wire.

4. Crank the engine for about 30 seconds.

5. If the fuel pump supplies the specified amount (refer to the fuel chapter later in this book), the trouble may be in the carburetor or fuel injection system. The fuel injection system should be tested by your dealer.

6. If there is no fuel present or the pump cannot supply the specified amount, either the fuel pump is defective or there is an obstruction in the fuel line. Replace the fuel pump and/or inspect the fuel lines for air leaks or obstructions.

7. Also pressure test the fuel pump by installing a T-fitting in the fuel line between the fuel pump and the carburetor. Connect a fuel pressure gauge to the fitting with a short tube (**Figure 22**).

8. Reconnect the coil wire, start the engine, and record the pressure. Refer to the fuel chapter later in this book for the correct pressure. If the pressure varies from that specified, the pump should be replaced.

9. Stop the engine. The pressure should drop off very slowly. If it drops off rapidly, the outlet valve in the pump is leaking and the pump should be replaced.

EMISSION CONTROL SYSTEMS

Major emission control systems used on nearly all U.S. models include the following:

a. Positive crankcase ventilation (PCV)

b. Thermostatic air cleaner

c. Air injection reaction (AIR)

d. Fuel evaporation control

e. Exhaust gas recirculation (EGR)

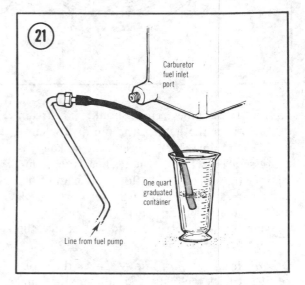

(21) Carburetor fuel inlet port

One quart graduated container

Line from fuel pump

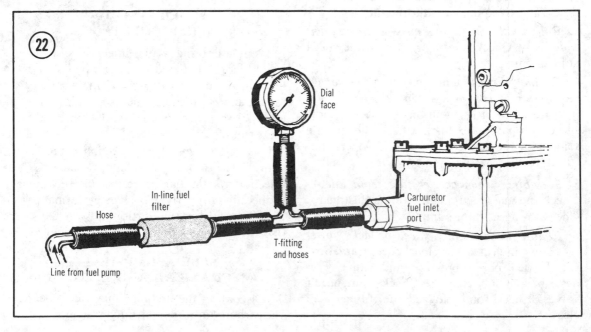

(22) Dial face

Carburetor fuel inlet port

In-line fuel filter

Hose

T-fitting and hoses

Line from fuel pump

Emission control systems vary considerably from model to model. Individual models contain variations of the four systems described here. In addition, they may include other special systems. Use the index to find specific emission control components in other chapters.

Many of the systems and components are factory set and sealed. Without special expensive test equipment, it is impossible to adjust the systems to meet state and federal requirements.

Troubleshooting can also be difficult without special equipment. The procedures described below will help you find emission control parts which have failed, but repairs may have to be entrusted to a dealer or other properly equipped repair shop.

With the proper equipment, you can test the carbon monoxide and hydrocarbon levels.

Figure 23 provides some sources of trouble if the readings are not correct.

Positive Crankcase Ventilation

Fresh air drawn from the air cleaner housing scavenges emissions (e.g., piston blow-by) from the crankcase, then the intake manifold vacuum draws emissions into the intake manifold. They can then be reburned in the normal combustion process. **Figure 24** shows a typical system. **Figure 25** provides a testing procedure.

Thermostatic Air Cleaner

The thermostatically controlled air cleaner maintains incoming air to the engine at a predetermined level, usually about 100°F or higher. It mixes cold air with heated air from the exhaust manifold region. The air cleaner in-

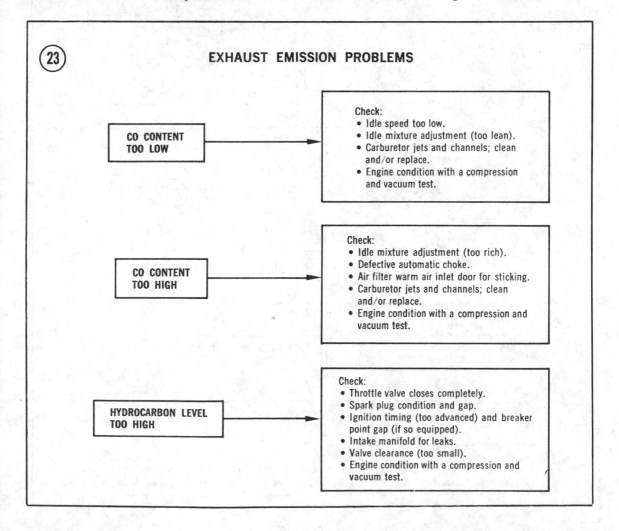

(23) **EXHAUST EMISSION PROBLEMS**

CO CONTENT TOO LOW

Check:
- Idle speed too low.
- Idle mixture adjustment (too lean).
- Carburetor jets and channels; clean and/or replace.
- Engine condition with a compression and vacuum test.

CO CONTENT TOO HIGH

Check:
- Idle mixture adjustment (too rich).
- Defective automatic choke.
- Air filter warm air inlet door for sticking.
- Carburetor jets and channels; clean and/or replace.
- Engine condition with a compression and vacuum test.

HYDROCARBON LEVEL TOO HIGH

Check:
- Throttle valve closes completely.
- Spark plug condition and gap.
- Ignition timing (too advanced) and breaker point gap (if so equipped).
- Intake manifold for leaks.
- Valve clearance (too small).
- Engine condition with a compression and vacuum test.

cludes a temperature sensor, vacuum motor, and a hinged door. See **Figure 26**.

The system is comparatively easy to test. See **Figure 27** for the procedure.

Air Injection Reaction System

The air injection reaction system reduces air pollution by oxidizing hydrocarbons and carbon monoxide as they leave the combustion chamber. See **Figure 28**.

The air injection pump, driven by the engine, compresses filtered air and injects it at the exhaust port of each cylinder. The fresh air mixes with the unburned gases in the exhaust and promotes further burning. A check valve prevents exhaust gases from entering and damaging the air pump if the pump becomes inoperative, e.g., from a fan belt failure.

Figure 29 explains the testing procedure for this system.

Fuel Evaporation Control

Fuel vapor from the fuel tank passes through the liquid/vapor separator to the carbon canister. See **Figure 30**. The carbon absorbs and

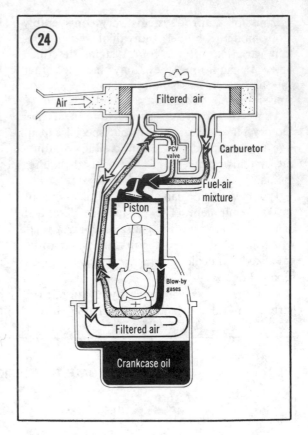

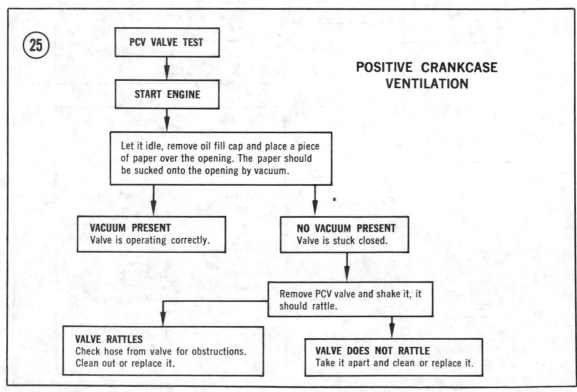

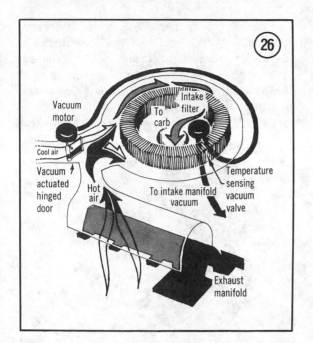

(26)

Intake
filter

To
carb

Vacuum
motor

Cool air

Vacuum
actuated
hinged
door

Hot
air

Temperature
sensing
vacuum
valve

To intake manifold
vacuum

Exhaust
manifold

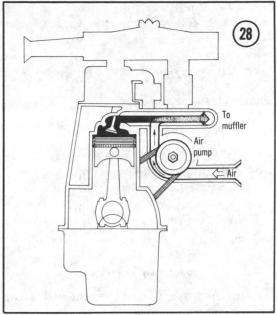

(28)

To
muffler

Air
pump

Air

2

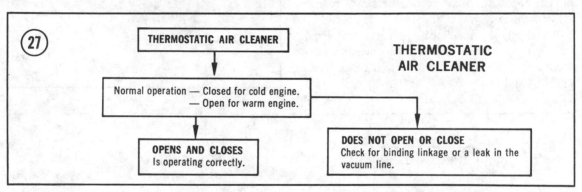

(27)

THERMOSTATIC AIR CLEANER

**THERMOSTATIC
AIR CLEANER**

Normal operation — Closed for cold engine.
— Open for warm engine.

OPENS AND CLOSES
Is operating correctly.

DOES NOT OPEN OR CLOSE
Check for binding linkage or a leak in the
vacuum line.

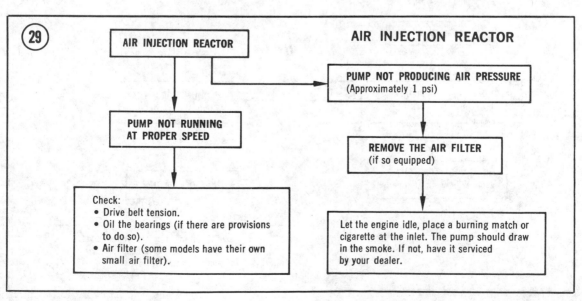

(29)

AIR INJECTION REACTOR

AIR INJECTION REACTOR

PUMP NOT PRODUCING AIR PRESSURE
(Approximately 1 psi)

**PUMP NOT RUNNING
AT PROPER SPEED**

REMOVE THE AIR FILTER
(if so equipped)

Check:
• Drive belt tension.
• Oil the bearings (if there are provisions
to do so).
• Air filter (some models have their own
small air filter).

Let the engine idle, place a burning match or
cigarette at the inlet. The pump should draw
in the smoke. If not, have it serviced
by your dealer.

stores the vapor when the engine is stopped. When the engine runs, manifold vacuum draws the vapor from the canister. Instead of being released into the atmosphere, the fuel vapor takes part in the normal combustion process.

Exhaust Gas Recirculation

The exhaust gas recirculation (EGR) system is used to reduce the emission of nitrogen oxides (NOx). Relatively inert exhaust gases are introduced into the combustion process to slightly reduce peak temperatures. This reduction in temperature reduces the formation of NOx.

Figure 31 provides a simple test of this system.

ENGINE NOISES

Often the first evidence of an internal engine trouble is a strange noise. That knocking, clicking, or tapping which you never heard before may be warning you of impending trouble.

While engine noises can indicate problems, they are sometimes difficult to interpret correctly; inexperienced mechanics can be seriously misled by them.

Professional mechanics often use a special stethoscope which looks similar to a doctor's stethoscope for isolating engine noises. You can do nearly as well with a "sounding stick" which can be an ordinary piece of doweling or a section of small hose. By placing one end in contact with the area to which you want to listen and the other end near your ear, you can hear

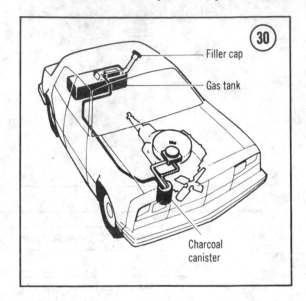

Filler cap

Gas tank

Charcoal canister

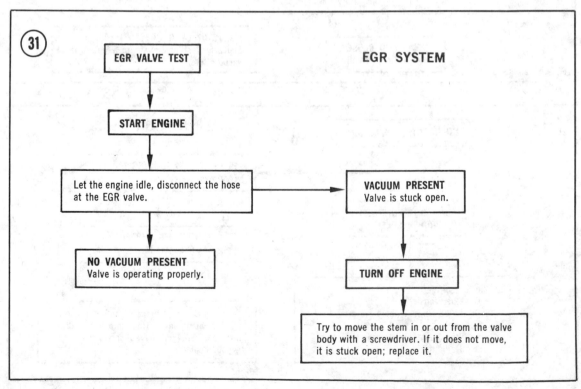

EGR VALVE TEST

EGR SYSTEM

START ENGINE

Let the engine idle, disconnect the hose at the EGR valve.

VACUUM PRESENT
Valve is stuck open.

NO VACUUM PRESENT
Valve is operating properly.

TURN OFF ENGINE

Try to move the stem in or out from the valve body with a screwdriver. If it does not move, it is stuck open; replace it.

sounds emanating from that area. The first time you do this, you may be horrified at the strange noises coming from even a normal engine. If you can, have an experienced friend or mechanic help you sort the noises out.

Clicking or Tapping Noises

Clicking or tapping noises usually come from the valve train, and indicate excessive valve clearance.

If your vehicle has adjustable valves, the procedure for adjusting the valve clearance is explained in Chapter Three. If your vehicle has hydraulic lifters, the clearance may not be adjustable. The noise may be coming from a collapsed lifter. These may be cleaned or replaced as described in the engine chapter.

A sticking valve may also sound like a valve with excessive clearance. In addition, excessive wear in valve train components can cause similar engine noises.

Knocking Noises

A heavy, dull knocking is usually caused by a worn main bearing. The noise is loudest when the engine is working hard, i.e., accelerating hard at low speed. You may be able to isolate the trouble to a single bearing by disconnecting

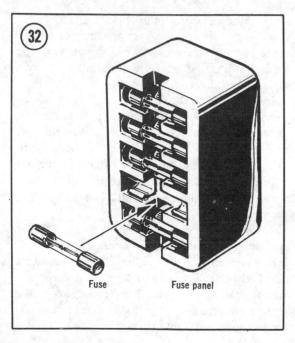

Fuse   Fuse panel

the spark plugs one at a time. When you reach the spark plug nearest the bearing, the knock will be reduced or disappear.

Worn connecting rod bearings may also produce a knock, but the sound is usually more "metallic." As with a main bearing, the noise is worse when accelerating. It may even increase further just as you go from accelerating to coasting. Disconnecting spark plugs will help isolate this knock as well.

A double knock or clicking usually indicates a worn piston pin. Disconnecting spark plugs will isolate this to a particular piston, however, the noise will *increase* when you reach the affected piston.

A loose flywheel and excessive crankshaft end play also produce knocking noises. While similar to main bearing noises, these are usually intermittent, not constant, and they do not change when spark plugs are disconnected.

Some mechanics confuse piston pin noise with piston slap. The double knock will distinguish the piston pin noise. Piston slap is identified by the fact that it is always louder when the engine is cold.

ELECTRICAL ACCESSORIES

Lights and Switches (Interior and Exterior)

1. *Bulb does not light* — Remove the bulb and check for a broken element. Also check the inside of the socket; make sure the contacts are clean and free of corrosion. If the bulb and socket are OK, check to see if a fuse has blown or a circuit breaker has tripped. The fuse panel (**Figure 32**) is usually located under the instrument panel. Replace the blown fuse or reset the circuit breaker. If the fuse blows or the breaker trips again, there is a short in that circuit. Check that circuit all the way to the battery. Look for worn wire insulation or burned wires.

If all the above are all right, check the switch controlling the bulb for continuity with an ohmmeter at the switch terminals. Check the switch contact terminals for loose or dirty electrical connections.

2. *Headlights work but will not switch from either high or low beam* — Check the beam selector switch for continuity with an ohmmeter

at the switch terminals. Check the switch contact terminals for loose or dirty electrical connections.

3. *Brake light switch inoperative* — On mechanically operated switches, usually mounted near the brake pedal arm, adjust the switch to achieve correct mechanical operation. Check the switch for continuity with an ohmmeter at the switch terminals. Check the switch contact terminals for loose or dirty electrical connections.

4. *Back-up lights do not operate* — Check light bulb as described earlier. Locate the switch, normally located near the shift lever. Adjust switch to achieve correct mechanical operation. Check the switch for continuity with an ohmmeter at the switch terminals. Bypass the switch with a jumper wire; if the lights work, replace the switch.

Directional Signals

1. *Directional signals do not operate* — If the indicator light on the instrument panel burns steadily instead of flashing, this usually indicates that one of the exterior lights is burned out. Check all lamps that normally flash. If all are all right, the flasher unit may be defective. Replace it with a good one.

2. *Directional signal indicator light on instrument panel does not light up* — Check the light bulbs as described earlier. Check all electrical connections and check the flasher unit.

3. *Directional signals will not self-cancel* — Check the self-cancelling mechanism located inside the steering column.

4. *Directional signals flash slowly* — Check the condition of the battery and the alternator (or generator) drive belt tension (**Figure 4**). Check the flasher unit and all related electrical connections.

Windshield Wipers

1. *Wipers do not operate* — Check for a blown fuse or circuit breaker that has tripped; replace or reset. Check all related terminals for loose or dirty electrical connections. Check continuity of the control switch with an ohmmeter at the switch terminals. Check the linkage and arms

for loose, broken, or binding parts. Straighten out or replace where necessary.

2. *Wiper motor hums but will not operate* — The motor may be shorted out internally; check and/or replace the motor. Also check for broken or binding linkage and arms.

3. *Wiper arms will not return to the stowed position when turned off* — The motor has a special internal switch for this purpose. Have it inspected by your dealer. Do not attempt this yourself.

Interior Heater

1. *Heater fan does not operate* — Check for a blown fuse or circuit breaker that has tripped. Check the switch for continuity with an ohmmeter at the switch terminals. Check the switch contact terminals for loose or dirty electrical connections.

2. *Heat output is insufficient* — Check the heater hose/engine coolant control valve usually located in the engine compartment; make sure it is in the open position. Ensure that the heater door(s) and cable(s) are operating correctly and are in the open position. Inspect the heat ducts; make sure that they are not crimped or blocked.

COOLING SYSTEM

The temperature gauge or warning light usually signals cooling system troubles before there is any damage. As long as you stop the vehicle at the first indication of trouble, serious damage is unlikely.

In most cases, the trouble will be obvious as soon as you open the hood. If there is coolant or steam leaking, look for a defective radiator, radiator hose, or heater hose. If there is no evidence of leakage, make sure that the fan belt is in good condition. If the trouble is not obvious, refer to **Figures 33 and 34** to help isolate the trouble.

Automotive cooling systems operate under pressure to permit higher operating temperatures without boil-over. The system should be checked periodically to make sure it can withstand normal pressure. **Figure 35** shows the equipment which nearly any service station has for testing the system pressure.

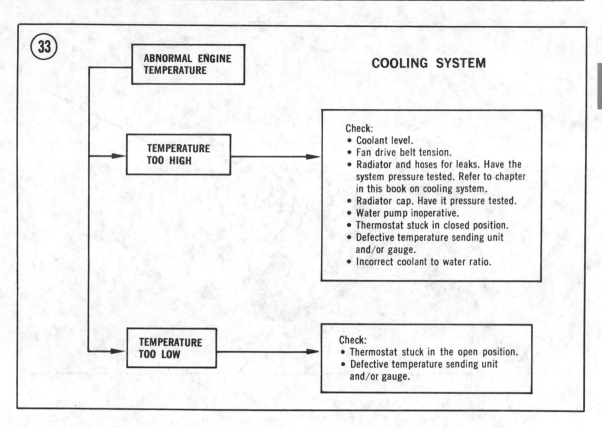

③③

ABNORMAL ENGINE
TEMPERATURE

COOLING SYSTEM

TEMPERATURE
TOO HIGH

Check:
• Coolant level.
• Fan drive belt tension.
• Radiator and hoses for leaks. Have the
  system pressure tested. Refer to chapter
  in this book on cooling system.
• Radiator cap. Have it pressure tested.
• Water pump inoperative.
• Thermostat stuck in closed position.
• Defective temperature sending unit
  and/or gauge.
• Incorrect coolant to water ratio.

TEMPERATURE
TOO LOW

Check:
• Thermostat stuck in the open position.
• Defective temperature sending unit
  and/or gauge.

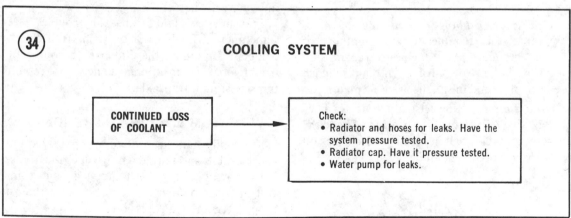

③④

COOLING SYSTEM

CONTINUED LOSS
OF COOLANT

Check:
• Radiator and hoses for leaks. Have the
  system pressure tested.
• Radiator cap. Have it pressure tested.
• Water pump for leaks.

CLUTCH

All clutch troubles except adjustments require transmission removal to identify and cure the problem.

1. *Slippage* — This is most noticeable when accelerating in a high gear at relatively low speed. To check slippage, park the vehicle on a level surface with the handbrake set. Shift to 2nd gear and release the clutch as if driving off. If the clutch is good, the engine will slow and stall. If the clutch slips, continued engine speed will give it away.

Slippage results from insufficient clutch pedal free play, oil or grease on the clutch disc, worn pressure plate, or weak springs.

2. *Drag or failure to release* — This trouble usually causes difficult shifting and gear clash, especially when downshifting. The cause may be excessive clutch pedal free play, warped or bent pressure plate or clutch disc, broken or

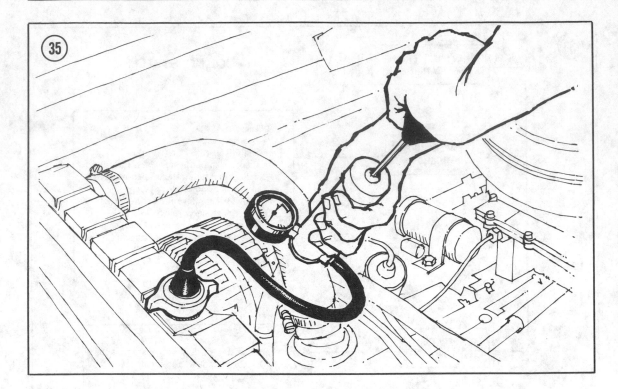

loose linings, or lack of lubrication in pilot bearing. Also check condition of transmission main shaft splines.

3. *Chatter or grabbing* — A number of things can cause this trouble. Check tightness of engine mounts and engine-to-transmission mounting bolts. Check for worn or misaligned pressure plate and misaligned release plate.

4. *Other noises* — Noise usually indicates a dry or defective release or pilot bearing. Check the bearings and replace if necessary. Also check all parts for misalignment and uneven wear.

MANUAL TRANSMISSION/TRANSAXLE

Transmission and transaxle troubles are evident when one or more of the following symptoms appear:

    a. Difficulty changing gears

    b. Gears clash when downshifting

    c. Slipping out of gear

    d. Excessive noise in NEUTRAL

    e. Excessive noise in gear

    f. Oil leaks

Transmission and transaxle repairs are not recommended unless the many special tools required are available.

Transmission and transaxle troubles are sometimes difficult to distinguish from clutch troubles. Eliminate the clutch as a source of trouble before installing a new or rebuilt transmission or transaxle.

AUTOMATIC TRANSMISSION

Most automatic transmission repairs require considerable specialized knowledge and tools. It is impractical for the home mechanic to invest in the tools, since they cost more than a properly rebuilt transmission.

Check fluid level and condition frequently to help prevent future problems. If the fluid is orange or black in color or smells like varnish, it is an indication of some type of damage or failure within the transmission. Have the transmission serviced by your dealer or competent automatic transmission service facility.

BRAKES

Good brakes are vital to the safe operation of the vehicle. Performing the maintenance speci-

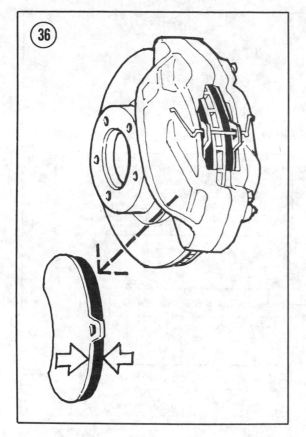

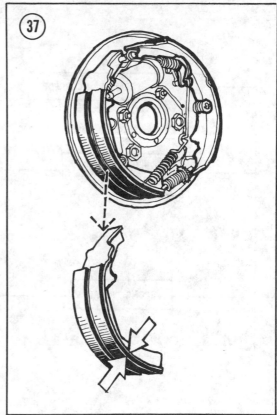

fied in Chapter Three will minimize problems with the brakes. Most importantly, check and maintain the level of fluid in the master cylinder, and check the thickness of the linings on the disc brake pads (**Figure 36**) or drum brake shoes (**Figure 37**).

If trouble develops, **Figures 38 through 40** will help you locate the problem. Refer to the brake chapter for actual repair procedures.

STEERING AND SUSPENSION

Trouble in the suspension or steering is evident when the following occur:

a. Steering is hard
b. Car pulls to one side
c. Car wanders or front wheels wobble
d. Steering has excessive play
e. Tire wear is abnormal

Unusual steering, pulling, or wandering is usually caused by bent or otherwise misaligned suspension parts. This is difficult to check without proper alignment equipment. Refer to the suspension chapter in this book for repairs that you can perform and those that must be left to a dealer or suspension specialist.

If your trouble seems to be excessive play, check wheel bearing adjustment first. This is the most frequent cause. Then check ball-joints (refer to Suspension chapter). Finally, check tie rod end ball-joints by shaking each tie rod. Also check steering gear, or rack-and-pinion assembly to see that it is securely bolted down.

TIRE WEAR ANALYSIS

Abnormal tire wear should be analyzed to determine its causes. The most common causes are the following:

a. Incorrect tire pressure
b. Improper driving
c. Overloading
d. Bad road surfaces
e. Incorrect wheel alignment

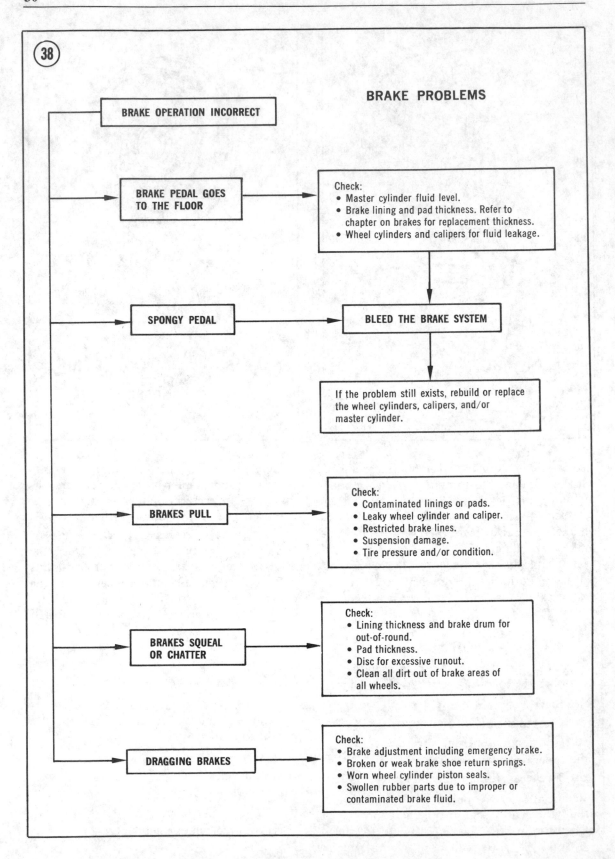

BRAKE PROBLEMS

BRAKE OPERATION INCORRECT

BRAKE PEDAL GOES TO THE FLOOR

Check:
- Master cylinder fluid level.
- Brake lining and pad thickness. Refer to chapter on brakes for replacement thickness.
- Wheel cylinders and calipers for fluid leakage.

SPONGY PEDAL

BLEED THE BRAKE SYSTEM

If the problem still exists, rebuild or replace the wheel cylinders, calipers, and/or master cylinder.

BRAKES PULL

Check:
- Contaminated linings or pads.
- Leaky wheel cylinder and caliper.
- Restricted brake lines.
- Suspension damage.
- Tire pressure and/or condition.

BRAKES SQUEAL OR CHATTER

Check:
- Lining thickness and brake drum for out-of-round.
- Pad thickness.
- Disc for excessive runout.
- Clean all dirt out of brake areas of all wheels.

DRAGGING BRAKES

Check:
- Brake adjustment including emergency brake.
- Broken or weak brake shoe return springs.
- Worn wheel cylinder piston seals.
- Swollen rubber parts due to improper or contaminated brake fluid.

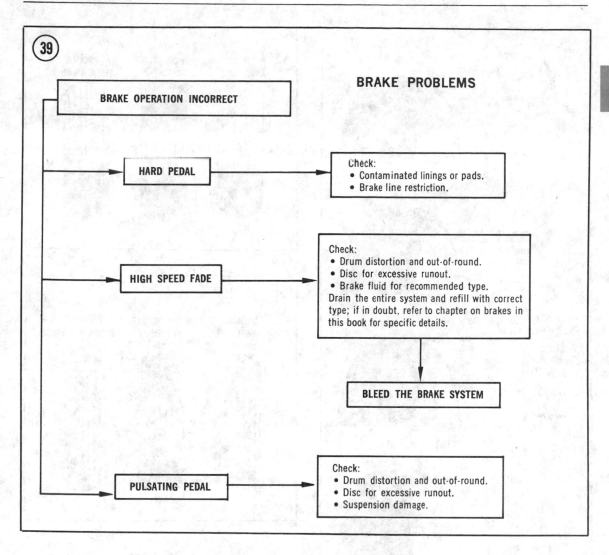

(39)

BRAKE PROBLEMS

BRAKE OPERATION INCORRECT

HARD PEDAL

Check:
• Contaminated linings or pads.
• Brake line restriction.

HIGH SPEED FADE

Check:
• Drum distortion and out-of-round.
• Disc for excessive runout.
• Brake fluid for recommended type.
Drain the entire system and refill with correct type; if in doubt, refer to chapter on brakes in this book for specific details.

BLEED THE BRAKE SYSTEM

PULSATING PEDAL

Check:
• Drum distortion and out-of-round.
• Disc for excessive runout.
• Suspension damage.

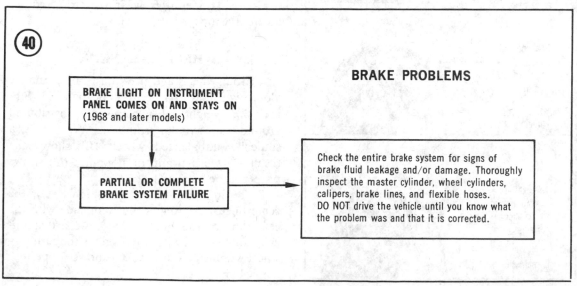

(40)

BRAKE PROBLEMS

BRAKE LIGHT ON INSTRUMENT PANEL COMES ON AND STAYS ON
(1968 and later models)

PARTIAL OR COMPLETE BRAKE SYSTEM FAILURE

Check the entire brake system for signs of brake fluid leakage and/or damage. Thoroughly inspect the master cylinder, wheel cylinders, calipers, brake lines, and flexible hoses.
DO NOT drive the vehicle until you know what the problem was and that it is corrected.

2

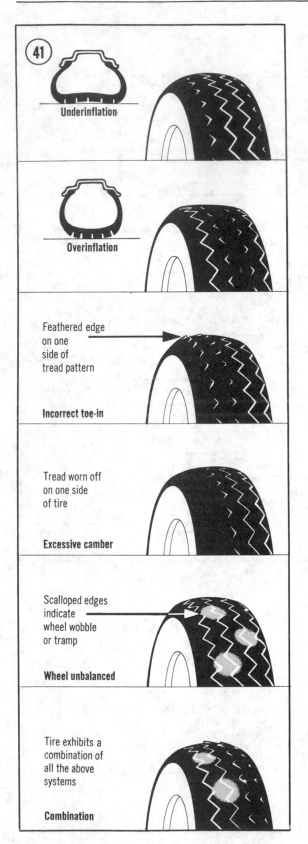

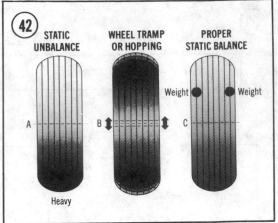

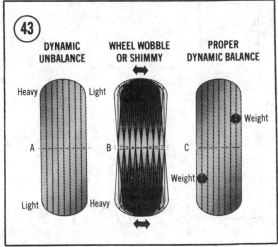

Figure 41 identifies wear patterns and indicates the most probable causes.

WHEEL BALANCING

All four wheels and tires must be in balance along two axes. To be in static balance (**Figure 42**), weight must be evenly distributed around the axis of rotation. (A) shows a statically unbalanced wheel; (B) shows the result — wheel tramp or hopping; (C) shows proper static balance.

To be in dynamic balance (**Figure 43**), the centerline of the weight must coincide with the centerline of the wheel. (A) shows a dynamically unbalanced wheel; (B) shows the result — wheel wobble or shimmy; (C) shows proper dynamic balance.

CHAPTER THREE

LUBRICATION, MAINTENANCE AND TUNE-UP

This chapter deals with the normal maintenance required to keep your vehicle running properly. **Table 1** gives the maintenance intervals for vehicles given normal use. Some procedures are done at fuel stops; others are done at specified mileage or time intervals.

Vehicles driven under severe conditions require more frequent maintenance. This is specified in **Table 1**. Such conditions include:

   a. Frequent short trips.
   b. Stop-and-go driving.
   c. Extremely cold weather.
   d. Trailer towing.
   e. Dust.

Some maintenance procedures are included under *Tune-up* in this chapter and detailed instructions will be found there. Other steps are described in the following chapters. Chapter references are included with these steps.

Tables 1-5 are at the end of the chapter.

HOISTING, JACKING AND LIFT POINTS

M-series vans are an integral body/frame construction using a welded steel box type frame with integral engine/front suspension and transmission crossmembers. This particular design requires that special precautions be taken when raising the vehicle with a jack or a hoist and when positioning jackstands. Incorrect jack or jackstand placement can cause suspension or drive train damage. The service jack provided with the vehicle is intended only for emergency use in changing a flat tire. Refer to the owner's manual when using this jack. Do not use it to lift the vehicle up while performing other services.

When lifting one wheel of the vehicle, as when changing a tire, dismantling a hub or removing a brake drum, make sure the vehicle is resting as level as possible and firmly block the wheels at the opposite end of the vehicle. Set the parking brake and place the transmission in PARK (automatic transmission) or REVERSE (manual transmission). Position the jack carefully to provide maximum contact under axles or spring hangers. The jack should be as close as possible to the wheel being raised and positioned exactly vertical.

Raise the jack until it just begins to support the axle. Loosen all wheel lug nuts about 1/4-1/2 turn. Continue to raise the jack slowly until the wheel just clears the ground and will rotate freely.

Unscrew the lug nuts and remove the wheel. When reinstalling the wheel, tighten the lug nuts securely, lower the vehicle to the ground and remove the jack, then tighten all of the lug nuts to specifications.

A floor jack or other type of hydraulic jack is recommended to raise the front or rear of the vehicle as required for service. Always place jackstands at the appropriate points to hold the vehicle stable. Relying upon a single jack to hold the vehicle without the use of jackstands can lead to serious physical injury.

The front of the vehicle can be safely lifted with a hydraulic jack placed under the center of the front crossmember, as shown in **Figure 1**. Make sure the jack does not lift against or contact any sheet metal, suspension or steering components or the bottom of the radiator. Check to see that it does not touch electrical leads, hydraulic lines or oil/fuel lines.

The rear of the vehicle can be safely lifted by placing the hydraulic jack under the center of the rear axle housing (**Figure 2**). After the vehicle has been lifted with the jack, support it on jackstands located under the frame rails or the rear axle. Do *not* run the engine when the rear wheels are jacked up if the vehicle is equipped with a limited-slip differential.

> *WARNING*
> *Never work beneath the vehicle when it is supported only by a jack.*

When raising the vehicle on a service station hoist, position the front hoist arms or lifting pads to provide maximum contact under the center of the lower suspension arms or spring supports as near the wheels as possible, making sure they do not touch the steering linkage. The rear hoist arms or pads should be positioned beneath the rear axle housing or the spring mounting pads, but not allowed to touch the shock absorber mounting brackets.

> *WARNING*
> *On vehicles equipped with an under-chassis mounted spare tire, remove the tire, wheel or tire carrier before raising the vehicle to a high-lift position. This will avoid any sudden weight release from the chassis that might affect vehicle positioning on the hoist.*

TOWING

> *CAUTION*
> *Tow a vehicle only as described in this chapter and with a minimal load. Improper towing techniques can result in serious transmission damage.*

As a general rule, the vehicles covered in this manual should be towed with their rear wheels off the ground. If the rear wheels cannot be raised, either disconnect the drive shaft or tow the vehicle with the aid of a dolly.

If the vehicle is towed with its front wheels on the ground, clamp the steering wheel in a straight-ahead position with a wheel clamping device designed for towing. Do *not* rely upon the steering column lock.

If the vehicle is towed with the front wheels off the ground, do not exceed speeds of 35 mph or distances of 50 miles unless the rear drive shaft is disconnected. Vehicles towed with the rear wheels off the ground should not exceed speeds of 35 mph (rough pavement) or 50 mph (smooth pavement).

WEEKLY CHECKS

Many of the following services were once routinely performed by service station attendants during a fuel stop. With the advent of the self-service station and the extra cost for "full service," you may want to perform the checks yourself. Although simple to perform, they are important, as such checks give an indication of the need for other maintenance.

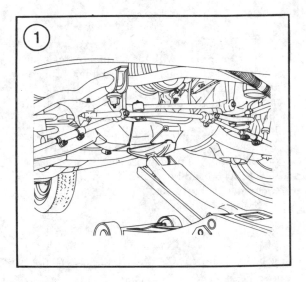

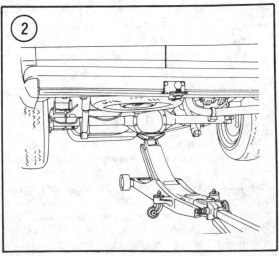

Engine Oil Level

Engine oil should be checked before the vehicle is started each day. At this time, all the oil is in the crankcase and the dipstick will give a true reading. If you find it necessary to check the oil after the engine has been started, let the vehicle sit for an hour to allow oil in the upper part of the engine to drain back into the crankcase.

With the engine cold and off, pull out the engine oil dipstick. See A, **Figure 3** (typical). Wipe the dipstick with a clean rag or paper towel and reinsert it in the dipstick tube. Be sure to push the dipstick all the way down. Pull the dipstick out again and check the oil level on the end of the dipstick. Reinsert the dipstick and push it all the way into the dipstick tube.

NOTE
Some dipsticks have ADD and FULL lines. Others may read ADD 1 QT. and OPERATING RANGE. In either case, keep the oil level above the ADD line.

Top up to the FULL or OPERATING RANGE mark on the dipstick, if necessary. Use *only* an SF,

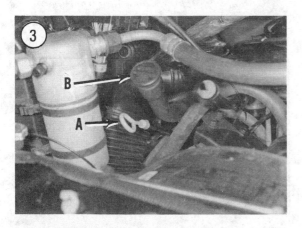

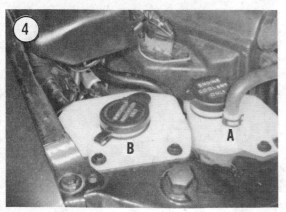

SF/CC or SF/CD grade oil (SF preferred). See **Table 2** for proper oil viscosity. Add oil through the valve cover opening or oil fill tube. See B, **Figure 3** (typical).

Coolant Level and Condition

WARNING
Do not remove the radiator cap when the engine is warm or hot, especially if an air conditioner has been in use. You may be seriously scalded or burned.

Check coolant level by observing the liquid level in the translucent recovery tank. See A, **Figure 4**. The radiator cap should *not* be removed. Coolant level should be near the FULL or MAX mark when the engine is hot and at the ADD or MIN mark when the engine is cold (the difference between the marks is approximately 1 quart).

NOTE
Some recovery tanks may have only one mark. Check the fluid level in such tanks when the engine is cold.

Top up as needed with a 50/50 mixture of ethylene glycol antifreeze and water, adding it to the recovery tank, not the radiator. If the recovery tank is empty, check the radiator level as well.

WARNING
Avoid removing the radiator cap when the engine is warm. If you must, wear heavy leather gloves. Turn the cap slowly counterclockwise against the first stop (about 1/4 turn). Let all pressure (hot coolant and steam) escape. Then depress the cap and turn counterclockwise to remove. If the cap is removed too soon, scalding coolant may escape and cause a serious burn.

Check the condition of the coolant. If it is dirty or rusty, drain the radiator and flush the cooling system as described in Chapter Seven, then refill it with fresh coolant.

Battery Electrolyte Level

Unsealed batteries have individual cell vent caps or 2 bars with vented plugs, each of which fits across 3 cells. To check electrolyte level with this type of battery, remove the vent caps or vent bars and observe the liquid level. With unsealed black batteries, it should be even with the bottom of the split vent wells. See **Figure 5**. On unsealed translucent batteries, it should be between the marks on the battery case (**Figure 6**).

If the level is low, add distilled water until the level contacts the bottom of the vent well. Do not overfill, as this will result in loss of electrolyte and shorten battery life. Carefully wipe any spilled water from the battery top before reinstalling the vent caps or bars.

Periodic electrolyte level checks are not required on Freedom II or other sealed, maintenance-free batteries.

Windshield Wipers and Washer

Check the wiper blades for breaks or cracks in the rubber. Blade replacement intervals will vary with age, the weather, amount of use and the degree of chemical reaction from road salt or tar.

Operate the windshield washer and wiper blades. At the same time, check the amount and direction of the sprayed fluid. If the blades do not clean the windshield satisfactorily, wash the windshield and the blades with a mild undiluted detergent. Rinse with water while rubbing with a clean cloth or paper towels.

If the wiper pattern is uneven and streaks over clean glass, replace the blades.

Check fluid level in the windshield washer reservoir. See B, **Figure 4** (typical). Fill the reservoir with a mixture of water and GM Optikleen windshield washer solvent or equivalent. The reservoir should be kept full, except during winter months when filling it only 3/4 full will allow for expansion if the fluid freezes. Never use radiator antifreeze in the windshield washer reservoir, as it can damage painted surfaces.

Brake Fluid Level

Clean the master cylinder housing and covers (**Figure 7**) to remove any possible contamination that might get into the fluid when the covers are removed. Grasp the cover tabs, depress the center of the cover and lift it off the reservoir housing (**Figure 8**). If the level is more than 1/4 in. below the reservoir, top up with a brake fluid marked DOT 3 and reinstall the cover by pressing down until it snaps in place.

WARNING
Do not use fluid from a previously opened container that is only part full. Brake fluid absorbs moisture from the air and moisture in the brake lines can reduce braking efficiency.

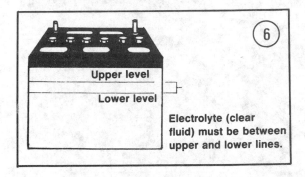

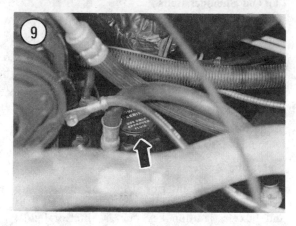

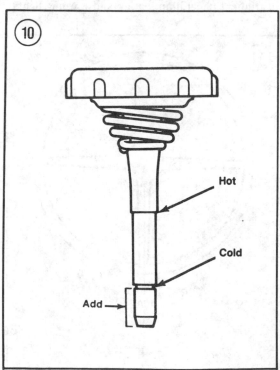

Hydraulic Clutch Fluid Level

Check the fluid level in the clutch master cylinder reservoir located near the master cylinder. The fluid level can be seen inside the translucent reservoir and should be above the embossed line on the side of the reservoir. If not, top up with DOT 3 brake fluid.

Power Steering Fluid Level

Check fluid level in the power steering pump reservoir, if so equipped. See **Figure 9** (typical). With the engine at normal operating temperature (upper radiator hose hot), turn the steering wheel lock-to-lock several times, then shut the engine off. Remove the pump reservoir cap with dipstick, wipe clean and reinsert. The fluid level should be between the HOT and COLD marks on the dipstick (**Figure 10**). Top up if necessary with power steering fluid. Reinstall the dipstick.

OWNER SAFETY CHECKS

The following simple checks should be performed on a daily basis during normal operation of the vehicle. Some are driveway checks. The others can be performed while driving. If any result in unsatisfactory operation, see your dealer to have the condition corrected.

Steering Column Lock

The ignition key should turn to LOCK position only when the transmission selector is in PARK (automatic transmission) or REVERSE (manual transmission).

Parking Brake and Transmission PARK Mechanism

Check holding ability by setting the parking brake with the vehicle on a fairly steep hill. Check the automatic transmission PARK mechanism by placing the transmission selector in PARK and releasing all brakes.

> *WARNING*
> *You should not expect the PARK mechanism to hold the vehicle by itself even on a level surface. **Always** set the parking brake **after** placing the transmission selector in PARK. When parking on an incline, you should also turn the wheels to the curb before shutting off the engine.*

Transmission Shift Indicator

Make sure the automatic transmission shift indicator accurately indicates the gear position selected.

Starter Safety Switch

The starter should operate only in PARK or NEUTRAL positions (automatic transmission) or in NEUTRAL with the clutch fully depressed (manual transmission).

Steering

With the vehicle on level ground, and with the front wheels lined up straight ahead, grasp the steering wheel and turn it from right to left to check for rotational free play. The free play should not exceed about one inch (**Figure 11**) and the steering should not make harsh sounds when turning or parking. try to move the steering wheel in and out to check for axial play. If any play is felt, check the tightness of the steering wheel center nut.

Attempt to move the steering wheel from side to side without turning it. Movement is an indication of loose steering column mounting bolts or worn column bushings. Check and tighten the mounting bolts if necessary, and if the movement is still present, take the vehicle to a dealer or front end specialist for corrective service.

Wheel Alignment and Balance

Wheel alignment and balance should be checked periodically by a dealer or an alignment specialist. Visually check the tires for abnormal wear. If the vehicle pulls either to the right or left on a straight, level road, an alignment problem is indicated. Excessive vibration of the steering wheel or front of the vehicle while driving at normal highway speeds usually indicates the need for wheel balancing.

Brakes

Observe brake warning light during braking action. Also check for changes in braking action, such as pulling to one side, unusual sounds or increased brake pedal travel. If the brake pedal feels spongy, there is probably air in the hydraulic system. Bleed the brakes (Chapter Twelve).

Exhaust System

Be alert to any smell of fumes in the vehicle or to any change in the sound of the exhaust system that might indicate leakage.

Defroster

Turn on the heater, then move the control to defrost (DEF) and check the amount of air directed to the windshield.

Rear View Mirror and Sun Visors

Make sure that the friction mounts are adjusted so that mirrors and visors stay in selected positions.

Horn

Check the horn to make sure that it works properly.

Lap and Shoulder Belts

Check all components for proper operation. Make sure that the anchor bolts are tight. Check the belts for fraying.

Head Restraints

If the seats are equipped with head restraints, check to see that they will adjust up and down properly and that no components are missing, loose or damaged.

Lights and Buzzers

Verify that all interior lights and buzzers are working. These include the seat belt reminder light and buzzer, ignition key buzzer, interior lights, instrument panel illumination and warning lights.

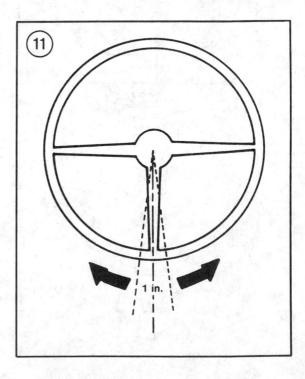

1 in.

Check all exterior lights for proper operation. These include the headlights, license plate lights, side marker lights, parking lights, turn or directional signals, backup lights and hazard warning lights.

Glass

Check for any condition that could obscure vision or be a safety hazard. Correct as required.

Door Latches

Verify positive closing, latching and locking action.

Fluid Leaks

Check under the vehicle after it has been parked for awhile for evidence of fuel, coolant or oil leaks. Water dripping from the air conditioner drain tube after use is normal. Immediately determine and correct the cause of any leaking gasoline fumes or liquids to avoid possible fire or explosion.

Tires and Wheels

Inspect the tire tread and sidewall condition. Original equipment and many replacement tires have tread wear indicators molded into the bottom of the tread grooves. Tread wear indicators will become visible as shown in **Figure 12** when tread depth becomes approximately 1/16 in. Tires should be replaced at this point. Wear patterns are a good indicator of chassis and suspension alignment. If detected early, alignment problems can be corrected before the tires have worn severely.

CAUTION
For satisfactory operation, all 4 wheels must be equipped with the same size tires, of equal circumference and identical or near identical tread pattern. In addition, bias ply and radial

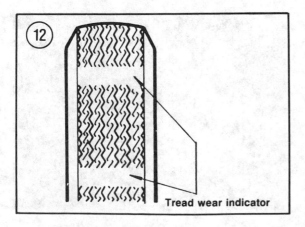

Tread wear indicator

tires should not be mixed; mixing will result in severe and even hazardous handling problems. Damage to the drive train components may also result.

Look for nails, cuts, excessive wear or other damage. Remove all stones or other objects wedged in the tread. Pay particular attention to signs of severe rock damage. This is usually found in the form of fractures and cuts in the tread and sidewalls. This type of damage presents an extreme driving hazard when the vehicle is operated at highway speeds. A damaged tire should be replaced as soon as possible.

WARNING
Do not repair a radial tire by installing a tube. Radial tires have cooling ridges cast inside the casing. Use of a tube prevents this cooling effect from taking place. Since air in the tires expands when heated, use of a tube in a radial tire will cause excessive pressure to develop and can result in a dangerous blowout at high speed.

Check the tire valves for air leaks; replace any leaking valve as soon as possible. Replace any missing valve caps. Check the tire pressure when the tires are cold in the morning or after the vehicle has been parked for at least 3 hours after being driven less than one mile. When the tires heat up from driving, the air inside them expands and gives false high-pressure readings.

NOTE
If tire pressure must be checked when the tires are warm, it will be about 3 psi higher following a low-speed drive and about 7 psi higher following a high-speed drive.

Use a reliable pressure gauge and adjust air pressure to agree with that specified for the tires. Pressure specifications for tires furnished with the vehicle are found on the tire placard attached to the rear edge of the driver's door lock pillar. Maintain the compact spare tire, if so equipped, at 60 psi.

NOTE
Because of the variety of tire types and makes used on the vehicles covered in this manual, it is impractical to print all possible tire pressure ranges. When buying tires other than original equipment sizes, check with the tire dealer for recommended pressures. In all cases, never exceed the maximum pressure embossed on the side of the tire.

SCHEDULED MAINTENANCE

Various services are required at the intervals stated to assure that the emission control systems are maintained at the levels required by law. The maintenance services and intervals provided in **Table 1** are a compilation and simplification of the manufacturer's schedule designed to offer maximum protection. If you follow this table, your vehicle will receive periodic maintenance that will meet all of the manufacturer's requirements.

Engine Oil and Filter

For average use, the engine oil and filter should be changed at the intervals stated in **Table 1** at the end of this chapter. If driving is primarily short distances and in stop-and-go traffic, change the oil and filter twice as often as for average use. If the vehicle is only driven a few hundred miles each month, change the oil and filter every 6-8 weeks. If the vehicle is driven for long periods in extremely cold weather (when the temperature is frequently below 10° F), change the oil and filter twice as often as for average use.

> *CAUTION*
> *Non-detergent, low-quality oil should never be used. The use of oil additives is unnecessary and not recommended.*

Engine oil should be selected to meet the demands of the temperatures and driving conditions anticipated. Refer to **Table 2** to select a viscosity that is appropriate for the temperatures you expect to encounter during the next maintenance interval. General Motors recommends the use of a high quality motor oil with an API classification of SF, SF/CC or SF/CD (API SF preferred) for all gasoline engines, regardless of the model year or previous oil recommendations. The rating and viscosity range are plainly marked on top of the can (**Figure 13**).

To drain the oil and change the filter, you will need:

a. Drain pan (6 quarts or more capacity).
b. Oil can spout or can opener and funnel.
c. Filter wrench.
d. Sufficient oil (see **Table 3**).
e. Adjustable wrench.
f. New oil filter.
g. Paper towels or shop cloths.

There are several ways to discard the old oil safely. The easiest way is to pour it from the drain pan into a gallon bleach or milk container. The oil can then be taken to a service station for dumping or, where permitted, thrown in your household trash. Oil disposal kits are available from auto parts stores. These contain a substance similar to sawdust which absorbs the oil for clean and easy disposal. After pouring the oil into the box, it can be disposed of in compliance with state and local regulations.

> *NOTE*
> *Some service stations accept oil for recycling. Check local regulations before disposing of oil in trash. Never let oil drain on the ground.*

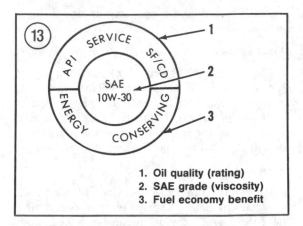

1. Oil quality (rating)
2. SAE grade (viscosity)
3. Fuel economy benefit

16

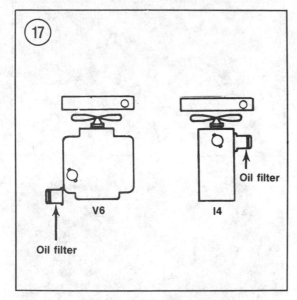

17

Oil filter

V6

I4

Oil filter

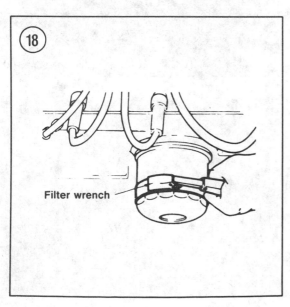

18

Filter wrench

The drain pan can be cleaned with solvent or paint thinner, if available. If not, hot water and dishwashing liquid will work satisfactorily.

1. With the vehicle on a level surface, warm the engine to operating temperature, then shut it off.

2. Set the parking brake and block the rear wheels so the vehicle will not roll in either direction.

3. Place a suitable container under the oil pan to serve as a drain pan.

4. Remove the oil filler cap on the valve cover (I4) or oil fill tube (V6) to promote faster draining. See **Figure 14** (I4) or **Figure 15** (V6).

5. Remove the dipstick (A, **Figure 3**) and wipe it clean with a cloth or paper towel.

6. Remove the drain plug with a suitable wrench or socket. See **Figure 16** (typical).

7. Clean the drain plug and check its gasket. Replace the gasket if damaged.

8. Allow the oil to drain completely (10-15 minutes), then reinstall the drain plug and gasket.

9. Relocate the drain pan beneath the oil filter. See **Figure 17**.

10. Unscrew the filter counterclockwise. Use a filter wrench (**Figure 18**) if the filter is too tight or too hot to remove by hand. Remove and discard the filter.

11. Wipe the engine mounting pad clean with a lint-free cloth or paper towel.

12. Coat the neoprene gasket on the new filter with a thin film of clean engine oil. Screw the filter in place *by hand* until it contacts the mounting pad surface. Tighten 3/4 turn further *by hand*. Do not overtighten, as this can cause an oil leak.

13. Fill the crankcase with oil through the filler cap or tube hole. Wipe up any spills on the valve cover or oil fill tube with a clean cloth or paper towel and reinstall the filler cap.

14. Reinstall the dipstick. Wait a few seconds, then withdraw the dipstick. The oil level on the dipstick should be very close to the correct mark if the proper quantity of oil was used in Step 13.

CAUTION
During the next step, do not operate the engine at more than idle speed until the oil has had a chance to circulate through the engine or damage may result.

15. Start the engine. The engine warning or oil pressure light will stay on for several seconds. Allow the engine to idle for several minutes.

16. Check the area under and around the drain plug and filter for leaks while the engine is idling. Shut the engine off.

3

Air Cleaner

A disposable paper element filter is used. Service to a paper element filter consists of replacement only. Elements should not be cleaned with an air hose, tapped, washed or oiled.

Air cleaner filters should be replaced at specified intervals. To change the filter:

1. Remove the engine cover. See Chapter Four (I4) or Chapter Five (V6).

2. Remove the flange nuts (fuel injected) or wing nut (carburetted) at the center of the air cleaner cover. See **Figure 19** (I4) or **Figure 20** (V6). Remove the cover.

3. Remove and discard the filter (**Figure 21**).

4. Wipe the inside of the air cleaner housing with a damp rag to remove any dust, dirt or debris.

5. Install a new filter element. Install the cover and tighten the flange nuts or wing nut securely. Check the air cleaner hoses and ducts when servicing the filter. Replace any hose or duct that is damaged. Check to make sure the air control valve in the air cleaner snorkel operates freely. Locate and correct any cause of valve binding or sticking.

Crankcase Ventilation Filter

The crankcase ventilation filter pack in the air cleaner housing (**Figure 22**) should be replaced each time the air cleaner filter is changed, if the air cleaner is so equipped. Disconnect the hose leading

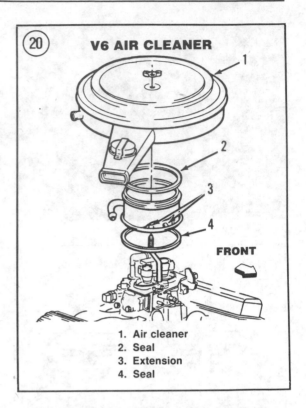

V6 AIR CLEANER

1. Air cleaner
2. Seal
3. Extension
4. Seal

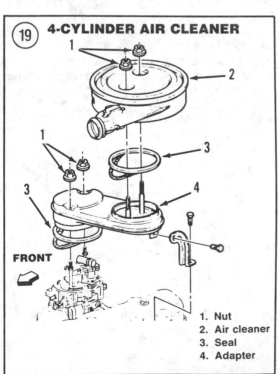

4-CYLINDER AIR CLEANER

1. Nut
2. Air cleaner
3. Seal
4. Adapter

to the filter pack, slide the retaining clip off and remove the filter pack from inside the air cleaner housing. Install a new filter pack through the air cleaner housing hole. Slide the retaining clip in place on the outside of the housing, making sure that it engages the groove in the filter pack assembly, then reconnect the hose.

Fuel Filter (Carburetted Engines)

Carburetted engines use a pleated paper fuel filter and check valve assembly (**Figure 23**) installed in the carburetor float bowl behind the fuel inlet nut. A dirty or restricted fuel filter will reduce fuel flow to the carburetor and cause a loss of engine power. Change the filter every 15,000 miles as follows:

1. Remove the air cleaner. See Chapter Six.

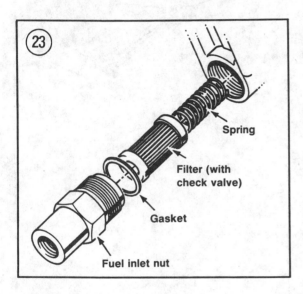

2. Place one open-end wrench on the carburetor inlet nut. Place second open-end wrench on the fuel line connector nut. Hold the fuel inlet nut from moving and loosen the connector nut.
3. Disconnect the fuel line from the inlet nut. Cap the line and move it out of the way.
4. Remove the fuel inlet nut. Remove the filter and spring assembly from the carburetor fuel inlet.
5. Remove and discard the inlet nut gasket.
6. Install the spring in the carburetor fuel inlet. Install the new filter element. The hole in the filter must face toward the nut.
7. Install a new gasket on the inlet nut. Install the nut to the carburetor and tighten to 25 ft.-lb. (34 N•m).
8. Uncap and connect the fuel line to the inlet nut. Start the connector by hand to avoid cross-threading and then tighten to 18 ft.-lb. (24 N•m) while holding the inlet nut with an open-end wrench.
9. Reinstall the air cleaner. See Chapter Six.
10. Start the engine and check for leaks.

Check all fuel lines for abrasion, cracks, pinched spots, etc. when the fuel filter is changed.

Fuel Filter
(Fuel Injected Engines)

The fuel filter is installed in the fuel feed line and is located in the engine compartment on 1985 models (**Figure 24**) or on the frame rail underneath the vehicle (**Figure 25**) on 1986 and later models.

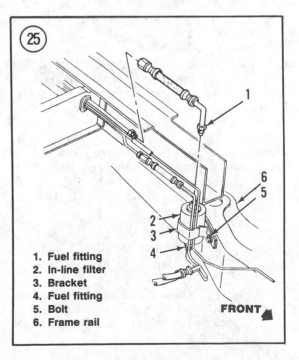

1. Fuel fitting
2. In-line filter
3. Bracket
4. Fuel fitting
5. Bolt
6. Frame rail

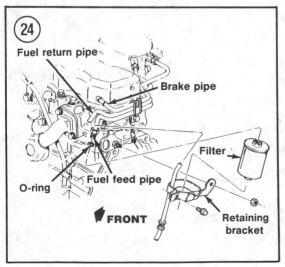

1. Relieve system pressure as described in Chapter Six.

2A. 1985—Remove the engine cover. See Chapter Four.

2B. 1986-on—Securely block both rear wheels so the vehicle will not roll in either direction. Raise the front of the vehicle with a jack and place it on jackstands.

3. Use one wrench to hold the fuel filter fitting and another wrench to loosen the fuel line nut. Disconnect and cap the fuel inlet and outlet lines.

4. Remove the bracket clamp screw. Remove the filter band bracket.

5. Check condition of the O-rings used on the inlet/outlet lines. Replace O-rings as required.

6. Install the new filter and bracket with the arrow stamped on the canister facing in the direction of fuel flow.

7. Tighten the bracket clamp screw, reconnect the lines to the canister and tighten fuel line fittings to 22 ft.-lb. (30 N•m).

Chassis/Suspension Lubrication

Inspect and lubricate the following components. If the vehicle is driven under severe service conditions as described in **Table 1**, perform this service every 3,000 miles or 3 months.

    a. Upper and lower control arm ball-joints (**Figure 26**).

    b. Steering linkage (**Figure 26**).

    c. Transmission shift linkage contacting faces (see Chapter Nine).

    d. Parking brake pulley, cable and linkage (see Chapter Twelve).

    e. Throttle linkage.

During winter weather, keep the vehicle in a heated garage for at least 30 minutes prior to lubrication so the joints will accept the lubricant.

Wipe around the grease fittings with a clean rag to remove any accumulated road dirt. On some vehicles, plugs may be installed instead of grease fittings. To lubricate such components, it is necessary to remove the plug and temporarily install a suitable grease or "zerk" fitting. When lubrication has been completed, remove the fitting and reinstall the plug.

> *CAUTION*
> *Do not overfill until lubricant escapes from boot. This will destroy the weathertight seal.*

Any lubricants used should be applied sparingly and the excess wiped away to prevent it from attracting dirt which will also accelerate wear and contribute to difficult operation.

Body Lubrication

All hood and door hinges, latches, locks and seat tracks should be lubricated periodically to ensure smooth operation and reduce wear. Recommended lubricants are given in **Table 4**.

1. Clean latch and hinge area of accumulated dirt or contamination.

2. Apply the specified lubricant sparingly, operating the mechanism several times to aid penetration.

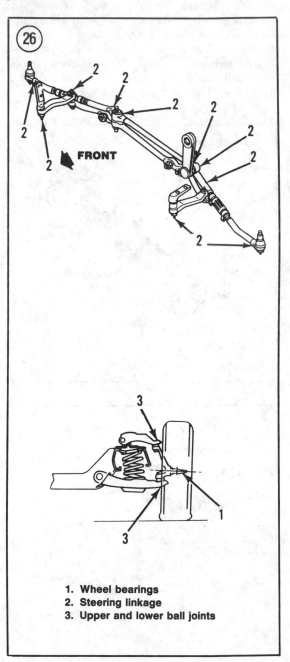

1. **Wheel bearings**
2. **Steering linkage**
3. **Upper and lower ball joints**

3. Wipe off any excess lubricant with a clean, dry cloth to prevent it from attracting dirt and from soiling clothes, carpeting or upholstery.

Positive Crankcase Ventilation (PCV) System

The PCV system should be checked for proper operation at the interval stated in **Table 1**. More frequent checks and/or replacement should be made if the vehicle is operated under severe service conditions.

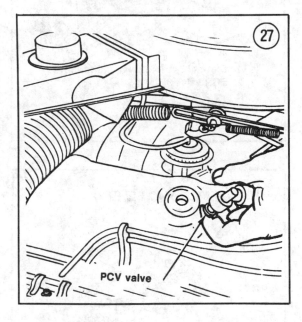

PCV valve

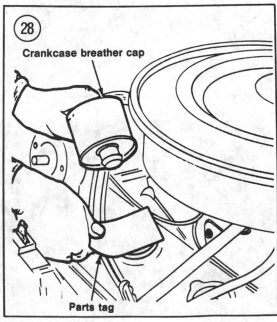

Crankcase breather cap

Parts tag

System Check

1. Start the engine and run at idle. Remove the PCV valve from the valve cover. A hissing noise should be heard as air passes through the valve and a strong vacuum should be felt when a finger is placed over the end of the valve (**Figure 27**). If not, check for plugged hoses. See Chapter Six. If the hoses are not plugged, replace the valve as described in this chapter.

2. Reinstall the PCV valve and remove the crankcase breather cap, vent retainer or fresh air inlet hose from the valve cover (this is located on the opposite valve cover of V6 engines). Hold a piece of stiff paper, such as a price tag or a 3x5 memo card, over the valve cover opening (**Figure 28**). Wait approximately 60 seconds for crankcase pressure to be reduced. Shortly thereafter, the paper should be sucked to the valve cover opening. If it is not, check for a plugged PCV hose (Chapter Six).

3. Shut the engine off. Reinstall the breather cap, vent retainer or fresh air inlet hose and remove the PCV valve from the valve cover a second time. Shake the valve and listen for the rattle of the check needle in the valve. If no rattle is heard, replace the valve as described in this chapter.

PCV Valve Replacement

The vehicles covered in this manual use PCV valves with different flow rates calibrated to the engine and model year. A new PCV valve should be of the same design and bear the same part number as the one being replaced.

1. Disconnect the hose from the PCV valve.

2. Remove the PCV valve from the valve cover grommet with an upward rotating motion. Discard the valve.

> *NOTE*
> *Do not attempt to clean and reuse a plugged PCV valve.*

3. Check the condition of the valve cover grommet and replace as required.

4. Install the new valve in the valve cover grommet with a downward rotating motion.

5. Position the valve with the vacuum nipple facing the PCV hose. Reconnect the hose to the valve.

Exhaust Gas Recirculation (EGR) System

The EGR valve is mounted on an adapter housing on the intake manifold (I4) or at the rear of an intake manifold riser near the carburetor or TBI unit (V6). See **Figure 29** (I4) or **Figure 30** (V6). Test the system (Chapter Six) at the intervals stated in **Table 1**. If the valve does not function as described, remove it and inspect the orifice hole for deposits. EGR valves should be replaced, not cleaned. At the same time, inspect and clean the EGR passages in the intake manifold as required.

Evaporative Emission Canister (EEC)

Canister size, design and location differ according to model year and engine application. **Figure 31** shows a typical design located in the engine compartment.

Inspect the canister lines and connections, as well as the fuel tank filler cap, when checking the evaporative emission control system as specified in **Table 1**.

Early Fuel Evaporation (EFE) Valve (Exhaust Heat Control Valve)

A butterfly valve controlled by a vacuum diaphragm is installed between the exhaust pipe and manifold flange (**Figure 32**). This exhaust heat control or EFE valve decreases engine warm-up time and aids in vaporization of fuel when the engine is cold. If the valve sticks, engine performance and fuel economy will be impaired.

Remove the vacuum line at the EFE diaphragm and connect a hand vacuum pump to the diaphragm nipple. Apply 7-10 in. Hg vacuum while watching the linkage for movement. If the linkage does not move, the diaphragm is defective. Lubricate the shaft with a suitable heat control valve lubricant.

Drive Belt Condition and Tension

Check the alternator, water pump, AIR pump, air conditioning and power steering pump drive belts for fraying, glazing or cracking of the contact surfaces. Belts that are damaged or deteriorated should be replaced (Chapter Seven) before they fail and cause serious problems from engine overheating, electrical system failure or reduction of steering control.

Check and adjust (if necessary) the tension of all drive belts (Chapter Seven). A belt that is too loose will cause the driven components to operate at less than required efficiency. A belt that is adjusted too tightly will wear rapidly and place unnecessary side

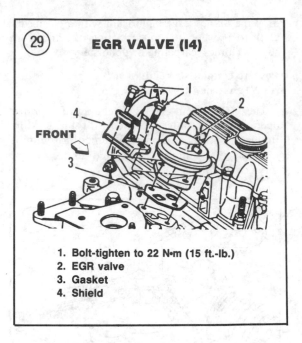

EGR VALVE (I4)

1. Bolt-tighten to 22 N•m (15 ft.-lb.)
2. EGR valve
3. Gasket
4. Shield

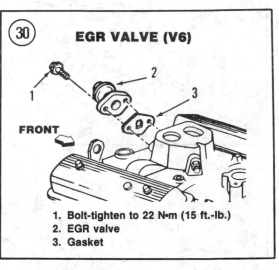

EGR VALVE (V6)

1. Bolt-tighten to 22 N•m (15 ft.-lb.)
2. EGR valve
3. Gasket

loads on the bearings of driven components, which can cause premature wear or failure of the components.

Brake System

Check the brake master cylinder fluid level as described in this chapter.

Inspect all brake lines, hoses and fittings for abrasion, kinks, leakage and other damage; replace as necessary. Any line that is less than perfect should be replaced immediately.

Check all connections to make sure they are tight and look for any signs of leakage which might indicate a cracked or otherwise unserviceable connection. As with lines and hoses, any connections that are less than perfect should be replaced.

Always bleed the brakes after opening a system connection. See Chapter Twelve.

Check all brake shoe linings (disc and drum) for signs of brake fluid, oil or grease contamination on the friction material. If any contamination is present, the linings must be replaced regardless of how much material remains.

Measure the linings to determine their serviceability. If any brake shoe lining (disc or drum) has worn down to within 1/32 in. of a rivet head (**Figure 33**) or the backing plate on bonded shoes, replace the linings on both wheels.

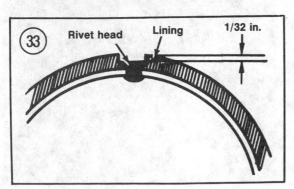

Power Steering

Check the power steering fluid level in the pump reservoir as described in this chapter.

Check all power steering hoses and lines for proper connections, leaks or deterioration. If abrasion or excessive wear is evident, locate and correct the cause immediately.

Manual Steering Gearbox Seal

The steering gearbox is permanently lubricated and should require no service other than checking around the Pitman arm and housing for seal leakage and oozing. Leakage (solid grease, not just an oily film) should be corrected immediately.

Cooling System

> *WARNING*
> *Personal injury is possible. Perform cooling system service when the engine is cold.*

Clean exterior of radiator and air conditioning condenser with compressed air and inspect radiator hoses at least once a year for cracks, checks, swelling or other signs of deterioration. Make sure that all hoses are correctly routed and installed and that all clamps are tight. Replace hoses at every coolant change.

Remove the radiator cap and check the condition of the coolant. If it is dirty or rusty, the system should be drained, flushed and refilled with fresh coolant regardless of the mileage. Replace the coolant every 24 months or 30,000 miles. See Chapter Seven.

Manual Transmission and Rear Axle Lubricant Level

Manual transmission fluid should be changed at 7,500 miles, then at every 30,000 mile interval. Periodic or seasonal rear axle lubricant changes are not required but the fluid level should be checked each time the crankcase oil is changed. Top up if necessary with the recommended lubricant (**Table 1**).

1. Drive the vehicle several miles to bring the lubricant to normal operating temperature.
2. Set the parking brake and block the drive wheels (transmission check) or front wheels (rear axle check).
3. Raise the front or rear of the vehicle as required with a jack and place it on jackstands.

4. Clean all dirt and grease from the fill/level or fill plug. See **Figure 34** (manual transmission) or **Figure 35** (rear axle) for typical plug locations.

5. Unscrew and remove the fill/level or fill plug. The lubricant level should be even with the bottom of the fill/level plug hole (manual transmission) or within 3/8 in. of the bottom of the fill hole (rear axle). If not, top up with the recommended lubricant (**Table 4**) and reinstall the plug. Wipe any excess lubricant from the transmission case or differential housing.

6. Remove the jackstands and lower the vehicle to the ground. Remove the wheel chocks.

**Manual Transmission and
Rear Axle Lubricant Change**

If the vehicle has been driven only a few hundred miles each month, the lubricant should be changed more frequently than indicated in **Table 1**, as in the case where the vehicle is operated in extremely cold weather when the temperature is frequently below 10° F. Acids that form in the lubricant during short-haul driving or during operation in extremely cold weather are injurious to moving parts. In addition, lubricants should be changed whenever water has entered the component and contaminated the oil.

With limited slip rear axles, drain and refill to level of fill plug hole at first 7,500 miles. Change lubricant at 15,000-mile intervals when using vehicle to pull a trailer. Add 4 oz. of GM lubricant additive (part No. 1052358) or equivalent, then fill with GM gear lubricant part No. 1052271 or equivalent.

1. Drive the vehicle several miles to bring the lubricant to normal operating temperature.

2. Set the parking brake and block the wheels that will remain on the ground.

3. Raise the front or rear of the vehicle as appropriate with a jack and place it on jackstands.

4. Clean all dirt and grease from around the fill/level or fill plug. See **Figure 34** or **Figure 35** as required.

5. Manual transmission:
   a. Place a drain pan under the transmission and remove the drain plug. Let the lubricant drain for 10-15 minutes.
   b. Clean and reinstall the drain plug snugly.
   c. Fill the transmission with the recommended lubricant (**Table 4**). The level is correct when the fluid just starts to seep from the fill/level hole.

d. Clean and reinstall the fill/level plug snugly.
e. Wipe any excess lubricant from the transmission case.

6. Rear axle:
   a. Unscrew and remove the filler plug.
   b. Remove the old oil with a suction pump.
   c. If a suction pump is not available, place a drain pan under the differential and loosen the

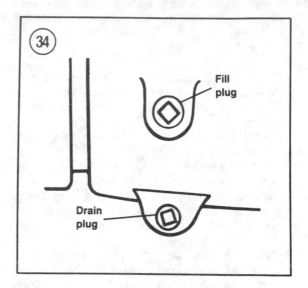

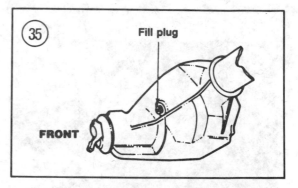

3

rear cover bolts several turns. Tap the edge of the cover to break it loose and let the oil drain for 10-15 minutes.

d. Remove the cover and discard the gasket. Clean all gasket residue from the cover and differential flange. Reinstall the cover with a new gasket, tightening the bolts in a crisscross pattern. See Chapter Eleven.

e. Fill the differential with the appropriate type of lubricant until the level reaches the bottom of the filler hole and just starts to seep out.

f. Clean and reinstall the filler plug. Tighten the plug snugly but do not overtighten or you may strip the threads on the differential housing. Wipe any excess lubricant from the differential housing.

7. Remove the jackstands and lower the vehicle to the ground.

8. After driving the vehicle about 100 miles, check for leaks around the drain plug. If leakage is found, correct the problem and recheck the oil level as described in this chapter.

Automatic Transmission Service

Automatic transmission fluid will deliver 100,000 miles of service at normal operating temperature (approximately 175° F) before

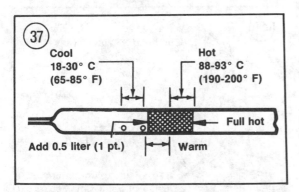

Figure 37

Cool
18-30° C
(65-85° F)

Hot
88-93° C
(190-200° F)

Full hot

Add 0.5 liter (1 pt.)   Warm

Figure 38

oxidation occurs. When a transmission operates at above normal temperature, the service life of its fluid is cut in half with each 20° F increase in temperature. See **Table 5**.

If fluid operating temperature is allowed to reach 500° F, the metals inside the transmission will start to warp rapidly. For this reason, rocking a vehicle out of snow, mud or sand by rapidly shifting from FORWARD to REVERSE and back should be avoided if at all possible. If attempted, do not rock the vehicle for more than 1-2 minutes.

Fluid color and smell are no longer valid indicators of fluid condition. DEXRON II turns dark early in its service life and will emit a burned smell after only a few hundred miles of use.

Level Check

1. Check the fluid level with the transmission at operating temperature, engine running and the vehicle parked on level ground with the parking brake set and the transmission selector in PARK.

2. Clean all dirt from the transmission dipstick cap. See **Figure 36** (typical). Pull the dipstick from the tube, wipe with a clean, lint-free cloth and reinsert until the cap seats fully. Wait a few seconds, then remove the dipstick a second time and note the reading (**Figure 37**).

3. If the fluid level is low, add sufficient automatic transmission fluid of the recommended type (**Table 4**) to bring it to the proper level on the dipstick. Reinsert the dipstick and make sure it is fully seated in the tube.

> *CAUTION*
> *Do not overfill the transmission. Too much fluid can damage the transmission.*

Fluid Change

Under normal circumstances, automatic transmission fluid is changed at 100,000 mile intervals. If the vehicle has been subjected to constant severe service such as those stated in **Table 1**, change the fluid and strainer at 30,000 mile intervals.

1. Drive the vehicle several miles to bring the lubricant to normal operating temperature.

2. Set the parking brake and block the rear wheels.

3. Raise the front of the vehicle with a jack and place it on jackstands.

4. Place a drain pan underneath the transmission.

5. Loosen all pan attaching bolts (**Figure 38**) a few turns. Tap one corner of the pan with a rubber hammer to break it loose and let the fluid drain.

6. When the fluid has drained to the level of the pan flange, remove the pan bolts at the rear of the pan (**Figure 39**). This will let the pan drop at the rear and drain slowly.

7. When all fluid has drained, remove the pan and let the strainer drain.

8. Remove any gasket or sealant residue from the pan and transmission case mating flanges.

9. Discard the gasket and clean the pan thoroughly with solvent and lint-free cloths or paper towels.

10. Remove the strainer attaching screws (**Figure 40**). Remove the strainer from the transmission valve body. Check the attaching nipple on the strainer for an O-ring seal. If it is not on the strainer, remove it from the valve body bore.

11. Install a new O-ring on the new strainer nipple. Install the strainer to the valve body bore and tighten the attaching screws securely.

12. Apply a 1/16 in. bead of RTV sealant to the pan mounting flange. See **Figure 41**.

NOTE
*If the pan flange has a raised rib as shown in **Figure 42**, do not use RTV sealant. This pan design requires the use of a gasket.*

13. Install the pan on the transmission and tighten the attaching bolts to 10-13 ft.-lb. (14-18 N•m) in a crisscross pattern.

14. Insert a clean funnel containing a fine-mesh filter in the filler tube and pour approximately 4 quarts of fresh DEXRON II automatic transmission fluid into the transmission.

15. Start the engine and let it idle for 2 minutes with the gear selector in PARK. Increase the engine speed to approximately 1,200 rpm and let it run until it reaches normal operating temperature.

16. Depress and hold the foot brake. Slowly move the selector lever through each gear range, pausing long enough for the transmission to engage. Return to the PARK position.

17. Remove the dipstick and wipe it with a clean, lint-free cloth. Reinsert the dipstick in the filler tube until it seats completely.

CAUTION
Do not overfill the transmission. Too much fluid is harmful. If the fluid level is above the specified mark on the dipstick with the fluid at normal operating temperature, drain enough fluid to correct the level.

18. Remove the dipstick and check the fluid level. Add sufficient fluid as required to bring the fluid to the appropriate level on the dipstick (**Figure 37**).

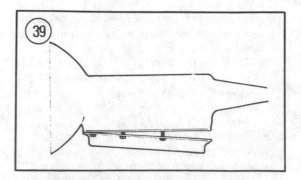

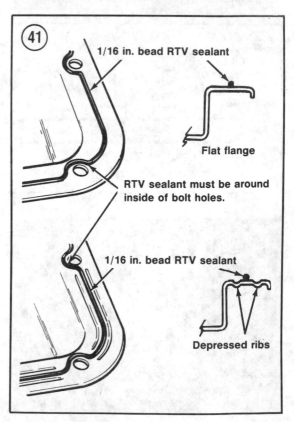

1/16 in. bead RTV sealant

Flat flange

RTV sealant must be around inside of bolt holes.

1/16 in. bead RTV sealant

Depressed ribs

19. Once the fluid level is correct, check for and correct any leaks at the filler tube connection and around the edge of the oil pan.

20. Road test the vehicle to make sure the transmission operates properly. After driving the vehicle approximately 100 miles, recheck the fluid level and correct, if necessary.

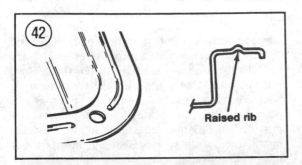

Raised rib

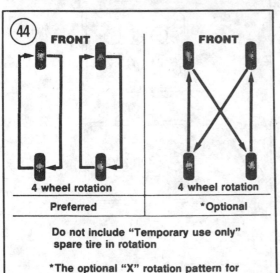

4 wheel rotation | 4 wheel rotation
Preferred | *Optional

Do not include "Temporary use only" spare tire in rotation

*The optional "X" rotation pattern for radials is acceptable when required for more uniform tire wear

Carburetor Choke and Vacuum Lines

Make sure that the choke and vacuum break diaphragm(s) work properly and freely. Inspect vacuum lines for proper routing and connection. Check vacuum line condition and replace any that are cracked, split or deteriorated.

Carburetor Choke and Throttle Linkage

Inspect the choke and vacuum break linkage (Figure 43) for proper operation. Spray the choke linkage and shaft with choke or carburetor cleaner to remove any gum or varnish. Check the carburetor linkage for damaged or missing parts. Work the throttle lever back and forth to check for interference or binding. Correct as required. Spray the linkage with carburetor cleaner and lubricate with WD-40.

Carburetor or Throttle Body Mounting Fasteners

Check mounting fastener torque. Tighten long carburetor fasteners to 7 ft.-lb. (9 N•m) and short fasteners to 11 ft.-lb. (15 N•m). Tighten I4 throttle body fasteners to 13 ft.-lb. (18 N•m) and V6 fasteners to 12 ft.-lb. (16 N•m).

Exhaust System

Check the entire exhaust system from exhaust manifold to tailpipe. Look for broken, damaged, missing, corroded or misaligned components, open seams, holes, loose connections or any other defect that could allow exhaust gases to enter the passenger compartment.

Inspect the catalytic converter heat shields (if so equipped) for looseness or damage. Tighten or replace as required. Remove any debris that may have lodged or accumulated in or around the shields. Make sure there is adequate clearance between the exhaust system components and nearby body areas.

Whenever the muffler requires replacement, replace the exhaust pipe and resonator (if so equipped) to the rear of the muffler to maintain exhaust system integrity.

Tire Rotation

Inspect the tires for cracks, bumps, bulges or other defects. Look for signs of excessive wear. Rotate radial tires at the first 7,000 miles, then every 15,000 miles thereafter. Rotate bias-belted tires every 6,000 miles. Refer to Figure 44 for recommended rotation patterns.

Front Wheel Bearings

Clean, repack and adjust bearings. See Chapter Ten.

Oxygen Sensor

Replace the sensor as required. See *Emission Control Systems* in Chapter Six.

Idle Stop Solenoid

On carburretted models, check operation of the idle stop solenoid (if so equipped).

1. Turn the ignition switch ON but do not start the engine. If equipped with air conditioning, turn the air conditioner ON.

2. Open the throttle until the solenoid plunger fully extends, then close the throttle. Unplug the solenoid electrical lead and the plunger should move away from the throttle lever.

3. Reconnect the solenoid lead and the plunger should extend again until it touches the throttle lever. If it does not, connect a test lamp between the solenoid feed wire and ground.

    a. If the test lamp lights, replace the solenoid.

    b. If it does not light, look for an open circuit in the feed wire and correct the condition.

Fuel Tank, Cap and Lines

Inspect the fuel tank, cap and lines for leaks or damage. Remove the fuel cap and check the gasket for an even filler neck imprint.

ENGINE TUNE-UP

A tune-up consists of a series of inspections, adjustments and parts replacements to compensate for normal wear and deterioration of engine components. Regular tune-ups are important for proper emission control and fuel economy.

Since proper engine operation depends upon a number of interrelated system functions, a tune-up consisting of only one or two corrections will seldom give lasting results. For improved power, performance and operating economy, a thorough and systematic procedure of analysis and correction is necessary.

Vehicle Emission Control Information (VECI) Decal

Federal government regulations require that a VECI decal be located on the valve cover or elsewhere in the engine compartment. This decal contains the required tune-up specifications and procedures necessary to keep the engine emissions within specified levels for the make, model and model year vehicle. Since running changes which affect emission control are instituted at the factory, these specifications and procedures may vary considerably during a model year. For this reason, it is important that you consult the VECI decal for your vehicle to obtain the proper specifications and procedures. If either varies from the information provided in this manual, *always* follow the decal instructions, as they represent the most current information available concerning your vehicle.

Tune-Up Sequence

Because different systems in an engine interact, the tune-up should be carried out in the following order.

    a. Compression check.

    b. Ignition system work.

    c. Fuel system inspection and adjustment.

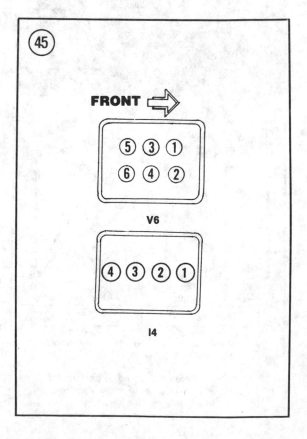

Compression Test

An engine with low or uneven compression cannot be properly tuned. Whenever the spark plugs are removed from the engine, it is a good idea to run a compression test. A compression test measures the compression pressure built up in each cylinder. Its results can be used to assess general cylinder and valve condition. In addition, it can warn of developing problems inside the engine.

1. Warm the engine to normal operating temperature (upper radiator hose hot). Shut the engine off. Make sure the choke and throttle valves are wide open on carburetted models.
2. Remove all spark plugs as described in this chapter.
3. Disconnect the pink wire between the HEI distributor and the ignition coil.
4. Connect a remote start switch to the starter solenoid according to manufacturer's instructions. Leave the ignition key in the OFF position.
5. Connect a compression tester to the No. 1 cylinder according to manufacturer's instructions.

NOTE
*The No. 1 cylinder is the front cylinder on the I4 engine and the front cylinder on the left (driver's side) bank on the V6. See **Figure 45**.*

6. Crank the engine at least 5 turns with the remote start switch or until there is no further increase in compression shown on the tester gauge.

7. Remove the compression tester and record the reading. Relieve the tester pressure valve.
8. Test the remaining cylinders in the same manner.

When interpreting the results, actual readings are not as important as the differences in readings. The lowest must be within 75 percent of the highest. A greater difference indicates worn or broken rings, leaking or sticking valves or a combination of these problems.

If the compression test indicates a problem (excessive variation in readings), isolate the cause with a wet compression test. This is done in the same way as the dry compression test, except that about 1 teaspoon of oil is poured down the spark plug hole before performing Steps 5-7. If the wet compression readings are much greater than the dry compression readings, the trouble is probably due to worn or broken rings. If there is little difference between the wet and dry readings, the problem is probably due to leaky or sticking valves. If 2 adjacent cylinders read low in both tests, the head gasket may be leaking.

Spark Plug Replacement

Spark plugs should be replaced at intervals specified in **Table 1**.

CAUTION
Whenever the spark plugs are removed, dirt from around them can fall into the spark plug holes. This can cause expensive engine damage.

1. Blow out any foreign matter from around the spark plugs with compressed air. Use a compressor if you have one. Cans of compressed inert gas are available from photo stores.
2. Disconnect the spark plug wires by twisting the wire boot back and forth on the plug insulator while pulling upward (**Figure 46**). Pulling on the wire instead of the boot may cause internal damage to the wire. Wire removal with spark plug terminal pliers (**Figure 46**) is recommended where there is enough clearance for their use.
3. Remove the plugs with a 5/8 in. spark plug socket. Keep the plugs in order so you know which cylinder each one came from.

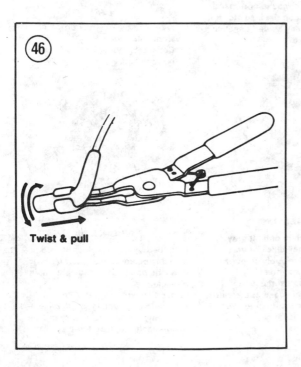

Twist & pull

SPARK PLUG CONDITION

NORMAL
- Identified by light tan or gray deposits on the firing tip.
- Can be cleaned.

GAP BRIDGED
- Identified by deposit buildup closing gap between electrodes.
- Caused by oil or carbon fouling. If deposits are not excessive, the plug can be cleaned.

OIL FOULED
- Identified by wet black deposits on the insulator shell bore and electrodes.
- Caused by excessive oil entering combustion chamber through worn rings and pistons, excessive clearance between valve guides and stems, or worn or loose bearings. Can be cleaned. If engine is not repaired, use a hotter plug.

CARBON FOULED
- Identified by black, dry fluffy carbon deposits on insulator tips, exposed shell surfaces and electrodes.
- Caused by too cold a plug, weak ignition, dirty air cleaner, too rich a fuel mixture, or excessive idling. Can be cleaned.

LEAD FOULED
- Identified by dark gray, black, yellow, or tan deposits or a fused glazed coating on the insulator tip.
- Caused by highly leaded gasoline. Can be cleaned.

WORN
- Identified by severely eroded or worn electrodes.
- Caused by normal wear. Should be replaced.

FUSED SPOT DEPOSIT
- Identified by melted or spotty deposits resembling bubbles or blisters.
- Caused by sudden acceleration. Can be cleaned.

OVERHEATING
- Identified by a white or light gray insulator with small black or gray brown spots and with bluish-burnt appearance of electrodes.
- Caused by engine overheating, wrong type of fuel, loose spark plugs, too hot a plug, or incorrect ignition timing. Replace the plug.

PREIGNITION
- Identified by melted electrodes and possibly blistered insulator. Metallic deposits on insulator indicate engine damage.
- Caused by wrong type of fuel, incorrect ignition timing or advance, too hot a plug, burned valves, or engine overheating. Replace the plug.

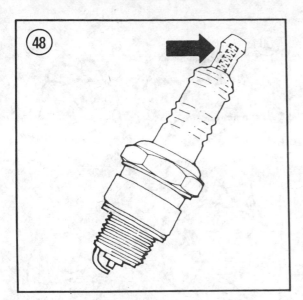

3

4. Examine each spark plug. Compare its condition with **Figure 47**. Spark plug condition indicates engine condition and can warn of developing trouble.

5. Discard the plugs. Although they could be cleaned, regapped and reused if in good condition, they seldom last very long. New plugs are inexpensive and far more reliable.

6. Remove the plugs from the box. Tapered plugs do not use gaskets. Some plug brands may have small end pieces that must be screwed on (**Figure 48**) before the plugs can be used.

7. Determine the correct gap setting from the VECI decal. Use a spark plug gapping tool to check the gap. **Figure 49** shows two common types. Insert the appropriate size wire gauge between the electrodes. If the gap is correct, there will be a slight drag as the wire is pulled through. If there is no drag or if the wire will not pull through, bend

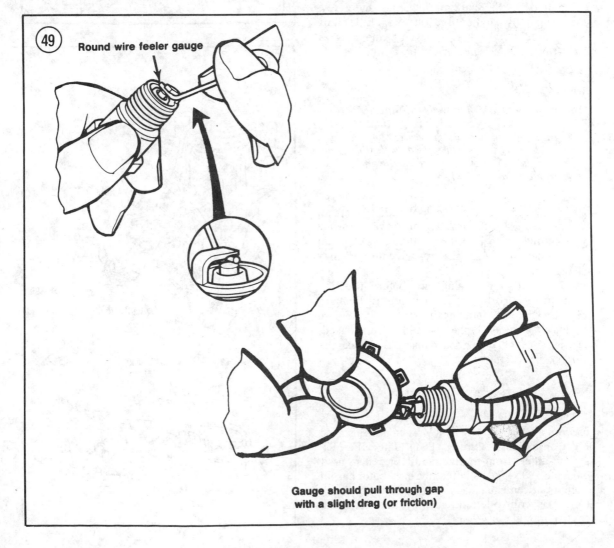

Round wire feeler gauge

Gauge should pull through gap
with a slight drag (or friction)

the side electrode with the gapping tool (**Figure 50**) to change the gap and then remeasure with the wire gauge.

> *NOTE*
> *Never try to close the electrode gap by tapping the spark plug on a solid surface. This can damage the plug internally. Always use a spark plug tool to open and close the gap.*

8. Check spark plug hole threads and clean with an appropriate size spark plug thread chaser, if necessary, before installing plugs. This will remove any corrosion, carbon build-up or minor flaws from the threads. Coat the chaser with grease to catch chips or foreign matter. Use care to avoid cross-threading.

9. Apply a thin film of engine oil or anti-seize compound to the spark plug threads and screw each plug in by hand until it seats. Very little effort is required. If force is necessary, the plug is cross-threaded. Unscrew it and try again.

> *NOTE*
> *On V6 engines, access to the rear cylinder spark plug wells is limited. To install such plugs more easily, slip a 10 in. length of fuel line hose over the end of the plug. This will serve as a flexible handle and allow you to screw the plugs in easily and quickly.*

10. After seating the plug by hand, tighten an additional 1/4-3/8 turn. If you have a torque wrench, tighten to 7-15 ft.-lb. (10-20 N•m). Do not overtighten the plugs, as excessive torque may change the gap setting.

11. Inspect the spark plug wires before installing them to their correct cylinder locations. Refer to **Figure 51** for 4-cylinder engine routing and **Figure 52** for V6 routing. If the insulation is oil soaked, brittle, torn or otherwise damaged, replace the wire(s).

IGNITION SERVICE

The Delco High Energy Ignition (HEI) system is used on all gasoline engines. Most engines also use Electronic Spark Timing (EST). The HEI-EST system differs from the standard HEI system used on some 1985 models in that the distributor has no vacuum or centrifugal advance mechanisms. Spark timing is controlled directly by the electronic control module or ECM.

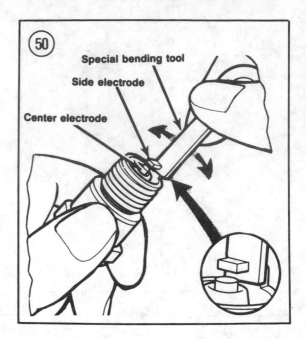

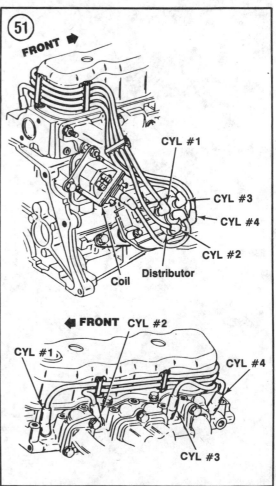

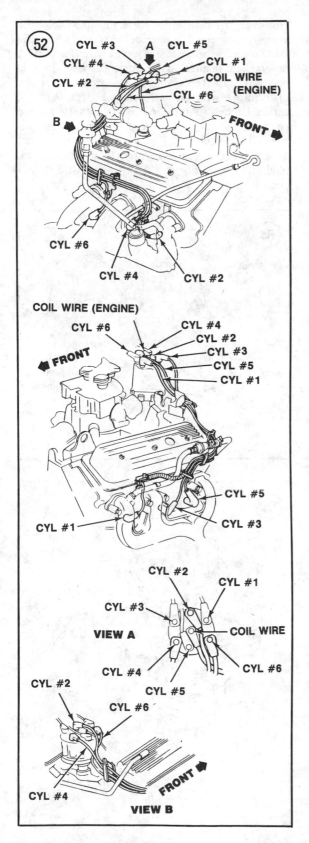

Fuel injected V6 engines use a modified HEI system with Electronic Spark Control (ESC) and/or EST. The ESC system controls engine detonation by automatically retarding ignition timing by as much as 15° whenever a knock sensor detects vibrations caused by detonation. The sensor signals a solid-state controller which in turns signals the distributor module to adjust timing.

The HEI is a pulse-triggered, transistor controlled, inductive discharge system. Breaker points are not used. Principal system components are the ignition coil, electronic module, magnetic pickup assembly or Hall-effect switch and the centrifugal and vacuum advance mechanisms.

Ignition Coil

The HEI coil operates in basically the same way as a standard coil, but is smaller in size and generates a higher secondary voltage. Some models use a remote coil; others have the coil mounted in the distributor cap (**Figure 53**).

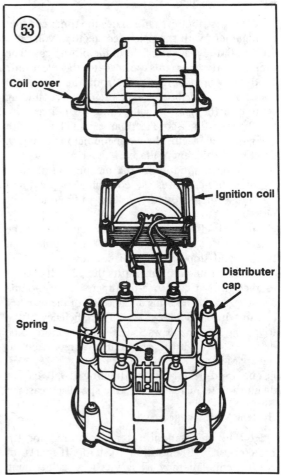

Electronic Module

The electronic module is contained within the distributor housing (**Figure 54**). Circuits within the module perform 5 basic functions: spark triggering, switching, current limiting, dwell control and distributor pickup. Modules used in EST or ESC distributors also control timing advance. The standard HEI module has 4 terminals; the HEI/EST module has 7 terminals.

Magnetic Pickup Assembly or Hall-effect Switch

The magnetic pickup assembly consists of a timer core with external teeth (one for each cylinder) which is rotated by the distributor shaft, a stationary pole piece with internal teeth bottom plate. The Hall-effect vane switch used in some late model distributors contains a stator assembly with one window in the vane for each cylinder assembly. Some distributors may use both assemblies. **Figure 55** shows the Hall-effect switch.

System Operation

As the distributor shaft rotates the timer core out of alignment with the pole piece teeth, a voltage is created in the magnetic field of the pickup coil. The pickup coil sends this voltage to the electronic module, which determines from the rotational speed of the distributor shaft when to start building current in the ignition coil primary windings.

When the timer core teeth are again aligned with the pole piece teeth, the magnetic field is changed, creating a different voltage. This signal is sent to the electronic module by the pickup coil primary circuit. This collapses the coil magnetic field and induces a high secondary voltage to fire one spark plug.

The Hall-effect switch uses the windows in the rotating stator assembly to signal the module when to start and stop primary current flow.

The electronic module limits the 12-volt current to the ignition coil to 5-6 amperes. The module also triggers the opening and closing of the primary circuit with zero energy loss. The efficiency of the triggering system allows 35,000 volts or more to be delivered through the secondary wiring system to the spark plugs.

The module circuit controlling dwell causes dwell time to increase as engine speed increases.

System Maintenance

Routine maintenance is not required for the breakerless HEI ignition system. If parts or components fail, they are serviced by replacement.

However, the distributor cap and rotor should be visually inspected at periodic intervals. At the same time, inspect the spark plug wires for burned or cracked insulation or other damage. If it is necessary to replace one or more wires on distributors with an integral coil, depress the 2 spring latches (**Figure 56**). Half of the wires are connected to the connector; the other half remain connected to the cap. Replace one wire at a time. This will prevent any confusion as to which spark plug and distributor cap terminal the wire should connect to.

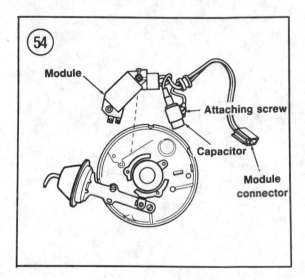

Module
Attaching screw
Capacitor
Module connector

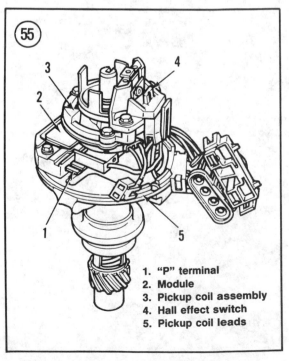

1. "P" terminal
2. Module
3. Pickup coil assembly
4. Hall effect switch
5. Pickup coil leads

The HEI system uses large (8 mm) diameter, silicone-insulated spark plug wires. While these are more heat resistant and less vulnerable to deterioration than standard wires, they should not be mistreated. When removing wires from spark plugs, grasp them only by the boots. Twist the boot 1/2 turn in either direction to break the seal, then pull to remove. Use of spark plug wire pliers (**Figure 46**) is recommended for wire removal.

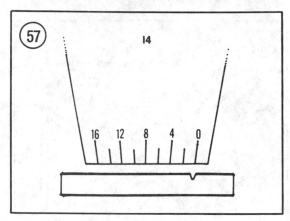

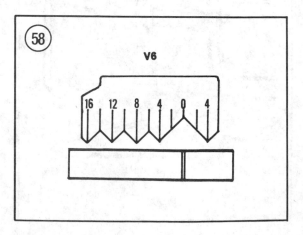

The only adjustments possible on the HEI distributor are centrifugal and vacuum advance, both of which should be entrusted to a dealer or automotive ignition system specialist. On models equipped with EST, ESC or EST/ESC, the distributor contains no advance mechanisms. Distributor advance is electronically controlled by the ignition module.

Suspected ignition trouble with the HEI ignition should be referred to a dealer or ignition specialist. Testing requires special equipment and skills and an otherwise good electronic circuit can be damaged by an incorrect test connection.

Distributor Cap, Wires and Rotor

The distributor cap, wires and rotor should be inspected at intervals specified in **Table 1**.
1. Depress the distributor cap latch screws with a suitable screwdriver and turn 90°. Lift the cap straight up and off to prevent rotor blade damage.
2. Check the carbon button and electrodes inside the distributor cap for dirt, corrosion or arcing. Check the cap for cracks. Replace the cap and rotor as a set, if necessary.
3. Replace the wires if the insulation is melted, brittle or cracked.
4. Loosen the 2 rotor screws. Lift the rotor straight up and off the distributor shaft.
5. Wipe the rotor with a clean, damp cloth. Check for burns, arcing, cracks or other defects. Replace the cap and rotor as a set, if necessary.
6. Reinstall the rotor and tighten the attaching screws.
7. Reinstall the distributor cap. Depress and rotate the cap latch screws 90° to lock the cap in place.

Ignition Timing

Use the following procedure to adjust basic timing on engines equipped with the HEI ignition:
1. Set the parking brake and place the transmission in PARK (automatic) or NEUTRAL (manual).
2. Check the VECI decal to determine the timing specifications, if this information is not already known.
3. Clean the timing marks with a stiff brush. See **Figure 57** (I4) or **Figure 58** (V6) for typical timing marks.
4. Mark the timing mark and pointer with white paint or chalk for better visibility. The paint makes the marks easier to see under the timing light.
5. Disconnect and plug any distributor vacuum advance line(s) with a common pencil or golf tee.
6. Connect an inductive timing light and tachometer to the No. 1 cylinder according to

manufacturer's instructions. Refer to **Figure 59** for I4 engine No. 1 cylinder plug wire and **Figure 60** for V6 No. 1 cylinder plug wire. Use only a clamp-on or inductive timing light with the HEI ignition. The distributor cap has a special terminal marked TACH. Connect one lead of the tachometer to this terminal and the other to ground. Check the test equipment manufacturer's instructions before making connections. Some engines have a special TACH pigtail to permit easy access for connecting test equipment.

WARNING
Keep your hands and hair clear of all drive belts and pulleys. Although they seem to be standing still when viewed with a timing light, they are actually spinning at more than 10 times per second and can cause serious injury.

7. Start the engine and let it warm to normal operating temperature (upper radiator hose hot). Check the curb idle speed and compare to specifications on the VECI decal in the engine compartment. Also note any changes in procedure that differ from the steps given here. If there are differences, follow the VECI decal. If idle speed is incorrect, take the vehicle to a dealer (idle speed is computer-controlled).

8. Aim the timing light at the timing marks. They will appear to stand still or waver slightly under the light. If the timing marks are aligned, the timing is satisfactory.

9. If the timing is incorrect, loosen the distributor hold-down clamp bolt enough to rotate the

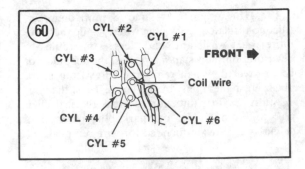

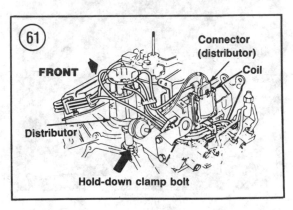

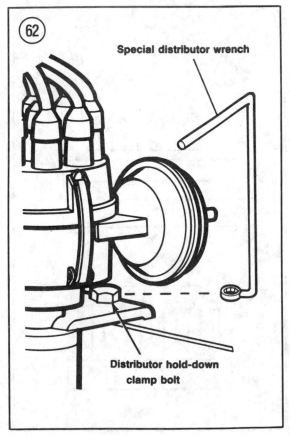

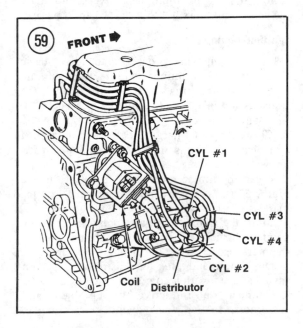

distributor body. See **Figure 61** (V6 shown). The use of a distributor wrench (**Figure 62**) is recommended.

> *WARNING*
> *Never touch the distributor's thick wires when the engine is running. This can cause a painful shock, even if the insulation is in perfect condition.*

10. Grasp the distributor cap and rotate the body clockwise or counterclockwise as required to align the timing marks. When the marks are properly aligned, tighten the hold-down clamp bolt to 17-25 ft.-lb. (23-33 N•m).

11. Recheck timing and shut the engine off.

12. Disconnect and remove the test equipment. Unplug and reconnect the vacuum line to the distributor, if so equipped.

FUEL SYSTEM ADJUSTMENTS

Base idle, fast idle and idle mixture on carburetted and fuel injected engines used with the vehicles covered in this manual are controlled by the Computer Command Control (CCC) electronic control module (ECM) and no attempt at adjustments should be made by the owner/mechanic. If the carburetor or injection system requires adjustment for any reason, see your Chevrolet or GMC dealer.

Table 1 MAINTENANCE SCHEDULE

Every 7,500 miles (12 months)	• **Engine oil change*** • **Chassis/suspension lubrication*** • **Check manual transmission** • **Check exhaust system** • **Check brake system** • **Check power steering system** • **Check rear axle lubricant level*** **Drain/refill limited-slip differential @ first 7,500 miles** • **Check and adjust drive belts**
First 7,500 miles, then every 15,000 miles	• **Check and rotate tires** • **Change engine oil filter***
First 7,500 miles, then every 30,000 miles	• **Change manual transmission fluid** • **Inspect EFE system** • **Check carburetor or TBI unit fastener torque** • **Inspect carburetor choke and hoses**
Every 12,000 miles	• **Check air cleaner operation** • **Check parking brake system**
Annually	• **Check cooling system operation** • **Check coolant condition and protection**
Every 15,000 miles	• **Replace fuel filter** • **Check PCV system operation** • **Check vacuum hose condition** • **Check/adjust drive belts**
Every 2 years	• **Drain, flush and refill cooling system** • **Replace cooling system hoses**
Every 30,000 miles	• **Replace spark plugs*** • **Check spark plug and ignition coil wires, distributor cap and rotor** • **Check EFE valve operation** • **Clean, repack and adjust wheel bearings***

(continued)

Table 1 MAINTENANCE SCHEDULE (cont.)

Every 30,000 miles (cont.)	• Check EGR system operation • Check ignition timing • Inspect fuel tank, cap and lines (Evaporative emission control system) • Check AIR system operation • Replace air cleaner filter • Replace crankcase vent filter • Replace PCV valve* • Check manual steering gear housing seals
Every 100,000 miles	• Change automatic transmission fluid and strainer*

* SEVERE SERVICE OPERATION: If the vehicle is operated under any of the following conditions, change engine oil @ 3,000 miles or 3 month intervals and oil filter @ alternate oil changes. Repack wheelbearings every 15,000 miles.Change rear axle lubricant every 15,000 miles. Change PCV valve every 15,000 miles. Clean and regap spark plugs every 6,000 miles. Lubricate chassis and suspension every 6,000 miles. Change automatic transmission fluid and strainer every 30,000 miles.
a. Extended idle or low-speed operation (short trips, stop-and-go driving).
b. Trailer towing.
c. Operation @ temperatures below 10° F for 60 days or more with most trips under 10 miles.
d. Very dusty or muddy conditions.

Table 2 OIL VISCOSITY

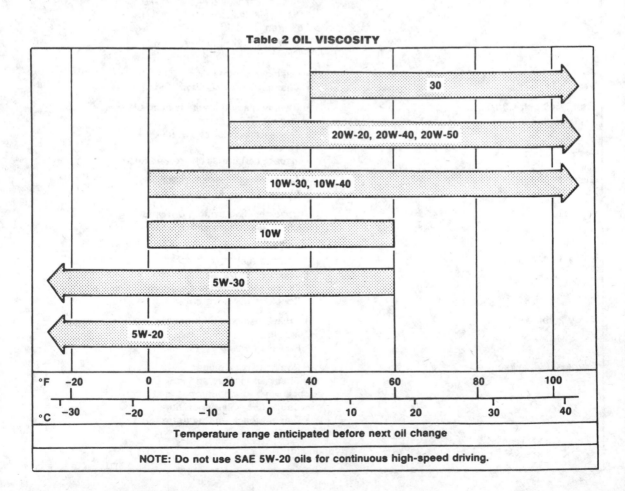

Temperature range anticipated before next oil change

NOTE: Do not use SAE 5W-20 oils for continuous high-speed driving.

Table 3 APPROXIMATE REFILL CAPACITIES

	qt.	pt.
Engine oil		
I4 (with or without filter)	3	
V6		
With filter	5.0	
Without filter	4.0	
Automatic transmission**		
After rebuild		23.0
After fluid change		10.0
Manual transmission		
4-speed	1.3	
5-speed	2.2	
Differential		
7 1/2 in.		3.5
Cooling system*		
I4	10	
V6	13.5	

* If equipped with rear heater, add 2.84 qt.

Table 4 RECOMMENDED LUBRICANTS

Engine crankcase	API Service SF, SF/CC or SF/CD oil
Engine coolant	Prestone II or equivalent
Brake fluid	Delco Supreme 11 or other DOT 3 or DOT 4 fluid
Power steering pump	GM power steering fluid or equivalent
Manual steering gear	GM lubricant part No. 1051052 or equivalent
Manual transmission	SAE 80W or SAE 80W/90 GL-5 gear lubricant
Rear axle (standard)	SAE 80W or SAE 80W/90 GL-5 gear lubricant
Rear axle (limited slip)	GM part No. 1052271 or equivalent plus 4 oz. GM part No. 1052358 additive or equivalent
Automatic transmission	DEXRON II automatic transmission fluid
Shift linkage	Engine oil
Front wheel bearings	GM lubricant part No. 1051344 or equivalent
Chassis lubrication	GM chassis grease meeting 6031-M specification
Hood latch, all hinges	Engine oil
Windshield washer	GM Optikleen washer solvent or equivalent
Key lock cylinders	WD-40 or equivalent

Table 5 AUTOMATIC TRANSMISSION FLUID OXIDATION

Temperature (degrees F)	Life expectancy (in miles)
175	100,000
195	50,000
212	25,000
235	12,000
255	6,250
275	3,000
295	1,500
315	750
335	325
355	160
375	80
390	40
415	Less than 30 minutes

CHAPTER FOUR

4-CYLINDER ENGINE

The basc enginc is a 151 cid (2.5 liter) 4-cylinder engine of cast iron manufactured by Pontiac. The engine is mounted longitudinally in the engine compartment, with the No. 1 cylinder at the front of the vehicle. The firing order is 1-3-4-2.

The cast iron cylinder head contains intake and exhaust valves with integral valve guides. Rocker arms are retained on individual threaded shoulder bolts. A ball pivot valve train is used, with camshaft motion transferred through hydraulic roller lifters to the rocker arms by pushrods. The gear-driven camshaft is supported by 3 bearings.

The oil pump is driven by the camshaft and is mounted at the bottom of the engine block.

The crankshaft is supported by 5 main bearings. The No. 5 bearing provides the crankshaft thrust surfaces.

The cylinder block is cast iron with full length water jackets around each cylinder.

Figure 1 shows the cylinder head assembly. **Figure 2** shows the cylinder block assembly.

Engine specifications (**Table 1**) and tightening torques (**Table 2**) are at the end of the chapter.

ENGINE IDENTIFICATION

An engine identification number is located on a pad at the rear of the block below the exhaust manifold. The pad also contains the Vehicle Identification Number or VIN. See **Figure 3** for typical location. This information indicates if there are unique parts or if internal changes have been made during the model year. It is important when ordering replacement parts for The engine.

The engine code is the 8th digit/letter of the Vehicle Identification Number (VIN). The VIN is the official identification for title and vehicle registration. The VIN is stamped on a gray-colored plate fastened to the upper left corner of the instrument panel close to the windshield on the driver's side (**Figure 4**). It can be read from outside the vehicle.

GASKET SEALANT

Gasket sealant is used instead of pre-formed gaskets between numerous mating surfaces on the

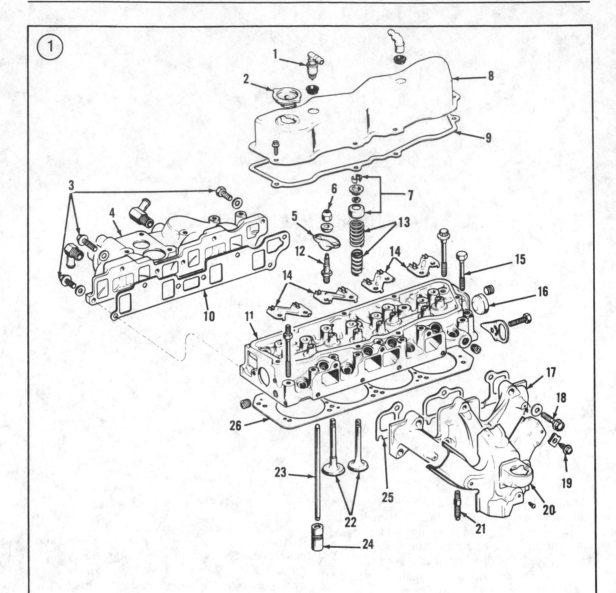

CYLINDER HEAD (I4 ENGINE)

1. PCV valve
2. Oil filler cap
3. Intake manifold attaching screws
4. Intake manifold
5. Rocker arm
6. Rocker arm pivot ball and nut
7. Valve spring retainer assembly
8. Cylinder head cover (rocker cover)
9. Cylinder head cover gasket
10. Intake manifold gasket
11. Cylinder head
12. Rocker arm stud
13. Valve spring
14. Pushrod guide
15. Cylinder head bolts
16. Cylinder head core plug
17. Exhaust manifold
18. Exhaust manifold bolt
19. Oil level indicator tube attaching screw
20. Exhaust manifold heat shroud (heat shield)
21. Exhaust manifold to exhaust pipe stud
22. Valves
23. Pushrod
24. Lifter
25. Exhaust manifold gasket
26. Cylinder head gasket

CYLINDER BLOCK (I4 ENGINE)

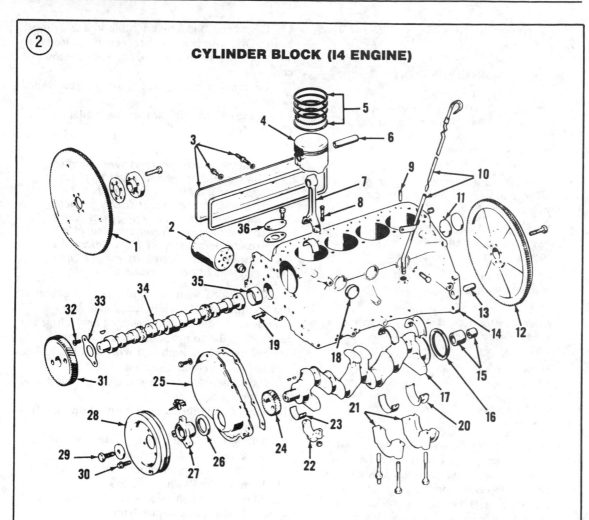

1. **Drive plate and ring (automatic transmission)**
2. **Oil filter**
3. **Pushrod cover and bolts**
4. **Piston**
5. **Piston ring**
6. **Piston pin**
7. **Connecting rod**
8. **Connecting rod bolt**
9. **Dowel**
10. **Oil level indicator and tube**
11. **Camshaft plug**
12. **Flywheel and ring gear (manual transmission)**
13. **Dowel**
14. **Cylinder block**
15. **Pilot and/or converter bushing**
16. **Rear oil seal**
17. **Crankshaft**
18. **Block core plug**
19. **Timing chain oiler**
20. **Main bearings**
21. **Main bearing caps**
22. **Connecting rod bearing cap**
23. **Connecting rod bearing**
24. **Crankshaft gear**
25. **Timing cover (front)**
26. **Timing cover oil seal**
27. **Crankshaft pulley hub**
28. **Crankshaft pulley**
29. **Crankshaft pulley hub bolt**
30. **Crankshaft pulley bolt**
31. **Camshaft pulley bolt**
32. **Camshaft thrust plate screw**
33. **Camshaft thrust plate**
34. **Camshaft**
35. **Camshaft bearing**
36. **Oil pump driveshaft retainer plate, gasket and bolt**

engines covered in this chapter. See *Gasket Sealant*, Chapter One.

ENGINE REMOVAL

WARNING
The engine is heavy, awkward to handle and has sharp edges. It may shift or drop suddenly during removal. To prevent serious injury, always observe the following precautions.

1. Never place any part of your body where a moving or falling engine may trap, cut or crush you.

2. If you must push the engine during removal, use a board or similar tool to keep your hands out of danger.

3. Be sure the hoist is designed to lift engines and has enough load capacity for your engine.

4. Be sure the hoist is securely attached to safe lifting points on the engine.

5. The engine should not be difficult to lift with a proper hoist. If it is, stop lifting, lower the engine back onto its mounts and make sure the engine has been completely separated from the vehicle.

1. Open and support the hood. Relieve fuel system pressure as described in Chapter Six. Disconnect the negative battery cable, then the positive cable.
2. Remove the 4 center console bolts, unsnap the 2 latches at the base of the engine cover and remove the 2 bolts from under the hood which hold the engine cover in place. Remove the engine cover.
3. Remove the headlamp bezels, grille, radiator lower close-out panel and support brace.
4. Remove the lower tie bar. Remove the cross brace.
5. Remove the hood latch mechanism.
6. Remove the upper radiator core support.
7. Drain the cooling system. See Chapter Seven.
8. Disconnect the radiator hoses at the radiator and remove the filler panels. Remove the radiator and fan shroud as a unit. See Chapter Seven.
9. Disconnect the engine wiring harness at the bulkhead connector. Disconnect the harness at the electronic control module and pull it through the bulkhead.
10. Disconnect the heater hoses at the heater core fittings.
11. Disconnect the throttle cable at the throttle body injection unit. Disconnect the transmission TV (throttle valve) and/or speed control cables at the TBI unit, if so equipped.

12. Disconnect the ground cable at the cylinder head. Disconnect all other electrical leads or vacuum lines connected to non-engine mounted components.
13. Disconnect the purge hose at the vapor canister.
14. Remove the air cleaner and adapter. See Chapter Six.

WARNING
The air conditioning system contains pressurized refrigerant which can cause frostbite if it touches skin and blindness if it touches the eyes. If discharged near an open flame, the refrigerant forms poisonous gas. Never disconnect air conditioning system lines unless the system has been discharged and evacuated by a professional.

15. If equipped with air conditioning, disconnect the compressor electrical leads and remove the compressor without disconnecting any refrigerant lines. Place the compressor out of the way.
16. Securely block both rear wheels so the vehicle will not roll in either direction.
17. Raise the front of the vehicle with a jack and place it on jackstands.
18. Disconnect the exhaust pipe at the exhaust manifold.
19. Disconnect the wiring harness at the transmission, starter motor and frame.
20. Remove the starter motor. See Chapter Eight.
21. Remove the flywheel shield.
22. **Manual transmission—Remove the clutch slave cylinder. See Chapter Nine.**

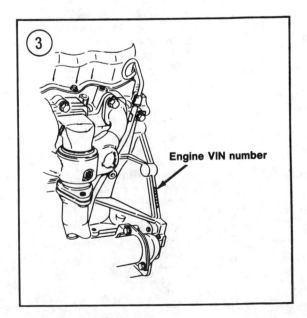

Engine VIN number

23. Automatic transmission—Make matching chalk marks on the converter and flywheel for alignment during installation. Remove the bolts holding the torque converter to the flywheel.
24. Disconnect the fuel hoses at the fuel lines. Plug the hoses and cap the lines to prevent leakage.
25. Remove the motor mount through bolts.
26. Remove the bell housing bolts.
27. Drain the crankcase oil. See Chapter Three.
28. Remove the jackstands and lower the vehicle to the ground.
29. Remove the thermostat housing.
30. Position a floor jack with a block of wood under the transmission housing for support.

NOTE
Double check to make sure all electrical leads, vacuum lines and control links between the engine and engine compartment have been disconnected or removed. Check also to make sure that the air conditioning lines, oil lines and wiring harness will not snag on the engine when it is removed.

31. Attach a suitable lifting device to the engine. With an assistant's help from inside the vehicle, carefully raise the engine up, forward and out of the engine compartment through the front of the vehicle.

ENGINE INSTALLATION

Engine installation is the reverse of removal, plus the following:
1. Position the engine into the vehicle. Leave the lifting device attached and holding the assembly until all mounts and mount fasteners have been installed and tightened to specifications (**Table 2**).

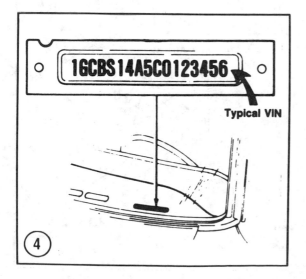

Typical VIN

2. Fill the engine with an oil recommended in Chapter Three.
3. Fill the cooling system and adjust the drive belts. See Chapter Seven.
4. Adjust the ignition timing as required. See Chapter Three.

ENGINE MOUNTS AND SUPPORTS

WARNING
The engine is heavy and may shift or drop suddenly. Never place your hands or any part of your body where the moving engine may trap or crush you. If you can't remove the mounts without placing your hands where the moving engine may injure them, support the engine with a jackstand as well as a hoist to be certain the engine can't fall on you.

Engine mounts are non-adjustable and rarely require service. Replace any broken or deteriorated mounts immediately to reduce strain on remaining mounts and drive line components.

Checking Front Mounts

1. Attach a lifting device and raise the engine enough to remove its weight from the mount.
2. Check the rubber surface of the mount for:
   a. Heat check cracks.
   b. Separation from the metal plate.
   c. Splitting through the center.
3. If any of these defects are noted, replace the mounts as described in this chapter.
4. If movement of the mount relative to the frame is noted during this procedure, lower the engine to place its weight back on the mounts and retighten the mount fasteners.
5. Remove the lifting device.

Checking Rear Mounts

1. Securely block both rear wheels so the vehicle will not roll in either direction.
2. Raise the front of the vehicle with a jack and place it on jackstands.
3. Watch the transmission mount while pushing up and pulling downward on the transmission extension housing. Replace the mount if the rubber separates from the metal plate or if the extension housing moves up but not downward.
4. If movement of the mount relative to the crossmember is noted during this procedure, retighten the mount fasteners.

Front Mount Replacement

Refer to **Figure 5** for this procedure.
1. Securely block the rear wheels so the vehicle will not roll in either direction.
2. Raise the front of the vehicle with a jack and place it on jackstands.
3. Play a hydraulic jack under the engine oil pan. Insert a wooden block between the jack and oil pan.
4. Remove the engine mount through bolt.
5. Raise the engine with the hydraulic jack enough to remove the mount-to-frame bracket bolts. Remove the mount.
6. Install a new engine mount to the frame bracket. Tighten fasteners to specifications (**Table 2**).
7. Lower the engine until the through bolt can be installed. Tighten the through bolt to specifications (**Table 2**).

8. Remove the hydraulic jack and jackstands, then lower the vehicle to the ground.

Rear Mount Replacement

Refer to **Figure 6** for this procedure.
1. Raise the vehicle with a jack and place it on jackstands.
2. Remove the mount-to-crossmember support nut.
3. Position a jack under the rear of the engine and raise it enough to relieve the weight from the rear mount and allow access to the mount-to-transmission bolts.
4. Remove the mount-to-transmission bolts. Remove the mount.
5. Install a new mount to the transmission. Tighten the fasteners to specifications (**Table 2**).

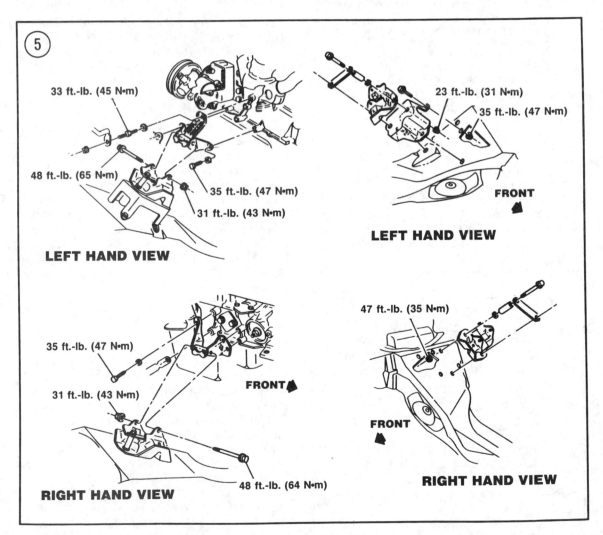

(5)

33 ft.-lb. (45 N•m)

48 ft.-lb. (65 N•m)

35 ft.-lb. (47 N•m)

31 ft.-lb. (43 N•m)

LEFT HAND VIEW

23 ft.-lb. (31 N•m)

35 ft.-lb. (47 N•m)

FRONT

LEFT HAND VIEW

35 ft.-lb. (47 N•m)

31 ft.-lb. (43 N•m)

FRONT

48 ft.-lb. (64 N•m)

RIGHT HAND VIEW

47 ft.-lb. (35 N•m)

FRONT

RIGHT HAND VIEW

6. Lower the engine slowly, aligning the mount stud to the crossmember support hole. Install the mount nut and tighten to specifications (**Table 2**).
7. Remove the jack from under the engine. Remove the jackstands and lower the vehicle to the ground.

DISASSEMBLY CHECKLISTS

To use the checklists, remove and inspect each part in the order mentioned. To reassemble, go through the checklists backwards, installing the parts in order. Each major part is covered in its own section in this chapter, unless otherwise noted.

Decarbonizing or Valve Service

1. Remove the valve cover.
2. Remove the intake and exhaust manifolds.
3. Remove the rocker arms.
4. Remove the cylinder head.
5. Have valves removed and inspected. Have valve guides and seats inspected, repairing or replacing as required.
6. Assemble by reversing Steps 1-4.

Valve and Ring Service

1. Perform Steps 1-5 of *Decarbonizing or Valve Service.*
2. Remove the oil pan and oil pump.

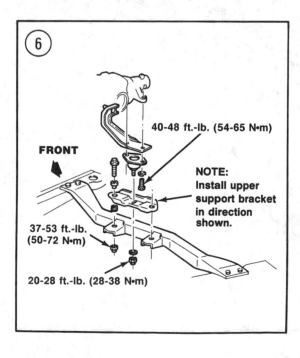

6

FRONT

40-48 ft.-lb. (54-65 N•m)

**NOTE:
Install upper
support bracket
in direction
shown.**

37-53 ft.-lb.
(50-72 N•m)

20-28 ft.-lb. (28-38 N•m)

3. Remove the pistons with connecting rods.
4. Remove the piston rings. It is not necessary to separate the pistons from the connecting rods unless a piston, connecting rod or piston pin needs repair or replacement.
5. Assemble by reversing Steps 1-4.

General Overhaul

1. Remove the engine. Remove the clutch from manual transmission vehicles.
2. Remove the flywheel (manual) or drive plate (automatic).
3. Remove the mount brackets and oil pressure sending unit from the engine.
4. If available, mount the engine on an engine stand. These can be rented from equipment rental dealers. The stand is not absolutely necessary, but it will make the job much easier.
5. Remove the following accessories or components from the engine, if present:
   a. Air injection (AIR) system and brackets.
   b. Alternator and mounting bracket.
   c. Power steering pump and mounting bracket.
   d. **Spark plug wires and distributor cap.**
   e. Throttle body injection (TBI) unit and fuel lines.
   f. Oil filter.
6. Check the engine for signs of coolant or oil leaks.
7. Clean the outside of the engine.
8. Remove the distributor. See Chapter Eight.
9. Remove all hoses and tubes connected to the engine.
10. Remove the intake and exhaust manifolds.
11. Remove the thermostat housing/water outlet adapter. See Chapter Seven.
12. Remove the valve cover and rocker arms.
13. Remove the crankshaft pulley, front hub, front cover and timing gear.
14. Remove the camshaft sprocket and camshaft.
15. Remove the water pump. See Chapter Seven.
16. Remove the cylinder head.
17. Remove the oil pan and oil pump.
18. Remove the pistons and connecting rods.
19. Remove the crankshaft.
20. Inspect the cylinder block.
21. Assemble by reversing Steps 1-19.

VALVE COVER

Removal/Installation

Refer to **Figure 7** for this procedure.

1. Open and support the hood . Disconnect the negative battery cable, then the positive cable.

2. Remove the glovebox assembly.

3. Remove the 4 center console bolts, unsnap the 2 latches at the base of the engine cover and remove the 2 bolts from under the hood which hold the engine cover in place. Remove the engine cover.

4. Remove the air cleaner assembly. See Chapter Six.

5. Disconnect the spark plug wires and remove them from the valve cover looms. See **Figure 8**.

6. Remove the PCV and EGR valves.

7. Remove the oil filler tube, if so equipped.

8. Disconnect the vacuum pipe rail at the intake manifold and thermostat housing.

9. Remove the valve cover bolts. Tap the end of the valve cover with a rubber mallet to break the RTV seal. Remove the valve cover.

10. Clean all RTV sealant residue from the cylinder head and valve cover with degreaser and a putty knife.

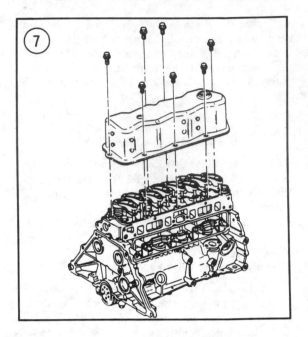

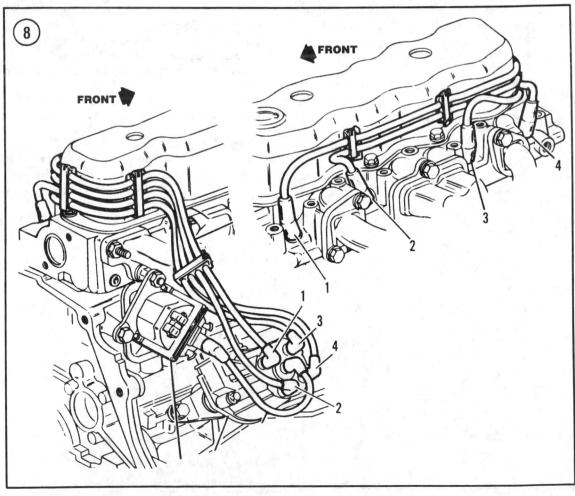

CAUTION
Keep sealant out of bolt holes in Step 11 to prevent a hydraulic lock which could damage the cylinder head.

11. Apply a continuous 3/16 in. (5 mm) bead of RTV sealant on the valve cover flange sealing surface. Flow the RTV on the inside of the bolt holes. See **Figure 9**.
12. Install the valve cover while the RTV is wet. Tighten the fasteners to 7 ft.-lb. (10 N•m).
13. Reverse Steps 1-8 to complete cover installation.

INTAKE MANIFOLD

The intake manifold is located on the right-hand (passenger) side of the engine. A coolant passage allows engine coolant to warm the manifold. An EGR passage is also provided.

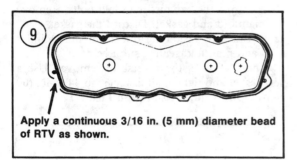

Apply a continuous 3/16 in. (5 mm) diameter bead of RTV as shown.

Removal/Installation

Refer to **Figure 10** for this procedure.
1. Open and support the hood. Disconnect the negative battery cable, then the positive cable.
2. Remove the glovebox assembly.
3. Remove the 4 center console bolts, unsnap the 2 latches at the base of the engine cover and remove the 2 bolts from under the hood which hold the engine cover in place. Remove the engine cover.
4. Remove the air cleaner assembly. See Chapter Six.

CAUTION
Drain the cooling system completely in Step 5. If coolant remains in the engine, it will flow into the cylinder head when the intake manifold is removed.

5. Drain the cooling system. See Chapter Seven.
6. Disconnect the vacuum pipe rail at the exhaust manifold and thermostat housing.
7. Disconnect all vacuum lines and electrical connectors from the intake manifold.
8. Disconnect the throttle cable at the Throttle body injection (TBI) unit. Disconnect the transmission TV (throttle valve) and/or speed control cables at the TBI unit, if so equipped.
9. Remove the fuel line bracket at the intake manifold.

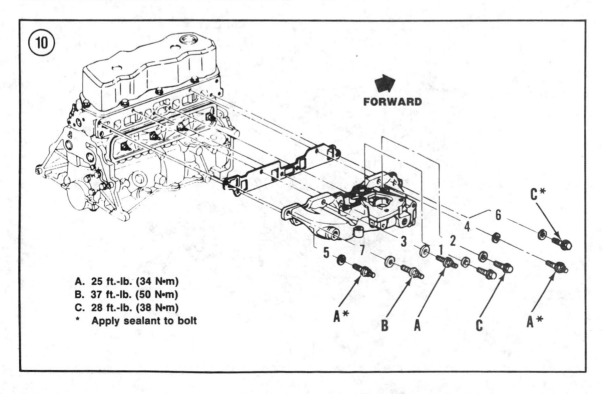

FORWARD

A. 25 ft.-lb. (34 N•m)
B. 37 ft.-lb. (50 N•m)
C. 28 ft.-lb. (38 N•m)
* Apply sealant to bolt

10. Disconnect the coolant hoses at the intake manifold.

11. Unbolt and remove the alternator. Place alternator to one side out of the way.

12. Disconnect the ignition coil leads. Unbolt and remove the coil. See **Figure 11**.

13. Remove the intake manifold bolts and studs. Remove the manifold.

14. Remove and discard the manifold gasket. Clean all gasket residue from the intake manifold and cylinder head sealing surface.

15. Installation is the reverse of removal. Use a new gasket. Apply sealant to the studs and bolts as specified in **Figure 10** and tighten the fasteners to specifications. Refill the cooling system (Chapter Seven).

EXHAUST MANIFOLD

The exhaust manifold is a single take-down design of cast iron mounted on the left-hand (driver) side of the engine. It has a manifold cover to provide heated air to the air cleaner.

Removal/Installation

Refer to **Figure 12** for this procedure.

1. Open and support the hood. Disconnect the negative battery cable, then the positive cable.

2. Remove the glovebox assembly.

3. Remove the 4 center console bolts, unsnap the 2 latches at the base of the engine cover and remove the 2 bolts from under the hood which hold the engine cover in place. Remove the engine cover.

4. Disconnect the air cleaner heat tube at the manifold.

5. Unplug the oxygen sensor connector at the wiring harness.

6. Securely block both rear wheels so the vehicle will not roll in either direction.

7. Raise the front of the vehicle with a jack and place it on jackstands.

8. Disconnect the exhaust pipe from the exhaust manifold.

9. Unbolt and remove the air conditioning compressor rear mounting bracket.

10. Remove the exhaust manifold bolts. Remove the manifold and gasket. Discard the gasket.

11. Clean any gasket residue from the cylinder head and manifold sealing surfaces.

12. Installation is the reverse of removal. Use a new gasket and tighten all fasteners to 44 ft.-lb. (60 N•m) in the sequence shown in **Figure 12**.

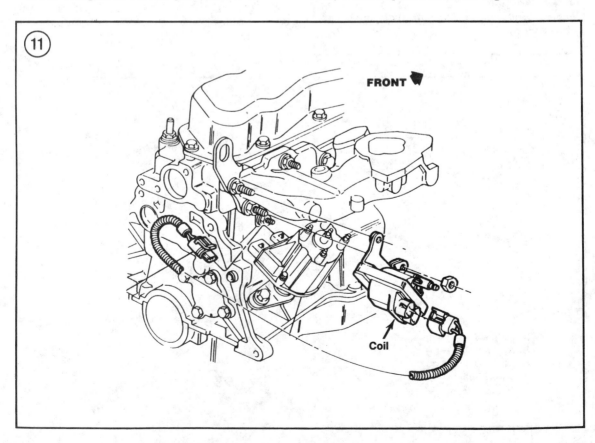

FRONT

Coil

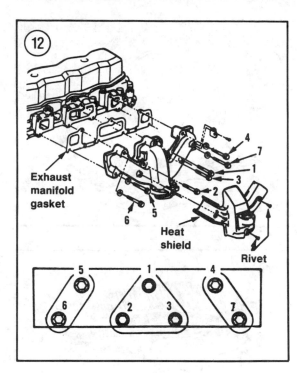

Exhaust manifold gasket

Heat shield

Rivet

MANIFOLD INSPECTION

1. Check the intake and exhaust manifolds for cracks or distortion. Replace if distorted or if cracks are found.
2. Check the gasket surfaces for nicks or burrs. Small burrs may be removed with an oilstone.
3. Place a straightedge across the manifold flange/gasket surfaces. If there is any gap between the straightedge and surface, measure it with a flat feeler gauge. Measure each manifold from end to end and from corner to corner. If the gasket surface is not flat within 0.006 in. (0.15 mm) per foot of manifold length, replace the manifold.
4. Check the EFE valve on exhaust manifolds. If the valve does not operate freely, apply a penetrating solvent to the valve shaft. If it still does not function properly, replace the EFE valve.

CRANKSHAFT PULLEY AND FRONT HUB

Refer to **Figure 13** for this procedure.
1. Loosen all accessory units and remove the drive belts. See Chapter Seven.
2. Remove the center bolt from the pulley hub. Remove the hub and pulleys.
3. Installation is the reverse of removal. Tighten the crankshaft bolt to specification (**Table 2**). Adjust all drive belts (Chapter Seven).

TIMING GEAR COVER

Removal/Installation

1. Open and support the hood. Disconnect the negative battery cable.
2. Drain the cooling system. See Chapter Seven.
3. Remove the power steering reservoir at the fan shroud without disconnecting any hydraulic lines.
4. Remove the upper fan shroud, cooling fan and pulley. See Chapter Seven.
5. Remove the alternator mounting brackets, brace and alternator. Place alternator to one side out of the way.
6. Remove the crankshaft pulley and front hub as described in this chapter.
7. Disconnect the lower radiator hose at the water pump.
8. Remove the 2 oil pan-to-timing gear cover screws. Remove the cover-to-block fasteners. Remove the timing gear cover.
9. Clean all RTV residue from the engine block, timing gear cover and oil pan mating surfaces with degreaser and a putty knife.
10. Run a continuous bead of RTV sealant on the timing gear cover sealing flange. See **Figure 14**.

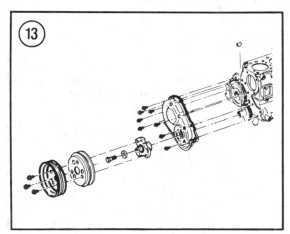

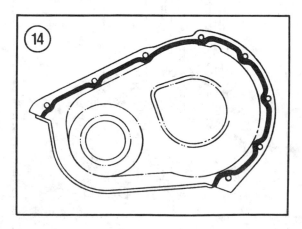

NOTE
The use of a centering tool in Step 11 is recommended to assure that the timing gear cover is properly aligned. If it is not, the crankshaft pulley hub may damage the seal when it is reinstalled.

11. Install centering tool part No. J-34995 in the timing gear cover seal and position the cover on the block (**Figure 15**).

12. Install and partially tighten the 2 oil pan-to-cover screws. Tighten cover fasteners to specifications (**Table 2**), then finish tightening the oil pan-to-cover screws. Remove the centering tool.

13. Reverse Steps 1-7 to complete installation.

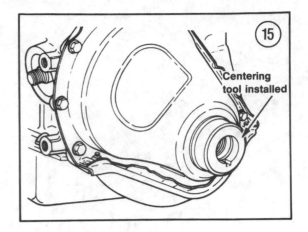

TIMING GEAR REPLACEMENT

This procedure requires a press and support tools. If you don't have them, a machine shop can press the gear off and on for a small fee.

1. Remove the camshaft as described in this chapter.

NOTE
Make sure the thrust plate is aligned with the Woodruff key in the camshaft before performing Step 2.

2. Install the camshaft in a press plate and use an arbor press to remove the camshaft from the gear.

3. Installation is the reverse of removal. Press the gear onto the camshaft until it bottoms against the gear spacer ring.

4. Check the thrust plate end clearance with a flat feeler gauge as shown in **Figure 16**. It should be 0.0015-0.0050 in. (0.038-0.127 mm). If less than 0.0015 in. (0.038 mm), replace the spacer plate. If greater than 0.0050 in. (0.127 mm), replace the thrust plate.

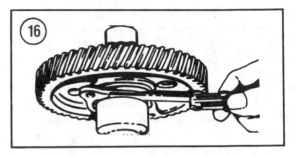

ROCKER ARMS AND PUSHROD COVER

Rocker Arm Removal/Installation

Each rocker arm moves on its own pivot ball. The rocker arm and pivot ball are retained by a capscrew. It is not necessary to remove the rocker arm for pushrod replacement; simply loosen the capscrew and twist the rocker arm away from the pushrod. Refer to **Figure 17** for this procedure.

1. Remove the valve cover as described in this chapter.

2. Remove the rocker arm capscrew and ball.

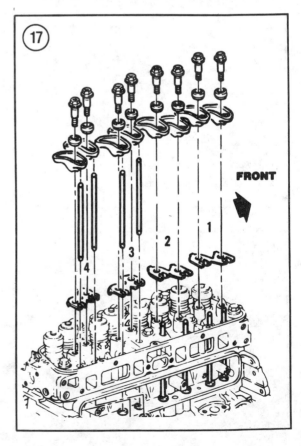

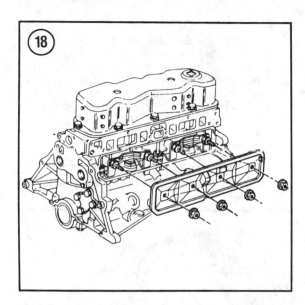

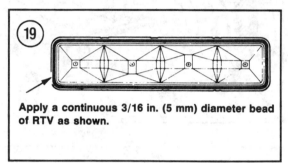

Apply a continuous 3/16 in. (5 mm) diameter bead of RTV as shown.

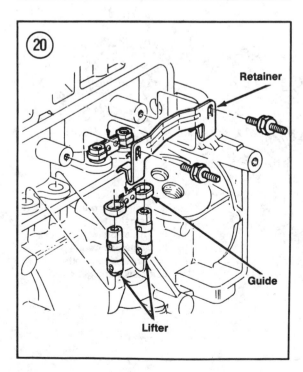

Retainer

Guide

Lifter

3. Remove the rocker arm. Remove the pushrod. If removing more than one assembly, place in order of removal so that the same rocker arm and pushrod can be reinstalled in its original location.
4. Installation is the reverse of removal. Make sure pushrod engages lifter. Tighten the capscrew to 20 ft.-lb. (27 N•m).

Rocker Arm Inspection

Clean all parts with solvent and use compressed air to blow out the oil passage in each pushrod. Check each rocker arm, pivot ball and pushrod for scuffing, pitting or excessive wear. If the pushrod is worn from lack of oil, it will be necessary to replace the hydraulic lifter and rocker arm as well.

Pushrod Cover Removal/Installation

Refer to **Figure 18** for this procedure.
1. Open and support the hood. Disconnect the negative battery cable.
2. Remove the alternator and mounting bracket.
3. Remove the brace between the intake manifold and engine block.
4. Drain the cooling system. See Chapter Seven.
5. Disconnect the lower radiator and heater hoses at the engine.
6. Disconnect and remove the oil pressure sending unit.
7. Remove the wiring harness brackets from the pushrod cover.
8. Remove the pushrod cover attaching nuts. Remove the cover and gasket. Discard the gasket.
9. Clean all gasket residue from the pushrod cover and cylinder block sealing surfaces.
10. Run a continuous 3/16 in. (5 mm) bead of RTV sealant along the pushrod cover flange as shown in **Figure 19**.
11. Install the cover to the block. Tighten the attaching nuts to 75 in.-lb. (10 N•m).
12. Reverse Steps 1-7 to complete installation.

**Hydraulic Valve Lifter
Removal/Installation**

Refer to **Figure 20** for this procedure.
1. Remove the valve cover as described in this chapter.
2. Remove the pushrod cover as described in this chapter.
3. Loosen the rocker arms and remove the pushrods as described in this chapter.
4. Remove the guide plate and clamp. Remove the valve lifter with a pencil-type magnet.
5. Installation is the reverse of removal. Make sure the lifter fits into its boss properly before installing the guide plate and clamp.

CAMSHAFT AND TIMING GEARS

Removal

1. Remove the pushrod cover as described in this chapter.

2. Disconnect and remove the power steering reservoir from the fan shroud. Remove the upper fan shroud.

3. Loosen all accessory units and remove the drive belts. Remove the cooling fan and pulley. See Chapter Seven.

4. Remove the crankshaft pulley and hub as described in this chapter.

5. Remove the timing gear cover as described in this chapter.

6. **Remove the distributor. See Chapter Eight.**

7. Remove the oil pump drive shaft and cover.

8. Remove the air cleaner assembly. Remove the EGR valve. See Chapter Six.

9. Disconnect the vacuum lines at the intake manifold and thermostat housing.

10. Remove the pushrods and hydraulic valve lifters as described in this chapter.

11. Remove the radiator. See Chapter Seven.

12. Remove the 2 camshaft thrust plate bolts through the holes in the camshaft gear. See **Figure 21.**

WARNING
The air conditioning system contains pressurized refrigerant which can cause frostbite if it touches skin and blindness if it touches the eyes. If discharged near an open flame, the refrigerant forms poisonous gas. Never disconnect air conditioning system lines unless the system has been discharged and evacuated by a professional.

13. If equipped with air conditioning, remove the condenser baffles, then unbolt the condenser. Raise

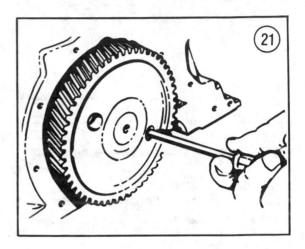

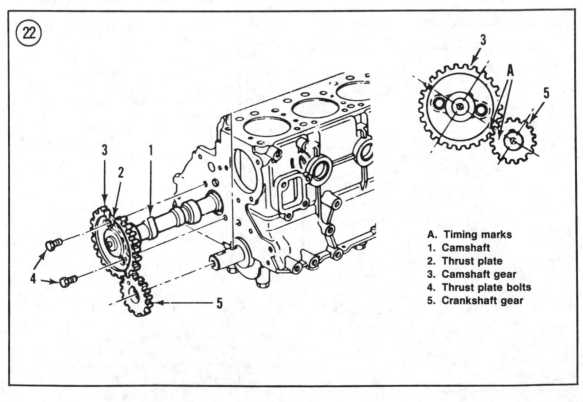

A. Timing marks
1. Camshaft
2. Thrust plate
3. Camshaft gear
4. Thrust plate bolts
5. Crankshaft gear

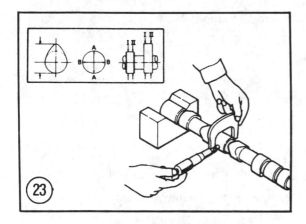

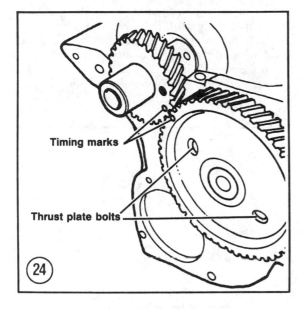

Timing marks

Thrust plate bolts

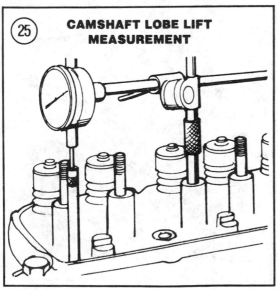

CAMSHAFT LOBE LIFT MEASUREMENT

condenser enough to provide access and secure it in place.

14. Remove the head lamp bezel, grille and bumper filler panel.

15. Carefully withdraw the camshaft and gear assembly from the front of the engine block with a rotating motion. See **Figure 22**.

Inspection

1. Check the journals and lobes for signs of wear or scoring. Lobe pitting in the toe area is not sufficient reason for replacement unless the lobe lift loss exceeds specifications.

NOTE
If you do not have precision measuring equipment, have Step 2 done by a machine shop.

2. Measure the camshaft journal diameters with a micrometer (**Figure 23**) and compare to specifications (**Table 1**). Replace the camshaft if the journals are more than 0.0009 in. (0.025 mm) out-of-round.

Installation

NOTE
When installing a new camshaft, coat the lobes with GM EOS lubricant or equivalent.

1. Lubricate the camshaft journals with SAE 30W engine oil.

2. Carefully install the camshaft in the engine block with a rotating motion.

3. Rotate the crankshaft and camshaft as required to align the valve timing marks on the gear teeth. See **Figure 22** and **Figure 24**.

4. Reverse Steps 1-15 of *Removal* in this chapter to complete installation. Tighten thrust plate screws to 75 in.-lb. (10 N•m).

Lobe Lift Measurement

Camshaft lobe lift can be measured with the camshaft in the block and the cylinder head in place. The lifters must be bled down slowly in Step 5 or the readings will be incorrect.

1. Remove the valve cover as described in this chapter.

2. Remove the rocker arms and pivot assemblies as described in this chapter.

3. Remove the spark plugs.

4. Install a dial indicator on the end of a pushrod. A piece of rubber tubing will hold the dial indicator plunger in place on the center of the pushrod. See **Figure 25** (typical).

5. Rotate the crankshaft in the normal direction of rotation until the valve lifter seats on the heel or base of the cam lobe. This positions the pushrod at its lowest point.

6. Set the dial indicator at zero, then slowly rotate the crankshaft until the pushrod reaches its maximum travel. Note the indicator reading. Correct cam lobe lift is 0.398 in. (10.3124 mm) for both intake and exhaust.

7. Repeat Steps 4-6 for each pushrod. If all lobes are within specifications in Step 6, reinstall the rocker arm assemblies.

8. If one or more lobes are worn beyond specifications, replace the camshaft.

9. Remove the dial indicator and reverse Steps 1-3.

OIL PAN

1. Open and support the hood. Disconnect the negative battery cable.

2. Securely block both rear wheels so the vehicle will not roll in either direction.

3. Raise the vehicle with a jack and place it on jackstands.

4. Drain the crankcase. See Chapter Three.

5. Disconnect the wires at the starter motor.

6. Remove the flywheel shield.

7. Remove the starter motor. See Chapter Eight.

8. Disconnect the exhaust pipe at the exhaust manifold. Disconnect the exhaust hangers and move the exhaust system to one side to provide access for oil pan removal. Suspend exhaust system from the suspension with wire.

9. Unbolt and remove the oil pan. See **Figure 26.**

10. Clean any RTV residue from the oil pan rail on the engine block. Clean the oil pan sealing flange.

11. Apply RTV sealant along the entire oil pan sealing flange as shown in **Figure 27.**

12. Install the oil pan and tighten the pan bolts to specifications (**Table 2**).

13. Reverse Steps 1-8 to complete installation.

OIL PUMP AND
DRIVE SHAFT

Oil Pump Removal/Installation

1. Remove the oil pan as described in this chapter.

2. Remove the pickup tube support bracket nut.

3. Remove the 2 flange mounting bolts and the nut from the main bearing cap. Remove the oil pump and pickup assembly as a unit.

4. To reinstall, align pump gear shaft tang with pump drive shaft slot.

5. Install pump-to-block positioning bracket over the oil pump drive shaft lower bushing.

NOTE
The oil pump should slide into place easily. If it does not, remove the shaft and realign the slot.

6. Install the pump attaching bolts and nut. Tighten to 22 ft.-lb. (30 N•m).

7. Install the pickup tube support bracket nut. Tighten to 37 ft.-lb. (50 N•m).

8. Install the oil pan as described in this chapter.

Oil Pump Disassembly/Assembly

Refer to **Figure 28** for this procedure.

1. Remove the cover screws, cover and gasket (if so equipped). Discard the gasket.

2. Mark the gear teeth for reassembly indexing and then remove the idler and drive gear with shaft from the pump body.

3. Remove the pressure regulator valve pin, regulator, spring and valve.

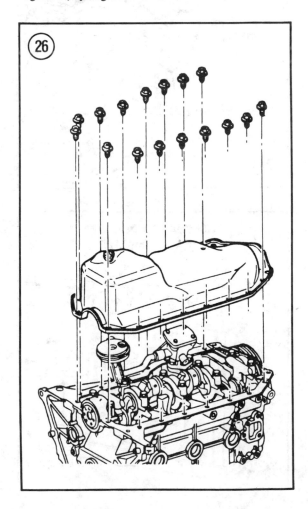

(26)

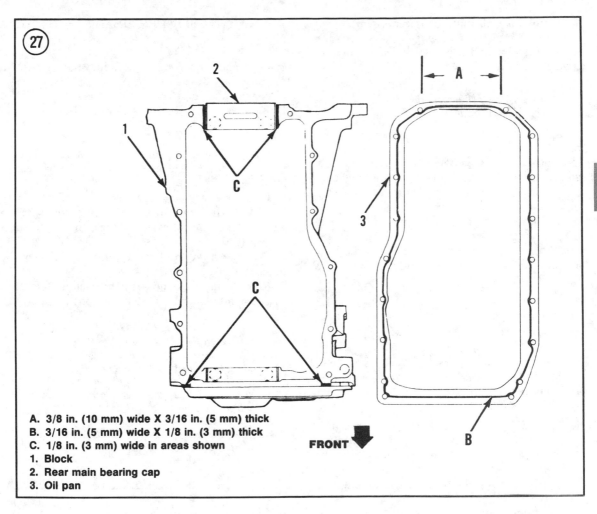

A. 3/8 in. (10 mm) wide X 3/16 in. (5 mm) thick
B. 3/16 in. (5 mm) wide X 1/8 in. (3 mm) thick
C. 1/8 in. (3 mm) wide in areas shown
1. Block
2. Rear main bearing cap
3. Oil pan

FRONT

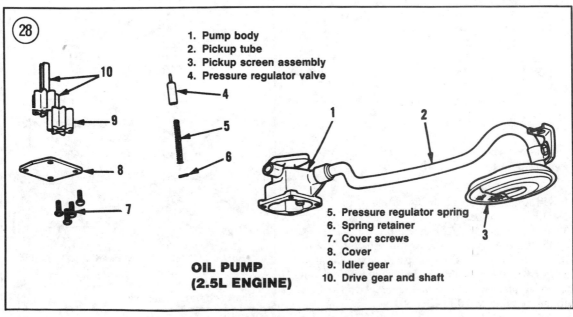

1. Pump body
2. Pickup tube
3. Pickup screen assembly
4. Pressure regulator valve

5. Pressure regulator spring
6. Spring retainer
7. Cover screws
8. Cover
9. Idler gear
10. Drive gear and shaft

**OIL PUMP
(2.5L ENGINE)**

4. Remove the pickup tube/screen assembly *only* if it needs replacement. Secure the pump body in a soft-jawed vise and separate the tube from the cover.

CAUTION
Do not twist, shear or collapse the tube when installing it in Step 5.

5. If the pickup tube/screen assembly was removed, install a new one. Secure the pump body in a soft-jawed vise. Apply sealer to the new tube and gently tap in place with a soft-faced mallet.
6. Lubricate all parts thoroughly with clean engine oil before reassembly.
7. Assembly is the reverse of disassembly. Index the gear marks, install a new cover gasket and rotate the pump drive shaft by hand to check for smooth operation. Tighten cover screws to 6-9 ft.-lb. (8-12 N•m).

Oil Pump Inspection

NOTE
The pump assembly and gears are serviced as an assembly. If one or the other is worn or damaged, replace the entire pump. No wear specifications are provided by GM.

1. Clean all parts thoroughly in solvent. Brush the inside of the body and the pressure regulator chamber to remove all dirt and metal particles. Dry with compressed air, if available.
2. Check the pump body and cover for cracks or excessive wear.
3. Check the pump gears for damage or excessive wear.
4. Check the drive gear shaft-to-body fit for excessive looseness.
5. Check the inside of the pump cover for wear that could allow oil to leak around the ends of the gears.
6. Check the pressure regulator valve for a proper fit.

Oil Pump Drive Shaft
Replacement

Refer to **Figure 29** for this procedure.
1. Unbolt and remove the cover plate.
2. Remove the bearing.
3. Remove the shaft/gear assembly.
4. Installation is the reverse of removal. Rotate shaft until it indexes the camshaft gear and pilots properly in the oil pump body. Apply RTV sealant to cover plate as shown in **Figure 29** and tighten attaching bolts to 10 ft.-lb. (14 N•m).

CYLINDER HEAD

Removal

1. Open and support the hood. Relieve fuel system pressure as described in Chapter Six, then disconnect the negative battery cable.
2. Remove the valve cover as described in this chapter.
3. Drain the cooling system. See Chapter Seven.
4. Disconnect all vacuum line, cooling system hoses and electrical connectors from the cylinder head.
5. Disconnect the throttle cable at the TBI unit. Disconnect the transmission TV (throttle valve) and/or speed control cables at the TBI unit, if so equipped.
6. Disconnect the front coolant hose at the intake manifold.
7. Remove the alternator, rear bracket and brace. Place the alternator to one side out of the way.

WARNING
Refrigerant causes freezing temperatures when it evaporates. This can cause frostbite if it touches the skin, and blindness if it touches the eyes. If discharged near an open flame, R-12 creates poisonous gas. If the refrigerant can is hooked up to the pressure side of the compressor, it may explode. Always wear safety goggles and gloves when working with R-12.

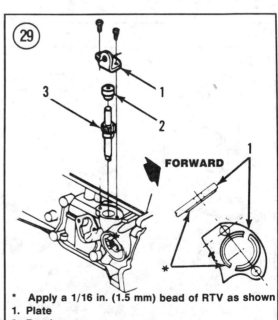

* **Apply a 1/16 in. (1.5 mm) bead of RTV as shown**
1. **Plate**
2. **Bearing**
3. **Shaft and gear assembly**

8. If equipped with air conditioning, remove the compressor without disconnecting any refrigerant lines and place to one side out of the way.

9. Remove the thermostat housing from the cylinder head.

10. Disconnect the ignition coil leads. Unbolt and remove the coil. See **Figure 11**.

11. Remove the fuel line bracket at the intake manifold.

12. Tag and disconnect all vacuum lines and electrical connectors at the TBI unit.

13. Securely block both rear wheels so the vehicle will not roll in either direction.

14. Raise the front of the vehicle with a jack and place it on jackstands.

15. Disconnect the exhaust pipe at the exhaust manifold.

16. Unplug the oxygen sensor connector at the wiring harness.

17. Remove the jackstands and lower the vehicle to the ground.

18. Back off the rocker arm capscrews and swivel the rocker arms to one side. Remove the pushrods and place them on a clean workbench in the order of removal.

19. Loosen and remove the cylinder head bolts in the reverse of the sequence shown in **Figure 30**.

NOTE
Place the head on its side in Step 20 to prevent damage to the spark plugs or head gasket surface.

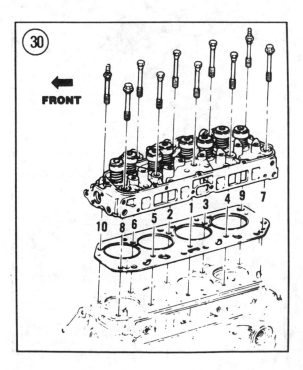

20. With the help of an assistant, remove the head with the intake/exhaust manifolds attached.

21. Remove the intake/exhaust manifolds from the cylinder head, if required.

22. Remove and discard the head gasket. Clean any residue from the head and block surfaces.

Installation

1. Make sure the cylinder head and block gasket surfaces and bolt holes are clean. Dirt in the block bolt holes or on the head bolt threads will affect bolt torque.

2. Check all visible oil and water passages for cleanliness.

3. Reinstall the intake/exhaust manifolds, if removed.

4. Install a new head gasket on the cylinder block dowel pins.

5. Carefully lower the cylinder head in place on the dowel pins and gasket.

6. Coat the head bolt threads with sealing compound and install the bolts finger-tight.

7. Tighten the head bolts following the sequence shown in **Figure 30** to 92 ft.-lb. (125 N•m).

8. Reverse Steps 1-18 of *Removal* in this chapter.

Decarbonizing

1. Without removing the valves, remove all deposits from the combustion chambers, intake ports and exhaust ports. Use a fine wire brush dipped in solvent or make a scraper from hardwood. Be careful not to scratch or gouge the combustion chambers.

2. After all carbon is removed from the combustion chambers and ports, clean the entire head in solvent.

3. Clean away all carbon on the piston tops. Do not remove the carbon ridge at the top of the cylinder bore.

4. Clean the bolt holes. Use a cleaning solvent to remove dirt and grease.

Inspection

1. Check the cylinder head for signs of oil or water leaks before cleaning.

2. Clean the cylinder head thoroughly in solvent. While cleaning, look for cracks or other visible signs of damage. Look for corrosion or foreign material in the oil and water passages.

3. Clean the passages with a stiff spiral brush, then blow them out with compressed air.

4. Check the cylinder head studs for damage and replace if necessary.

5. Check the flatness of the cylinder head-to-block surface with a straightedge and feeler gauge (**Figure 31**). Measure diagonally, as well as end to end. If the gap exceeds 0.0078-0.0157 in. (0.2-0.4 mm), have the head resurfaced by a machine shop. If the gap exceeds 0.004 in. (0.102 mm), replace the head.

VALVES AND VALVE SEATS

Servicing the valves, guides and valve seats requires special knowledge and expensive machine tools. A general practice among those who do their own service is to remove the cylinder head, perform all disassembly except valve removal and take the head to a dealer or machine shop for inspection and service. Since the cost is low relative to the required effort and equipment, this is usually the best approach, even for experienced mechanics.

PISTON/CONNECTING ROD ASSEMBLY

Piston/Connecting Rod Removal

1. Remove the cylinder head and oil pan as described in this chapter.

2. Rotate the crankshaft until one piston is at bottom dead center. Pack the cylinder bore with clean shop rags. Remove the carbon ridge at the top of the cylinder bores with a ridge reamer. These can be rented for use. Vacuum out the shavings, then remove the shop rages.

3. Rotate the crankshaft until the connecting rod is centered in the bore. Measure the clearance between the connecting rod and the crankshaft with a flat feeler gauge (**Figure 32**). If the clearance exceeds specifications (**Table 1**), replace the connecting rod during reassembly.

NOTE
Mark the cylinder number on the top of each piston with quick-drying paint. Check the cylinder numbers or identification marks on the connecting rod and cap. If they are not visible, make your own **Figure 33**.

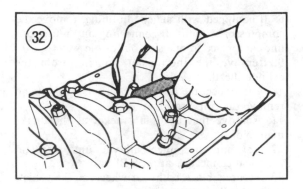

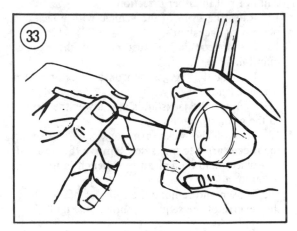

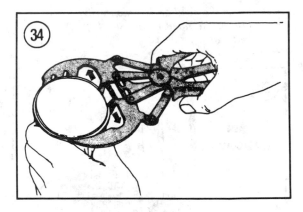

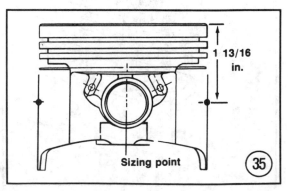

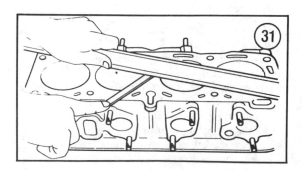

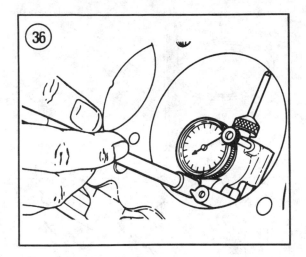

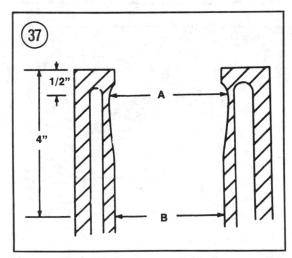

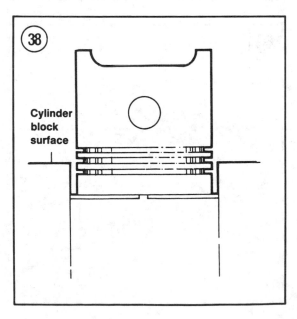

4. Remove the nuts holding the connecting rod cap. Lift off the cap, together with the lower bearing insert.

> *NOTE*
> *If the connecting rod caps are difficult to remove, tap the studs with a wooden hammer handle.*

5. Use the wooden hammer handle to push the piston and connecting rod from the bore.
6. Remove the piston rings with a ring remover (**Figure 34**).
7. Repeat Steps 1-6 for all remaining connecting rods.

Piston Pin Removal/Installation

The piston pins are press-fitted to the connecting rods and hand-fitted to the pistons. Removal requires the use of a press and support stand. This is a job for a dealer or machine shop equipped to fit the pistons to the pins, ream the pin bushings to the correct diameter and install the pistons and pins on the connecting rods.

Piston Clearance Check

Unless you have precision measuring equipment and know how to use it properly, have this procedure done by a machine shop.

1. Measure the piston diameter with a micrometer at the sizing points shown in **Figure 35**.
2. Measure the cylinder bore diameter with a bore gauge (**Figure 36**). **Figure 37** shows the points of normal cylinder wear. If dimension A exceeds dimension B by more than 0.003 in., the cylinder must be rebored and a new piston/ring assembly installed.
3. Subtract the piston diameter from the largest cylinder bore reading. If it exceeds the specifications in **Table 1**, the cylinder must be rebored and an oversized piston installed.

> *NOTE*
> *Obtain the new piston and measure it to determine the correct cylinder bore oversize dimension.*

Piston Ring Fit/Installation

1. Check the ring gap of each piston ring. To do this, position the ring in the cylinder bore and square it by tapping gently with an inverted piston. See **Figure 38**.

> *NOTE*
> *If the cylinders have not been rebored, check the gap at the bottom of the ring travel, where the cylinder is least worn.*

2. Measure the ring gap with a feeler gauge as shown in **Figure 39**. Compare with specifications in **Table 1**. If the measurement is not within specifications, the rings must be replaced as a set. Check gap of new rings as well. If the gap is too small, file the ends of the ring to correct it (**Figure 40**).

3. Check the side clearance of the rings as shown in **Figure 41**. Place the feeler gauge alongside the ring all the way into the groove. If the measurement is not within specifications (**Table 1**), either the rings or the ring grooves are worn. Inspect and replace as required.

4. Using a ring expander tool (**Figure 42**), carefully install the oil control ring, then the compression rings. Oil rings consists of 3 segments. The wavy segment goes between the flat segments to act as a spacer. Upper and lower flat segments are interchangeable. The second compression ring is tapered. The top of each compression ring is marked and must face upward.

5. Position the ring gaps as shown in **Figure 43**.

Connecting Rod Inspection

Have the connecting rods checked for straightness by a dealer or machine shop. When installing new connecting rods, have them checked for misalignment before installing the piston and piston pin. Connecting rods can spring out of alignment during shipping or handling.

Connecting Rod Bearing
Clearance Measurement

1. Place the connecting rods and upper bearing halves on the proper connecting rod journals.

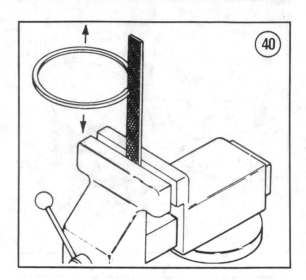

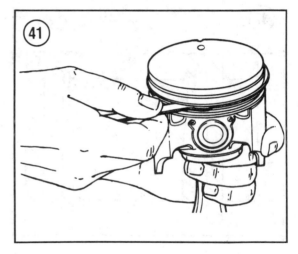

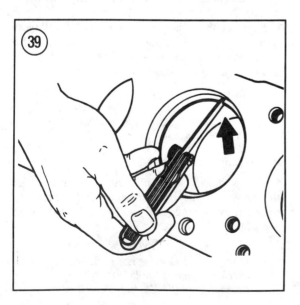

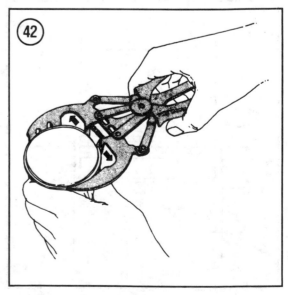

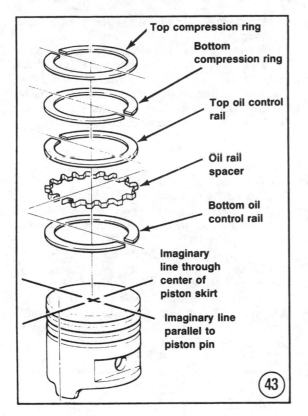

Top compression ring

Bottom compression ring

Top oil control rail

Oil rail spacer

Bottom oil control rail

Imaginary line through center of piston skirt

Imaginary line parallel to piston pin

43

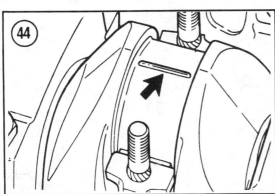

44

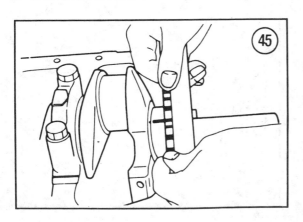

45

2. Cut a piece of Plastigage the width of the bearing. Place the Plastigage on the journal (**Figure 44**), then install the lower bearing half and cap.

NOTE
Do not place Plastigage over the journal oil hole.

3. Tighten the connecting rod cap to specifications (**Table 2**). Do not rotate the crankshaft while the Plastigage is in place.

4. Remove the connecting rod caps. Bearing clearance is determined by comparing the width of the flattened Plastigage to the markings on the envelope (**Figure 45**). If the clearance is excessive, the crankshaft must be reground and undersize bearings installed.

Piston/Connecting Rod Installation

1. Make sure the pistons are correctly installed on the connecting rods, if they were separated. The raised notch side of the rod at the bearing end must be opposite the notch in the piston (**Figure 46**). When installed in the block, the notch cast in the top of the piston head must face the front of the engine. See **Figure 47** (typical).

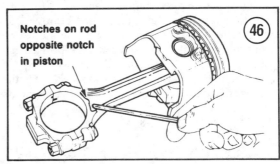

Notches on rod opposite notch in piston

46

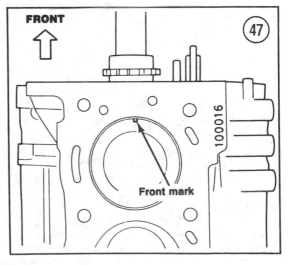

FRONT

47

100016

Front mark

2. Make sure the ring gaps are positioned as shown in **Figure 43**.

3. Slip short pieces of hose over the connecting rod studs to prevent them from nicking the crankshaft. Tape will work if you do not have the right diameter hose, but it is more difficult to remove.

4. Immerse the entire piston in clean engine oil. Coat the cylinder wall with oil.

> *CAUTION*
> *Use extreme care in Step 5 to prevent the connecting rod from nicking the crankshaft journal.*

5. Install the piston/connecting rod assembly in its cylinder with a piston ring compressor as shown in **Figure 48**. Tap lightly with a wooden hammer handle to insert the piston. Make sure the notch at the top of the piston (**Figure 47**) faces toward the front of the engine and that the piston number (painted on top before removal) corresponds to the cylinder number, counting from the front of the engine.

6. Clean the connecting rod bearings carefully, including the back sides. Coat the journals and bearings with clean engine oil. Place the bearings in the connecting rod and cap.

7. Pull the connecting rod and bearing into position against the crankpin. Remove the protective hose or tape and lightly lubricate the connecting rod bolt threads with SAE 30W engine oil.

8. Install the connecting rod cap. Make sure the rod and cap marks align. Install the cap nuts finger-tight.

9. Repeat Steps 4-8 for each remaining piston/connecting rod assembly.

10. Tighten the cap nuts to specifications (**Table 2**).

11. Check the connecting rod big-end play as described under *Piston/Connecting Rod Removal* in this chapter.

REAR MAIN OIL SEAL

The one-piece rear main bearing oil seal can be replaced with the engine in the vehicle and without removing the oil pan or crankshaft.

Removal/Installation

1. Set the parking brake. Securely block both rear wheels so the vehicle will not roll in either direction.

2. Raise the vehicle with a jack and place it on jackstands. Support the engine with a jack.

3. Remove the transmission. See Chapter Nine.

4. Remove the flywheel as described in this chapter.

5. Insert an awl or small screwdriver blade through the seal dust lip as shown in **Figure 49** and pry the seal out with a revolving motion. Work carefully to prevent damage to the outer diameter of the crankshaft with the pry tool.

6. Check the inner diameter of the seal bore for nicks, burring or other defects. Correct as required.

7. Check crankshaft for burring or surface nicks on area which touches the seal. Repair or replace crankshaft as required.

8. Lubricate a new seal with clean engine oil and install seal on installer tool part No. J-34924. Slide seal on installer mandrel until dust lip bottoms against tool collar. See **Figure 50**.

9. Align tool dowel pin with hole in crankshaft. Install tool to crankshaft and tighten attaching screws to 2-5 ft.-lb.

10. Rotate the installer handle so collar will push seal into the seal bore. Continue turning handle until collar fits tightly against the case, indicating that the seal has seated properly.

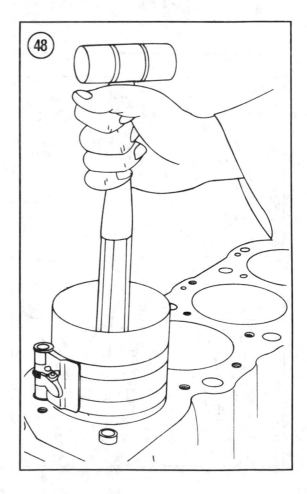

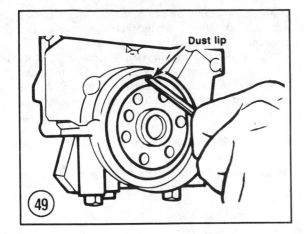

(49) Dust lip

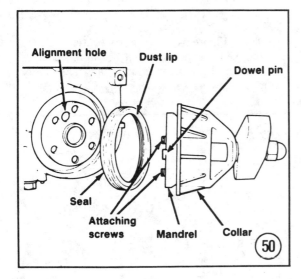

Alignment hole   Dust lip

Dowel pin

Seal

Attaching screws   Mandrel   Collar

(50)

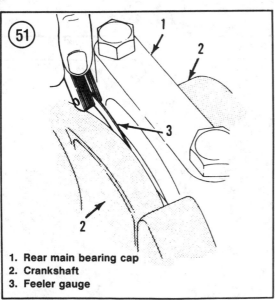

(51)

1
2
3
2

1. **Rear main bearing cap**
2. **Crankshaft**
3. **Feeler gauge**

11. Loosen the installer handle and remove the tool.

12. Check that the seal is seated completely and squarely in the bore.

13. Reverse Steps 1-4 to complete the installation.

CRANKSHAFT

End Play Measurement

1. Pry the crankshaft to the front of the engine with a large screwdriver.

2. Measure the crankshaft end play at the front of the No. 5 main bearing with a flat feeler gauge. See **Figure 51**. Compare to specifications in **Table 1**.

3. If the end play is excessive, replace the No. 5 main bearing. If less than specified, check the bearing faces for imperfections.

Removal

1. Remove the engine as described in this chapter.

2. Remove the flywheel as described in this chapter.

3. Mount the engine on an engine stand, if available.

4. Invert the engine to bring the oil pan to an upright position.

5. Remove the oil pan and oil pump as described in this chapter.

6. Remove the timing gear cover as described in this chapter.

7. Remove the spark plugs to per mit easy rotation of the crankshaft.

8. Rotate the crankshaft to position one connecting rod at the bottom of its stroke.

9. Remove the connecting rod bearing cap and bearing. Move the piston/rod assembly away from the crankshaft.

10. Repeat Step 8 and Step 9 for each piston/rod assembly.

11. Check the caps for identification numbers or marks. If none are visible, clean the caps with a wire brush. If marks still cannot be seen, make your own with quick-drying paint.

12. Unbolt and remove the main bearing caps and bearing inserts.

> *NOTE*
> *If the caps are difficult to remove, lift the bolts partway out, then pry them from side to side.*

13. Carefully lift the crankshaft from the engine block and place it on a clean workbench.

14. Remove the bearing inserts from the block. Place the bearing caps and inserts in order on a clean workbench.

Inspection

1. Clean the crankshaft thoroughly with solvent. Blow out the oil passages with compressed air.

NOTE
If you do not have precision measuring equipment, have a machine shop perform Step 2.

2. Check the crankpins and main bearing journals for wear, scoring or cracks. Check all journals against specifications (**Table 1**) for out-of-roundness and taper. See **Figure 52**. Have the crankshaft reground, if necessary.

Main Bearing Clearance Measurement

Main bearing clearance is measured with Plastigage in the same manner as the connecting rod bearing clearance described in this chapter. Excessive clearance requires that the bearings be replaced, the crankshaft be reground or both.

Installation

1. Install the main bearing inserts in the cylinder block. Bearing oil holes must align with block oil holes and bearing tabs must seat in the block tab slots.

NOTE
Check cap bolts for thread damage before reuse. If damaged, replace the bolts.

2. Lubricate the bolt threads with SAE 30W engine oil.
3. Install the bearing inserts in each cap.
4. Lubricate the bearings with a generous coat of clean engine oil. Carefully lower the crankshaft into position in the block. Coat the crankshaft journals with clean engine oil.
5. Install the bearing caps in their marked positions with the arrows pointing toward the front of the engine and the number mark aligned with the corresponding mark on the journals. See **Figure 53**.
6. Install and tighten all bolts finger-tight. Recheck end play as described in this chapter, then tighten all bolts to specifications (**Table 2**).
7. Rotate the crankshaft to make sure it turns smoothly at the flywheel rim. If not, remove the bearing caps and crankshaft and check that the bearings are clean and properly installed.

PILOT BEARING

An oil-impregnated bearing is located inside the rear end of the crankshaft to support the transmission input shaft on manual transmission vehicles. It should be inspected whenever the transmission is removed.

1. Check the bearing for visible signs of wear or damage. Rotate the bearing with a finger and make sure it turns easily. If wear, damage or stiff movement are found, remove with tool part No. J-1448 or an equivalent puller.
2. Position a new bearing in the crankshaft bore and install with tool part No. J-1522 or an equivalent driver.
3. Lubricate the bearing with a few drops of machine oil.

FLYWHEEL/DRIVE PLATE

Removal/Installation

Refer to **Figure 54** for this procedure.
1. Remove the engine as described in this chapter.
2. Remove the clutch on manual transmission vehicles. See Chapter Nine.

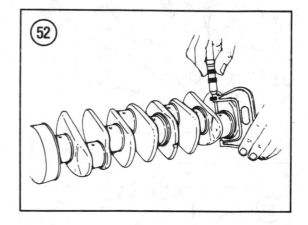

(52)

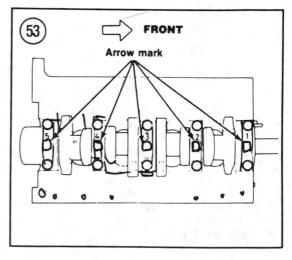

(53)   FRONT

Arrow mark

3. Unbolt the flywheel or drive plate from the crankshaft. Remove the bolts gradually in a diagonal pattern.

4. Visually check the flywheel or drive plate surfaces for cracks, deep scoring, excessive wear, heat discoloration and checking. If the surface is glazed or slightly scratched, have the flywheel/drive plate resurfaced by a machine shop.

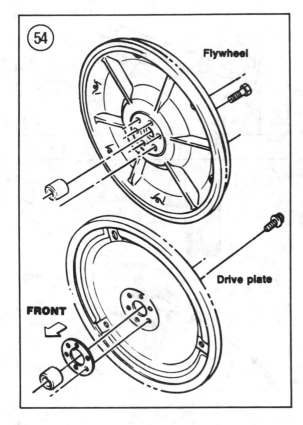

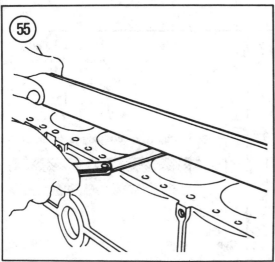

5. Inspect the ring gear for cracks, broken teeth or excessive wear. If severely worn, check the starter motor drive teeth for similar wear or damage. Replace as required.

6. Installation is the reverse of removal. Tighten bolts to specifications (**Table 2**) in a crisscross pattern. Wipe all oil, grease and other contamination from the flywheel surface before installing the clutch on manual transmission vehicles.

CYLINDER BLOCK

Cleaning and Inspection

1. Clean the block thoroughly with solvent. Remove any RTV sealant residue from the machined surfaces. Check all core plugs for leaks and replace any that are suspect. See *Core Plug Replacement* in this chapter. Remove any plugs that seal oil passages. Check oil and coolant passages for sludge, dirt and corrosion while cleaning. If the passages are very dirty, have the block boiled out by a machine shop. Blow out all passages with compressed air. Check the threads in the head bolt holes to be sure they are clean. If dirty, use a tap to true up the threads and remove any deposits.

2. Examine the block for cracks. To confirm suspicions about possible leak areas, use a mixture of 1 part kerosene and 2 parts engine oil. Coat the suspected area with this solution, then wipe dry and immediately apply a solution of zinc oxide dissolved in wood alcohol. If any discoloration appears in the treated area, the block is cracked and should be replaced.

3. Check flatness of the cylinder block deck or top surface. Place an accurate straightedge on the block. If there is any gap between the block and straightedge, measure it with a flat feeler gauge (**Figure 55**). Measure from end to end and from corner to corner. Have the block resurfaced if it is warped more than 0.004 in. (0.102 mm).

4. Measure cylinder bores with a bore gauge for out-of-roundness or excessive wear as described in *Piston Clearance Check* in this chapter. If the cylinders exceed maximum tolerances, they must be rebored. Reboring is also necessary if the cylinder walls are badly scuffed or scored.

> *CAUTION*
> *If one cylinder is bored out, the others must be bored to the same diameter. Before boring, install all main bearing caps and tighten the cap bolts to specifications in **Table 2**.*

CORE PLUG REPLACEMENT

The condition of all core plugs in the block and cylinder head should be checked whenever the engine is out of the vehicle for service. If any signs of leakage or corrosion are found around one core plug, replace them all.

Removal/Installation

CAUTION
Do not drive core plugs into the engine casting. It will be impossible to retrieve them and they can restrict coolant circulation, resulting in serious engine damage.

1. Tap the bottom edge of the core plug with a hammer and drift. Use several sharp blows to push the bottom of the plug inward, tilting the top out (**Figure 56**).
2. Grip the top of the plug firmly with pliers. Pull the plug from its bore (**Figure 57**) and discard.

NOTE
Core plugs can also be removed by drilling a hole in the center of the plug and prying them out with an appropriate size drift or pin punch. On large core plugs, the use of a universal impact slide hammer is recommended.

3. Clean the plug bore thoroughly to remove all traces of the old sealer. Inspect the bore for any damage that might interfere with proper sealing of the new plug. If damage is evident, true the surface by boring for the next oversize plug.

NOTE
Oversize plugs can be identified by an "OS" stamped in the flat on the cup side of the plug.

4. Coat the inside diameter of the plug bore and the outer diameter of the new plug with sealer. Use an oil-resistant sealer if the plug is to be installed in an oil gallery or a water-resistant sealer for plugs installed in the water jacket.
5. Install the new core plug with an appropriate size core plug replacer tool (**Figure 58**), driver or socket. The sharp edge of the plug should be at least 0.02 in. (0.5 mm) inside the lead-in chamfer.
6. Repeat Steps 1-5 to replace each remaining core plug.

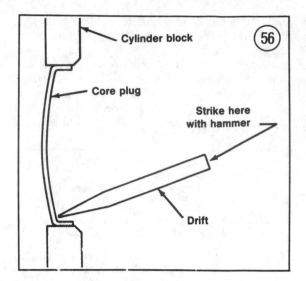

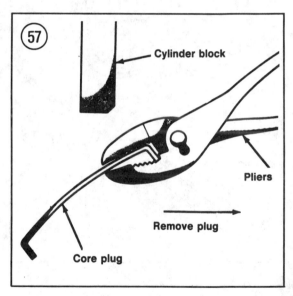

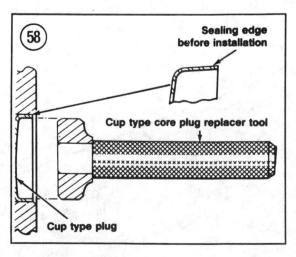

Table 1 I4 ENGINE SPECIFICATIONS

Engine type	Inline 4-cylinder
Bore	4.00 in. (101.6 mm)
Stroke	3.00 in. (76.2 mm)
Displacement	151 cid (2.5 liter)
Firing order	1-3-4-2
Cylinder arrangement	1-2-3-4
Engine code	E
Cylinder bore	
Diameter	4.00 In. (101.6 mm)
Out-of-round (maximum)	0.0014 in. (0.0356 mm)
Taper (maximum)	0.0005 in. (0.0127 mm)
Piston	
Clearance-to-bore	
Top	0.0025-0.0033 in. (0.635-0.838 mm)
Bottom	0.0017-0.0041 in. (0.043-0.1041 mm)
Piston rings	
Side clearance	
Compression rings	0.0015-0.0030 in. (0.0762-0.0381 mm)
Ring gap	
Top	0.010-0.022 in. (0.254-0.635 mm)
Second	0.010-0.027 in. 0.254-0.4826 mm)
Oil	0.015-0.055 in. (0.381-1.397 mm)
Piston pin	
Diameter	0.938-0.942 in. (23.8252-23.9268 mm)
Length	3.00 in. (76.2 mm)
Pin-to-piston clearance	0.0003-0.0005 in. (0.00762-0.01270 mm)
Fit in rod	Press
Camshaft	
Lobe lift	0.398 in. (10.3124 mm)
Journal diameter	1.869 in. (47.4726 mm)
Journal clearance	0.0007-0.0027 in. (0.1778-0.0685 mm)
End play	0.0015-0.0050 in. (0.0381-0.127 mm)
Crankshaft	
Main journal diameter	2.300 in. (59.182 mm)
Taper (maximum)	0.0005 in. (0.0127 mm)
Out-of-round (maximum)	0.0005 in. (0.0127 mm)
Main bearing clearance	0.0005-0.0022 in. (0.0127-0.05588 mm)
End play	0.0035-0.0085 in. (0.889-0.2159 mm)
Crankpin	
Diameter	2.000 in. (50.8 mm)
Taper (maximum)	0.0005 in. (0.0127 mm)
Out-of-round (maximum)	0.0005 in. (0.0127 mm)

4

(continued)

Table 1 I4 ENGINE SPECIFICATIONS (cont.)

Connecting rod	
Bearing clearance	0.0005-0.0026 in.
	(0.0127-0.06604 mm)
Side clearance	0.006-0.022 in.
	(0.1524-0.5588 mm)
Valve train	
Lifter	Hydraulic
Rocker arm ratio	1.75:1
Valve lash	Zero lash
Pushrod length	9.754 in. (242.316 mm)
Face angle	45°
Seat angle	
Intake	46°
Exhaust	45°
Seat width	
Intake	0.0353-0.0747 in.
	(0.986-1.897 mm)
Exhaust	0.058-0.0971 in.
	(1.468-2.468 mm)
Stem clearance	
Intake	0.0010-0.0027 in.
	(0.0254-0.06858 mm)
Exhaust	
Top	0.0010-0.0027 in.
	(0.0254-0.06858 mm)
Bottom	0.0020-0.0037 in.
	(0.0508-0.09398 mm)
Head diameter	
Intake	1.72 in. (43.688 mm)
Exhaust	1.50 in. (38.1 mm)
Stem diameter	
Intake and exhaust	0.3418-0.3425 in.
	(8.68172-8.6995 mm)
Valve spring	
Installed height	1.69 in. (42.926 mm)
Load	
Closed	78-86 lb. @ 1.66 in.
Open	122-180 lb. @ 1.254 in.

Table 2 I4 TIGHTENING TORQUES

Fastener	ft.-lb.	N·m
Camshaft thrust plate	7	10
Connecting rod caps	32	44
Crankshaft pulley bolt	160	220
Cylinder head bolts	92	125
Distributor hold-down clamp	22	30
EGR valve	10	14

(continued)

Table 2 I4 TIGHTENING TORQUES (cont.)

Fastener	ft.-lb.	N·m
Engine mounts		
Front		
To block		
Bolt	35	47
Stud	33	45
Through-bolt	48	65
To frame	35	47
Rear		
Manual transmission		
To transmission	40-48	54-65
To support bracket	20-28	28-38
Support bracket	37-53	50-72
Automatic transmission	25-33	35-45
Exhaust manifold		
1985	37	50
1986-on		
Inner bolts	36	50
Outer bolts	32	43
Fan and pulley	18	24
Flywheel	44	60
Intake manifold		
Studs		
Upper rear end	37	50
All others	25	34
Bolts	28	38
Main bearing caps	70	95
Oil pump		
To block	22	30
Cover	10	14
Oil screen support	37	50
Oil pan		
Drain plug	25	34
To crankcase	4	6
To front cover	7	10
Pushrod cover	7	10
Rocker arm bolt	20	27
TBI assembly	15	20
Thermostat housing	20	27
Timing gear cover	7	10
Valve cover	6	8
Water outlet	20	27
Water pump	25	34
Standard torque values (Grade 5 fasteners)		
1/4-20	8	11
1/4-28	8	11
5/16-18	17	23
5/16-24	20	27
3/8-16	30	40
3/8-24	35	47
7/16-14	50	68
7/16-20	55	75
1/2-13	75	100
1/2-20	85	115
9/16-12	105	142
9/16-18	115	156

4

CHAPTER FIVE

V6 ENGINE

A 262 cid (4.3 liter) V6 engine manufactured by Chevrolet is optional in Astro and Safari vehicles. Derived from the Chevrolet 350 cid V8, the engine is mounted longitudinally in the engine compartment, with the No. 1 cylinder at the front of the left bank (passenger side). The cylinders are numbered from front to rear: 1-3-5 on the left bank and 2-4-6 on the right bank. The firing order is 1-6-5-4-3-2.

The cast iron cylinder heads contain intake and exhaust valves with integral valve guides. Rocker arms are retained on individual threaded shoulder bolts. A ball pivot valve train is used, with camshaft motion transferred through hydraulic lifters to the rocker arms by pushrods. No lash adjustment is necessary in service or during assembly unless some component in the valve train has been removed or replaced.

The chain-driven camshaft is located above the crankshaft between the 2 cylinder banks and supported by 4 bearings. The oil pump mounted at the bottom of the engine block is driven by the camshaft via the distributor.

The crankshaft is supported by 4 main bearings, with the No. 4 bearing providing the crankshaft thrust surfaces.

The cylinder block is cast iron with full length water jackets around each cylinder.

Engine specifications (**Table 1**) and tightening torques (**Table 2** and **Table 3**) are at the end of the chapter.

ENGINE IDENTIFICATION

An engine identification number is stamped on a pad at the front of the block under the cylinder head (**Figure 1**). The pad also contains the Vehicle Identification Number or VIN. This information indicates if there are unique parts or if internal changes have been made during the model year. It is important when ordering replacement parts for the engine.

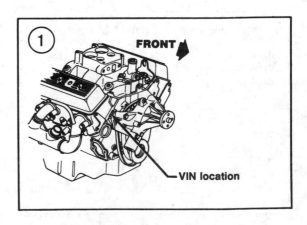

FRONT

VIN location

The engine code is the 8th digit/letter of the Vehicle Identification Number (VIN). The VIN is the official identification for title and vehicle registration. The VIN is stamped on a gray-colored plate fastened to the upper left corner of the instrument panel close to the windshield on the driver's side (**Figure 2**). It can be read from outside the vehicle.

GASKET SEALANT

Gasket sealant is used instead of pre-formed gaskets between numerous mating surfaces on the engine covered in this chapter. See *Gasket Sealant*, Chapter One.

ENGINE REMOVAL

WARNING
The engine is heavy, awkward to handle and has sharp edges. It may shift or drop suddenly during removal. To prevent serious injury, always observe the following precautions.

1. Never place any part of the body where a moving or falling engine may trap, cut or crush you.

2. If you must push the engine during removal, use a board or similar tool to keep your hands out of danger.

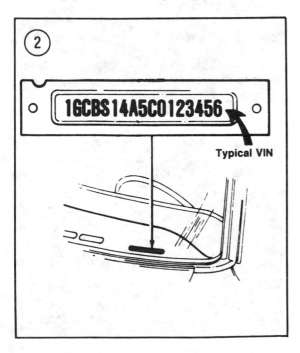

② **Typical VIN**

1GCBS14A5C0123456

3. Be sure the hoist is designed to lift engines and has enough load capacity for your engine.

4. Be sure the hoist is securely attached to safe lifting points of the engine.

5. The engine should not be difficult to lift with a proper hoist. If it is, stop lifting, lower the engine back onto its mounts and make sure the engine has been completely separated from the vehicle.

WARNING
If the vehicle is equipped with air conditioning, have the system discharged by an air conditioning specialist before beginning this procedure.

1. Open and support the hood.

WARNING
Do not disconnect fuel injection lines unless fuel system pressure has been relieved.

2. On fuel injected models, relieve fuel system pressure as described in **Chapter Six**.
3. Disconnect the negative battery cable, then the positive cable.
4. Remove the 4 center console bolts, unsnap the 2 latches at the base of the engine cover and remove the 2 bolts from under the hood which hold the engine cover in place. Remove the engine cover.
5. Remove the headlamp bezels, grille, radiator lower close-out panel and support brace.
6. Remove the lower tie bar. Remove the cross brace.
7. Remove the hood latch mechanism.
8. Drain the cooling system. See Chapter Seven.
9. Securely block both rear wheels so the vehicle will not roll in either direction.
10. Raise the front of the vehicle with a jack and place it on jackstands.
11. Disconnect the exhaust crossover pipe at the exhaust manifolds. Unplug the oxygen sensor electrical connector at the wiring harness.
12. Automatic transmission—Disconnect the strut rods at the flywheel inspection cover. Remove the inspection cover.
13. Manual transmission—Remove the slave cylinder. See Chapter Nine.
14. Automatic transmission—Make matching chalk marks on the converter and flywheel for alignment during installation. Remove the bolts holding the torque converter to the flywheel.

5

15. Disconnect the wiring harness at the transmission (**Figure 3**), starter motor and frame. Remove the starter motor (**Figure 4**). See Chapter Eight.

16. Disconnect the fuel hoses at the frame. Disconnect automatic transmission oil cooler lines, if so equipped, at the oil pan.

17. Drain the engine oil and remove the oil filter. See Chapter Three.

18. Disconnect the lower oil cooler and transmission cooler lines, if so equipped, at the radiator. Disconnect the lower radiator hose. See **Figure 5** and Chapter Seven.

19. Remove the lower fan shroud fasteners.

20. Remove the motor mount through-bolts.

21. Remove the bell housing bolts.

22. Remove the jackstands and lower the vehicle to the ground.

23. Remove the brake master cylinder (**Figure 6**). See Chapter Twelve.

24. Remove the upper fan shroud (Chapter Seven) and upper radiator core support.

25. Disconnect the upper oil cooler and transmission cooler lines, if so equipped, at the radiator. Disconnect the upper radiator hose and remove the radiator. See Chapter Seven.

26. Remove the radiator filler panels.

> *WARNING*
> *The air conditioning system contains pressurized refrigerant which can cause frostbite if it touches skin and blindness if it touches the eyes. If discharged near an open flame, the refrigerant forms poisonous gas. Never disconnect air conditioning system lines unless the system has been discharged and evacuated by a professional.*

27. Remove the air conditioning compressor rear brace, disconnect the AC hose at the accumulator and remove the compressor and bracket assembly.

28. Remove the power steering pump. Cap the lines and fittings to prevent leakage or the entry of contamination.

29. Disconnect the ground cable at the cylinder head. Label and disconnect all other electrical leads or vacuum lines connected to non-engine mounted components.

30. Disconnect the engine wiring harness at the bulkhead connector. Remove the right kick panel and disconnect the harness at the ESC module, then push it through the bulkhead.

31. Disconnect the heater hoses at the heater core fittings.

32. Remove the distributor cap. See Chapter Eight.

33. Remove the air conditioning accumulator, if so equipped.

34. Disconnect the fuel line(s) at the fuel pump (carburetted) or TBI unit (fuel injected). Plug the lines and cap the fittings to prevent leakage or the entry of contamination.

35. Disconnect the throttle cable at the carburetor or TBI unit. Disconnect the transmission TV

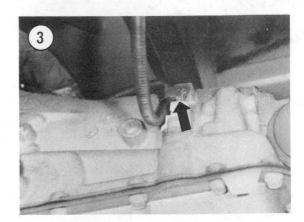

(throttle valve) and/or speed control cables at the carburetor or TBI unit, if so equipped.

36. Remove the air management or diverter valve (A, **Figure 7**) and AIR check valves (B, **Figure 7** and **Figure 8**).

37. Disconnect the transmission dipstick tube, if equipped with an automatic transmission. Remove the engine oil filler tube, if so equipped.

38. Remove the horn. See Chapter Eight.

39. Remove the air cleaner and adapter. See Chapter Six.

40. Position a floor jack with a block of wood under the transmission housing for support.

NOTE
Double check to make sure all electrical leads, vacuum lines and control links between the engine and engine compartment have been disconnected or removed. Check also to make sure that the air conditioning lines, oil lines and wiring harness will not snag on the engine when it is removed.

41. Attach a suitable lifting device to the engine. With an assistant's help from inside the vehicle, carefully raise the engine up, forward and out of the engine compartment through the front of the vehicle.

5

ENGINE INSTALLATION

Engine installation is the reverse of removal, plus the following:

1. Position the engine into the vehicle. Leave the lifting device attached and holding the assembly until all mounts and mount fasteners have been installed and tightened to specifications (**Figure 9**).

2. Fill the engine with an oil recommended in Chapter Three.

3. Fill the cooling system and adjust the drive belts. See Chapter Seven.

4. Adjust the ignition timing as required. See Chapter Three.

ENGINE MOUNTS AND SUPPORTS

WARNING
The engine is heavy and may shift or drop suddenly. Never place your hands or any part of your body where the moving engine may trap or crush you. If you can't remove the mounts without placing your hands where the moving engine may injure them, support the engine with a jackstand as well as a hoist to be certain the engine can't fall on you.

Engine mounts are non-adjustable and rarely require service. Replace any broken or deteriorated mounts immediately to reduce strain on remaining mounts and drive line components.

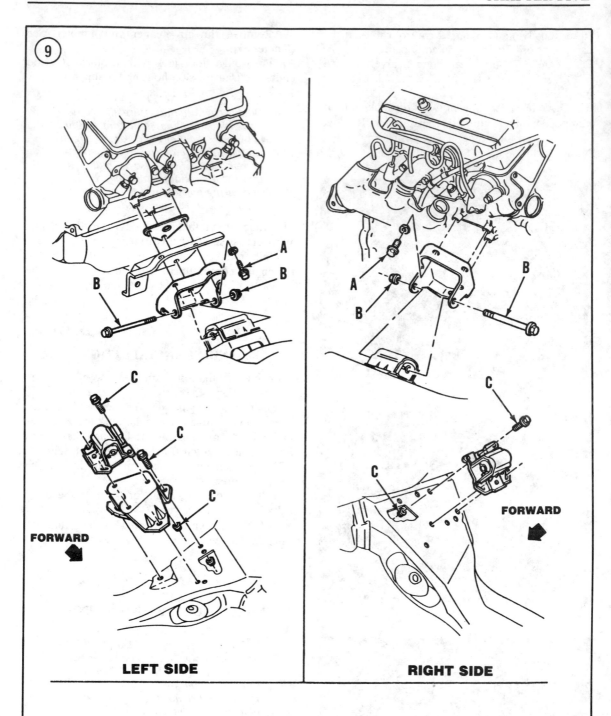

LEFT SIDE   **RIGHT SIDE**

A. 36 ft.-lb. (50 N•m)
B. Torque bolt to 75 ft.-lb. (100 N•m) or nut to 50 ft.-lb.
(68 N•m)
C. Torque bolt to 45 ft.-lb. (60 N•m) or nut to 36 ft.-lb.
(50 N•m)

Checking Front Mounts

1. Attach a lifting device and raise the engine enough to remove its weight from the mount.
2. Check the rubber surface of the mount for:
   a. Heat check cracks.
   b. Separation from the metal plate.
   c. Splitting through the center.
3. If any of these defects are noted, replace the mounts as described in this chapter.
4. If movement of the mount relative to the frame is noted during this procedure, lower the engine to place its weight back on the mounts and retighten the mount fasteners.
5. Remove the lifting device.

Checking Rear Mounts

1. Securely block both rear wheels so the vehicle will not roll in either direction.
2. Raise the front of the vehicle with a jack and place it on jackstands.

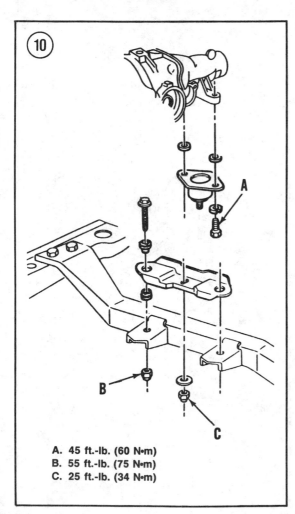

A. 45 ft.-lb. (60 N•m)
B. 55 ft.-lb. (75 N•m)
C. 25 ft.-lb. (34 N•m)

3. Watch the transmission mount while pushing up and pulling downward on the transmission extension housing. Replace the mount if the rubber separates from the metal plate or if the extension housing moves up but not downward.
4. If movement of the mount relative to the crossmember is noted during this procedure, retighten the mount fasteners.

Front Mount Replacement

Refer to **Figure 9** for this procedure.
1. Securely block the rear wheels so the vehicle will not roll in either direction.
2. Raise the front of the vehicle with a jack and place it on jackstands.
3. Place a hydraulic jack under the engine oil pan. Insert a wooden block between the jack and oil pan.
4. Raise the engine with the hydraulic jack enough to remove the engine mount through-bolt.
5. Remove the mount-to-frame bracket bolts. Remove the mount.
6. Install a new engine mount to the frame bracket. Tighten fasteners to specifications (**Table 2**).
7. Lower the engine until the through-bolt can be installed. Tighten the through-bolt to specifications (**Figure 9**).
8. Remove the hydraulic jack and jackstands, then lower the vehicle to the ground.

Rear Mount Replacement

Refer to **Figure 10** for this procedure.
1. Raise the vehicle with a jack and place it on jackstands.
2. Remove the mount-to-crossmember support nut.
3. Position a jack under the rear of the engine and raise it enough to relieve the weight from the rear mount and allow access to the mount-to-transmission bolts.
4. Remove the mount-to-transmission bolts. Remove the mount.
5. Install a new mount to the transmission. Tighten the fasteners to specifications (**Figure 10**).
6. Lower the engine slowly, aligning the mount stud to the crossmember support hole. Install the mount nut and tighten to specifications (**Table 2**).
7. Remove the jack from under the engine. Remove the jackstands and lower the vehicle to the ground.

DISASSEMBLY CHECKLISTS

To use the checklists, remove and inspect each part in the order mentioned. To reassemble, go through the checklists backwards, installing the parts in order. Each major part is covered in its own section in this chapter, unless otherwise noted.

Decarbonizing or Valve Service

1. Remove the valve covers.
2. Remove the intake and exhaust manifolds.
3. Remove the rocker arms.
4. Remove the cylinder heads.
5. Have valves removed and inspected. Have valve guides and seats inspected, repairing or replacing as required.
6. Assemble by reversing Steps 1-4.

Valve and Ring Service

1. Perform Steps 1-5 of *Decarbonizing or Valve Service*.
2. Remove the oil pan and oil pump.
3. Remove the pistons with connecting rods.
4. Remove the piston rings. It is not necessary to separate the pistons from the connecting rods unless a piston, connecting rod or piston pin needs repair or replacement.
5. Assemble by reversing Steps 1-4.

General Overhaul

1. Remove the engine. Remove the clutch from manual transmission vehicles.
2. Remove the flywheel (manual) or drive plate (automatic).
3. Remove the mount brackets, knock sensor and oil pressure sending unit from the engine.
4. If available, mount the engine on an engine stand. These can be rented from equipment rental dealers. The stand is not absolutely necessary, but it will make the job much easier.
5. Remove the following accessories or components from the engine, if present:
   a. Air injection (AIR) system and brackets.
   b. Alternator and mounting bracket.
   c. Power steering pump and mounting bracket.
   d. Spark plug wires and distributor cap.
   e. Carburetor or TBI unit and fuel lines.
   f. Oil dipstick and tube.

6. Check the engine for signs of coolant or oil leaks.
7. Clean the outside of the engine.
8. Remove the distributor. See Chapter Eight.
9. Remove all hoses and tubes connected to the engine.
10. Carburetted engine—Remove the fuel pump. See Chapter Six.
11. Remove the intake and exhaust manifolds.
12. Remove the thermostat housing/water outlet adapter. See Chapter Seven.
13. Remove the valve covers and rocker arms.
14. Remove the crankshaft pulley, front hub, front cover and water pump.
15. Remove the camshaft sprocket and camshaft.
16. Remove the cylinder heads.
17. Remove the oil pan and oil pump.
18. Remove the pistons and connecting rods .

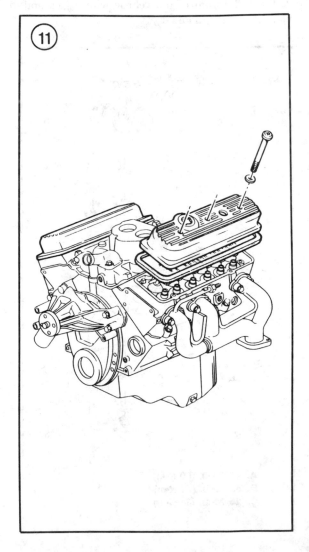

19. Remove the crankshaft.
20. Inspect the cylinder block.
21. Assemble by reversing Steps 1-19.

VALVE COVERS

Removal/Installation
Right Side

Refer to **Figure 11** for this procedure.
1. Open and support the hood. Disconnect the negative battery cable.
2. Remove the 4 center console bolts, unsnap the 2 latches at the base of the engine cover and remove the 2 bolts from under the hood which hold the engine cover in place. Remove the engine cover.
3. Remove the air cleaner assembly. See Chapter Six.
4. Disconnect the spark plug wires and remove them from the valve cover looms. Remove the distributor wires and plug wires. See **Figure 12**.

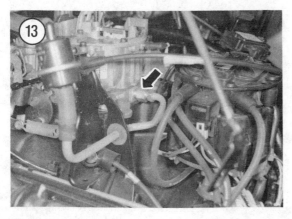

5. Disconnect and remove the air management or diverter valve. See A, **Figure 7**.
6. Disconnect the crankcase oil filler tube and transmission oil filler tube (if so equipped) at the alternator bracket.
7. Remove the PCV valve.
8. Remove the bolts holding the AIR pipes at the rear of the right cylinder head, then move the hose out of the way.
9. Remove the valve cover bolts. Tap the end of the valve cover with a rubber mallet to break the gasket seal. Remove the valve cover and discard the gasket.
10. Clean all gasket residue from the cylinder head and valve cover with degreaser and a putty knife.
11. Install the valve cover with a new gasket. Tighten the fasteners to specifications (**Table 2**).
12. Reverse Steps 1-8 to complete cover installation.

Removal/Installation
Left Side

Refer to **Figure 11** for this procedure.
1. Open and support the hood. Disconnect the negative battery cable.
2. Remove the 4 center console bolts, unsnap the 2 latches at the base of the engine cover and remove the 2 bolts from under the hood which hold the engine cover in place. Remove the engine cover.
3. Remove the air cleaner assembly. See Chapter Six.
4A. Carburetted engine—Disconnect the vacuum pipe at the carburetor (**Figure 13**).
4B. Fuel injected engine—Disconnect the vacuum lines at the TBI unit.
5. Unplug the electrical connector at the wire harness.
6. Remove the valve cover bolts.
7. Disconnect the throttle cable at the carburetor or TBI unit. Disconnect the transmission TV (throttle valve) and speed control cables at the carburetor or TBI unit, if so equipped. Unbolt and remove the cable bracket from the intake manifold.
8. Tap the end of the valve cover with a rubber mallet to break the gasket seal. Remove the valve cover and discard the gasket.
9. Clean all gasket residue from the cylinder head and valve cover with degreaser and a putty knife.
10. Install the valve cover with a new gasket. Tighten the fasteners to specifications (**Table 2**).
11. Reverse Steps 1-7 to complete cover installation.

5

INTAKE MANIFOLD

The single level cast iron intake manifold contains an EGR port to permit the recirculation of exhaust gases. The exhaust gas is combined with the incoming air-fuel mixture.

Removal/Installation

Refer to **Figure 14** for this procedure.
1. Open and support the hood. Relieve fuel system pressure on fuel injected models, then disconnect the negative battery cable.
2. Remove the glovebox assembly.
3. Remove the 4 center console bolts, unsnap the 2 latches at the base of the engine cover and remove the 2 bolts from under the hood which hold the engine cover in place. Remove the engine cover.
4. Remove the air cleaner assembly. See Chapter Six.
5. Partially drain the cooling system. See Chapter Seven. If coolant is to be reused, drain it into a suitable container.

> ### WARNING
> *Antifreeze is poisonous and may attract animals. Do not leave the drained coolant where it is accessible to children or pets.*

6. Remove the distributor. See Chapter Eight.

7. Disconnect the throttle cable at the carburetor or TBI unit. Disconnect the transmission TV (throttle valve) and speed control cables at the carburetor or TBI unit, if so equipped. Unbolt and remove the cable bracket from the intake manifold.
8. If equipped with air conditioning, remove the compressor rear brace.
9. Disconnect the crankcase oil filler tube and transmission oil filler tube (if so equipped) at the alternator bracket.
10. If equipped with air conditioning, remove the idler pulley at the alternator brace, then remove the alternator brace.
11. Disconnect the fuel line(s) at the carburetor or TBI unit. See Chapter Six. Plug the lines and cap the fittings to prevent leakage or the entry of contamination.
12. Label and disconnect all vacuum lines and electrical connectors at the carburetor or TBI unit.
13. Disconnect and remove the AIR hoses and brackets.
14. Disconnect the heater hose at the intake manifold.
15. If carburetor or TBI unit is to be removed, do so at this point. See Chapter Six.
16. Loosen and remove the intake manifold bolts. Carefully loosen the intake manifold with a suitable pry bar (taking care not to damage any sealing surfaces) and remove the manifold from the engine.

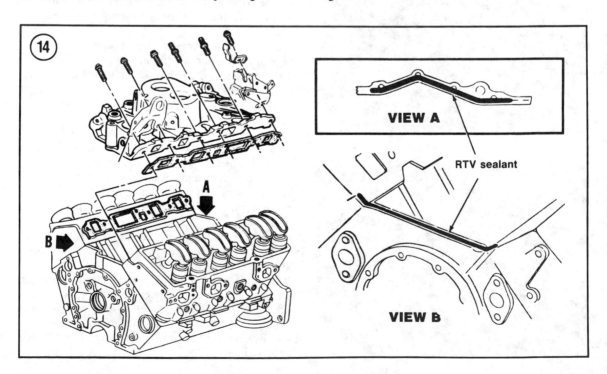

VIEW A

RTV sealant

VIEW B

17. Remove and discard the manifold gaskets and seals.

18. Clean all gasket and RTV sealant residue from the manifold, engine block and cylinder head sealing surfaces with degreaser and a putty knife.

19. If the manifold is to be replaced, transfer all components and fittings on the old manifold to the new one. Make sure fittings are properly installed and positioned.

20. Install new gaskets on the cylinder heads and new end seals on the block. Run a 3/16 in. bead of RTV sealant on the front and rear ridges of the cylinder block. Extend the bead about 1/2 in. up each cylinder head to hold and seal the manifold side gaskets. See **Figure 14**. Use sealing compound around the water passages.

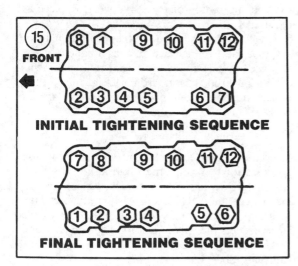

21. Install the manifold on the cylinder block. Install the manifold bolts and tighten to 25 ft.-lb. (34 N•m) following the initial tightening sequence shown in **Figure 15**. When all bolts have been tightened, retighten to 35 ft.-lb. (47 N•m) following the final sequence shown in **Figure 15**.

22. Reverse Steps 1-15 to complete installation. Tighten all fasteners to specifications (**Table 2**).

EXHAUST MANIFOLDS

Stainless steel exhaust manifolds are used to transfer exhaust gases from the engine's combustion chambers to the exhaust system. The right manifold has a heat shield or stove to provide heated air to the air cleaner.

Removal/Installation

Refer to **Figure 16** for this procedure.

1. Open and support the hood. Disconnect the negative battery cable.

2. Securely block both rear wheels so the vehicle will not roll in either direction.

3. Raise the front of the vehicle with a jack and place it on jackstands.

4. Disconnect the exhaust crossover pipe at the exhaust manifold(s) to be removed.

5. Left side:
   a. Disconnect the AIR pipe bracket at the cylinder head.
   b. Disconnect the air cleaner heat tube at the manifold.
   c. Unbolt and remove the exhaust manifold.

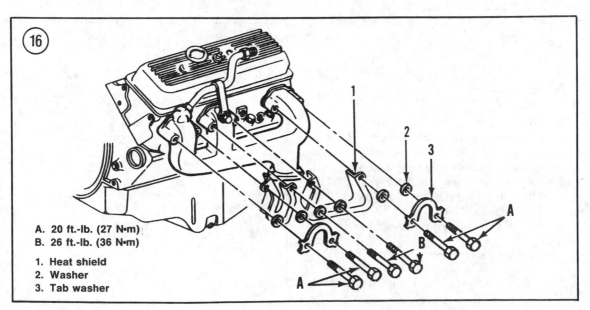

A. 20 ft.-lb. (27 N•m)
B. 26 ft.-lb. (36 N•m)

1. Heat shield
2. Washer
3. Tab washer

6. Right side:
   a. Remove the jackstands and lower the vehicle to the ground.
   b. Remove the glovebox assembly.
   c. Remove the 4 center console bolts, unsnap the 2 latches at the base of the engine cover and remove the 2 bolts from under the hood which hold the engine cover in place. Remove the engine cover.
   d. Unbolt and remove the exhaust manifold. Remove the manifold and gasket. Discard the gasket.
7. Clean the cylinder head and exhaust manifold mating surfaces.
8. Installation is the reverse of removal. Use a new gasket and tighten all fasteners to specifications as shown in **Figure 16**.

MANIFOLD INSPECTION

1. Check the intake and exhaust manifolds for cracks or distortion. Replace if distorted or if cracks are found.
2. Check the mating surfaces for nicks or burrs. Small burrs may be removed with an oilstone.
3. Place a straightedge across the manifold flange/mating surfaces. If there is any gap between the straightedge and surface, measure it with a flat feeler gauge. Measure each manifold from end to end and from corner to corner. If the mating surface is not flat within 0.006 in. (0.15 mm) per foot of manifold length, replace the manifold.
4. Check the EFE valve on exhaust manifolds so equipped. If the valve does not operate freely, apply a penetrating solvent to the valve shaft. If it still does not function properly, replace the EFE valve assembly.

ROCKER ARMS

Removal/Installation

Each rocker arm moves on its own pivot ball. The rocker arm and pivot ball are retained by a nut. It is not necessary to remove the rocker arm for pushrod replacement; simply loosen the nut and move the arm away from the pushrod. To remove the entire assembly, refer to **Figure 17** and proceed as follows.
1. Remove the valve cover as described in this chapter.
2. Remove the rocker arm nut and ball.
3. Remove the rocker arm.
4. Remove the valve pushrod from the cylinder block.

5. Repeat Steps 2-4 for each remaining rocker arm. Place each rocker arm and pushrod assembly in a separate container or use a rack to keep them separated for reinstallation in the same position from which they were removed.
6. Installation is the reverse of removal. If new rocker arms or balls are being installed, coat contact surfaces with engine oil or Molykote. Make sure pushrods fit into lifter sockets. Tighten each nut securely. Adjust the valve clearance as described in this chapter.

Inspection

1. Clean all parts with solvent and use compressed air to blow out the oil passages in the pushrods.
2. Check each rocker arm, ball, nut and pushrod for scuffing, pitting or excessive wear. Replace as required.
3. Check pushrods for straightness by rolling them across a flat, even surface such as a pane of glass. Replace any pushrods that do not roll smoothly.
4. If a pushrod is worn from lack of lubrication, replace the corresponding lifter and rocker arm as well.

Valve Clearance Adjustment

Stem-to-rocker arm clearance must be within specifications when the hydraulic lifter is completely collapsed. If valve clearance is insufficient, the valve opens early and closes late, resulting in a rough engine idle. Excessive clearance lets the valve open too late and close too early, causing valve bounce and damage to the camshaft lobe.

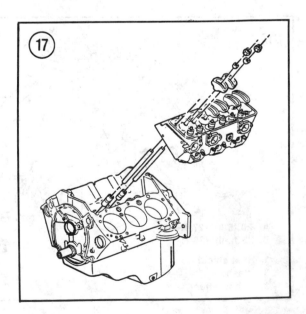

Valve adjustment is required only when the cylinder head valve train has been disassembled. Adjust the valves with the lifter on the base circle of the camshaft lobe.

1. Rotate the crankshaft until the pulley notch aligns with the zero mark on the timing tab. This positions the No. 1 cylinder at TDC. This position can be verified by placing a finger on the No. 1 rocker arms as the pulley notch nears the zero mark. If the rocker arms are moving, the engine is in the No. 4 firing position; rotate the crankshaft pulley one full turn to reach the No. 1 firing position.

2. With the engine in the No. 1 firing position, refer to **Figure 18** and adjust the No. 1, 2 and 3 intake and the No. 1, 5 and 6 exhaust valves.

3. To adjust each valve, back off the adjusting nut until lash is felt at the pushrod, then turn the nut to remove all lash. When lash has been removed, the pushrod will not rotate. Turn the nut in one additional full turn to center the lifter plunger. See **Figure 19**.

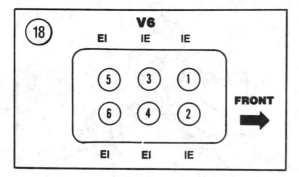

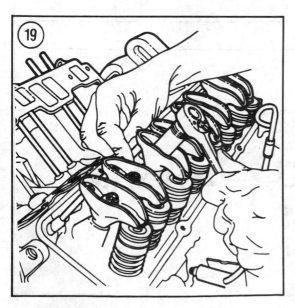

4. Rotate the crankshaft one full turn to realign the pulley notch and the timing tab zero mark in the No. 4 firing position. Refer to **Figure 18** and adjust the No. 4, 5 and 6 intake and the No. 2, 3 and 4 exhaust valves.

CAMSHAFT

Removal/Installation

1. Open and support the hood. Relieve fuel system pressure on fuel injected models, then disconnect the negative battery cable.

2. Remove the glovebox assembly.

3. Remove the 4 center console bolts, unsnap the 2 latches at the base of the engine cover and remove the 2 bolts from under the hood which hold the engine cover in place. Remove the engine cover.

4. Remove the air cleaner assembly. See Chapter Six.

5. Drain the cooling system. See Chapter Seven. If coolant is to be reused, drain it into a suitable container.

> *WARNING*
> *Antifreeze is poisonous and may attract animals. Do not leave the drained coolant where it is accessible to children or pets.*

6. Remove the distributor. See Chapter Eight.

7. Remove the carburetor or TBI unit. See Chapter Six.

8. Remove the intake manifold as described in this chapter.

9. Remove the upper fan shroud.

10. Remove the power steering and AIR pumps. Remove the AIR pump bracket.

11. Remove the cooling fan and pulley. Remove the water pump. See Chapter Seven.

12. Remove the torsional damper as described in this chapter.

13. Remove the timing cover and timing chain/camshaft gear as described in this chapter.

14. Carburetted engine—Remove the fuel pump and pushrod. See Chapter Six.

15. Disconnect the oil cooler lines at the radiator. Remove the lower fan shroud. See Chapter Seven.

16. Loosen the rocker arm adjusting nuts, swivel the arms off the pushrods and remove the pushrods. Identify each pushrod for reinstallation in its original location.

17. Remove the valve lifters with a pencil-type magnet. Place lifters in a rack in order of removal for reinstallation in their original location.

18. Rotate the crankshaft to position the No. 1 piston at TDC with the camshaft and crankshaft marks aligned as shown in **Figure 20**.

19. Remove the camshaft sprocket bolts. The sprocket is a light press fit and should come off easily. If not, lightly tap the lower edge of the sprocket with a plastic hammer to dislodge it from the camshaft. Remove the sprocket and timing chain.

20. Install two 5/16-18X4 in. bolts in the camshaft sprocket bolt holes at the end of the camshaft.

> *CAUTION*
> *Do not cock the camshaft during removal. This can damage the camshaft or its bearing thrust surfaces.*

21. Carefully withdraw the camshaft from the front of the engine with a rotating motion to avoid damage to the bearings.

22. Installation is the reverse of removal. Coat the camshaft lobes with GM EOS lubricant or equivalent and the journals with heavy engine oil before reinstalling in the block. Check and adjust ignition timing (Chapter Three).

Inspection

1. Check the journals and lobes for signs of wear or scoring. Lobe pitting in the toe area is not sufficient reason for replacement unless the lobe lift loss exceeds specifications.

> *NOTE*
> *If you do not have precision measuring equipment, have Step 2 done by a machine shop.*

2. Measure the camshaft journal diameters with a micrometer (**Figure 21**) and compare to

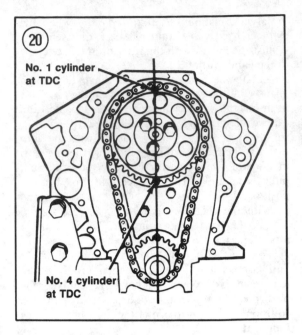

No. 1 cylinder at TDC

No. 4 cylinder at TDC

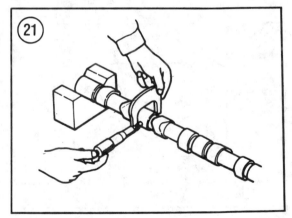

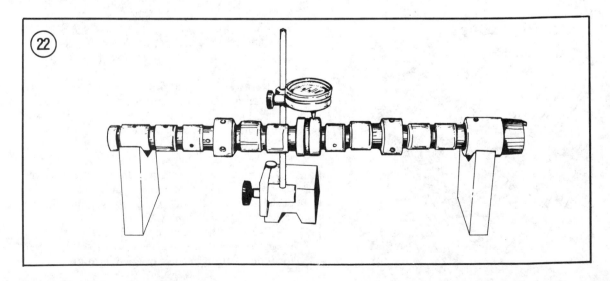

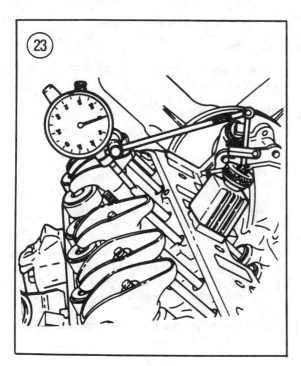

specifications (**Table 1**). Replace the camshaft if the journals are more than 0.0009 in. (0.025 mm) out-of-round.

3. Suspend the camshaft between V-blocks and check for warpage with a dial indicator. See **Figure 22**. Replace if the runout is greater than 0.015 in.

Lifter Inspection

Keep the lifters in proper sequence for installation in their original position in the head. Clean lifters in solvent and wipe dry with a clean, lint-free cloth. Inspect and test the lifters separately to prevent intermixing of their internal parts. If any part requires replacement, replace the entire lifter.

Inspect all parts. If any lifter shows signs of pitting, scoring, galling, non-rotation or excessive wear, discard it. Check the lifter plunger. It should drop to the bottom of the body by its own weight when dry and assembled.

Lobe Lift Measurement

Camshaft lobe lift can be measured with the camshaft in the block and the cylinder head in place. The lifters must be bled down slowly in Step 6 or the readings will be incorrect.

1. Remove the valve cover as described in this chapter.

2. Remove the rocker arms and pivot assemblies as described in this chapter.

3. Remove the spark plugs.

4. Install a dial indicator on the end of a pushrod. A piece of rubber tubing will hold the dial indicator plunger in place on the center of the pushrod. See **Figure 23** (typical).

5. Rotate the crankshaft in the normal direction of rotation until the valve lifter seats on the heel or base of the cam lobe (**Figure 24**). This positions the pushrod at its lowest point.

6. Set the dial indicator at zero, then slowly rotate the crankshaft until the pushrod reaches its maximum travel. Note the indicator reading and compare to specifications (**Table 1**).

7. Repeat Steps 4-6 for each pushrod. If all lobes are within specifications in Step 6, reinstall the rocker arm assemblies and adjust the valves as described in this chapter.

8. If one or more lobes are worn beyond specifications, replace the camshaft as described in this chapter.

9. Remove the dial indicator and reverse Steps 1-3.

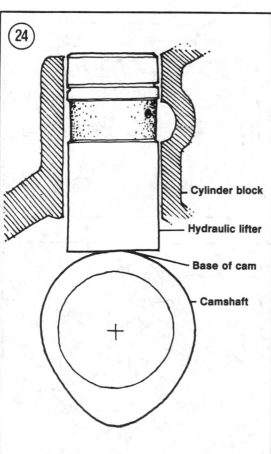

- Cylinder block

- Hydraulic lifter

- Base of cam

- Camshaft

Bearing Replacement

Camshaft bearings can be replaced without complete engine disassembly. Replace bearings in complete sets. Camshaft bearing and installer tool part No. J-6098 is required for bearing replacement. If you don't have the special tool, take the engine to a machine shop for camshaft bearing replacement.

1. Remove the camshaft as described in this chapter.
2. Remove the crankshaft as described in this chapter . Leave pistons in cylinder bores.
3. Drive the camshaft welch plug from the rear of the cylinder block.
4. Secure the connecting rods to the side of the engine to keep them out of the way while replacing the cam bearings.
5. Install the nut and thrust washer to tool part No. J-6098. Index the tool pilot in the front cam bearing. Install the puller screw through the pilot.
6. Install tool part no. J-6098 with its shoulder facing the front intermediate bearing and the threads engaging the bearing.
7. Hold the puller screw with one wrench. Turn the nut with a second wrench until the bearing has been pulled from its bore. See **Figure 25**.
8. When bearing has been removed from bore, remove tool and bearing from puller screw.
9. Repeat Steps 5-8 to remove the center bearing.
10. Remove the tool and index it to the rear bearing to remove the rear intermediate bearing from the block.
11. Remove the front and rear bearings by driving them toward the center of the block.

> *CAUTION*
> *Improper alignment of the rear bearing during Step 12 will restrict oil pressure reaching the valve train.*

12. Installation is the reverse of removal. Use the same tool to pull the new bearings into their bores. Bearing oil holes must align with those in the block. Since the oil hole is on the top of the bearings (and cannot be seen during installation), align bearing oil hole with hole in bore and mark opposite side of bearing and block at bore to assist in positioning the oil hole during installation as follows—Position the No. 1 bearing oil holes at an equal distance from the 6 o'clock position. Align No. 5 bearing oil hole with the 12 o'clock position.
13. Wipe a new camshaft welch plug with an oil-resistant sealer and install it flush to 1/32 in. deep to maintain a level surface on the rear of the block.

TORSIONAL DAMPER

Removal/Installation

1. Remove the fan shroud, cooling fan and pulley. See Chapter Seven.

> *NOTE*
> *On some installations, it may be necessary to drain the cooling system and remove the radiator to provide clearance for damper removal. See Chapter Seven.*

2. Unbolt and remove the drive pulley from the torsional damper.
3. Remove the damper retaining bolt.
4. Install puller part No. J-23523 to the damper with the pulley attaching bolts and remove the torsional damper. See **Figure 26** (typical).
5. Lubricate the front cover seal lip and that area on the damper where the seal contacts it with clean engine oil.
6. Position the damper over the crankshaft key.

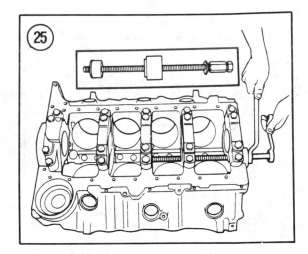

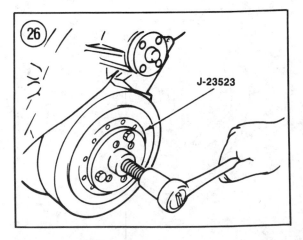

7. Install threaded end of tool part No. J-23523 in the crankshaft so that at least 1/2 in. of the tool threads are engaged. Install plate, thrust bearing and nut to complete tool installation.

8. Pull damper into position as shown in **Figure 27** (typical).

9. Remove the tool, install the damper retaining bolt and tighten to specifications (**Table 2**).

10. Reverse Step 1 and Step 2 to complete installation. Adjust drive belts as necessary. See Chapter Seven.

CRANKCASE FRONT COVER AND OIL SEAL

Cover Removal/Installation

1. Remove the torsional damper as described in this chapter.

2. Remove the water pump. See Chapter Seven.

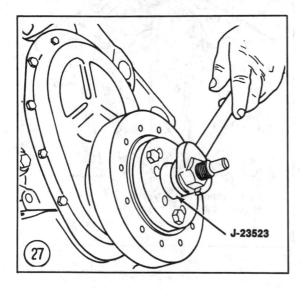

J-23523

27

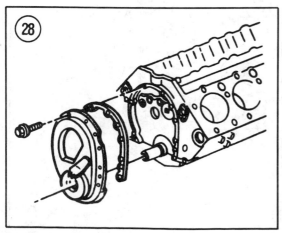

28

3. Remove the front cover attaching screws. Remove the front cover and gasket. See **Figure 28**. Discard the gasket.

4A. 1985—Cut away any excess oil pan gasket material protruding at the oil pan-to-block joint.

4B. 1986-on—Check the condition of the exposed part of the one-piece oil pan gasket. If satisfactory, it can be reused; if not, replace the oil pan gasket as described in this chapter when reinstalling the front cover.

5. Clean the block and front cover sealing surfaces of all oil and grease. Apply a 1/8 in. (3 mm) bead of RTV sealant to the joint formed at the oil pan and cylinder block on each side.

6. Install the gasket to the cover with gasket sealant.

7. Install the cover-to-oil pan seal. Coat the bottom of the seal with engine oil.

8. Position cover over crankshaft end and loosely install the cover-to-block upper screws.

NOTE
Do not force cover on dowels in Step 9 so the cover flange or holes are distorted.

9. Press downward on the cover to align the block dowels with their corresponding cover holes, then tighten the screws in a crisscross pattern.

10. Install remaining cover screws and tighten to specifications (**Table 2**).

11. Install the water pump. See Chapter Seven.

12. Install the torsional damper as described in this chapter.

Seal Replacement

The seal can be replaced without removing the front cover. If the cover has been removed and seal replacement is necessary, support the cover on a clean workbench and perform Steps 2-4.

1. Remove the torsional damper as described in this chapter.

2. Pry the old seal from the cover with a large screwdriver. Work carefully to prevent damage to the cover seal surface.

3. Clean the seal recess in the cover with solvent and blow dry with compressed air.

4. Position a new seal in the cover recess with its open end facing the inside of the cover. Drive seal into place with installer part No. J-23042.

5. Install the torsional damper as described in this chapter.

5

TIMING CHAIN AND SPROCKETS

Removal

Refer to **Figure 29** for this procedure.
1. Remove the spark plugs. See Chapter Three.
2. Remove the torsional damper as described in this chapter.
3. Remove the front cover as described in this chapter.
4. Rotate the crankshaft to position the No. 1 piston at TDC with the camshaft and crankshaft sprocket marks aligned as shown in **Figure 30**.
5. Remove the camshaft sprocket bolts. The sprocket is a light press fit and should come off easily. If not, lightly tap the lower edge of the sprocket with a plastic hammer to dislodge it from the camshaft. Remove the sprocket and timing chain.
6. If crankshaft sprocket is to be removed, use puller part No. J-5825 or equivalent (**Figure 31**).

Installation

Refer to **Figure 29** for this procedure.
1. Install the crankshaft sprocket, if removed, with sprocket installer part No. J-5590 or equivalent. See **Figure 32**.
2. Install the timing chain on the camshaft sprocket.
3. Hold the sprocket vertically with the chain hanging down. Align the camshaft and crankshaft sprocket marks as shown in **Figure 30**.
4. Align the camshaft dowel with the sprocket hole. Install the sprocket on the camshaft.
5. Install the camshaft sprocket mounting bolts. Tighten bolts to draw the sprocket onto the camshaft, then tighten to specifications (**Table 2**).
6. Lubricate the timing chain with SAE 30W engine oil.
7. Install the front cover and torsional damper as described in this chapter.
8. Reinstall the spark plugs. See Chapter Three.

OIL PAN

Refer to **Figure 33** for this procedure.
1. Open and support the hood. Disconnect the negative battery cable.
2. Securely block both rear wheels so the vehicle will not roll in either direction.
3. Raise the vehicle with a jack and place it on jackstands.
4. Drain the crankcase. See Chapter Three.
5. Disconnect the exhaust crossover pipe at the exhaust manifolds. Disconnect the exhaust hangers and move the exhaust system to one side to

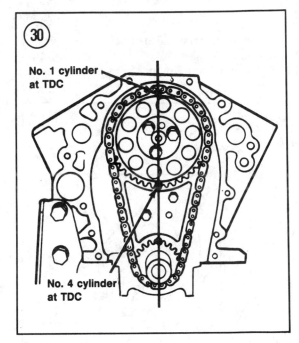

No. 1 cylinder at TDC

No. 4 cylinder at TDC

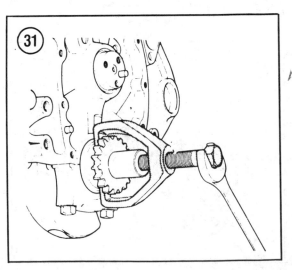

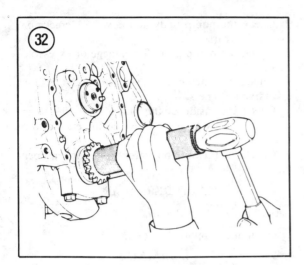

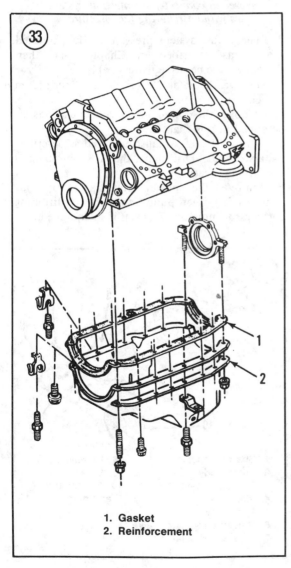

1. Gasket
2. Reinforcement

provide access for oil pan removal. Suspend exhaust system from the suspension with wire.

6. Disconnect the strut rods at the flywheel cover or motor mounts, as required.

7. Remove the flywheel cover.

8. Remove the starter motor. See Chapter Eight.

9. Position a floor jack under the torsional damper. Place a wooden block between the jack head and torsional damper. Raise the engine enough to provide sufficient access for oil pan removal.

10. Remove the oil pan bolts and reinforcement strips. Make sure that the forward crankshaft throw or counterbalance weight does not extend downward and block pan removal. If necessary, rotate crankshaft to place throw on a horizontal plane. Remove the oil pan.

11. Remove and discard the one-piece pan gasket.

12. Clean any gasket residue from the oil pan rail on the engine block and the oil pan sealing flange with degreaser and a putty knife.

13. Clean the pan thoroughly in solvent and check for dents or warped gasket surfaces. Straighten or replace the pan as required.

14. Install the oil pan with a new gasket and tighten the pan bolts to specifications (**Table 2**).

15. Reverse Steps 1-9 to complete installation.

OIL PUMP

Removal/Installation

1. Remove the oil pan as described in this chapter.

NOTE
The oil pump pickup tube and screen are a press fit in the pumphousing and should not be removed unless replacement is required.

2. Remove the nut holding the pump to the rear main bearing cap (**Figure 34**). Remove the pump, gasket (if used) and extension shaft.

3. To install, align the slot on the extension shaft top with the drive tang on the lower end of the distributor drive shaft.

> *NOTE*
> *The bottom edge of the oil pump pickup screen should be parallel to the oil pan rails when pump is installed in Step 4.*

4. Install pump to rear main bearing cap with a new gasket (if used). Tighten pump nut to specifications (**Table 2**).
5. Reinstall the oil pan as described in this chapter.

Disassembly/Assembly

Refer to **Figure 35** for this procedure.
1. Remove the cover screws, cover and gasket. Discard the gasket.
2. Mark the gear teeth for reassembly indexing and then remove the idler and drive gear with shaft from the body.
3. Remove the pressure regulator valve pin, regulator, spring and valve.
4. Remove the pickup tube/screen assembly *only* if it needs replacement. Secure the pump body in a soft-jawed vise and separate the tube from the cover.

> *CAUTION*
> *Do not twist, shear or collapse the tube when installing it in Step 5.*

5. If the pickup tube/screen assembly was removed, install a new one. Secure the pump body in a soft-jawed vise. Apply sealer to the new tube and gently tap in place. See **Figure 36**.
6. Lubricate all parts thoroughly with clean engine oil before reassembly.
7. Assembly is the reverse of disassembly. Index the gear marks, install a new cover gasket and rotate the pump drive shaft by hand to check for smooth operation. Tighten cover bolts to specifications (**Table 2**).

Inspection

> *NOTE*
> *The pump assembly and gears are serviced as an assembly. If one or the other is worn or damaged, replace the entire pump. No wear specifications are provided by GM.*

1. Clean all parts thoroughly in solvent. Brush the inside of the body and the pressure regulator chamber to remove all dirt and metal particles. Dry with compressed air, if available.

2. Check the pump body and cover for cracks or excessive wear.
3. Check the pump gears for damage or excessive wear.
4. Check the drive gear shaft-to-body fit for excessive looseness.
5. Check the inside of the pump cover for wear that could allow oil to leak around the ends of the gears.
6. Check the pressure regulator valve for a proper fit.

CYLINDER HEAD

Left Cylinder Head Removal

1. Open and support the hood.

> *WARNING*
> *Never disconnect fuel injection system lines without relieving fuel pressure.*

2. Relieve fuel system pressure on fuel injected models as described in Chapter Six, then disconnect the negative battery cable.
3. Remove the intake manifold as described in this chapter.
4. Remove the valve cover and pushrods as described in this chapter.
5. Remove the left exhaust manifold as described in this chapter. Disconnect the AIR plumbing at the cylinder head.
6. Remove the power steering pump, air conditioning idler pulley and air conditioning compressor mounting bracket, if so equipped.

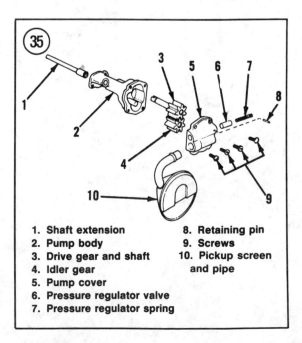

1. Shaft extension
2. Pump body
3. Drive gear and shaft
4. Idler gear
5. Pump cover
6. Pressure regulator valve
7. Pressure regulator spring
8. Retaining pin
9. Screws
10. Pickup screen and pipe

7. Disconnect the spark plug wires at the cylinder head, then remove the spark plugs. See Chapter Six.

8. Loosen the cylinder head bolts, working from the center of the head to the end in each direction.

9. Remove the head bolts. Tap the end of the head with a plastic mallet to break the gasket seal. Remove the head from the engine.

CAUTION
Place the head on its side to prevent damage to the head gasket surface.

10. Remove and discard the head gasket. Clean all gasket residue from the head and block mating surfaces.

Right Cylinder Head Removal

1. Remove the intake manifold as described in this chapter.

2. Remove the right exhaust manifold as described in this chapter.

3. Disconnect the spark plug wires at the cylinder head, then remove the spark plugs.

4. Remove the valve cover and pushrods as described in this chapter.

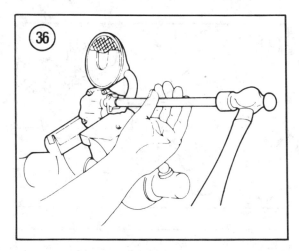

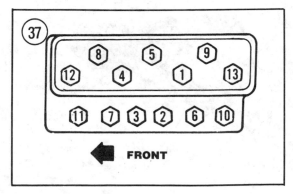

5. Disconnect the AIR pipe, wiring harness and engine ground wire at the rear of the cylinder head.

6. Remove the alternator. See Chapter Eight.

7. Loosen the cylinder head bolts, working from the center of the head to the end in each direction.

8. Remove the head bolts. Tap the end of the head with a plastic mallet to break the gasket seal. Remove the head from the engine.

CAUTION
Place the head on its side to prevent damage to the head gasket surface.

9. Remove and discard the head gasket. Clean all gasket residue from the head and block mating surfaces.

Installation

1. Make sure the cylinder head and block gasket surfaces and bolt holes are clean. Dirt in the block bolt holes or on the head bolt threads will affect bolt torque.

2. Check all visible oil and water passages for cleanliness.

3A. Steel gasket—Apply gasket sealant to both sides of the gasket with a paint roller to assure a thin, even coat.

3B. Steel asbestos gasket—Install without gasket sealer.

4. Place the new head gasket over the cylinder head dowel pins in the block with the gasket bead facing upward.

5. Carefully lower the head onto the cylinder block, engaging the dowel pins.

6. Wipe all head bolt threads with sealing compound part No. 1052080 or equivalent. Install and tighten the head bolts finger-tight.

7. Tighten the head bolts to specifications (**Table 2**) in several stages, following the sequence shown in Figure 37.

8. To complete installation, reverse Steps 1-6 (right cylinder head) or Steps 1-7 (left cylinder head). Adjust the valves as described in this chapter. Check and adjust ignition timing as required. See Chapter Three.

Decarbonizing

1. Without removing the valves, remove all deposits from the combustion chambers, intake ports and exhaust ports. Use a fine wire brush dipped in solvent or make a scraper from hardwood. Be careful not to scratch or gouge the combustion chambers.

2. After all carbon is removed from the combustion chambers and ports, clean the entire head in solvent.

3. Clean away all carbon on the piston tops. Do not remove the carbon ridge at the top of the cylinder bore.

4. Clean the bolt holes. Use a cleaning solvent to remove dirt and grease.

Inspection

1. Check the cylinder head for signs of oil or water leaks before cleaning.

2. Clean the cylinder head thoroughly in solvent. While cleaning, look for cracks or other visible signs of damage. Look for corrosion or foreign material in the oil and water passages.

3. Clean the passages with a stiff spiral brush, then blow them out with compressed air.

4. Check the cylinder head studs for damage and replace if necessary.

5. Check the flatness of the cylinder head-to-block surface with a straightedge and feeler gauge (**Figure 38**). Measure diagonally, as well as end to end. If the gap exceeds 0.005 in. (0.125 mm), have the head resurfaced by a machine shop. If head resurfacing is necessary, do not remove more than 0.010 in. Replace the head if a greater amount must be removed to correct warpage.

VALVES AND VALVE SEATS

Servicing the valves, guides and valve seats requires special knowledge and expensive machine tools. A general practice among those who do their own service is to remove the cylinder head, perform all disassembly except valve removal and take the head to a dealer or machine shop for inspection and service. Since the cost is low relative to the required effort and equipment, this is usually the best approach, even for experienced mechanics.

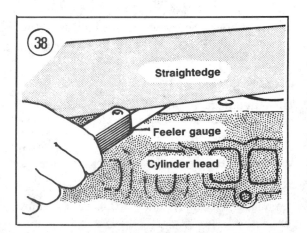

PISTON/CONNECTING ROD ASSEMBLY

Piston/Connecting Rod Removal

1. Remove the cylinder head and oil pan as described in this chapter.

2. Rotate the crankshaft until one piston is at bottom dead center. Pack the cylinder bore with

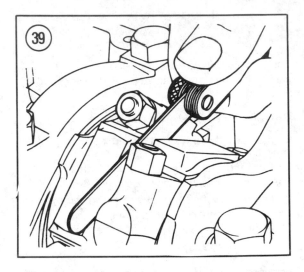

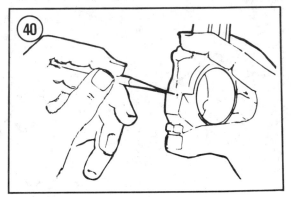

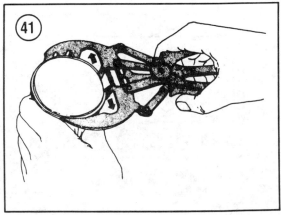

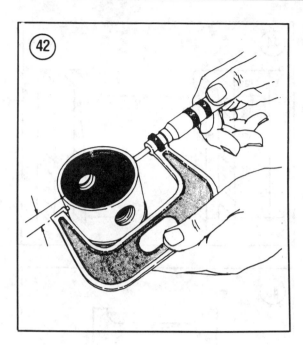

(42)

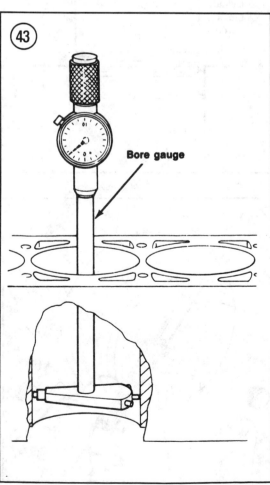

(43)

Bore gauge

clean shop rags. Remove the carbon ridge at the top of the cylinder bores with a ridge reamer. These can be rented for use. Vacuum out the shavings, then remove the shop rags.

3. Rotate the crankshaft until the connecting rod is centered in the bore with the piston at the bottom of its travel. Measure side clearance between the connecting rod and the crankshaft with a flat feeler gauge (**Figure 39**). If the clearance exceeds specifications (**Table 1**), replace the connecting rod during reassembly.

NOTE
Mark the cylinder number on the top of each piston with quick-drying paint. Check for cylinder numbers or identification marks on the connecting rod and cap. If they are not visible, make your own (Figure 40).

4. Remove the nuts holding the connecting rod cap. Lift off the cap, together with the lower bearing insert.

NOTE
If the connecting rod caps are difficult to remove, tap the studs with a wooden hammer handle.

5. Use the wooden hammer handle to push the piston and connecting rod from the bore.
6. Remove the piston rings with a ring remover (**Figure 41**).
7. Repeat Steps 1-6 for all remaining connecting rods.

Piston Pin Removal/Installation

The piston pins are press-fitted to the connecting rods and hand-fitted to the pistons. Removal requires the use of a press and support stand. This is a job for a dealer or machine shop equipped to fit the pistons to the pins, ream the pin bushings to the correct diameter and install the pistons and pins on the connecting rods.

Piston Clearance Check

Unless you have precision measuring equipment and know how to use it properly, have this procedure done by a machine shop.
1. Measure the piston diameter with a micrometer (**Figure 42**) just below the rings at right angles to the piston pin bore.
2. Measure the cylinder bore diameter with a bore gauge (**Figure 43**). **Figure 44** shows the points of normal cylinder wear. If dimension A exceeds dimension B by more than 0.003 in., the cylinder must be rebored and a new piston/ring assembly installed.

3. Subtract the piston diameter from the largest cylinder bore reading. If it exceeds the specifications in **Table 1**, the cylinder must be rebored and an oversized piston installed.

> *NOTE*
> *Obtain the new piston and measure it to determine the correct cylinder bore oversize dimension.*

Piston Ring Fit/Installation

1. Check the ring gap of each piston ring. To do this, position the ring at the bottom of the ring travel area and square it by tapping gently with an inverted piston. See **Figure 45**.

> *NOTE*
> *If the cylinders have not been rebored, check the gap at the bottom of the ring travel, where the cylinder is least worn.*

2. Measure the ring gap with a feeler gauge as shown in **Figure 46**. Compare with specifications in **Table 1**. If the measurement is not within specifications, the rings must be replaced as a set. Check gap of new rings as well. If the gap is too small, file the ends of the ring to correct it (**Figure 47**).

3. Check the side clearance of the rings as shown in **Figure 48**. Place the feeler gauge alongside the ring all the way into the groove. If the measurement is not within specifications (**Table 1**), either the rings or the ring grooves are worn. Inspect and replace as required.

4. Using a ring expander tool (**Figure 41**), carefully install the oil control ring, then the compression rings. Oil rings consist of 3 segments. The wavy segment goes between the flat segments to act as a spacer. Upper and lower flat segments are interchangeable. The second compression ring is tapered. The top of each compression ring is marked and must face upward.

5. Position the ring gaps as shown in **Figure 50**.

Connecting Rod Inspection

Have the connecting rods checked for straightness by a dealer or machine shop. When installing new connecting rods, have them checked for misalignment before installing the piston and piston pin. Connecting rods can spring out of alignment during shipping or handling.

**Connecting Rod Bearing
Clearance Measurement**

1. Place the connecting rods and upper bearing halves on the proper connecting rod journals.

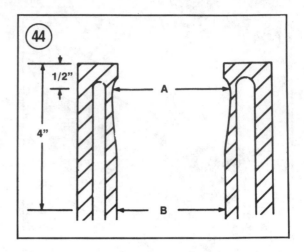

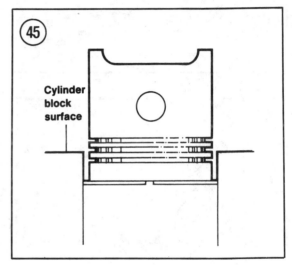

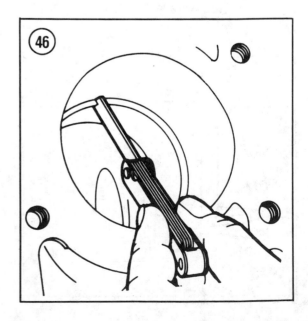

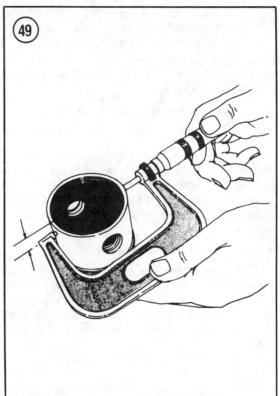

47

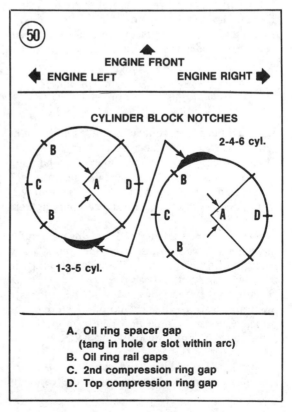

49

5

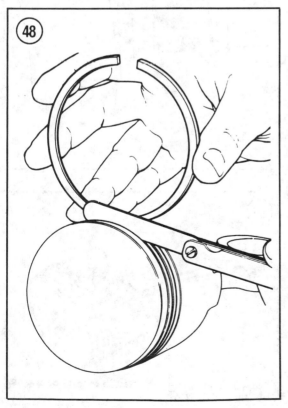

48

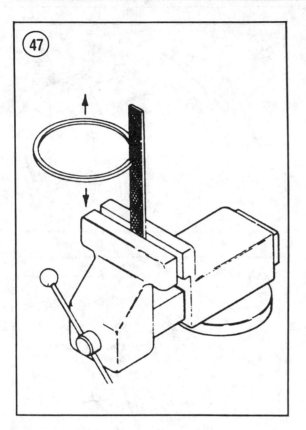

50

▲
ENGINE FRONT
◀ **ENGINE LEFT**   **ENGINE RIGHT** ▶

CYLINDER BLOCK NOTCHES

2-4-6 cyl.

1-3-5 cyl.

A. Oil ring spacer gap
   (tang in hole or slot within arc)
B. Oil ring rail gaps
C. 2nd compression ring gap
D. Top compression ring gap

2. Cut a piece of Plastigage the width of the bearing. Place the Plastigage on the journal (**Figure 51**), then install the lower bearing half end cap.

> *NOTE*
> *Do not place Plastigage over the journal oil hole.*

3. Tighten the connecting rod cap to specifications (**Table 2**). Do not rotate the crankshaft while the Plastigage is in place.

4. Remove the connecting rod caps. Bearing clearance is determined by comparing the width of the flattened Plastigage to the markings on the envelope (**Figure 52**). If the clearance is excessive, the crankshaft must be reground and undersize bearings installed.

Piston/Connecting Rod Installation

1. Make sure the pistons are correctly installed on the connecting rods, if they were separated. The machined hole or cast notch on the top of the piston (**Figure 53**) and the oil hole on the side of the connecting rod must both face in the same direction.

2. Make sure the ring gaps are positioned as shown in **Figure 50**.

3. Slip short pieces of hose over the connecting rod studs to prevent them from nicking the crankshaft. Tape will work if you do not have the right diameter hose, but it is more difficult to remove.

4. Immerse the entire piston in clean engine oil. Coat the cylinder wall with oil.

> *CAUTION*
> *Use extreme care in Step 5 to prevent the connecting rod from nicking the crankshaft journal.*

5. Install the piston/connecting rod assembly in its cylinder with a piston ring compressor as shown in **Figure 54**. Tap lightly with a wooden hammer handle to insert the piston. Make sure that the piston number (painted on top before removal) corresponds to the cylinder number, counting from the front of the engine.

6. Clean the connecting rod bearings carefully, including the back sides. Coat the journals and bearings with clean engine oil. Place the bearings in the connecting rod and cap.

7. Pull the connecting rod and bearing into position against the crankpin. Remove the protective hose or tape and lightly lubricate the connecting rod bolt threads with SAE 30W engine oil.

8. Install the connecting rod cap. Make sure the rod and cap marks align. Install the cap nuts finger-tight.

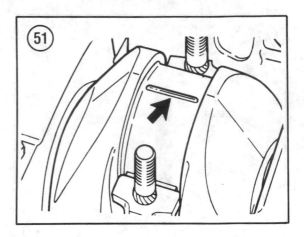

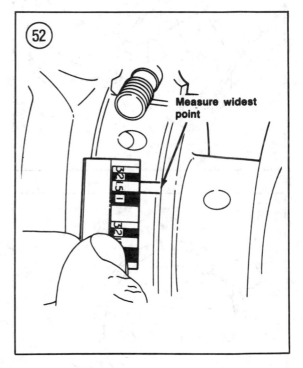

Measure widest point

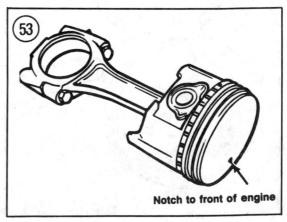

Notch to front of engine

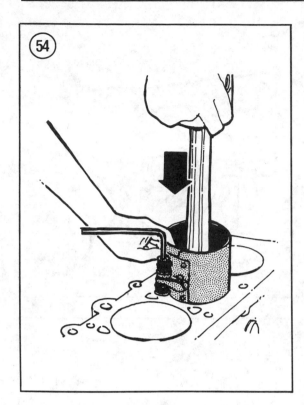

(54)

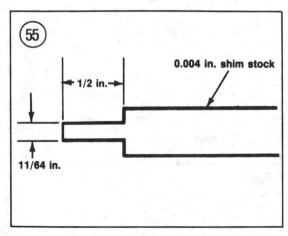

(55)

0.004 in. shim stock

1/2 in.

11/64 in.

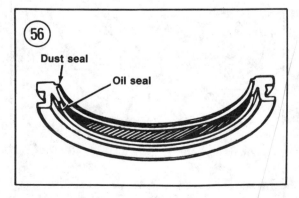

(56)

Dust seal

Oil seal

9. Repeat Steps 4-8 for each remaining piston/connecting rod assembly.

10. Tighten the cap nuts to specifications (**Table 2**).

11. Check the connecting rod big-end play as described under *Piston/Connecting Rod Removal* in this chapter.

REAR MAIN OIL SEAL

A split lip-type type seal located under the rear main bearing cap is used on 1985 engines.

A 1-piece oil seal located in a cast aluminum retainer installed on the rear of the block is used on 1986 and later engines. Whenever the retainer is removed, a new seal and retainer gasket must be installed. The seal can be replaced with the engine in the vehicle without removing the oil pan or crankshaft.

Replacement
(Split Lip-type)

1. Fabricate a seal installation tool as shown in **Figure 55** to protect the seal bead when positioning the new seal.

2. Remove the oil pan and oil pump as described in this chapter.

3. Remove the rear main bearing cap. Pry the oil seal from the bottom of the cap with a small screwdriver.

4. Remove the upper half of the seal with a brass pin punch. Tap the punch on one end of the seal until its other end protrudes far enough to be removed with pliers.

5. Clean all sealant from the bearing cap and crankshaft with a non-abrasive cleaner.

6. Coat the lips and bead of a new seal with light engine oil. Do not let oil touch seal mating ends.

7. Position tip of seal installer tool (fabricated in Step 1) between crankcase and seal seat. Position seal between crankshaft and tip of tool so seal bead touches tool tip. Make sure oil seal lip faces toward front of engine. See **Figure 56**.

8. Use seal installer tool as a shoehorn and roll seal around crankshaft, protecting seal bead from sharp corners of seal seat surfaces. Keep tool in position until seal is properly seated, with both ends flush with the block.

9. Remove the tool carefully to prevent pulling seal out with it.

10. Use seal installer tool as a shoehorn again and install seal half in bearing cap. Feed seal into cap with light thumb and finger pressure.

5

11. Apply sealant to the areas shown in **Figure 57**. Keep sealant off the seal split line.

12. Install rear main bearing cap with seal and tighten to 10-12 ft.-lb. (14-16 N•m). Tap end of crankshaft to the rear, then to the front to align the thrust surfaces.

13. Retighten bearing cap to specifications (**Table 2**).

Seal Replacement
(1-piece Seal)

To replace the seal:

1. Set the parking brake. Securely block both rear wheels so the vehicle will not roll in either direction.

2. Raise the vehicle with a jack and place it on jackstands. Support the engine with a jack.

3. Remove the transmission. See Chapter Nine.

4. Remove the flywheel as described in this chapter.

5. Pry the old seal from the retainer with a small screwdriver or awl (**Figure 58**). Use the pry notches provided in the retainer (**Figure 59**) and work carefully to avoid scratching the outer diameter of the crankshaft with the pry tool.

6. Carefully clean and inspect the inner diameter of the seal bore and the outer diameter of the crankshaft for nicks and burrs which could affect seal performance. If any are found, the engine must be removed, disassembled and the defects corrected before a new seal is installed.

7. Lubricate the inner diameter of a new seal with clean engine oil. Install seal on mandrel of tool part No. J-35621 until it bottoms against the tool collar. See **Figure 60**.

8. Align the tool with the rear of the crankshaft and thread tool screws in place. Tighten securely with a screwdriver to make sure the seal will be installed squarely.

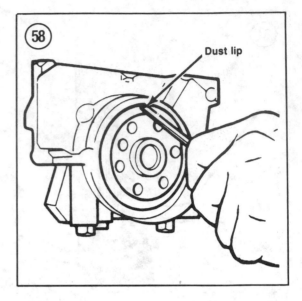

(58) Dust lip

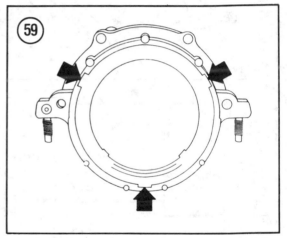

(59)

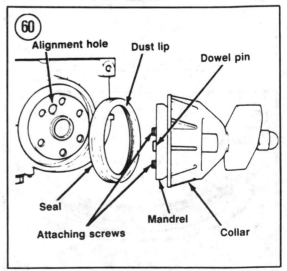

(60) Alignment hole   Dust lip   Dowel pin

Seal   Mandrel   Collar

Attaching screws

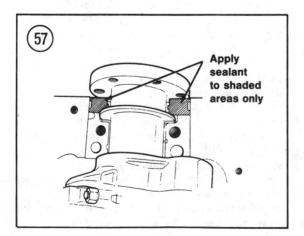

(57) Apply sealant to shaded areas only

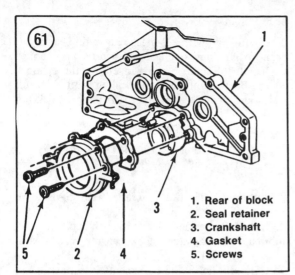

1. Rear of block
2. Seal retainer
3. Crankshaft
4. Gasket
5. Screws

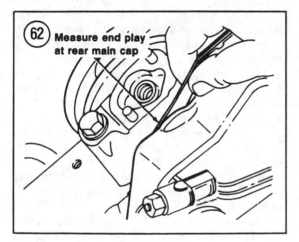

⑥2 Measure end play at rear main cap

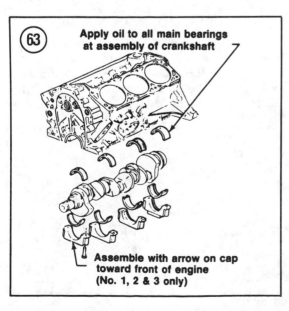

⑥3 Apply oil to all main bearings at assembly of crankshaft

Assemble with arrow on cap toward front of engine (No. 1, 2 & 3 only)

9. Turn the tool handle until the collar is tightly against the block and the handle has bottomed. This will push the seal into its bore and seat it properly.

10. Back the tool handle off until it stops. Remove tool from crankshaft.

11. Check seal to make sure it is seated squarely in the bore, then reverse Steps 1-4 to complete installation.

To replace the retainer, refer to **Figure 61** and proceed as follows:

1. Securely block both rear wheels so the vehicle will not roll in either direction.

2. Raise the front of the vehicle with a jack and place it on jackstands.

3. Support the engine with a jack. Position the jack so the oil pan can be removed later. Remove the transmission. See Chapter Nine.

4. Remove the oil pan and flywheel as described in this chapter.

5. Unbolt and remove the retainer/seal assembly. Remove and discard the gasket.

6. Clean all gasket residue from the retainer and block mating surfaces.

7. Fit a new gasket over the studs on the block and install the retainer. Tighten bolts to 120-150 in.-lb. (13-16 N•m).

8. Apply a small quantity of sealer part No. 1052751 or equivalent to the front and rear corners of the oil pan, then reinstall pan with the same gasket.

9. Install a new seal as described in this chapter.

CRANKSHAFT

End Play Measurement

1. Pry the crankshaft to the front of the engine with a large screwdriver.

2. Measure the crankshaft end play at the front of the No. 4 main bearing with a flat feeler gauge. See **Figure 62**. Compare to specifications in **Table 1**.

3. If the end play is excessive, replace the No. 4 main bearing. If less than specified, check the bearing faces for imperfections.

Removal

Refer to **Figure 63** for this procedure.

1. Remove the engine as described in this chapter.

2. Remove the flywheel as described in this chapter.

3. Mount the engine on an engine stand, if available.

4. Invert the engine to bring the oil pan to an upright position.

5

5. Remove the oil pan and oil pump as described in this chapter.

6. Remove the front cover and timing chain as described in this chapter.

7. Remove the spark plugs to permit easy rotation of the crankshaft.

8. Measure crankshaft end play as described in this chapter.

9. Rotate the crankshaft to position one connecting rod at the bottom of its stroke.

10. Remove the connecting rod bearing cap and bearing. Move the piston/rod assembly away from the crankshaft.

11. Repeat Steps 9-11 for each remaining piston/rod assembly.

12. Check the caps for identification numbers or marks. If none are visible, clean the caps with a wire brush. If marks still cannot be seen, make your own with quick-drying paint.

13. Unbolt and remove the main bearing caps and bearing inserts.

NOTE
If the caps are difficult to remove, lift the bolts partway out, then pry them from side to side.

14. Carefully lift the crankshaft from the engine block and place it on a clean workbench.

15. Remove the bearing inserts from the block. Place the bearing caps and inserts in order on a clean workbench.

Inspection

1. Clean the crankshaft thoroughly with solvent. Blow out the oil passages with compressed air.

NOTE
If you do not have precision measuring equipment, have a machine shop perform Step 2.

2. Check the crankpins and main bearing journals for wear, scoring or cracks. Check all journals against specifications (**Table 1**) for out-of-roundness and taper. See **Figure 64**. Have the crankshaft reground, if necessary.

Main Bearing Clearance Measurement

Main bearing clearance is measured with Plastigage in the same manner as the connecting rod bearing clearance described in this chapter. Excessive clearance requires that the bearings be replaced, the crankshaft be reground or both.

Installation

1. If equipped with a 2-piece rear main bearing oil seal, install a new one as described in this chapter.

2. Install the main bearing inserts in the cylinder block. Bearing oil holes must align with block oil holes and bearing tabs must seat in the block tab slots.

NOTE
Check cap bolts for thread damage before reuse. If damaged, replace the bolts.

3. Lubricate the bolt threads with SAE 30W engine oil.

4. Install the bearing inserts in each cap. Liberally lubricate the cap and block bearing inserts with clean engine oil.

5. Carefully lower the crankshaft into position in the block.

6. Install the bearing caps in their marked positions with the arrows pointing toward the front of the engine and the number mark aligned with the corresponding mark on the journals.

7. Install and tighten all bolts finger-tight. Recheck end play as described in this chapter, then tighten all bolts to specifications (**Table 2**).

8. Rotate the crankshaft to make sure it turns smoothly at the flywheel rim. If not, remove the bearing caps and crankshaft and check that the bearings are clean and properly installed.

9. If equipped with a one-piece rear main bearing oil seal, install a new one as described in this chapter.

10. Reverse Steps 1-10 of *Removal* in this chapter to complete the installation.

PILOT BEARING

An oil-impregnated bearing is located inside the rear end of the crankshaft to support the transmission input shaft on manual transmission vehicles. It should be inspected whenever the transmission is removed.

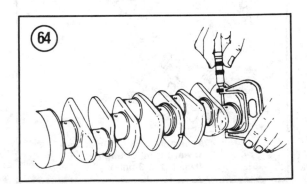

1. Check the bearing for visible signs of wear or damage. Rotate the bearing with a finger and make sure it turns easily. If wear, damage or stiff movement are found, remove with tool part No. J-1448 or an equivalent puller.

2. Position a new bearing in the crankshaft bore and install with tool part No. J-1522 or an equivalent driver.

3. Lubricate the bearing with a few drops of machine oil.

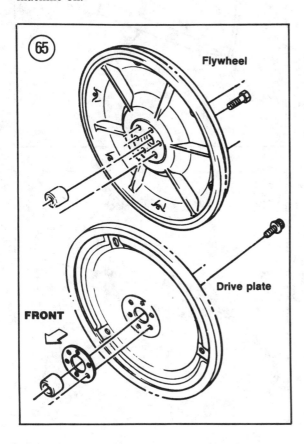

Flywheel

Drive plate

FRONT

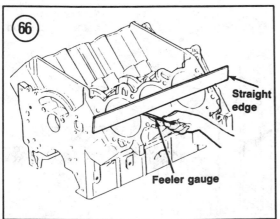

Straight edge

Feeler gauge

FLYWHEEL/DRIVE PLATE

Removal/Installation

Refer to **Figure 65** for this procedure.

1. Remove the engine as described in this chapter.

2. Remove the clutch on manual transmission vehicles. See Chapter Nine.

3. Unbolt the flywheel or drive plate from the crankshaft. Remove the bolts gradually in a diagonal pattern.

4. Visually check the flywheel or drive plate surfaces for cracks, deep scoring, excessive wear, heat discoloration and checking. If the surface is glazed or slightly scratched, have the flywheel/drive plate resurfaced by a machine shop.

5. Inspect the ring gear for cracks, broken teeth or excessive wear. If severely worn, check the starter motor drive teeth for similar wear or damage. Replace as required.

6. Installation is the reverse of removal. Tighten bolts to specifications (**Table 2**) in a crisscross pattern. Wipe all oil, grease and other contamination from the flywheel surface before installing the clutch on manual transmission vehicles.

CYLINDER BLOCK

Cleaning and Inspection

1. Clean the block thoroughly with solvent. Remove any RTV sealant residue from the machined surfaces. Check all core plugs for leaks and replace any that are suspect. See *Core Plug Replacement* in this chapter. Remove any plugs that seal oil passages. Check oil and coolant passages for sludge, dirt and corrosion while cleaning. If the passages are very dirty, have the block boiled out by a machine shop. Blow out all passages with compressed air. Check the threads in the head bolt holes to be sure they are clean. If dirty, use a tap to true up the threads and remove any deposits.

2. Examine the block for cracks. To confirm suspicions about possible leak areas, use a mixture of 1 part kerosene and 2 parts engine oil. Coat the suspected area with this solution, then wipe dry and immediately apply a solution of zinc oxide dissolved in wood alcohol. If any discoloration appears in the treated area, the block is cracked and should be replaced.

3. Check flatness of the cylinder block deck or top surface. Place an accurate straightedge on the block. If there is any gap between the block and straightedge, measure it with a flat feeler gauge (**Figure 66**). Measure from end to end and from

corner to corner. Have the block resurfaced if it is warped more than 0.004 in. (0.102 mm).

4. Measure cylinder bores with a bore gauge for out-of-roundness or excessive wear as described in *Piston Clearance Check* in this chapter. If the cylinders exceed maximum tolerances, they must be rebored. Reboring is also necessary if the cylinder walls are badly scuffed or scored.

> *NOTE*
> *Before boring, install all main bearing caps and tighten the cap bolts to specifications in Table 2.*

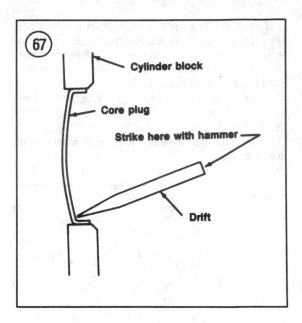

CORE PLUG REPLACEMENT

The condition of all core plugs in the block and cylinder head should be checked whenever the engine is out of the vehicle for service. If any signs of leakage or corrosion are found around one core plug, replace them all.

Removal/Installation

> *CAUTION*
> *Do not drive core plugs into the engine casting. It will be impossible to retrieve them and they can restrict coolant circulation, resulting in serious engine damage.*

1. Tap the bottom edge of the core plug with a hammer and drift. Use several sharp blows to push the bottom of the plug inward, tilting the top out (**Figure 67**).

2. Grip the top of the plug firmly with pliers. Pull the plug from its bore (**Figure 68**) and discard.

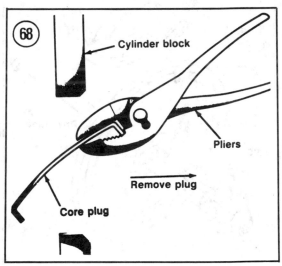

> *NOTE*
> *Core plugs can also be removed by drilling a hole in the center of the plug and prying them out with an appropriate size drift or pin punch. On large core plugs, the use of a universal impact slide hammer is recommended.*

3. Clean the plug bore thoroughly to remove all traces of the old sealer. Inspect the bore for any damage that might interfere with proper sealing of

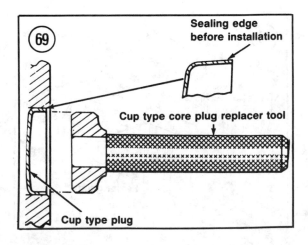

the new plug. If damage is evident, true the surface by boring for the next oversize plug.

NOTE
Oversize plugs can be identified by an "OS" stamped in the flat on the cup side of the plug.

4. Coat the inside diameter of the plug bore and the outer diameter of the new plug with sealer. Use an oil-resistant sealer if the plug is to be installed in an oil gallery or a water-resistant sealer for plugs installed in the water jacket.

5. Install the new core plug with an appropriate size core plug replacer tool (**Figure 69**), driver or socket. The sharp edge of the plug should be at least 0.02 in. (0.5 mm) inside the lead-in chamfer.

6. Repeat Steps 1-5 to replace each remaining core plug.

5

Tables are on the following pages.

Table 1 V6 ENGINE SPECIFICATIONS

Engine type	90° V6
Bore	4.00 in.
Stroke	3.480 in.
Displacement	262 cid (4.3 liter)
Firing order	1-6-5-4-3-2
Cylinder arrangement	
Left bank	1-3-5
Right bank	2-4-6
Engine code	
Carburetted	N
Fuel injected	Z
Cylinder bore	
Diameter	3.9995-4.0025 in.
Out-of-round	
Production	0.001 in. max.
Service	0.002 in. max.
Taper	
Production	
Thrust side	0.0005 in. max.
Relief side	0.001 in. max.
Service	0.001 in. max.
Piston clearance	
Production	0.0007-0.0017 in. max.
Service	0.0027 in. max.
Piston ring	
Ring side clearance	
Compression	0.0012-0.0032 in.
Oil	0.002-0.007 in.
Ring gap	
Top	0.010-0.020 in.
2nd	0.010-0.025 in.
Oil	0.015-0.055 in.
Piston pin	
Diameter	0.9270-0.9273 in.
Clearance	
In piston	0.00025-0.00035 in.
Fit in rod	0.0008-0.0016 (interference)
Camshaft	
Lobe lift	
Intake	0.357 in.
Exhaust	0.390 in.
Journal diameter	1.8682-1.8692 in.
Runout	0.0015 in.
End play	0.004-0.012 in.
Crankshaft	
Main journal diameter	
No. 1	2.4484-2.4493 in.
No. 2 and No. 3	2.4481-2.4490 in.
No. 4	2.4479-2.4488 in.
Taper	
Production	0.0002 in.
Service	0.001 in.
Out-of-round	
Production	0.0002 in.
Service	0.001 in.

(continued)

Table 1 V6 ENGINE SPECIFICATIONS (cont.)

Crankshaft (cont.)	
Main bearing clearance	
Production	
No. 1	0.0008-0.0020 in.
No. 2 and No. 3	0.0011-0.0023 in.
No. 4	0.0017-0.0032 in.
Service	
No. 1	0.001-0.0015 in.
No. 2 and No. 3	0.001-0.0020 in.
No. 4	0.0025-0.0030 in.
End play	0.002-0.006 in.
Crankpin	
Diameter	2.2487-2.2497 in.
Taper	
Production	0.0002 in.
Service	0.0005 in. max.
Out-of-round	
Production	0.0002 in.
Service	0.0005 in. max.
Connecting rod	
Bearing clearance	
Production	0.0010-0.0032 in.
Service	0.002-0.0030 in.
Side clearance	0.007-0.015 in.
Valve train	
Lifter	Hydraulic
Rocker arm ratio	1.5:1
Valve lash	1 turn down from zero lash
Face angle	45°
Seat angle	46°
Seat width	
Intake	1/32-1/16 in.
Exhaust	1/16-1/32 in.
Stem clearance	0.0010-0.0027 in.
Valve spring	
Free length	2.03 in.
Installed height	1 23/32 in.
Damper free length	1.86 in.
Load	
Closed	76-84 lb. @ 1.70 in.
Open	194-206 lb. @ 1.25 in.

Table 2 V6 TIGHTENING TORQUES

Fastener	ft.-lb.	N·m
Camshaft sprocket	18	24
Connecting rod caps	45	60
Cylinder head bolts	65	90
Exhaust manifold		
Center 2 bolts	26	36
All others	20	27
Flywheel-to-crankshaft	75	100
Flywheel housing	32	44
Front cover	7	10
Intake manifold	36	48
Main bearing caps	75	100
Oil filter adapter bolts	15	20
Oil pan		
Nuts	8	11
Bolts	16	22
Oil pump		
Attaching bolts	65	90
Cover screws	6.5	9
Rear oil seal retainer screws	10	15
Torsional damper	70	95
Valve cover	7	10
Water outlet	21	28
Water pump	30	40

Table 3 STANDARD TORQUE VALUES

Fastener	ft.-lb.	N·m
Grade 5		
1/4-20	8	11
1/4-28	8	11
5/16-18	17	23
5/16-24	20	27
3/8-16	30	40
3/8-24	35	47
7/16-14	50	68
7/16-20	55	75
1/2-13	75	100
1/2-20	85	115
9/16-12	105	142
9/16-18	115	156
Grade 6		
1/4-20	10.5	14
1/4-28	12.5	17
5/16-18	22.5	31
5/16-24	25	54
3/8-16	40	34
3/8-24	45	60
7/16-14	65	90
7/16-20	70	95
1/2-13	100	136
1/2-20	110	149
9/16-12	135	183
9/16-18	150	203

FUEL, EXHAUST AND EMISSION CONTROL SYSTEMS

This chapter consists of service procedures for the air cleaner, carburetor, throttle body injection (TBI) unit, fuel pump, fuel tank and lines, exhaust system and fuel-related emission controls.

THERMOSTATICALLY CONTROLLED (THERMAC) AIR CLEANER

A dry air cleaner containing a replaceable air filter element is standard on all engines. The filter element can be changed without removing the air cleaner housing from the engine. Many air cleaners also contain a replaceable crankcase ventilation filter element.

The air cleaner is attached to the top of the carburetor or TBI unit. Various sensors, switches and a vacuum-operated control valve or door in the air cleaner snorkel control intake air temperature.

The air cleaner furnishes temperature-regulated air to the carburetor or TBI unit to reduce emissions and improve driveability. The air cleaner snorkel is connected to a fresh air inlet hose and to a hot air hose/heat stove assembly surrounding the intake manifold. Air flow from these 2 sources is controlled by a valve in the snorkel. This valve is operated by a vacuum motor mounted on the snorkel. The door and motor are connected by mechanical linkage inside the snorkel. A temperature sensor inside the air cleaner housing modulates vacuum to the motor according to air cleaner air temperature. **Figure 1** shows the major components of the typical air cleaner system used.

When the engine is first started, the air cleaner draws hot air from near the exhaust manifold through the hot air hose (A, **Figure 2**). As the engine warms up, the control valve changes position to partially block off air from the hot air hose (B, **Figure 2**). Once the air cleaner temperature reaches a specified value, the control valve closes off the hot air hose completely. This allows the air cleaner to draw intake air through the snorkel from the fresh air inlet duct (C, **Figure 2**).

During periods of high engine compartment temperature, a hot idle compensator (if so equipped) in the air cleaner opens to route air into the intake manifold. This prevents an excessively rich mixture that could result in a rough idle and high emissions.

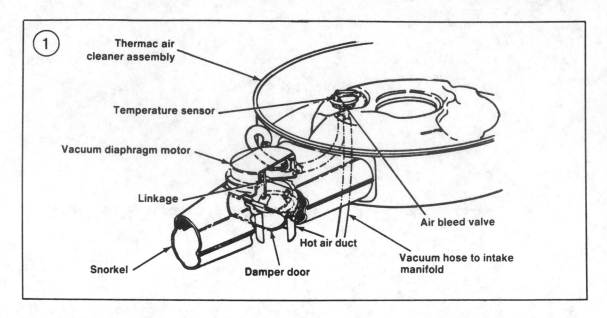

① Thermac air
cleaner assembly

Temperature sensor

Vacuum diaphragm motor

Linkage

Air bleed valve

Snorkel

Hot air duct

Damper door

Vacuum hose to intake
manifold

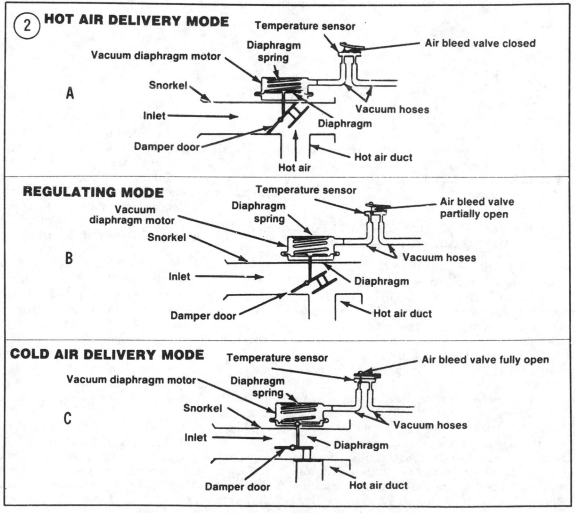

② **HOT AIR DELIVERY MODE**

Temperature sensor

Diaphragm
spring

Air bleed valve closed

Vacuum diaphragm motor

Snorkel

A

Inlet

Vacuum hoses

Diaphragm

Damper door

Hot air duct

Hot air

REGULATING MODE

Temperature sensor

Diaphragm
spring

Vacuum
diaphragm motor

Air bleed valve
partially open

Snorkel

B

Vacuum hoses

Inlet

Diaphragm

Damper door

Hot air duct

COLD AIR DELIVERY MODE

Temperature sensor

Air bleed valve fully open

Vacuum diaphragm motor

Diaphragm
spring

Snorkel

C

Vacuum hoses

Inlet

Diaphragm

Damper door

Hot air duct

Air Cleaner Removal/Installation
(1985 I4 Engine)

Refer to **Figure 3** for this procedure.

> *NOTE*
> *Leave the filter element inside the air cleaner housing during removal. This will prevent dirt and debris from dropping into the TBI unit.*

1. Remove the engine cover. See Chapter Four.
2. Remove the air cleaner cover wing nuts.
3. Unsnap the intake duct clamp and remove the duct hose from the air cleaner snorkel.
4. Disconnect the heat stove tube at the air cleaner snorkel. If the manifold is to be removed, remove the clamp holding the heat stove tube at the manifold and remove the tube.
5. Remove the air cleaner cover and filter. Remove the retaining clamp holding the manifold absolute pressure (MAP) sensor to the housing. Remove the MAP sensor. Disconnect any other vacuum lines connected to the housing, then reinstall the filter and cover.

6. Tilt the air cleaner housing up and disconnect the temperature sensor vacuum lines.
7. Remove the air cleaner assembly and place on a clean flat surface.
8. Check to see if the crankcase separator remained in the valve cover or was removed with the air cleaner housing. The separator also serves as a support for the air cleaner snorkel.
9. Check the air cleaner seal. If it is not found on the throttle body air horn, it may be attached to the underside of the air cleaner housing.

> *NOTE*
> *Step 10 is critical to proper engine operation in climates where temperatures vary considerably or remain below 68° F for long periods of time.*

10. Check condition of the flexible duct. If cracked, torn or otherwise damaged, disconnect the other end at the duct assembly and install a new length of flexible ducting.
11. Installation is the reverse of removal. If the old mounting seal is damaged or missing, install a new one to prevent a vacuum leak. Tighten the attaching nuts securely.

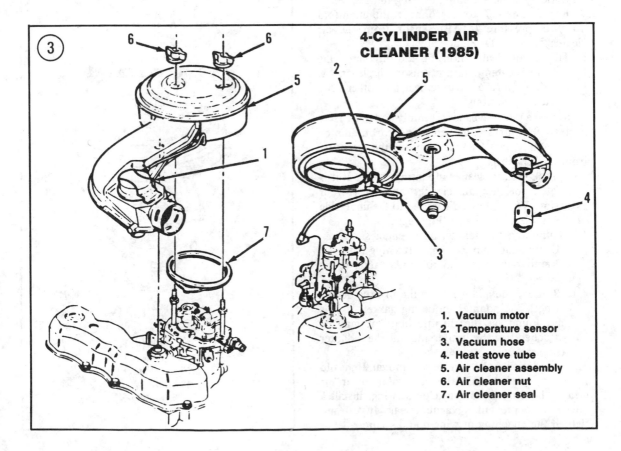

4-CYLINDER AIR CLEANER (1985)

1. Vacuum motor
2. Temperature sensor
3. Vacuum hose
4. Heat stove tube
5. Air cleaner assembly
6. Air cleaner nut
7. Air cleaner seal

Air Cleaner Removal/Installation
(All Except 1985 I4 Engine)

Refer to **Figure 4** for typical I4 and V6 air cleaner assemblies.

> *NOTE*
> *Leave the filter element inside the air cleaner housing during removal. This will prevent dirt and debris from dropping into the carburetor or TBI unit.*

1. Remove the engine cover. See Chapter Four (I4) or Chapter Five (V6). Open and support the hood.
2. Unscrew and remove the air cleaner cover attaching or wing nut(s).
3. Unsnap the intake duct clamp and remove the duct hose from the air cleaner snorkel.
4. Disconnect the hot air hose at the manifold heat stove.
5. Remove the air cleaner filter (A, **Figure 5**), then disconnect the PCV breather hose at the side of the air cleaner housing. See B, **Figure 5**.
6. Remove the clamp holding the vacuum line fitting to the air cleaner housing (C, **Figure 5**). Pull the fitting out of the housing and set the clamp to one side with the attaching or wing nut(s).
7. Repeat Step 7 to disconnect the manifold absolute pressure (MAP) sensor from the air cleaner housing (D, **Figure 5**).
8. Tilt the air cleaner housing and disconnect the lines from the temperature sensor nipple on the underside (**Figure 6**). Disconnect any other lines connected to the housing.
9. Remove the air cleaner assembly and place it on a clean flat surface. If removing carburetor or throttle body on V6 engine, remove the extension from the air horn.
10. Check the air cleaner mounting gasket. If it is not found on the air cleaner adapter (I4) or extension (V6), it may be attached to the underside of the air cleaner housing (**Figure 3**).
11. To remove the adapter on I4 engines:
   a. Loosen and remove the 2 attaching nuts.
   b. Remove the screw holding the adapter to the brace.
   c. Remove the adapter from the throttle body.
   d. Check the adapter mounting gasket. If it is not found on the throttle body, it may be attached to the underside of the adapter (**Figure 4**).
12. Installation is the reverse of removal. If the old mounting gasket on either the adapter or air cleaner housing is damaged or missing, install a new one to prevent a vacuum leak. Install and tighten the attaching or wing nut(s) securely.

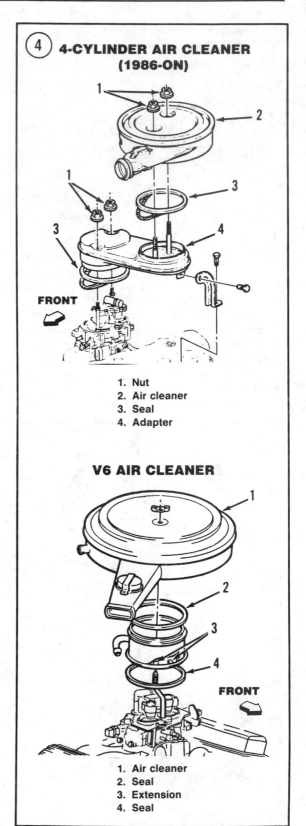

(4) 4-CYLINDER AIR CLEANER (1986-ON)

FRONT

1. Nut
2. Air cleaner
3. Seal
4. Adapter

V6 AIR CLEANER

FRONT

1. Air cleaner
2. Seal
3. Extension
4. Seal

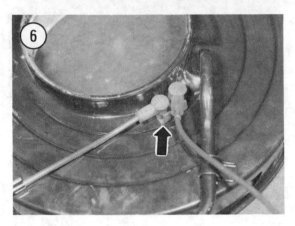

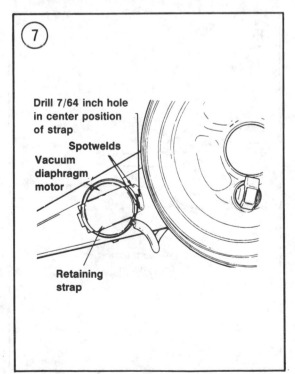

Drill 7/64 inch hole in center position of strap

Spotwelds

Vacuum diaphragm motor

Retaining strap

Control Valve Function Test

1. Unsnap the intake duct clamp and disconnect the duct hose from the air cleaner snorkel (**Figure 4**).

2. Disconnect the vacuum line at the vacuum motor on the air cleaner snorkel. Connect a hand vacuum pump to the motor nipple.

3. Apply at least 7 in. Hg vacuum. The control valve should move to block off the snorkel passage completely.

4. Bend the vacuum pump hose to trap the vacuum. The control valve should remain closed. If it does not, check for binding linkage between the vacuum motor and valve.

5. If the linkage is not corroded and does not bind, replace the vacuum motor assembly.

Vacuum Motor Replacement

1. Remove the air cleaner from the engine as described in this chapter.

2. Place the air cleaner on a clean flat surface. Remove the cover and filter element.

3. Disconnect the vacuum line at the vacuum motor.

NOTE
Support the air cleaner housing and snorkel in Step 4 to prevent damage to the snorkel during drilling.

4. Drill the 2 spot welds holding the motor retaining strap (**Figure 7**) with a 1/16 in. drill bit. Enlarge the drill hole as required to remove the retaining strap.

5. Lift the vacuum motor up and tilt it as necessary to unhook the linkage from the control valve. Remove the motor.

6. Drill a 7/64 in. hole in the snorkel, midway between the spotwelds.

7. Install the new vacuum motor, tilting it to connect the linkage to the control valve.

8. Install the new retaining strap with the sheet metal screw provided with the new motor.

NOTE
Make sure the sheet metal screw does not interfere with control valve operation when installed. If it does, cut off the end of the screw.

9. Reconnect the vacuum motor line. Install the filter element and air cleaner cover.

10. Install the air cleaner on the engine as described in this chapter.

Air Cleaner Sensor Operational Check

NOTE
Perform this procedure with the engine off and cold.

1. Set the parking brake and block the front wheels.
2. Unscrew and remove the air cleaner cover wing nuts. Remove the cover and filter element.
3. Check the hot air and intake duct hoses for cracks or other damage. Repair or replace as necessary.
4. Disconnect the intake duct hose from the snorkel. Lift the air cleaner housing up enough to see into the snorkel.
5. Look inside the snorkel. The control valve should be in the open or full fresh air position (**Figure 8**).
6. Depress the control valve with one finger and check for binding or sticking.
7. Tape a candy thermometer as close as possible to the temperature sensor (**Figure 9**) on the air inlet side of the sensor. Install the air cleaner cover without the wing nuts.
8. Start the engine. The air cleaner temperature must be below 86° F (30° C). The control valve should move to the closed or full heat position (A, **Figure 2**). If it does not, shut off the engine, cool the temperature sensor below 86° F with an ice pack and retest. If the valve still does not close, check the vacuum lines for leakage.

NOTE
Some temperature sensors incorporate a delay valve in the vacuum line between the sensor and vacuum motor to delay control valve opening. See ***Figure 10****. The lower the temperature, the longer the delay.*

9. If the control valve moves to the closed or full heat position, let the engine run for 5 minutes. Watch the control valve. When it starts to open, remove the air cleaner cover and note the thermometer reading. It should be approximately 131° F (55° C).
10. If the door does not move, remove the air cleaner cover and read the temperature. If the temperature is above 100° F (38° C), the sensor is defective.
11. A temperature of less than 100° F (38° C) is not sufficient to operate the valve. Install the air cleaner cover and let the engine continue to run. If the control valve still has not moved with the temperature above 100° F (38 ° C), replace the sensor.

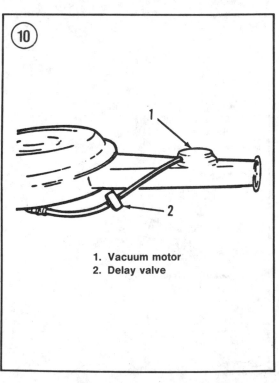

1. Vacuum motor
2. Delay valve

Sensor Replacement

1. Remove the air cleaner as described in this chapter.

2. Disconnect the 2 vacuum lines at the sensor (**Figure 6**). 3. Pry open the sensor retaining clip tabs (**Figure 11**). Note the positioning of the old sensor and remove it from the air cleaner housing.

4. Install a new sensor in the same relative position. Press down on the sensor edges and install the retaining clip on the hose connectors.

5. Reconnect the 2 vacuum lines to the sensor nipples from which they were removed.

6. Reinstall the air cleaner as described in this chapter.

FUEL QUALITY

Gasoline blended with alcohol is widely available, although it is not legally required to be labeled as such in many states. A mixture of 10 percent ethyl alcohol and 90 percent unleaded gasoline is called gasohol.

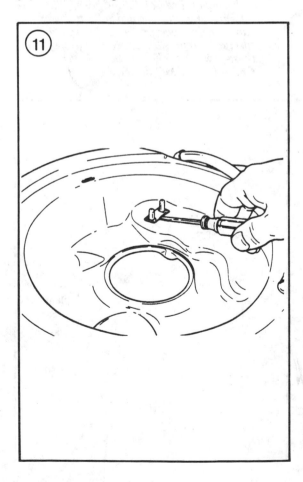

Fuels with an alcohol content tend to absorb moisture from the air. When the moisture content of the fuel reaches approximately one percent, it combines with the alcohol and separates from the fuel. This water-alcohol mixture settles at the bottom of the fuel tank where the fuel pickup carries it into the fuel line to the carburetor or fuel injectors.

The greatest problem with gasohol is its cleaning effect on service station storage tanks, as well as the vehicle's fuel tank. As a result of this cleaning action, a combination of dust, a jelly-like sludge and metallic particles pass into the automotive fuel system. These substances cause reduced fuel flow through the filter and will eventually plug the carburetor or injector passageways.

Some methods of blending alcohol with gasoline now make use of cosolvents as a suspension agent to prevent the water-alcohol from separating from the gasoline. Regardless of the method used, however, alcohol mixed with gasoline in any manner can cause numerous and serious problems with an automotive fuel system, including:

a. Corrosion formation on the inside of fuel tanks, steel fuel lines, fuel pumps, carburetors and fuel injectors.

b. Deterioration of the plastic liner used in some fuel tanks, resulting in eventual plugging of the in-tank filter.

c. Deterioration and failure of synthetic rubber or plastic materials such as O-ring seals, diaphragms, inlet needle tips, accelerator pump cups and gaskets.

d. Premature failure of fuel line hoses.

e. Hot weather driveability problems.

The problem of gasoline blended with alcohol has become so prevalent around the United States that Miller Tools (32615 Park Lane, Garden City, MI 48135) and Kent-Moore (28635 Mound Road, Warren, MI 48092) now offer Alcohol Detection Kits (Miller part No. C-4846; Kent-Moore part No. J-34353) so that owners can determine the quality of fuel being used.

The detection procedure is performed with water as a reacting agent. However, if cosolvents have been used as a suspension agent in alcohol blending, the test will not show the presence of alcohol unless ethylene glycol (automotive antifreeze) is used instead of water as a reacting agent. It is suggested that a gasoline sample be tested twice using the detection kit: first with water and then with ethylene glycol (automotive antifreeze).

The procedure cannot differentiate between types of alcohol (ethanol, methanol, etc.) nor is it considered to be absolutely accurate from a scientific standpoint, but it is accurate enough to determine whether or not there is enough alcohol in the fuel to cause the user to take precautions. Maintaining a close watch on the quality of fuel used can save hundreds of dollars in engine and fuel system repairs.

CARBURETOR

The 1985 V6 uses a Rochester E4ME or E4MED 4-barrel carburetor on California engines and a Rochester M4ME on Federal engines. All other engines are fuel-injected. The prefix E indicates that the carburetor is used in an electronic engine control system; the prefix M indicates that the carburetor is a modified primary metering or open-loop design. The suffix C or E indicates that the carburetor is equipped with either a hot air choke (C) or electric choke (E). Carburetors with the suffix D have a dual capacity pump.

Carburetors designated as electronic (E4ME or E4MED) use an electrically operated mixture control solenoid (MCS) which is mounted in the float bowl. This solenoid controls air and fuel metered by the stepped primary metering rods to the idle and main metering systems upon command from the Electronic Control Module (ECM). The ECM evaluates data from several sensors and cycles the solenoid plunger 10 times per second to control the air-fuel mixture for maximum performance and economy, and minimum emissions.

A throttle position sensor (TPS) mounted on the carburetor signals the ECM whenever changes occur in the throttle position. The ECM holds the last-known air-fuel mixture ratio during throttle position changes.

An idle speed control (ISC) assembly controls the carburetor idle speed on command from the ECM. Since the curb idle speed is programmed into the ECM, idle speed is automatic and cannot be adjusted.

CAUTION
Do not attempt to adjust idle speed on electronic carburetors by adjusting the ISC plunger. To prevent unauthorized adjustment, the plunger head is

designed to require the use of a special tool. Attempting to turn the plunger head without the tool can result in damage to the lSC unit.

Certain carburetor adjustments are prevented on 1981 and later carburetors by the use of tamper-resistant features according to Federal law.

A single or dual vacuum break system may be used to control choke operation.

The vacuum break rods are a non-bendable design and the choke cap is riveted to the housing. These tamper-resistant features are designed to prevent changes in the factory-adjusted choke setting.

The idle mixture screw in the throttle body is recessed and sealed with a metal plug to prevent unauthorized changes in the factory adjustment.

WARNING
Tampering with a sealed carburetor is a violation of Federal law. Choke, idle mixture and other sealed adjustments can legally be made only under specified circumstances. Adjustment of these systems should be left to a Chevrolet or GMC dealer.

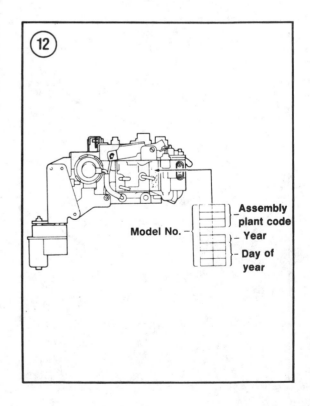

Removal and installation procedures are provided for all carburetors. Carburetor specifications vary with point of first sale and engine/transmission application. This means that specifications will differ according to whether the engine is a Federal (49-state), California or high altitude model. The necessary specifications are provided on instruction sheets accompanying overhaul kits, along with specific procedures required for proper adjustment. Such instruction sheets also incorporate any recent changes authorized by the factory in adjustment specifications.

Model Identification

The model identification code on all Rochester carburetors is stamped vertically on the float bowl (**Figure 12**). The letters and numbers identify the specific carburetor, model year and calibration. To obtain the correct carburetor overhaul kit, write down all information on the identification pad and give it to the parts department of any Chevrolet or GMC dealer or auto parts store.

Carburetor Removal/Installation

1. Disconnect the negative battery cable.
2. Remove the air cleaner as described in this chapter.

> *NOTE*
> *Alphabetical code letters are cast into the carburetor vacuum fittings on late-model carburetors to assist in proper vacuum line reconnection.*

3. Label and disconnect all vacuum lines and electrical connectors.

4. Hold the fuel inlet nut with a suitable open-end wrench and use a second wrench to break the fuel line fitting nut loose at the inlet nut. Disconnect the fuel line from the inlet nut. See **Figure 13**. Plug the line to prevent leakage.
5. Disconnect the throttle cable. Disconnect the cruise control cable and/or automatic transmission detent cable, if so equipped.
6. Remove the carburetor retaining bolts. Remove the carburetor and gasket or insulator/shield sandwich from the intake manifold.
7. Stuff a clean shop cloth in the intake manifold opening to prevent the entry of contamination.
8. Installation is the reverse of removal. If the insulator is damaged, install a new one. Tighten attaching fasteners in a clockwise pattern to prevent carburetor base warpage. With E4ME and E4MED, torque long bolts to 7 ft.-lb. (9 N•m) and short bolts to 11 ft.-lb. (15 N•m). With all other models, torque bolts to 12 ft.-lb. (16 N•m).

Preparation for Overhaul

Before removing and disassembling any carburetor, be sure you have the proper overhaul kit, a sufficient quantity of fresh carburetor cleaner and the proper tools. Work slowly and carefully, follow the disassembly/assembly procedures, refer to the exploded drawing of your carburetor when necessary and do not apply excessive force at any time.

It is not necessary to disassemble the carburetor linkage or remove linkage adjusting screws when overhauling a carburetor. Solenoids, dashpots and other diaphragm-operated assist devices attached to the carburetor body should be removed, as carburetor cleaner will damage them. Wipe such parts with a cloth to remove road film, grease and other contamination.

Use carburetor legs to prevent throttle plate damage while working on the carburetor. If legs are not available, thread a nut on each of four 2 1/4 in. bolts. Install each bolt in a flange hole and thread another nut on the bolt. These will hold the bolts securely to the carburetor and serve the same purpose as legs.

> *WARNING*
> *Tampering with a sealed carburetor is a violation of Federal law. Choke, idle mixture and other sealed adjustments*

6

can legally be made only under specified circumstances. Adjustment of these systems should be left to a Chevrolet or GMC dealer.

The carburetors used on the vehicles covered in this manual have riveted choke housings and plug seals over the idle mixture needles in accordance with Federal regulations. These adjustments are factory-set and should not be changed by the home mechanic. If the engine will not run properly after the carburetor is cleaned, reassembled and installed, it is advisable to install a rebuilt carburetor.

Cleaning and Inspection

Dirt, varnish, gum or other contamination in or on the carburetor are often the cause of unsatisfactory performance. Gaskets and accelerating pump cups may swell or leak, resulting in carburetion problems. Efficient carburetion depends upon careful cleaning, inspection and proper installation of new parts. All parts provided in the carburetor overhaul kit (except the idle mixture needle) should be installed when overhauling the carburetor.

Wash all parts except the choke cap, diaphragms, dashpots, solenoids and other vacuum or electrically operated assist devices in a cleaning solvent. Immersion-type carburetor cleaners are often used to remove dirt, gum and varnish from carburetor parts, but the use of such cleaners can remove the sealing compound (dichromate finish) applied to the carburetor castings at the factory to prevent porosity. Cleaning with an aerosol type cleaner will do the job without damage to the sealing compound.

If a commercial cleaning solvent is used, suspend the air horn in the cleaner to prevent the solution from reaching the riveted choke cap and housing. Do not leave any parts in the cleaning solution longer than necessary to avoid removal of the sealing compound.

Rinse parts cleaned in solvent with kerosene. Blow all parts dry with compressed air. Wipe all parts which cannot be immersed in solvent with a soft cloth slightly moistened with solvent, then with a clean, dry cloth.

Force compressed air through all passages in the carburetor.

> *CAUTION*
> *Do not use a wire brush to clean any part. Do not use a drill or wire to clean out any opening or passage in the carburetor. A drill or wire may enlarge the hole or passage and change the calibration.*

Check the choke and throttle plate shafts for grooves, wear or excessive looseness or binding. Inspect the choke and throttle plates for nicked edges or burrs which prevent proper closure. Choke and throttle plates are positioned during production and should not be removed unless damaged.

Clean all gasket residue from the air horn, main body and throttle body sealing surfaces with a putty knife. Since carburetor castings are aluminum, a sharp instrument should not be used to clean the gasket residue or damage to the carburetor assemblies may result.

Inspect all components for cracks or warpage. Check floats for wear on the lip and hinge pin. Check hinge pin holes in air horn, bowl cover or float bowl for wear and elongation.

Check composition floats for fuel absorption by gently squeezing and applying fingernail pressure. If moisture appears, replace the float.

Replace the float if the arm needle contact surface is grooved. If the float or floats are serviceable, gently polish the needle contact surface of the arm with crocus cloth or steel wool. Replace the float if the shaft is worn.

> *NOTE*
> *Some gasolines contain additives that will cause the viton tip on the fuel inlet needle to swell. This problem is also caused by gasoline and alcohol blends. If carburetor problems are traced to a deformed inlet needle tip, change brands of gasoline used.*

Check the viton tip of the fuel inlet needle for swelling or distortion. Discard the needle if the overhaul kit contains a new needle for assembly.

Replace all screws and nuts that have stripped threads. Replace all distorted or broken springs. Inspect all gasket mating surfaces for nicks or burrs.

If main body requires replacement, check float bowl casting. If marked "MW," be sure to replace the main body with one marked "MW." This stands for Machined Pump Well and determines the type of pump used.

Reassemble all parts carefully. It should not be necessary to apply force to any parts. If force seems to be required, you are doing something wrong. Stop and refer to the exploded drawing for your carburetor.

See **Figure 14** (E4ME), **Figure 15** (E4MED) or **Figure 16** (M4MC and M4ME).

THROTTLE BODY INJECTION (TBI)

All I4 engines and the 1986-on 263 cid V6 are equipped with a Rochester throttle body injection (TBI) unit. The I4 uses a Rochester Model 300 TBI unit; the V6 is fitted with a Model 220 TBI unit. See **Figure 17** (Model 300) or **Figure 18** (Model 220). The TBI unit contains 1 (Model 300) or 2 (Model 220) electrically operated injectors that meter fuel into the intake air stream under the direction of the electronic control module (ECM). The ECM receives electrical signals from various sensors, refers to its stored program memory and calculates the precise amount of fuel and timing of fuel required by the engine. Fuel delivery time of the injectors is modified by the ECM to accommodate special engine conditions such as cranking, cold starts, altitude and acceleration or deceleration. The basic TBI assembly consists of 2 major aluminum castings;

a. The throttle body which contains the idle air control (IAC) valve and the throttle position sensor (TPS).

b. A fuel metering body assembly which contains an integral fuel pressure regulator and 1 or 2 injectors.

System Operation

Filtered fuel is supplied to the TBI unit by a high-pressure electric fuel pump mounted in the fuel tank. When the ignition switch is turned ON, a fuel pump relay mounted in the engine compartment (**Figure 19**) activates the in-tank pump for 1.5-2 seconds to prime the injectors. If the ECM does not receive a reference signal from the distributor within that time, it shuts down the fuel pump. However, to protect against a shutdown resulting from a relay failure, a backup circuit in the ECM will accept a voltage signal from the oil pressure switch installed in the engine block (the sender unit contains 2 circuits; one operates the oil pressure light or gauge while the other is a normally open circuit which closes when engine oil pressure is above approximately 4 psi (cranking pressure). **Figure 20** (I4) and **Figure 21** (V6) show the location of this switch.

Fuel flow is controlled by varying the duration of injection according to signals from the ECM. Excess fuel passes through a pressure regulator and is then returned to the fuel tank. A throttle position sensor (TPS) informs the ECM of throttle valve position. An idle air control (IAC) assembly maintains a pre-programmed idle speed according to directions from the ECM.

Since the system is electronically controlled, no attempt should be made to adjust the idle speed or fuel mixture by tampering with the TPS or IAC. Owner service should be limited to replacement only. If the system does not seem to be working properly, take the vehicle to a Chevrolet or GMC dealer for diagnosis and adjustment.

System Pressure Relief

The Model 220 TBI unit used with the V6 engine has a bleed in the pressure regulator to relieve fuel system pressure whenever the engine is turned off. The Model 300 TBI unit used on the I4 engine does not have this feature. Before opening any fuel connection on either TBI system, however, you should perform the following procedure to assure that all pressure is relieved.

NOTE
Wrap a shop cloth around the fitting while connecting the gauge in Step 1 to absorb any leakage.

1. Place the transmission in NEUTRAL (manual transmission) or PARK (automatic).

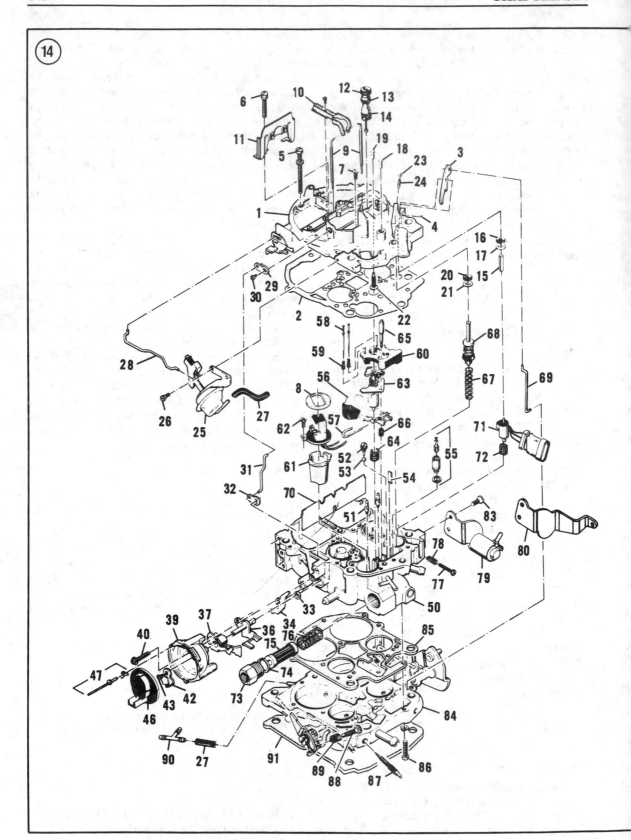

ROCHESTER E4ME CARBURETOR

AIR HORN PARTS:

1. Air horn assembly
2. Air horn gasket
3. Pump actuating lever
4. Pump lever hinge roll pin
5. Air horn long screw (2)
6. Air horn short screw
7. Air horn countersunk screw (2)
8. Solenoid connector to air horn gasket
9. Secondary metering rod (2)
10. Secondary metering rod holder and screw
11. Secondary air baffle
12. Idle air bleed valve
13. Idle air bleed valve O-ring (thick)
14. Idle air bleed valve O-ring (thin)
15. TPS actuator plunger
16. TPS plunger seal
17. TPS seal retainer
18. TPS adjusting screw
19. TPS screw plug
20. Pump plunger seal
21. Pump seal retainer
22. Solenoid plunger screw (rich stop)
23. Plunger stop screw plug (rich stop)
24. Solenoid adjusting plug (lean mixture)

CHOKE PARTS:

25. Front vacuum break control and bracket
26. Control attaching screw (2)
27. Vacuum hose
28. Air valve rod
29. Choke rod lever (upper)
30. Choke lever screw
31. Choke rod
32. Choke rod lever (lower)
33. Intermediate choke shaft seal
34. Secondary lockout lever
36. Int. choke shaft and lever
37. Fast idle cam
39. Choke housing kit
40. Choke housing to bowl screw
42. Choke coil lever
43. Choke coil lever screw
46. Stat cover and assembly (electric choke)
47. Stat cover attaching kit

FLOAT BOWL PARTS:

50. Float bowl assembly
51. Primary metering jet (2)
52. Pump discharge ball retainer
53. Pump discharge ball
54. Pump well baffle
55. Needle and seat assembly
56. Float assembly
57. Float assembly hinge pin
58. Primary metering rod (2)
59. Primary metering rod spring (2)
60. Float bowl insert
61. Bowl cavity insert
62. Connector attaching screw
63. Mixture control (M/C) solenoid and plunger assembly
64. Solenoid tension spring
65. Solenoid adjusting screw
66. Solenoid adjusting screw spring
67. Pump return spring
68. Pump assembly
69. Pump link
70. Secondary bores baffle
71. Throttle position sensor
72. TPS tension spring
73. Fuel inlet filter nut
74. Filter nut gasket
75. Fuel inlet filter
76. Fuel filter spring
77. Idle stop screw
78. Idle stop screw spring
79. Idle speed solenoid and bracket assembly
80. TPS bracket
83. Bracket attaching screw

THROTTLE BODY PARTS:

84. Throttle body assembly
85. Throttle body gasket
86. Throttle body screw
87. Idle needle and spring assembly (2)
88. Fast idle adjusting screw
89. Fast idle screw spring
90. Vacuum hose tee
91. Flange gasket

6

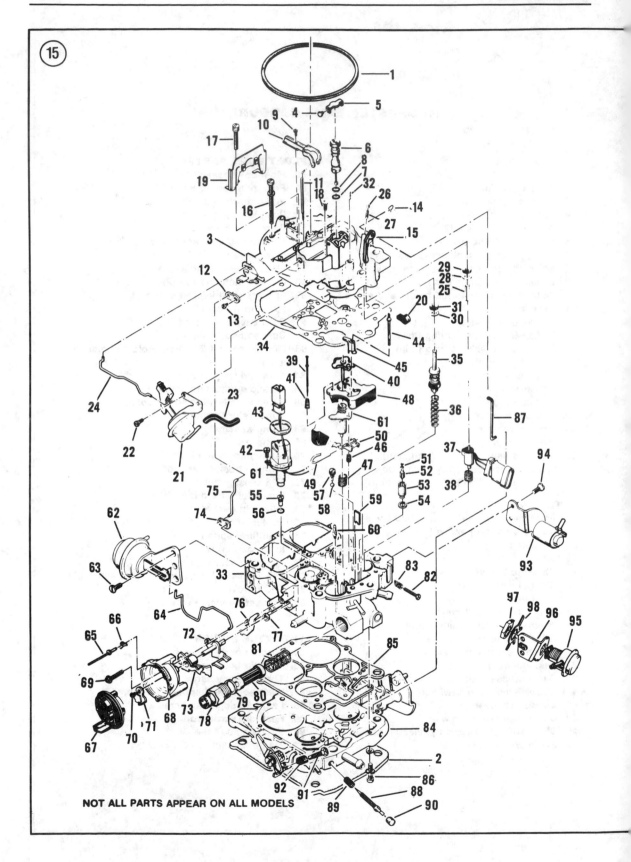

NOT ALL PARTS APPEAR ON ALL MODELS

ROCHESTER E4MED CARBURETOR

1. Air cleaner gasket
2. Flange gasket
3. Air horn
4. Cover rivet
5. Air bleed valve cover
6. Air bleed valve assembly
7. Lower air bleed valve O-ring
8. Upper air bleed valve O-ring
9. Secondary metering rod screw
10. Secondary metering rod screw
11. Secondary metering rod
12. Choke lever
13. Screw
14. Pump link retainer
15. Pump lever
16. Screw
17. Screw
18. Countersunk screw
19. Air horn baffle
20. MCS connector retainer
21. Primary (front) vacuum break assembly
22. Screw
23. Vacuum hose
24. Primary (front) vacuum break line
25. Sensor actuator plunger
26. TPS adjusting screw plug
27. TPS adjusting screw
28. TPS seal retainer
29. TPS plunger seal
30. Pump stem seal retainer
31. Pump stem seal
32. Solenoid adjusting screw plug
33. Float bowl
34. Gasket
35. Pump assembly
36. Pump return spring
37. TPS sensor
38. Sensor adjusting spring
39. Primary metering rod
40. Solenoid plunger
41. Primary metering rod spring
42. Solenoid connector screw
43. Solenoid connector gasket
44. Lean mixture adjusting screw spring
45. Rich stop limit
46. Solenoid adjusting screw spring
47. Solenoid return spring
48. Float bowl insert
49. Float hinge pin
50. Float
51. Inlet needle pull clip
52. Inlet needle
53. Inlet needle seat
54. Inlet needle seat gasket
55. Dual capacity pump valve assembly
56. Gasket
57. Pump discharge retainer plug
58. Pump discharge check ball
59. Pump well baffle
60. Primary metering jet
61. Mixture control/dual capacity pump solenoid
62. Rear vacuum break assembly
63. Screw
64. Rear vacuum break choke link
65. Choke cover rivet
66. Choke cover retainer
67. Electric choke cover
68. Choke housing
69. Screw
70. Screw
71. Choke lever
72. Intermediate choke shaft, lever and link
73. Fast idle cam assembly
74. Intermediate choke lever
75. Choke link
76. Secondary throttle lockout lever
77. Intermediate choke shaft seal
78. Fuel inlet nut
79. Fuel inlet nut gasket
80. Filter
81. Spring
82. Throttle stop screw
83. Spring
84. Throttle body assembly
85. Gasket
86. Screw
87. Pump link
88. Idle mixture needle
89. Spring
90. Idle mixture needle plug
91. Fast idle screw
92. Spring
93. Solenoid/bracket assembly
94. Screw
95. Throttle kicker assembly
96. Bracket
97. Nut
98. Lockwasher

6

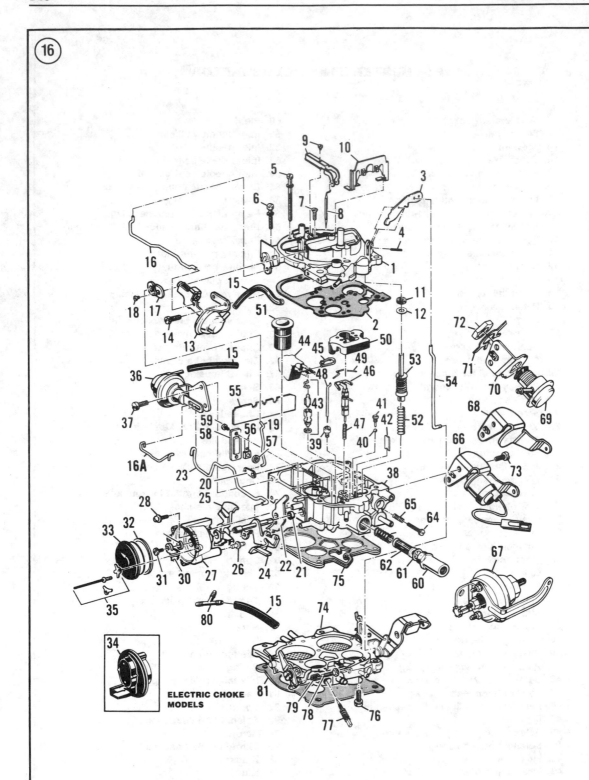

ELECTRIC CHOKE
MODELS

ROCHESTER M4MC AND M4ME CARBURETOR

AIR HORN PARTS

1. Air horn assembly
2. Gasket
3. Pump lever
4. Roll pin
5. Long air horn screw
6. Short air horn screw
7. Countersunk air horn screw
8. Secondary metering rod
9. Metering rod holder and screw
10. Secondary air baffle
11. Pump plunger seal
12. Pump seal retainer

CHOKE PARTS

13. Front vacuum break
14. Screw
15. Vacuum hose
16. Air valve rod
16A. Air valve rod
17. Upper choke rod lever
18. Choke lever screw
19. Choke rod
20. Lower choke rod lever
21. Intermediate choke shaft seal
22. Secondary lockout lever
23. Rear vacuum break link
24. Intermediate choke shaft and lever
25. Fast idle cam
26. Choke housing seal (M4MC)
27. Choke housing kit
28. Choke housing screw
29. Intermediate choke shaft seal (M4MC)
30. Choke coil lever
31. Screw
32. Gasket (M4MC)
33. Choke cover (M4MC)
34. Choke cover (M4ME)
35. Choke cover kit
36. Rear vacuum break
37. Screw

FLOAT BOWL PARTS

38. Float bowl assembly
39. Primary jet
40. Pump discharge check ball
41. Pump discharge ball retainer
42. Pump well baffle
43. Needle and seat assembly
44. Float assembly
45. Hinge pin
46. Power piston
47. Power piston spring
48. Primary metering rod
49. Metering rod retainer spring
50. Float bowl insert
51. Bowl cavity insert
52. Pump return spring
53. Pump assembly
54. Pump rod
55. Secondary bore baffle
56. Idle compensator assembly
57. Seal
58. Cover
59. Screw
60. Fuel inlet nut
61. Inlet nut gasket
62. Filter
63. Spring
64. Idle stop screw
65. Spring
66. Idle stop solenoid
67. Idle load compensator
68. Throttle return spring bracket
69. Throttle lever actuator
70. Actuator bracket
71. Washer
72. Nut
73. Screw

THROTTLE BODY PARTS

74. Throttle body assembly
75. Gasket
76. Screw
77. Idle mixture needle
78. Fast idle screw
79. Spring
80. Vacuum tee
81. Flange gasket

6

2. Set the parking brake and block the drive wheels.

3. Remove the fuel pump fuse from the fuse block.

4. Turn the ignition key to START. The engine will start and run for a few seconds until it runs out of fuel. Turn ignition key to START position again and hold for 3 seconds. This will dissipate fuel pressure and permit safe disconnection of fuel lines.

5. Once service has been completed, install fuel pump fuse and turn ignition key ON but do not start the engine. Inspect for leaks and repair if necessary before starting the engine.

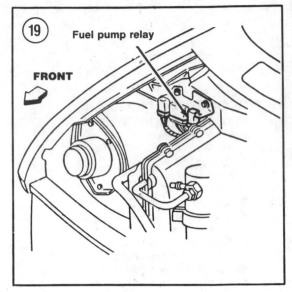

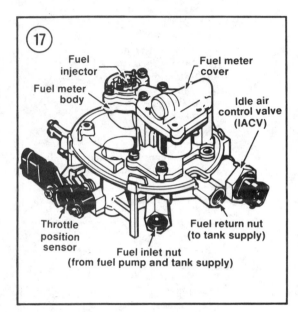

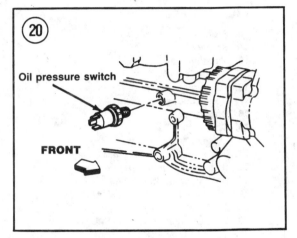

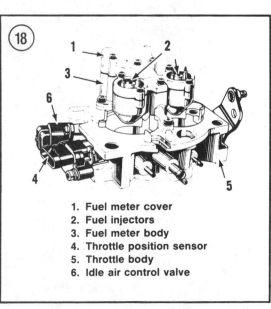

1. Fuel meter cover
2. Fuel injectors
3. Fuel meter body
4. Throttle position sensor
5. Throttle body
6. Idle air control valve

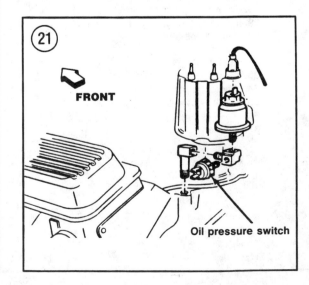

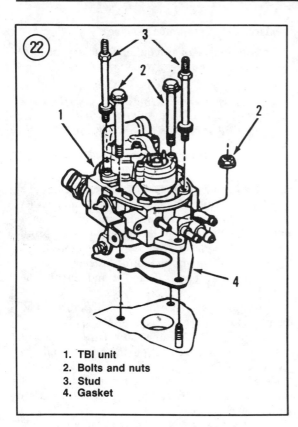

1. TBI unit
2. Bolts and nuts
3. Stud
4. Gasket

TBI Unit Removal/Installation

Refer to **Figure 22** (Model 300) or **Figure 23** (Model 220) for this procedure.

1. Relieve system pressure as described in this chapter.
2. Remove the air cleaner as described in this chapter.
3. Disconnect all electrical connectors at the TBI unit.
4. Disconnect the throttle linkage, return spring, transmission TV cable and speed control linkage (if so equipped).
5. Label and disconnect all vacuum lines at the TBI unit.
6. Disconnect the fuel supply and return lines at the TBI unit. Hold each inlet nut with a suitable open-end wrench and use a second wrench to break the fuel line fitting nuts loose. Plug both lines to prevent leakage or entry of contamination.
7. Remove the TBI mounting fasteners. Remove the TBI unit and gasket from the intake manifold. Discard the gasket.
8. Stuff a clean shop cloth in the intake manifold opening to prevent the entry of contamination.
9. Installation is the reverse of removal. Use a new gasket. Tighten Model 300 attaching fasteners to 13 ft.-lb. (18 N•m) and Model 220 fasteners to 12 ft.-lb. (16 N•m).

FUEL PUMP

Carburetted engines use a non-serviccable mechanical fuel pump (**Figure 24**) located at the right front of the engine. Fuel injected engines use an electric fuel pump located in the fuel tank. The pump is activated by a fuel pump relay bracket-mounted on the right inner fender in the engine compartment (**Figure 19**).

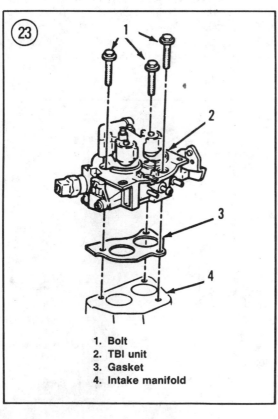

1. Bolt
2. TBI unit
3. Gasket
4. Intake manifold

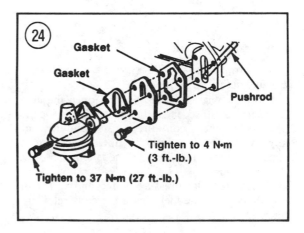

Gasket

Gasket

Pushrod

Tighten to 4 N•m (3 ft.-lb.)

Tighten to 37 N•m (27 ft.-lb.)

The 2 most common fuel pump problems are incorrect pressure and low volume. Low pressure results in a too-lean mixture and too little fuel at high speeds. High pressure will cause flooding and result in poor mileage. Low volume also results in too little fuel at high speeds.

If a fuel system problem is suspected, check the fuel filter first as described in Chapter Three. If the filter is not clogged or dirty, test the fuel pump on carburetted engines as described below.

Incorrect fuel line pressure with fuel-injected engines may be caused by a defective fuel pressure regulator or the in-tank fuel pump. Because of the complexity of the TBI system, have a Chevrolet or GMC dealer perform the necessary fuel pump and pressure regulator tests.

Pressure Test (Carburetted Engine)

1. Remove the air cleaner as described in this chapter.
2. Disconnect the fuel line at the carburetor fuel filter.
3. Connect a pressure gauge and a flexible hose with a restrictor clamp between the fuel line and filter inlet, as shown in **Figure 25**.
4. Place the end of the line in a clean quart-size container.
5. Start the engine and let it idle. Vent the system into the container by opening and closing the restrictor.
6. Let the pressure stabilize and read the gauge. It should read between 4 and 6 1/2 psi.
7. Slowly increase the idle speed and watch the gauge. The pressure should not vary considerably at different engine speeds.
8. If the pump pressure is not within specifications in Step 6 or if it varies considerably in Step 7, replace the pump.

Flow Test (Carburetted Engine)

1. Perform Steps 1-4 of *Pressure Test (Carburetted Engine)* described above.
2. Start the engine, let it idle, and open the hose restrictor for 30 seconds, then close the restrictor.
3. Check the container. It should be approximately 1/2 full. If not, check for a restriction in the fuel line. If none is found, replace the fuel pump.
4. Disconnect the pressure gauge and restrictor line. Reconnect the fuel line to the carburetor fuel filter.

Replacement (Carburetted Engine)

Refer to **Figure 24** as required for this procedure.
1. Disconnect the negative battery cable.

NOTE
If fuel pump fittings are on the underside of the pump, it will be necessary to raise the vehicle with a jack and place it on jackstands for Step 2 and Step 10. If so, securely block the wheels that remain on the ground.

2. Use 2 open-end wrenches to loosen and remove the fuel line nuts at the pump inlet and outlet fittings. If fuel hoses are used, remove the clamps and pull the hoses from the fittings. Unclamp and remove the vapor return hose, if so equipped.
3. Remove the pump mounting fasteners.
4. Remove the pump. Remove and discard the gasket.
5. Clean any gasket residue from the engine and pump mounting flanges with a putty knife.
6. If the pushrod came out with the pump, lubricate it with clean engine oil. Install the pushrod; if it does not fit all the way into the engine, rotate the crankshaft pulley nut with a suitable wrench to position the camshaft eccentric at its low point.
7. Install a new gasket to the pump mounting pad and insert the bolts through the pump flanges to hold the gasket in place.
8. Install the fuel pump and gasket to the engine block. Tighten the bolts to 15-18 ft.-lb. (20-24 N•m).

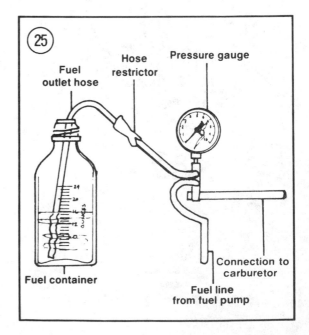

(25) Fuel outlet hose — Hose restrictor — Pressure gauge — Connection to carburetor — Fuel line from fuel pump — Fuel container

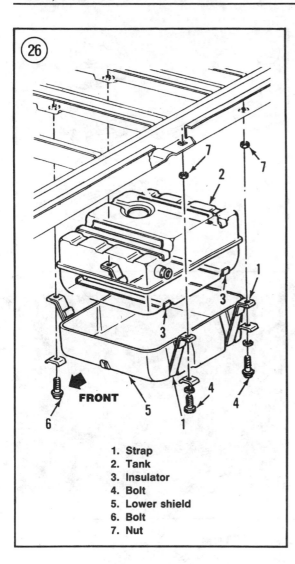

1. Strap
2. Tank
3. Insulator
4. Bolt
5. Lower shield
6. Bolt
7. Nut

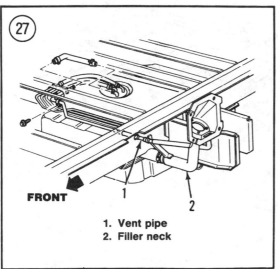

1. Vent pipe
2. Filler neck

9. Install new clamps on hoses and connect the inlet, outlet and vapor return lines (if so equipped). Tighten hose clamps securely. Tighten fuel line fittings to 20 ft.-lb. (27 N•m) using 2 open-end wrenches.

10. Reconnect the negative battery cable.

11. Start the engine and let it run for 2 minutes. Check for fuel leaks at the pump base and inlet/outlet connections.

FUEL TANK AND LINES

The fuel tank is located underneath the left center of the vehicle. Two metal straps attached to the underbody hold the tank in place. The inner bolt and jam nut are tightened to 26 ft.-lb. (35 N•m) and the outer bolt is tightened to 8 ft.-lb. (14 N•m). Insulation is used at various points between the top of the tank and the vehicle underbody to reduce rattles, squeaks and other noise. A lower shield may be installed over the tank to protect it from road damage. See **Figure 26** (typical).

Fuel Tank Removal/Installation

1. Disconnect the negative battery cable.

2. Remove the fuel tank filler cap. Insert a hand-operated pump device through the filler neck and into the tank. Remove as much fuel as possible with the pump.

> *WARNING*
> *Never store gasoline in an open container, since it is an extreme fire hazard. Store gasoline in a sealed metal container away from heat, sparks and flame.*

3. Securely block both front wheels so the vehicle will not roll in either direction.

4. Raise the vehicle with a jack and place it on jackstands.

5. Unclamp and disconnect the filler pipe neck and vent hoses. See **Figure 27**.

6. Disconnect the fuel meter wire connector. Remove the fuel meter ground wire screw.

7. Support the fuel tank with a jack and disconnect the retaining straps as required.

8. Lower the fuel tank enough to disconnect the sending unit wires, hoses and ground strap (if so equipped).

9. Remove the fuel tank from the vehicle.

10. Installation is the reverse of removal. Replace any deteriorated insulation or hoses as required. Use only hoses meeting GM specification 6163-M (identified with the word "Fluoroelastomer" marked on the hose).

Repairing Metal Fuel Tank Leaks

Fuel tank leaks can be repaired by soldering.

WARNING
The fuel tank is capable of exploding and killing anyone nearby. Always observe the following precautions when repairing a tank.

1. Have the tank steam-cleaned *inside* and *outside*.
2. Fill the tank with inert gas such as nitrogen or carbon dioxide, or fill the tank *completely* with water. Gasoline residue on the tank walls can form a highly explosive vapor if allowed to mix with air.
3. Have a dry chemical (Class B) fire extinguisher close by.
4. Whenever the tank is cleaned, the fuel meter on the top of the tank should be removed (**Figure 28**) and the strainer screen cleaned with compressed air.
5. After making the necessary repairs, pour the water out, put about one quart of gasoline in the tank and slosh it around. Pour the gasoline out, blow the tank dry with compressed air and reinstall in the vehicle.

EXHAUST SYSTEM

All models are fitted with a single muffler or resonator assembly, a single catalytic converter and connecting pipes. The exhaust pipe-to-manifold and rear converter connections are a ball type; all other connections are a slip-joint type. No gaskets are used in the exhaust system.

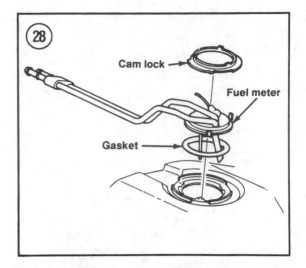

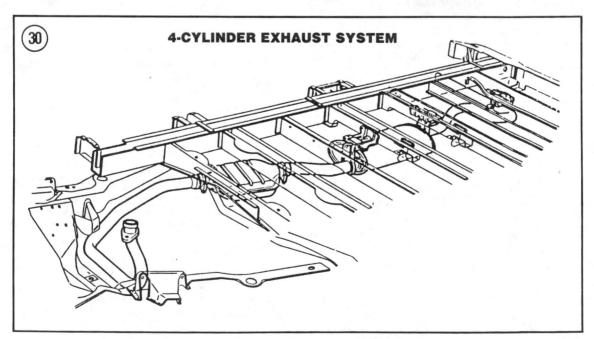

4-CYLINDER EXHAUST SYSTEM

The muffler inlet/outlet pipes are welded to the muffler. Replace the tailpipe whenever the muffler is replaced. Welded joints should be cut and the new connections clamped with U-bolts. See A, **Figure 29** (typical). Coat all slip joints (except at the converter) with an exhaust system sealer such as GM part No. 1051249 or equivalent (sealers will not withstand converter temperatures).

The exhaust system should be free of corrosion, leaks, binding, grounding or excessive vibration. Loose, broken or misaligned clamps, shields, brackets or pipes should be serviced as necessary to keep the exhaust system in a safe operating condition. See B, **Figure 29** (typical). Pay particular attention to the condition of heat shields designed to protect the underbody from excessive heat.

Figure 30 (I4) and **Figure 31** (V6) show the exhaust system arrangement and routing used on all models covered in this manual.

Removal/Installation

CAUTION
The exhaust system is extremely hot under normal operating conditions. To avoid the possibility of a bad burn, it is advisable to work on the system only when it is cool. Be especially careful around the catalytic converter. It

reaches temperatures of 600° F or greater after only a brief period of engine operation.

1. Prior to removal, soak all bolts, nuts and pipe joints with a penetrating oil such as WD-40.
2. Undo the required clamps and hanger brackets. See **Figure 29** (typical).
3. Replace the worn, damaged or corroded component(s).
4. Align the exhaust components. Start at the front of the system and tighten all fasteners securely.
5. Make sure there is adequate clearance between the exhaust system components and any pipes, hoses or other components that might be adversely affected by heat. There should also be sufficient clearance between the exhaust system and body/frame members to permit normal component movement without contact to prevent exhaust system rattle or noise.

EMISSION CONTROL SYSTEMS

All vehicles covered in this manual have a number of systems designed to minimize harmful emissions. Owner service to emission control systems is described in detail in this chapter and Chapter Three. Other service on vehicles equipped with CCC engine control systems is not recommended. Most of the components are non-adjustable and non-repairable. In many cases, expensive tools and test equipment, as well as considerable experience, are required.

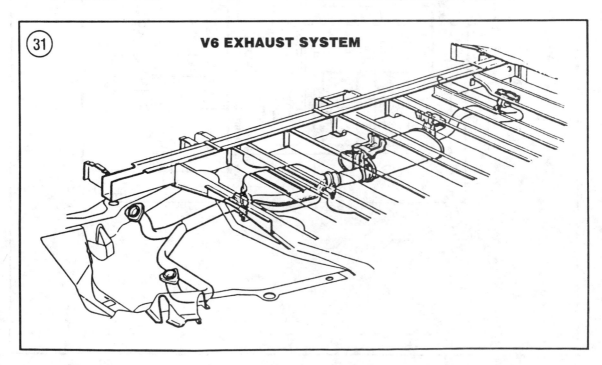
(31) V6 EXHAUST SYSTEM

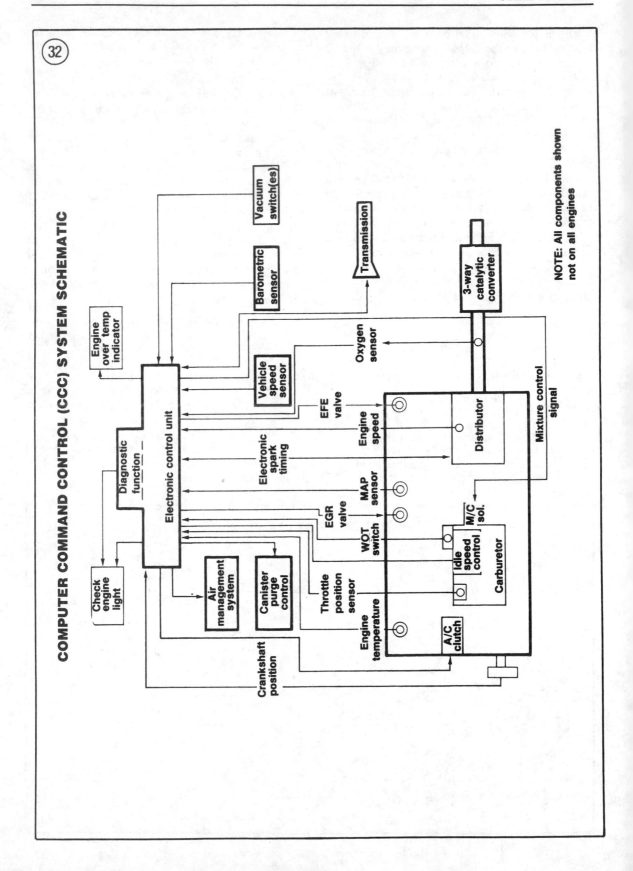

COMPUTER COMMAND CONTROL (CCC) SYSTEM SCHEMATIC

Computer Command Control (CCC) System

This electronically controlled system monitors up to 15 different engine/vehicle functions and may control as many as 9 different operations through an electronic control module (ECM) and various sensors. **Figure 32** is a schematic of the CCC system showing the sensors and the functions controlled. Note that not all engines will use all of the components shown in **Figure 32**.

The ECM receives data signals concerning cooling system temperature, crankshaft and distributor rpm, throttle shaft position, manifold pressure and exhaust gas oxygen content. It processes this information and sends back signals to control the air-fuel mixture, distributor advance, canister purge, air management system and other functions.

If a problem develops in the CCC system, a "Check Engine" or "Service Soon" lamp on the instrument panel will light. When this happens, return the vehicle to a Chevrolet or GMC dealer, who has the proper equipment and trained technicians to diagnose this complex system.

Evaporative Emission Control (EEC) System

This system is used on all models to prevent gasoline vapors from escaping into the atmosphere. Fuel vapors from the fuel tank pass through a vent restrictor to a carbon canister. Vapors from the carburetor float bowl are vented directly to the canister on 1985 V6 engines.

The carbon contained within the canister absorbs and stores the vapors when the engine is stopped. When the engine is running, manifold vacuum draws the vapors from the canister into the engine for burning. Instead of being released into the atmosphere, the fuel vapors become part of the normal combustion process. **Figure 33** (I4) and **Figure 34** (V6) show the components and operation of the EEC system on all except 1985 California V6 engines.

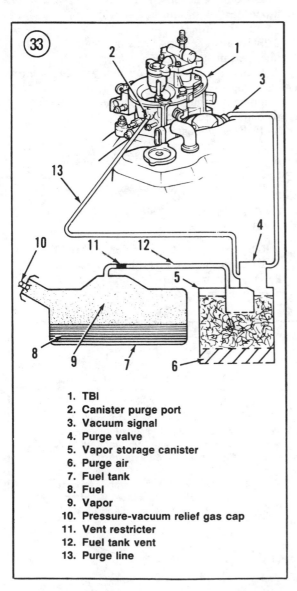

1. TBI
2. Canister purge port
3. Vacuum signal
4. Purge valve
5. Vapor storage canister
6. Purge air
7. Fuel tank
8. Fuel
9. Vapor
10. Pressure-vacuum relief gas cap
11. Vent restricter
12. Fuel tank vent
13. Purge line

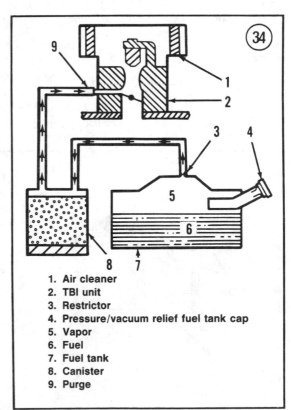

1. Air cleaner
2. TBI unit
3. Restrictor
4. Pressure/vacuum relief fuel tank cap
5. Vapor
6. Fuel
7. Fuel tank
8. Canister
9. Purge

6

The EEC system on 1985 California V6 engines is controlled by the Computer Command Control (CCC) system. The ECM controls vacuum to a canister purge valve through a solenoid valve. If the purge valve does not operate properly, the entire canister must be replaced. **Figure 35** shows the components and operation of this EEC system.

Two types of carbon canister are used: closed and open bottom. The closed bottom design is used with 1985 California V6 engines to prevent moisture from entering the bottom of the canister where it could freeze and restrict the flow of purge air. Purge air is drawn from the air cleaner with this type of canister. See **Figure 36**. The open bottom design contains a replaceable filter through which purge air must pass. This filter should be checked periodically and changed whenever it is dirty, plugged, damaged or deteriorated. See **Figure 37** (I4) or **Figure 38** (V6).

Other than replacing the open bottom canister filter, there is no scheduled maintenance of the system. Physical damage, leaks and missing components are the most common causes of evaporative system failures. If a poor idle condition, stalling or poor driveability is noted, the canister purge and vapor vent valves on non-CCC controlled systems should be checked as described in this chapter. Have a dealer check purge valve operation on 1985 California V6 engines equipped with Computer Command Control (CCC).

System inspection

1. Check the vapor lines for cracks or loose connections. Replace or tighten as necessary.
2. Check for a deformed fuel tank. Make sure the tank is not cracked and does not leak gasoline.

3. Inspect the canister for cracks or other damage.
4. Check the vapor hoses and tubes to make sure they slope downhill from the carburetor or throttle body to the canister.
5. Check the fuel filler cap for a damaged gasket.

CAUTION
Any damage or contamination which prevents the filler cap pressure-vacuum valve from working properly can result in deformation of the fuel tank.

Canister functional test
(non-CCC system except 1985 Federal V6)

Refer to **Figure 37** (I4) or **Figure 38** (V6) for this procedure.
1. Disconnect the hose at the canister purge valve lower fitting and connect a suitable length of clean hose to the fitting.
2. Blow into the hose. Little or no air should pass into the canister.
3. Connect a hand vacuum pump to the control valve (upper) tube. Apply 15 in. Hg vacuum. The diaphragm should hold vacuum for at least 20 seconds. If not, replace the canister.
4. If the diaphragm holds vacuum, repeat Step 2 with the vacuum applied. If air flow to the canister does not increase, replace the canister.

Canister purge control valve test
(1985 Federal V6)

Refer to **Figure 36** for this procedure.
1. Disconnect the hose at the canister purge valve lower fitting and connect a suitable length of clean hose to the fitting.

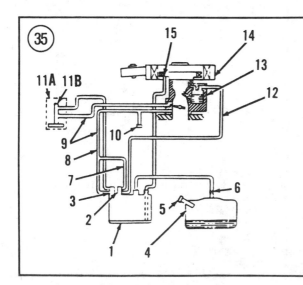

(35)

1. Canister
2. Vapor vent control valve
3. Canister purge control valve
4. Fuel tank
5. Fuel cap
6. Fuel tank vent line restriction
7. Vacuum signal for bowl vent valve
8. Vapor purge line (full manifold vacuum)
9. Ported manifold vacuum
10. PCV valve
11A. Thermal vacuum switch (Federal)
11B. Electric purge solenoid (California)
12. Carburetor bowl vent line
13. Carburetor
14. Air cleaner
15. Fuel vapor canister vent

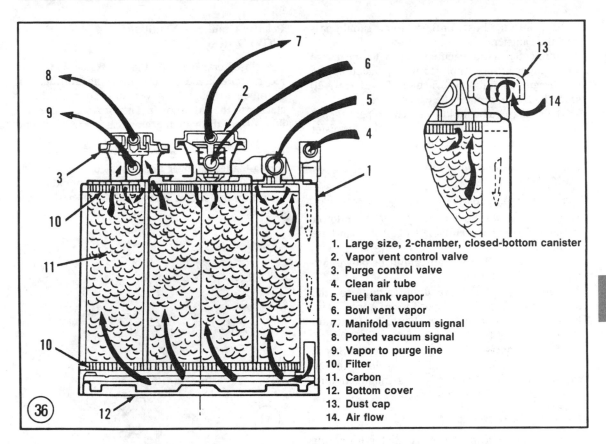

1. Large size, 2-chamber, closed-bottom canister
2. Vapor vent control valve
3. Purge control valve
4. Clean air tube
5. Fuel tank vapor
6. Bowl vent vapor
7. Manifold vacuum signal
8. Ported vacuum signal
9. Vapor to purge line
10. Filter
11. Carbon
12. Bottom cover
13. Dust cap
14. Air flow

36

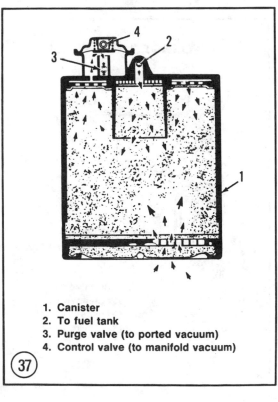

1. Canister
2. To fuel tank
3. Purge valve (to ported vacuum)
4. Control valve (to manifold vacuum)

37

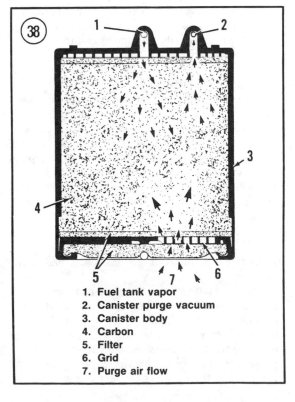

1. Fuel tank vapor
2. Canister purge vacuum
3. Canister body
4. Carbon
5. Filter
6. Grid
7. Purge air flow

38

2. Blow into the hose. Little or no air should pass into the canister.

3. Connect a hand vacuum pump to the purge valve upper fitting. Apply 15 in. Hg vacuum. The diaphragm should hold vacuum for at least 20 seconds. If not, replace the canister.

4. If the diaphragm holds vacuum, repeat Step 2 with the vacuum applied. If air flow to the canister does not increase, replace the canister.

Canister vapor vent valve test (1985 Federal V6)

Refer to **Figure 36** for this procedure.

1. Disconnect the hose at the vapor valve lower fitting and connect a suitable length of clean hose to the fitting.

2. Blow into the hose. If air cannot be blown into the canister, replace it.

3. Connect a hand vacuum pump to the diaphragm vapor valve upper fitting. Apply 15 in. Hg vacuum. The diaphragm should hold vacuum for at least 20 seconds. If not, replace the canister.

4. If the diaphragm holds vacuum, repeat Step 2 with the vacuum applied. If air flows to the canister, the vapor vent valve is malfunctioning and the canister must be replaced.

Canister filter replacement

1. Note the location of the canister hoses for reinstallation reference, then disconnect each from its canister fitting.

2. Loosen the canister mounting clamp screw and remove the canister.

3. Remove the filter from the bottom of the canister. See **Figure 39**.

4. Check and clean the canister hose fittings of any obstructions.

5. Install a new filter in the bottom of the canister.

6. Place the canister in the mounting clamp, rotating it as required to position the hose nipples in the same direction as originally installed.

7. Tighten the mounting clamp screw and reconnect the canister hoses to their appropriate fittings.

Canister replacement

1. Note the position of the hoses attached to the canister.

2. Disconnect the hoses from the canister.

3. Loosen the canister bracket clamp(s). Remove the canister.

4. Install the new canister and position the fittings in the same direction as the old canister.

5. Tighten the bracket clamp screw(s) and install the hoses to their correct canister fitting.

Positive Crankcase Ventilation (PCV) System

A closed crankcase ventilation system is used to recycle crankcase vapors into the combustion chambers for burning. A vent hose connects the air cleaner to the valve cover. This provides a positive flow of air through the crankcase. Fresh air and crankcase vapors are drawn into the intake manifold through a PCV valve containing a spring-loaded plunger and installed in the engine valve cover. PCV system components and operation are shown in **Figure 40** (I4) and **Figure 41** (V6).

㊴

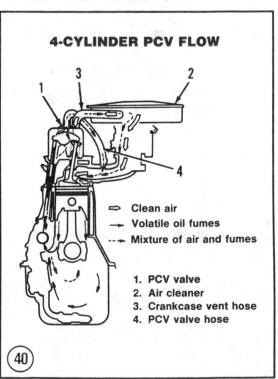

4-CYLINDER PCV FLOW

3   2
1
                 4

⇨ Clean air
→ Volatile oil fumes
--→ Mixture of air and fumes

1. PCV valve
2. Air cleaner
3. Crankcase vent hose
4. PCV valve hose

㊵

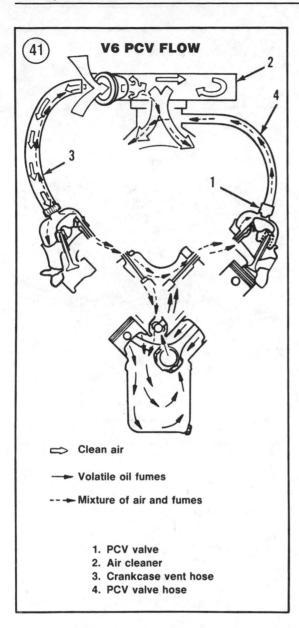

V6 PCV FLOW

⇨ Clean air

→ Volatile oil fumes

--→ Mixture of air and fumes

1. PCV valve
2. Air cleaner
3. Crankcase vent hose
4. PCV valve hose

The position of the check valve plunger in the PCV valve (**Figure 42**) varies according to engine vacuum and thus controls or meters the flow of crankcase vapors into the intake manifold, restricting flow during periods of high manifold vacuum.

The PCV system should be inspected and the PCV valve and air cleaner crankcase vent filter replaced at intervals specified in Chapter Three.

System check

Refer to **Figure 43** (I4) or **Figure 44** (V6) for this procedure.

1. Remove the PCV valve from the valve cover.
2. Start the engine and run at idle.

6

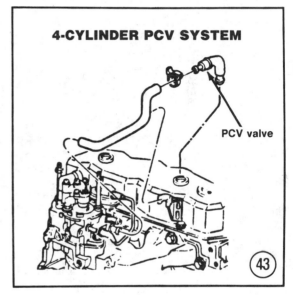

4-CYLINDER PCV SYSTEM

PCV valve

43

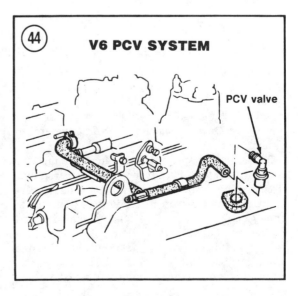

44

V6 PCV SYSTEM

PCV valve

Check valve

42

3. Place a thumb over the valve end to check for vacuum (**Figure 45**). If there is no vacuum, check for plugged hoses.

4. Shake the PCV valve. If the check needle inside the valve does not rattle, replace the valve.

5. Reinstall the PCV valve and disconnect the crankcase inlet hose at the valve cover.

6. Hold a parts tag or other stiff piece of paper over the opening (**Figure 46**). Within a minute, the crankcase pressure should subside and the paper should be sucked down against the hole. If not, check for a restricted vent hose between the PCV valve and intake manifold. Perform *System Maintenance* as described in this chapter.

7. Shut the engine off. Reinstall the PCV valve in the valve cover.

System Maintenance

1. Remove the PCV system components from the engine (PCV valve, hoses, tubes, elbows and grommets).

2. Clean rubber hoses by pushing a cleaning brush through them. Wash hoses in petroleum-based solvent, then blow dry with compressed air. Replace any hoses which show obvious signs of deterioration.

3. If system uses a crankcase ventilation filter in the air cleaner, service as described in Chapter Three.

4. Make sure all hoses, fittings and connections are free of obstructions. Check grommets for signs of deterioration and replace as required. Reinstall all components removed in Step 1.

Air Injection Reactor (AIR) System

V6 engines may use one of two types of AIR system. The I4 engine does not require an AIR system. The 1985 Federal V6 engine uses a standard or non-CCC controlled system. All other V6 engines use a "managed" or CCC controlled system.

The standard system injects fresh air into the exhaust manifold whenever the engine is running. The fresh air combines with the hot exhaust gases to create a more complete oxidation or burning of the gases, reducing carbon monoxide and hydrocarbon emissions.

The managed system is controlled by the Computer Command Control ECM and injects fresh air to the exhaust ports when first started,

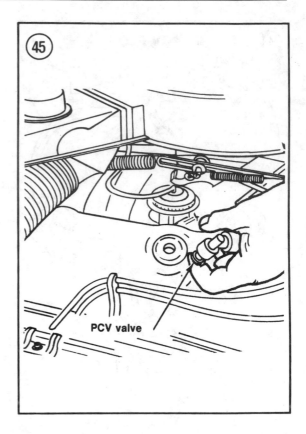

PCV valve

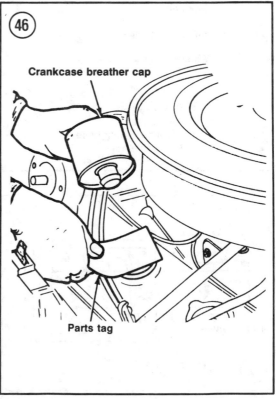

Crankcase breather cap

Parts tag

then switches air flow to a point in the catalytic converter between the reduction and oxidation catalysts when the engine goes into closed loop.

Both AIR systems consist of a belt-driven air pump, air diverter or electric air control valve, check valves, air injection tube/manifold and connecting hoses. Non-CCC controlled systems also use a gulp valve to prevent backfiring during deceleration.

Figure 47 (typical) shows the components used in the managed system; the standard system components are the same but a diverter valve is used instead of the electric air control or EAC valve and there is no connection to the ECM.

Intake air is drawn through a centrifugal filter fan at the front of the pump. This air is sent from the pump to the diverter valve, which directs it to the air injection manifold(s), to a point in the catalytic converter (ECM-controlled) or dumps it into the atmosphere, according to system application and engine operating conditions. The check valves prevent hot exhaust gases from reversing their flow in the system and causing pump damage.

Rough idling or poor perfromance can be caused by a leaking diverter or EAC valve vacuum line. Backfiring can be caused by a defective diverter or EAC valve or its connections. If there is no air flow to the exhaust ports, HC/CO emission levels will be excessive. On ECM-controlled systems, continual air flow to the exhaust ports will cause an incorrect oxygen sensor signal to the ECM. The ECM will respond by changing the air/fuel ratio when it is not necessary. The additional fuel and air will cause the catalytic converter temperature to rise, which can result in converter damage. For these reasons, AIR system maintenance is important.

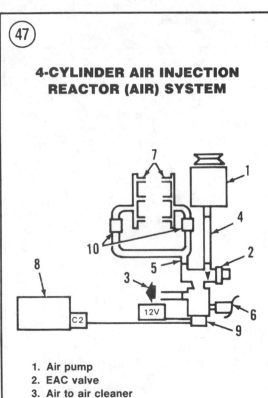

4-CYLINDER AIR INJECTION REACTOR (AIR) SYSTEM

1. Air pump
2. EAC valve
3. Air to air cleaner
4. Air to EAC valve
5. Air to exhaust ports
6. Manifold vacuum signal
7. Air injection pipes (air to exhaust ports)
8. ECM
9. EAC solenoid
10. Check valves

Air pump operation

The air pump can be distinguished from the alternator by the centrifugal filter fan located on the rotor shaft/drive hub. The pump is located on the front of the engine below the alternator and is serviced by replacement only. It should not be disassembled.

NOTE
There is a small vent hole at the top front of some pump housings. Do not mistake it for a lubrication point. Air pumps require no lubrication.

Air pumps are not noiseless in operation. Pump noise is normal and rises in pitch as engine speed increases. Three types of pump noise may be noticed:

  a. A chirp or squeak is often heard intermittently at low engine speeds. It is usually caused by the pump vanes rubbing in the housing bore, but may also be caused by drive belt slippage if the pump seizes.

  b. A rolling sound heard at all speeds is caused by the bearings. This sound is also normal, but can indicate bearing failure if it reaches an objectionable level.

  c. A continuous knocking noise indicates definite bearing failure. The pump must be replaced.

Air pump functional check

Refer to **Figure 48** (typical) for this procedure.

1. Check and adjust the drive belt tension, if required. See Chapter Seven.

2. Inspect all system hoses for cracking, burning or loose connections. Replace hoses or tighten connections as necessary.

3A. Non-CCC engine—Start the engine. Disconnect the pump output hose. There should be air flow. If not, replace the pump.

3B. CCC engine—Start the engine. Disconnect the hoses at the EAC valve side of the check valves. There should be air flow to the exhaust port outlet of the valve for several seconds, then the air flow should switch to the air cleaner outlet side.

4. Gradually increase engine speed to approximately 1,500 rpm. If air flow does not increase, replace the pump.

5. Reconnect the hoses. Increase engine speed to 2,000 rpm. Release the throttle quickly. If a backfire occurs, replace the gulp or EAC valve, as equipped.

6. Disconnect the check valve line and remove the check valve.

7. Try to blow and suck air through both ends of the valve. The valve should pass air in only one direction. If it passes air in both directions or does not pass air in either direction, install a new check valve.

8. Replace the pump if it does not perform as specified. Further air management system testing should be left to a dealer. Correct system operation is dependent on the ECM and its testing is best left to a qualified technician.

Air pump replacement

Refer to **Figure 49** for this procedure.

1. Securely block both rear wheels so the vehicle will not roll in either direction.

2. Raise the front of the vehicle with a jack and place it on jackstands.

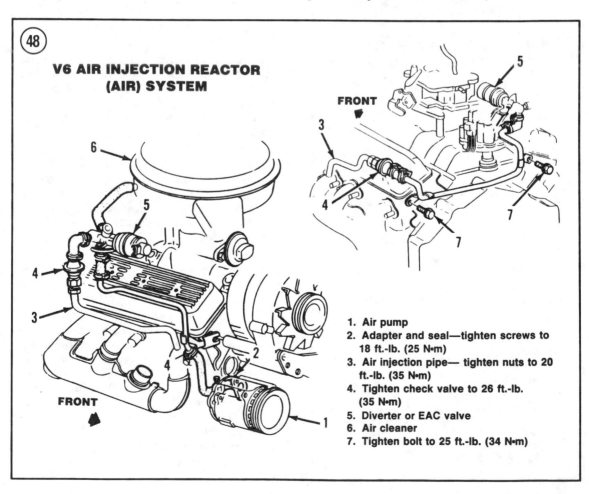

V6 AIR INJECTION REACTOR (AIR) SYSTEM

1. Air pump
2. Adapter and seal—tighten screws to 18 ft.-lb. (25 N•m)
3. Air injection pipe— tighten nuts to 20 ft.-lb. (35 N•m)
4. Tighten check valve to 26 ft.-lb. (35 N•m)
5. Diverter or EAC valve
6. Air cleaner
7. Tighten bolt to 25 ft.-lb. (34 N•m)

TYPICAL AIR PUMP COMPONENTS

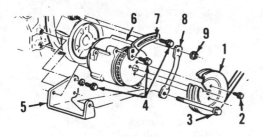

1. Pulley
2. Tighten bolt to 90 in.-lb. (10 N•m)
3. Tighten bolt to 32 ft.-lb. (45 N•m)
4. Tighten bolt to 25 ft.-lb. (34 N•m)
5. Support
6. Air pump
7. Bracket
8. Brace
9. Tighten nut to 25 ft.-lb. (34 N•m)

3. Compress the pump drive belt to hold the pump pulley from turning. Loosen the pump pulley bolts.

4. Loosen the pump mounting and adjusting bracket bolts.

5. Swivel the pump toward the engine and remove the drive belt.

6. Disconnect the pump output hose(s) at the rear of the pump housing.

7. Remove the pump pulley. Remove the pump mounting bolts. Remove the pump.

8. Installation is the reverse of removal. Adjust drive belt tension. See Chapter Seven.

Air injection pipe assembly, hoses and tubes

There is no periodic service for the air injection pipe assembly. Whenever the exhaust manifold(s) are removed for service, the injection pipes should be checked for carbon build-up and burned or warped pipes. Clean pipes with a wire rush. Remove pipes by liberally applying penetrating oil and disconnecting them from the exhaust manifold. See **Figure 48**.

Inspect hoses for cracking, burning or other deterioration. Replace any that are not satisfactory. AIR system hoses are manufactured from special materials to withstand high temperatures. Be sure to use the proper hose for replacement.

If leakage is suspected, check the connections to make sure they are tight. Test the pressure side of the system with a soapy water solution applied to each of the connections with the engine idling. Bubbling and foaming are indications that a connection is not tight and leak-free. Correct any leaks that are found.

Electric air control valve (CCC system)

Refer troubleshooting and service of the EAC valve in CCC-controlled systems to your Chevrolet or GMC dealer who has the appropriate test equipment and trained technicians to diagnose a managed AIR system.

Check valve

If a check valve is suspected of malfunctioning, disconnect its hose from the diverter or EAC valve and blow through it. There should be no resistance. Then, attempt to suck through the hose. If the valve is in good condition, this will not be possible. Replace the valve if it fails to perform satisfactorily in either direction. To prevent bending the air injection pipe when replacing a check valve, use two wrenches of comparable length for equal torque, as shown in **Figure 50**.

Exhaust Gas Recirculation (EGR) System

This system recirculates a small amount of exhaust gas into the incoming air-fuel mixture through an EGR valve at engine speeds above idle. See **Figure 51** (typical). This lowers the combustion temperature and reduces oxides of nitrogen (NOx) emissions.

The EGR system on all I4 engines is directly controlled by ported manifold vacuum taken from the TBI unit. See **Figure 52**. The 1985 Federal V6 system uses a thermostatic vacuum switch or TVS to control ported manifold vacuum taken from the carburetor (**Figure 53**). The EGR system on all other V6 engines is controlled by the Computer Command Control ECM through a solenoid (**Figure 54**). The ECM modulates exhaust gas flow by constantly turning the EGR solenoid on and off via the solenoid, varying the duration of flow according to data received from coolant temperature, throttle position and engine vacuum sensors.

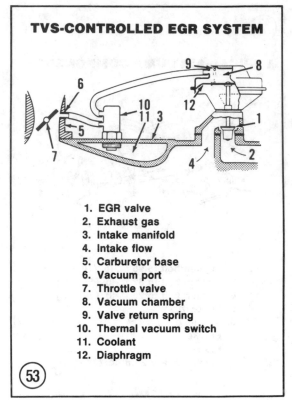

TVS-CONTROLLED EGR SYSTEM

1. EGR valve
2. Exhaust gas
3. Intake manifold
4. Intake flow
5. Carburetor base
6. Vacuum port
7. Throttle valve
8. Vacuum chamber
9. Valve return spring
10. Thermal vacuum switch
11. Coolant
12. Diaphragm

(53)

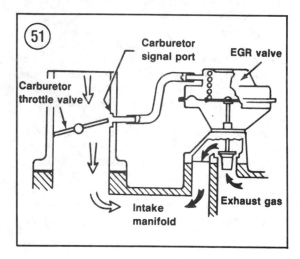

(51)

Carburetor signal port

EGR valve

Carburetor throttle valve

Exhaust gas

Intake manifold

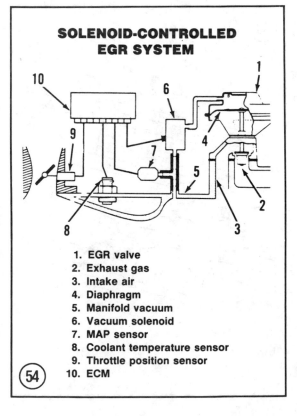

SOLENOID-CONTROLLED EGR SYSTEM

1. EGR valve
2. Exhaust gas
3. Intake air
4. Diaphragm
5. Manifold vacuum
6. Vacuum solenoid
7. MAP sensor
8. Coolant temperature sensor
9. Throttle position sensor
10. ECM

(54)

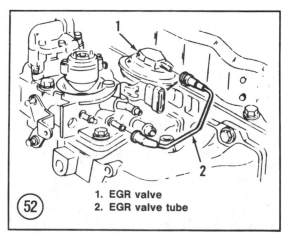

(52)

1. EGR valve
2. EGR valve tube

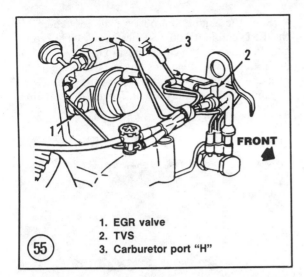

1. EGR valve
2. TVS
3. Carburetor port "H"

(55)

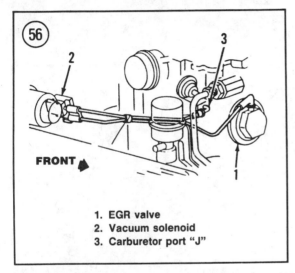

(56)

1. EGR valve
2. Vacuum solenoid
3. Carburetor port "J"

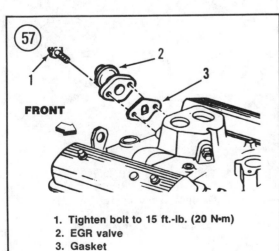

(57)

1. Tighten bolt to 15 ft.-lb. (20 N•m)
2. EGR valve
3. Gasket

The EGR valve is located on the intake manifold of I4 engines next to the TBI unit (**Figure 52**). On carburetted V6 engines, the valve is located externally on the intake manifold at the front of the carburetor. See **Figure 55** (Federal) or **Figure 56** (California). On fuel injected V6 engines, the EGR valve is located on the intake manifold at the rear of the TBI unit (**Figure 57**).

System operational check (non-CCC system)

1. With the engine off, grasp the top of the EGR valve and try to rotate it. If it is loose, replace the valve.
2. Place the transmission in PARK (automatic) or NEUTRAL (manual). Start the engine and run until it reaches normal operating temperature (upper radiator hose hot).
3. Reach under the EGR valve and push up on the diaphragm plate with an index finger. If there is not an immediate drop in engine speed, replace the valve.

> *NOTE*
> *The use of a small inspection mirror may be helpful in Step 4.*

4. Gradually increase engine speed to approximately 2,000 rpm while watching the EGR valve diaphragm stem for movement.
5. If the valve diaphragm stem does not move in Step 5, tee a vacuum gauge into the EGR valve vacuum line and gradually increase engine speed to approximately 2,000 rpm. If the gauge does not read more than 6 in. Hg, check the EGR valve vacuum line for restrictions, leaks or a poor connection. Correct any problems found. This completes diagnosis of the I4 EGR system.
6. 1985 Federal V6 with TVS control:
   a. If the EGR valve vacuum line is satisfactory, trace it to the thermal vacuum switch (TVS). Disconnect the vacuum line between the TVS and carburetor at the TVS and connect it to the vacuum gauge.
   b. Gradually increase engine speed to approximately 2,000 rpm while watching the gauge. If the gauge reading exceeds 10 in. Hg, replace the TVS. If the reading is less than 10 in. Hg, check for a restricted vacuum line or carburetor passage.

System operational check (CCC system)

The EGR system on V6 engines equipped with Computer Command Control (CCC) should be referred to your dealer for testing and diagnosis.

6

EGR valve service and inspection

EGR valves should be replaced, not cleaned. At the same time, inspect and clean the EGR passages in the intake manifold as required.

1. Unbolt and remove the EGR valve from the engine.

> **NOTE**
> *Do not sandblast the valve or wash it in solvent in Step 2.*

2. Inspect the valve passages for carbon build-up. Replace valve if passages are partially or completely plugged.
3. Depress the valve diaphragm. Check valve sealing and outlet areas (**Figure 58**).
4. Remove exhaust deposits from the manifold passages with a drill and wire brush or a screwdriver.
5. Clean intake manifold and valve mounting surfaces. Install the valve on the manifold with a new gasket. Tighten the mounting bolts to 15 ft.-lb. (22 N•m).
6. Check vacuum lines for damage or deterioration. Replace as required.

Early Fuel Evaporation (EFE) System

The EFE system is used on 1985 V6 engines. It provides heat to the intake manifold while the engine is cold in order to promote vaporization of the fuel. This reduces choke on-time and results in more complete burning of the fuel.

A butterfly valve installed between the exhaust manifold and exhaust pipe (**Figure 59**) diverts exhaust gas flow during cold engine operation to heat the intake manifold more rapidly. Valve operation is controlled by a vacuum diaphragm (EFE actuator) and a thermal vacuum switch (TVS) according to engine coolant temperature. See **Figure 60** for typical application.

If the EFE system does not operate, the engine will stumble and stall during warmup, requiring a longer time to reach operating temperature. An EFE system that remains on will cause reduced performance, a lack of power and may cause the engine to overheat.

Use the following procedure to check the butterfly valve system:

System check

Refer to **Figure 61** (Federal V6) or **Figure 62** (California V6) for the location of the TVS.

1. With the engine cold, place the transmission in PARK (automatic) or NEUTRAL (manual) and set the parking brake.

2. Start the engine and observe the movement of the EFE actuator rod and heat valve. The valve should move to the closed position.

3. If the valve does not move, disconnect the actuator vacuum line and check for the presence of vacuum. If vacuum is present, replace the actuator.

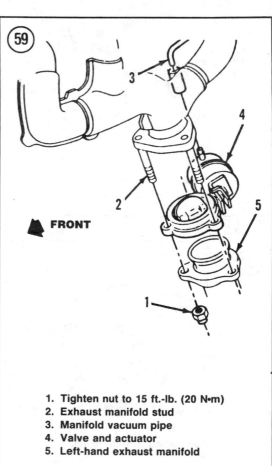

1. Tighten nut to 15 ft.-lb. (20 N•m)
2. Exhaust manifold stud
3. Manifold vacuum pipe
4. Valve and actuator
5. Left-hand exhaust manifold

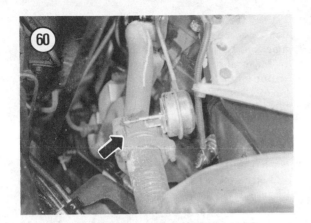

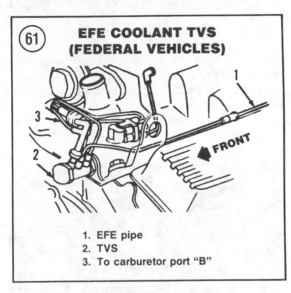

EFE COOLANT TVS (FEDERAL VEHICLES)

1. EFE pipe
2. TVS
3. To carburetor port "B"

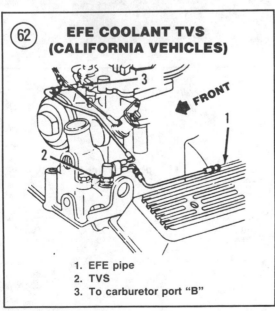

EFE COOLANT TVS (CALIFORNIA VEHICLES)

1. EFE pipe
2. TVS
3. To carburetor port "B"

4. If there is no vacuum present in Step 3, disconnect the vacuum input line at the TVS and check for vacuum. If vacuum is present, replace the TVS. If no vacuum is present, check the line for restrictions, leaking or deterioration. Replace the vacuum line as required.

5. If the valve closes in Step 2, run the engine until it reaches normal operating temperature (upper radiator hose hot).The exhaust heat valve should move to the open position. If it does not, disconnect the actuator vacuum line and check for the presence of vacuum. If no vacuum is present, replace the actuator. If vacuum is present, replace the TVS.

Valve and actuator replacement

Refer to **Figure 59** for this procedure.

1. Disconnect the vacuum line at the EFE actuator.

2. Securely block both rear wheels so the vehicle will not roll in either direction.

3. Raise the vehicle with a jack and place it on jackstands.

4. Disconnect the crossover pipe from the exhaust manifolds. Lower the pipe.

5. Remove the EFE valve and actuator assembly from the left hand exhaust manifold. Remove and discard any seals or gaskets used.

6. Installation is the reverse of removal. Install new seals and gaskets as required. Tighten exhaust flange nuts to 15 ft.-lb. (20 N•m).

TVS replacement

Refer to **Figure 61** (Federal V6) or **Figure 62** (California V6) for this procedure.

1. Drain the coolant below the level of the TVS. See Chapter Seven.

2. Label and disconnect the vacuum lines at the TVS.

3. Unscrew and remove the TVS. Check the base of the TVS to determine the calibration temperature.

4. Apply a soft-setting sealant on the replacement TVS threads. Do *not* apply sealant on the sensor end of the TVS.

5. Thread TVS in place and tighten to 120 in.-lb. (14 N•m), then turn it clockwise as required to align the vacuum ports with the vacuum lines.

6. Connect the vacuum lines to the TVS ports.

7. Refill the cooling system as required. See Chapter Seven.

6

Catalytic Converter

The catalytic converter is mounted in the exhaust system between the manifold exhaust pipe and the muffler. The converter may be either a bead-type or a monolithic converter.

The converter reduces carbon monoxide and unburned hydrocarbons in the exhaust gases. This process changes the harmful pollutants into harmless carbon dioxide and water. Oxides of nitrogen are reduced to pure nitrogen and oxygen. The converter contains beads or a monolithic honeycomb coated with a catalytic material containing platinum and palladium. The converter requires no maintenance other than the use of unleaded gasoline and replacement of the heat shield, if damaged.

It may become necessary to replace either the converter or catalyst beads. See *Exhaust System* in this chapter for converter replacement. Replacing the catalyst beads requires expensive special tools and special precautions must be taken in disposing of the old beads. For these reasons, it is more practical and economical to have the job done by a dealer or a qualified garage.

Oxygen Sensor

An oxygen sensor is installed in the exhaust manifold pipe on vehicles equipped with a CCC system. See **Figure 63**. This sensor monitors the oxygen content of the exhaust gas and sends a voltage signal to the electronic control module (ECM). The ECM evaluates this signal and adjusts the carburetor mixture control solenoid or TBI injector duration accordingly. See **Figure 64**. The use of leaded fuel or an attempt to measure the output voltage with a voltmeter will permanently damage an oxygen sensor.

Use the following procedure to replace a damaged sensor or transfer the sensor to a new manifold.

1. Make sure the engine is warm. Removing a sensor when engine temperature is below 120° F (48° C) may damage the exhaust manifold pipe threads.
2. Securely block both rear wheels so the vehicle will not roll in either direction.
3. Raise the front of the vehicle with a jack and place it on jackstands.
4. Locate the sensor in the exhaust manifold pipe (**Figure 63**), then unplug the sensor electrical connector at the wiring harness.
5. Remove the sensor with tool part No. J-29533 or equivalent.
6. If installing the same sensor, wipe its threads with an electrically conductive anti-seize compound (part No. 5613695 or equivalent). New sensors are pre-coated.
7. Thread the sensor in place by hand and tighten to 30 ft.-lb. (41 N•m).
8. Reconnect the sensor electrical connector to the wiring harness.

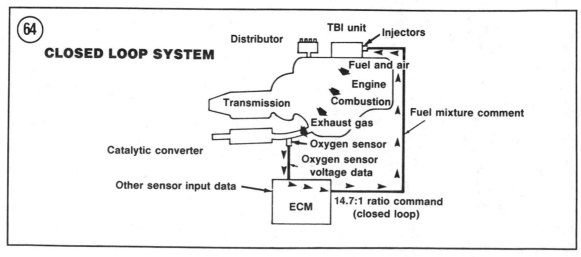

CHAPTER SEVEN

COOLING, HEATING AND AIR CONDITIONING

All vehicles covered in this manual use a pressurized cooling system (15 psi) sealed with a pressure-type radiator cap. The higher operating pressure of the system raises the boiling point of the coolant. This increases the efficiency of the radiator. Coolant circulation is thermostatically controlled. **Figure 1** shows a typical cooling system.

The cooling system consists of the radiator, water pump, cooling fan, thermostat, coolant recovery tank, temperature sensors and connecting hoses. The crossflow radiator is mounted on the engine compartment front body support panel.

The heater is a hot water type which circulates coolant through a small radiator (heater core) under the instrument panel.

The air conditioning system is a cycling clutch expansion tube (with fixed orifice) or CCOT design and uses outside air at all times, except during MAX A/C operation.

This chapter includes service procedures for the radiator, thermostat, water pump, cooling fan, heater and air conditioner. Cooling system flushing procedures are also described. **Tables 1-3** are at the end of the chapter.

COOLING SYSTEM

A crossflow radiator (**Figure 2**) is used on all models. The crossflow radiator is constructed in a tube and slit-fin-core arrangement with the tubes positioned horizontally between the header tanks for crossflow of the coolant. The header tanks on each side of the radiator provide uniform distribution of the coolant to the crossflow tubes. The right header tank contains the transmission oil cooler on automatic transmission models.

A coolant recovery system is incorporated in all cooling systems. This consists of a translucent plastic overflow reservoir connected to the radiator filler neck by a hose. See **Figure 3** (typical).

When coolant in the radiator expands to the overflow point, it passes through the filler neck and into the plastic reservoir. Once the coolant in the radiator cools down, it contracts. The vacuum created pulls coolant from the reservoir back into the radiator. This system prevents the radiator from boiling over. By remaining filled to capacity, cooling efficiency is maintained at all times.

COOLING SYSTEM FLUSHING

The recommended coolant is a 50/50 mixture of ethylene glycol antifreeze and low mineral content water, which provides a lower freezing point and higher boiling point than water alone.

The water pump circulates the coolant through the cooling system when the engine is running. When the engine is cold, the coolant is trapped inside the engine water jacket by the thermostat, which is located in the mouth of the hose leading to the radiator inlet tank. The thermostat remains closed until the coolant heats up to operating temperature. It then opens and the coolant flows through the hose into the radiator inlet tank. The coolant passes through the radiator tubes to the outlet tank, where it flows through the radiator outlet hose to the water pump inlet to start the cycle over again.

The cooling fan draws air through the radiator and removes excess heat from the coolant. Rigid or viscous clutch (thermostatic) fans are used, depending upon model year and air conditioning option. The viscous clutch fan uses a silicone-filled coupling that automatically increases or decreases fan speed according to temperature to provide proper engine cooling under all conditions.

All models have a shroud attached to the radiator to funnel air through the radiator more efficiently.

COOLING SYSTEM CHECKS

1. Visually inspect the cooling system and heater hoses for signs of cracking, checking, excessive

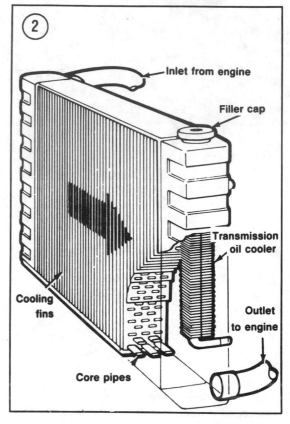

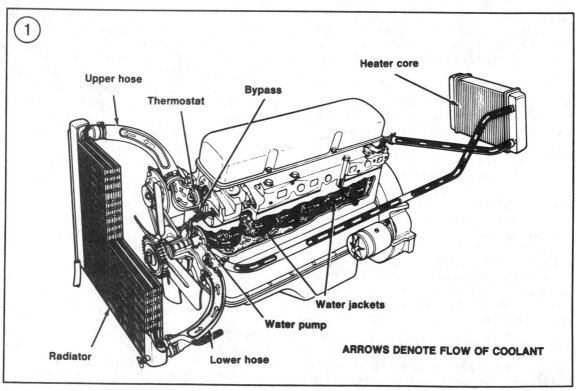

ARROWS DENOTE FLOW OF COOLANT

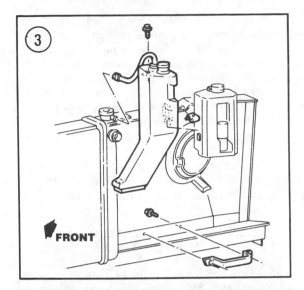

swelling or leakage. Restrictions in the cooling system may cause the radiator hoses to collapse, expand, vibrate or thump.

2. Check that all supporting or protective hose brackets or straps are properly positioned (**Figure 4**, typical) and that the hoses are correctly supported in the bracket or restrained by the strap.

3. Inspect the front and rear of the radiator core and tanks, all seams and the radiator drain valve for signs of seepage or leaks. See **Figure 5**.

4. Make sure all hose connections are tight and in good condition. See **Figure 6** (typical). Check the hoses carefully at their clamps for cuts or weakness. Overtightening strap-type clamps can cut the outer surface of a hose and weaken it.

5. Remove the radiator pressure cap. Check the rubber cap seal surfaces for tears or cracks (**Figure 7**). Check for a bent or distorted cap. Raise the vacuum valve and rubber seal and rinse the cap under warm tap water to flush away any loose rust or dirt particles.

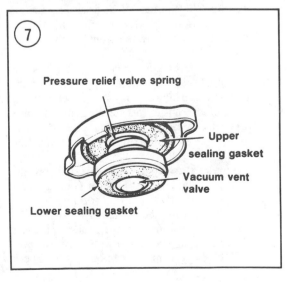

7

1. Inlet tank gasket
2. Core tubes
3. Outlet tank gasket
4. Drain valve
5. Oil cooler gaskets
6. Joint between tube and header

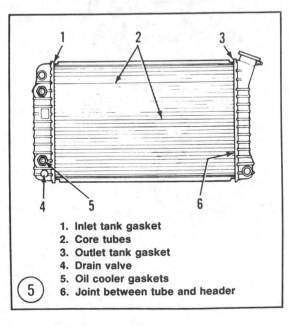

Pressure relief valve spring

Upper sealing gasket

Vacuum vent valve

Lower sealing gasket

6. Inspect the filler neck seat and sealing surface (**Figure 8**) for nicks, dents, distortion or contamination. Wipe the sealing surface with a clean cloth to remove any rust or dirt. Install the cap properly.

7. Start the engine and warm to normal operating temperature. Shut the engine off and carefully feel the radiator. Crossflow radiators should be hot along the left side and warm along the right side with an even temperature rise from right to left. Any cold spots indicate obstructed or clogged radiator sections.

8. Restart the engine and squeeze the upper radiator hose (**Figure 6**) to check water pump operation. If a pressure surge is felt, the water pump is functioning properly. If not, check for a plugged vent hole in the pump.

9. Visually check the area underneath the water pump for signs of leakage or corrosion. A defective water pump will usually leak through the vent hole at the bottom of the pump. The leakage will generally leave a white or greenish-white residue on the front of the block. If such residue is found, service the water pump at the first available opportunity.

10. Check the crankcase oil dipstick for signs of coolant in the engine oil. On automatic transmission models, check the coolant for signs of transmission fluid leaking from the oil cooler. Check the transmission lines which connect to the oil cooler.

11. If a cooling system suffers from overheating and none of the above steps point to the cause, perform the following diagnosis:

   a. Remove the water pump. Remove the rear cover of the pump and check internal passages with a penlight.

   b. Remove the thermostat as described in this chapter and check for restrictions in the crossover passage at the front of the intake manifold with a penlight.

   c. Remove the cylinder head(s) and check for restrictions in the coolant passages of the block with a penlight. All water jacket passages in the block can be inspected in this manner, so never assume the block is restricted unless you can visually determine that a restriction exists.

   d. If none of these steps locate a restriction, the cylinder head(s) is most likely at fault. Coolant passages in the head are very complex and are not as easily checked visually as those in the block or water pump. If the coolant passages in a cylinder head are blocked, they are most likely blocked in more than one place. Check the head(s) for a dark blue or black area, which results from overheating. If no discoloration is found, check the coolant passages visually with a penlight as best you can, then probe all accessible passages with a length of wire that is flexible enough to negotiate sharp turns. Since it may not be possible to satisfactorily inspect all of the coolant passages in this way, try to determine if any of the passages have rough or ragged internal surfaces. Even if no direct evidence of blockage can be found, a suspect cylinder head should be replaced and the new head checked in the same manner before installation.

COOLING SYSTEM LEAKAGE TEST

If the cooling system requires frequent topping up, it probably has a leak. Small cooling system leaks are not easy to locate; the hot coolant evaporates as fast as it leaks out, preventing the formation of tell-tale rusty or grayish-white stains. A pressure test of the cooling system will usually help to pinpoint the source of the leak. This test requires a reliable pressure tester and can be performed quickly and economically by your

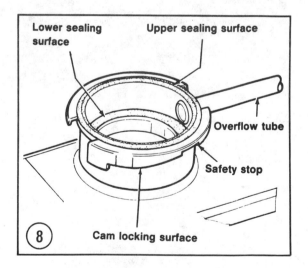

Lower sealing surface Upper sealing surface
Overflow tube
Safety stop
Cam locking surface
(8)

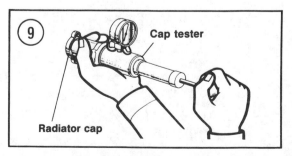

(9) Cap tester
Radiator cap

dealer or a radiator shop. The test should be performed if frequent additions of coolant are necessary to keep the cooling system topped up and your radiator is known to be in good condition.

1. Remove the radiator cap.

2. Dip the cap in water and attach a cooling system pressure tester, using the adapter supplied with the tester. See **Figure 9** (typical).

3. Pump the pressure to 15 psi. The cap relief valve should open at between 10.7-15 psi. If not, replace the cap.

4. Pump the pressure to 10 psi. If pressure drops rapidly below 8.5 psi, replace the cap.

5. Wipe the filler neck sealing surface on the radiator with a clean dry cloth. Make sure the coolant is within 1-1 1/2 in. of the cap seal seat in the filler neck.

6. Install the radiator cap and disconnect the overflow line at the filler neck nipple. See **Figure 10** (typical). Connect the pressure tester to the nipple and pump it up. If the radiator cap does not hold pressure at 8.5 psi and relieve it above 10.7 psi, the radiator cap seal is defective.

7. Remove the radiator cap and reconnect the overflow line. Connect the pressure tester to the

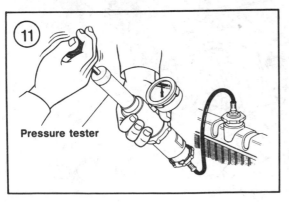

Pressure tester

filler neck (**Figure 11**). Pump the pressure to 12.8 psi. If it drops below 10 psi, check all system components for signs of leakage.

WARNING
Pressure builds up quickly in Step 8. Do not let it exceed 15 psi.

8. If the system will not hold at least 10 psi in Step 7 but no external leaks can be found, remove the tester but do not install the radiator cap. Start and run the engine until the upper radiator hose is hot. Reconnect the tester and pump the pressure to 12.8 psi.

   a. If the tester needle fluctuates, the head gasket is probably leaking.

   b. If the tester needle holds steady, rapidly open and close the throttle several times while an assistant checks for an abnormal amount of coolant or steam coming out of the tailpipe. This is caused by a defective head gasket or an engine block or cylinder head that is cracked.

   c. If the tester needle holds steady and the system does not emit coolant or steam in Step b, there may be an internal leak. Shut the engine off and remove the crankcase dipstick. Check the dipstick for signs of water mixed with the oil (milky-looking oil). If found, the engine must be removed and disassembled to locate and correct the leakage.

If the cooling system passes a pressure test but continues to lose coolant, check for an exhaust leak into the cooling system.

1. Drain the coolant until the level is just above the top of the cylinder head(s).

2. Disconnect the upper radiator hose and remove the thermostat and water pump drive belt.

CAUTION
Do not run the engine with the water pump belt disconnected for more than 30 seconds or the engine may overheat.

3. Add sufficient coolant to bring the level within 1/2 in. of the top of the thermostat housing.

4. Start the engine and open the throttle several times while observing the coolant. If the level rises noticeably or if bubbles appear in the coolant, exhaust gases are probably leaking into the cooling system. This probably means that the cylinder head gasket is defective.

5. Reinstall the thermostat and drive belt. Reconnect the upper radiator hose to the thermostat housing.

6. Add the coolant drained in Step 1 and adjust the drive belt tension.

COOLANT LEVEL CHECK

Always check coolant level with the engine and radiator cold. Coolant expands as it is heated and checking a hot or warm system will not give a true level reading.

Cooling systems equipped with a coolant recovery feature are checked at the reservoir instead of the radiator. Remove the reservoir cap. Add coolant as required to bring the level in the reservoir to a point midway between the "FULL" and "ADD" marks on the side of the reservoir. Install the reservoir cap.

COOLING SYSTEM FLUSHING

The recommended coolant is a 50/50 mixture of ethylene glycol antifreeze and water. GM recommends that only an antifreeze containing a silicate inhibitor and meeting GM specification 1825-M be used. GM Cooling System Fluid (part No. 1052753) and Prestone II are recommended coolants which meet this specification.

Recommended coolants are designed to prevent corrosion of aluminum components used in late-model engines and cooling systems. The use of antifreeze without the silicate inhibitor which does not meet GM specifications may cause a thermo-chemical reaction resulting in serious radiator and engine damage.

The radiator should be drained, flushed and refilled at the intervals specified in Chapter Three. After initial filling, the coolant level may drop by as much as one quart after engine operation due to the displacement of entrapped air.

CAUTION
Under no circumstances should a chemical flushing agent be used. Flush the cooling system with clear water only.

1. Coolant can stain concrete and harm plants. Park the vehicle over a gutter or similar area.
2. Move the heater temperature control on the instrument panel to its maximum heat position.
3. Loosen the radiator cap to its first detent and release the system pressure, then turn the cap to its second detent and remove it from the radiator.
4. Remove the cap from the coolant recovery tank.
5. Open the drain valve at the bottom of the radiator tank. See **Figure 5** (typical). Let the cooling system drain.
6. When the system has finished, open the engine drain tap(s). V6 engines have a drain tap on each side of the block. I4 engines have one drain tap at

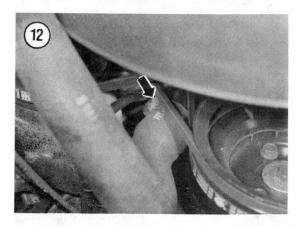

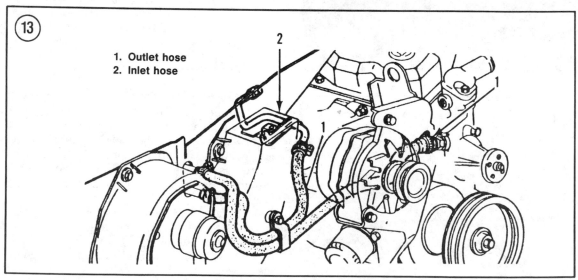

1. Outlet hose
2. Inlet hose

the left rear of the cylinder block. Let the engine block drain.

7. Loosen the clamp on the heater outlet hose at the water pump. Disconnect the hose and bend it down to aid in draining the heater.

8. Remove the thermostat as described in this chapter. Temporarily reinstall the thermostat housing.

9. Disconnect the top radiator hose from the radiator (**Figure 6**).

10. Disconnect the bottom hose from the water pump inlet (**Figure 12**).

11. Disconnect the heater inlet hose at the engine block. See **Figure 13** (I4) or **Figure 14** (V6) for hose location.

12. Connect a garden hose to the heater inlet hose. This does not have to be a positive fit, as long as most of the water enters the heater hose. Run water into the heater hose until clear water flows from the other heater hose.

13. If equipped with the optional rear heater, a water valve is installed in the heater inlet hose. Connect a hand vacuum pump to the vacuum fitting and apply 6-8 in. Hg vacuum to check valve operation. Make sure that it closes without water leakage. Disconnect the vacuum pump (the valve should open) and reconnect the vacuum line.

14. Insert the garden hose into the top radiator hose. Run water into the top hose until clear water flows from the bottom hose.

15. Insert the garden hose into the hose fitting at the bottom of the radiator. Run water into the radiator until clear water flows from the top fitting, then turn the water off.

16. Close the radiator drain valve and engine drain taps.

17. Disconnect the coolant recovery tank hose (**Figure 10**). Remove and drain the tank. See **Figure 3**. Flush the tank first with soapy water, then clean water. Drain and reinstall the tank. Connect the hose.

18. Reconnect all hoses to the water pump inlet, radiator and engine. Reinstall the thermostat.

19. Slowly pour 4 quarts of GM Cooling System Fluid or equivalent into the radiator.

20. Add sufficient water to bring the coolant level to the base of the filler neck. Do not install the radiator cap yet.

7

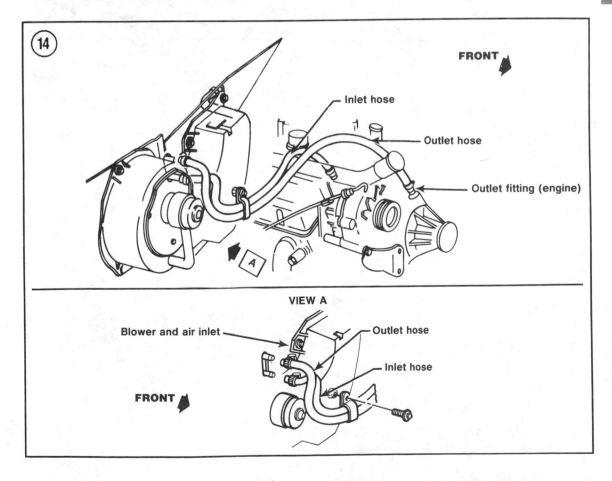

(14)

FRONT

Inlet hose

Outlet hose

Outlet fitting (engine)

A

VIEW A

Blower and air inlet

Outlet hose

Inlet hose

FRONT

21. Fill the coolant recovery tank to the FULL mark with coolant, then install the recovery tank cap.

22. Set the parking brake and block the drive wheels.

23. Place the transmission in NEUTRAL (manual) or PARK (automatic). Start the engine and run at a fast idle until the upper radiator hose is hot. Return the engine to normal idle.

24. Check the coolant level and add sufficient coolant to bring it back to the base of the filler neck. Install the radiator cap, aligning the cap arrow with the overflow tube.

25. After the vehicle has been driven, recheck the coolant level in the recovery tank when the radiator is cold. Top up as required with coolant to bring the level within specifications.

THERMOSTAT

Coolant flow to the radiator is blocked by the thermostat (**Figure 15**) when the engine is cold. As the engine warms up, the thermostat gradually opens, allowing coolant to circulate through the radiator. The thermostat heat range used depends upon model year and engine application. Check the thermostat when removed to determine its opening point; the heat range should be stamped on the thermostat flange. In most cases, it will be 195° F.

Removal and Testing

Refer to **Figure 16** (I4) or **Figure 17** (V6) for this procedure.

1. Make sure the engine is cool. Disconnect the negative battery cable.

2. Place a clean container under the radiator drain valve (**Figure 5**). Remove the radiator cap and open the drain valve. Drain sufficient coolant from the radiator to bring the coolant level below the thermostat housing. If the coolant is clean, save it for reuse.

3. Remove the air cleaner as described in Chapter Six, if necessary to provide working access to the thermostat housing.

4. Unclamp and disconnect the upper radiator hose at the thermostat housing. **Figure 18** shows the V6 housing; the I4 housing is similar.

5. Disconnect any electrical connectors at the thermostat housing.

NOTE
The thermostat housing on some installations may be obscured by vacuum or hydraulic lines. In such

cases, either work around or disconnect the lines as required in Step 6.

6. Remove the thermostat housing cover bolts. Lift the cover clear of the cylinder head (I4) or intake manifold (V6).

7. Remove the thermostat from the cylinder head (I4) or intake manifold (V6). Remove and discard the gasket.

8. Prepare a container of coolant mixed 1 part antifreeze to 3 parts water and suspend a thermometer in the container (**Figure 19**).

NOTE
Support the thermostat with wire so it does not touch the sides or bottom of the pan.

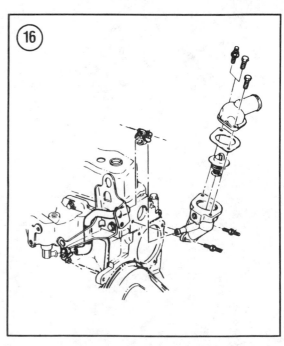

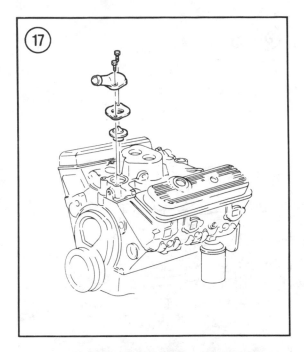

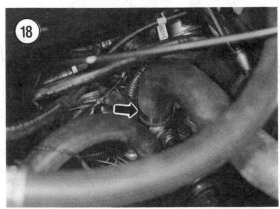

9. Heat the solution 25° F above the heat range stamped on the thermostat flange. Submerge the thermostat in the container of coolant and agitate the solution thoroughly. Replace the thermostat if the valve does not open fully.

10. Cool the solution 10° F below the temperature stamped on the thermostat flange. Replace the thermostat if the valve does not close completely.

11. Let the thermostat cool to room temperature. Hold it close to a light bulb and check for leakage. If light can be seen around the valve, the thermostat is defective.

Installation

Refer to **Figure 16** (I4) or **Figure 17** (V6) for this procedure.

1. If a new thermostat is being installed, test it as described in this chapter.

2. Stuff a clean shop cloth in the cylinder head (I4) or intake manifold (V6) to prevent gasket residue from entering the engine. Clean all gasket and RTV sealant residue from the mating surfaces with a putty knife.

3. Run a 1/8 in. bead of RTV sealant (part No. 1052289 or equivalent) in the thermostat housing sealing surface groove.

4. Install the thermostat in the cylinder head (I4) or intake manifold (V6). The copper element should face toward the engine and the thermostat flange must fit in the recess provided. See **Figure 20**.

5. Install the thermostat housing cover. Tighten the attaching bolts to specifications (**Table 1**).

6. Reinstall the upper radiator hose to the thermostat housing and tighten the clamp securely.

7. Reinstall the air cleaner, if removed.

8. Reconnect any vacuum lines, hydraulic lines or electrical connectors disconnected during removal.

9. Refill the cooling system to the specified level as described in this chapter.

10. Reconnect the negative battery cable.

11. Start the engine and check for leaks. Check coolant level and top up if required.

In-vehicle Testing

Thermostat operation can be tested without removing it from the engine. This procedure requires the use of 2 thermostat sticks available from GM dealers. A thermostat stick looks like a carpenter's pencil and is made of a chemically impregnated wax material which melts at a specific temperature.

This technique can be used to determine the thermostat's operation by marking the thermostat housing with 188 degree F stick (part No. J-24731-188) or 206 degree F stick (part No. J-24731-206), depending upon the problem. As the coolant reaches 188° F, the mark made by that stick will melt. The mark made by the 206° F stick will not melt until the coolant increases to that temperature.

Overheated engine

1. Carefully remove the radiator cap to relieve the cooling system pressure.
2. Rub the 206° F stick on the thermostat housing cover/water outlet.
3. Start the engine and run at a fast idle.
4. If no coolant flows through the upper radiator hose by the time the mark starts to melt, replace the thermostat.

Slow engine warmup

1. Carefully remove the radiator cap to relieve the cooling system pressure.
2. Rub the 188° F stick on the thermostat housing cover/water outlet.
3. Start the engine and run at a fast idle.
4. If coolant flows through the upper radiator hose before the mark starts to melt, replace the thermostat.

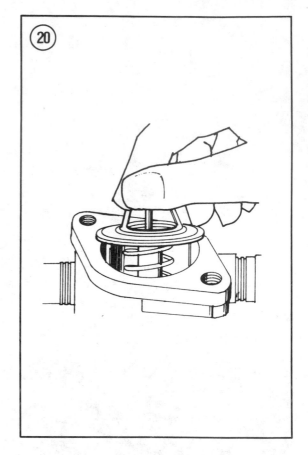

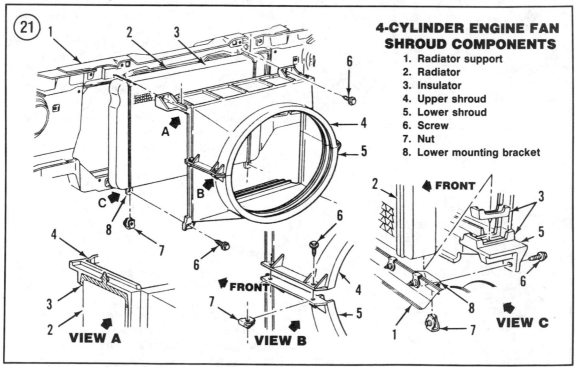

4-CYLINDER ENGINE FAN SHROUD COMPONENTS
1. Radiator support
2. Radiator
3. Insulator
4. Upper shroud
5. Lower shroud
6. Screw
7. Nut
8. Lower mounting bracket

RADIATOR

A vacuum brazed aluminum core radiator with nylon end tanks is used on all vehicles (instead of a copper/brass core radiator with metal header tanks). Work carefully when removing or installing hoses to a nylon end tank. If excessive pressure is applied, the fitting may crack or break. If this happens, the radiator must be removed and the end tank replaced.

Removal/Installation

Refer to **Figure 21** (I4) or **Figure 22** (V6) for this procedure.

1. Make sure that the engine is cool enough to touch comfortably.
2. Coolant can stain concrete and harm plants. Park the vehicle over a gutter or similar area. Place a clean container under the drain valve.
3. Remove the radiator cap and open the drain valve at the bottom of the radiator. See **Figure 5** (typical).
4. Disconnect and remove the brake master cylinder. See Chapter Twelve.
5. Disconnect the overflow tube at the radiator filler neck nipple (**Figure 10**).
6. Remove the screws holding the upper half of the fan shroud. Remove the lower fan shroud screws. Move shroud back and drape it over the fan.

7. Disconnect the upper hose at the radiator.
8. If equipped with an automatic transmission or engine oil cooler, disconnect the upper cooler line at the radiator fitting. Cap the fitting and line to prevent leakage.
9. On some models with limited access, it may be necessary to remove the fan retaining bolts and loosen the alternator adjusting and pivot bolts. If so, remove the fan, spacer, water pump pulley, drive belt and fan shroud (if so equipped).
10. Securely block both rear wheels so the vehicle will not roll in either direction.
11. Raise the front of the vehicle with a jack and place it on jackstands.
12. If equipped with an automatic transmission or engine oil cooler, disconnect the lower cooler line at the radiator fitting. Cap the fitting and line to prevent leakage.
13. Disconnect the lower hose at the radiator.
14. Remove any fasteners holding the radiator to its support assembly.
15. Tilt the radiator back as required, then lift it up and out of the lower mounting pads. Remove the radiator from the vehicle.
16. If the cooling fan was not removed, lift the shroud off the fan and remove it from the engine compartment.
17. Remove the lower radiator support pads and/or insulators (if used) and inspect for wear or damage. Replace as required.

7

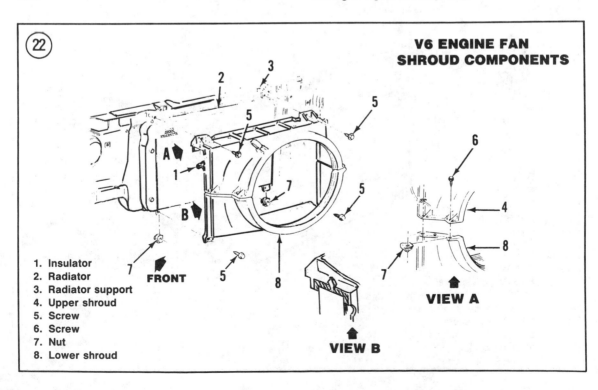

V6 ENGINE FAN SHROUD COMPONENTS

1. Insulator
2. Radiator
3. Radiator support
4. Upper shroud
5. Screw
6. Screw
7. Nut
8. Lower shroud

FRONT

VIEW A

VIEW B

18. Installation is the reverse of removal. Make sure the lower support pads and/or insulators (if used) are properly positioned and engage the radiator as it is lowered into place. Tighten all fasteners to specifications (**Table 1**). Reconnect the negative battery cable and pour all but one pint of the drained coolant into the radiator filler neck. Pour the remaining coolant into the coolant recovery tank. If the coolant is dirty or rusty, discard and install new coolant as described in *Cooling System Flushing* in this chapter.

End Tank Replacement

The aluminum tube radiator core is fitted with molded glass-filled nylon end tanks which incorporate radiator and fan shroud mounting brackets. Each end tank is attached to the core header by cinched metal tabs. A high-temperature rubber gasket between the tank and header acts as a seal. **Figure 23** shows the major components of the radiator assembly.

> *NOTE*
> *A small section of the header side may bend as the tabs are opened in the following procedure. A slight deformation of the header side is not harmful, as long as the tabs are opened just enough to permit tank removal.*

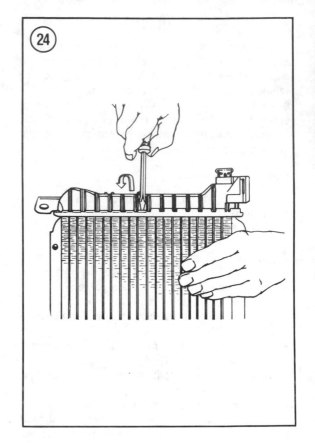

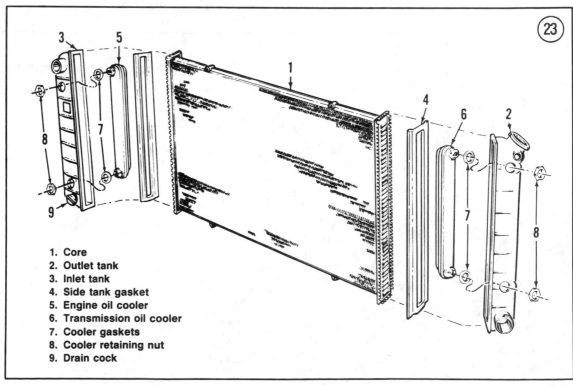

1. Core
2. Outlet tank
3. Inlet tank
4. Side tank gasket
5. Engine oil cooler
6. Transmission oil cooler
7. Cooler gaskets
8. Cooler retaining nut
9. Drain cock

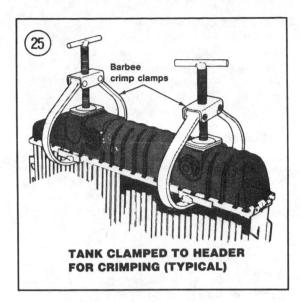

Barbee
crimp clamps

**TANK CLAMPED TO HEADER
FOR CRIMPING (TYPICAL)**

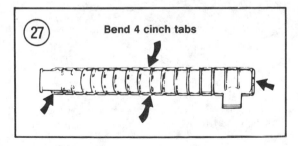

Bend 4 cinch tabs

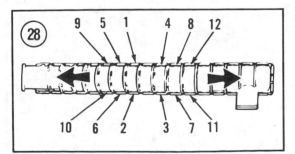

*Such deformation will generally return
to a normal position once the tabs are
recrimped when the tank is reinstalled.*

1. Remove the radiator as described in this chapter.

2. Insert a screwdriver tip between the tank and the end of the header tab, as shown in **Figure 24**. Carefully pry each tab away from the tank edge (except those under the inlet, outlet and/or filler neck) just enough for tank removal. Do not overbend the tabs or they may break off. If more than 3 tabs are broken on one side of the header or more than 2 adjacent tabs are broken, replace the core.

3. Carefully lift the tank enough to slide it out from underneath the remaining tabs that are still cinched. Remove the rubber gasket from the header and discard it. A new gasket must be installed whenever the tank and header are separated.

4. Clean the header and gasket groove to remove all contamination and gasket residue. Clean the sealing edge of the end tank.

5. Check the tank flange and header gasket surface for signs of leakage. Clean or repair the surfaces as required to remove any dirt, burrs or bumps.

6. If the outlet tank of an automatic transmission model is being replaced, transfer the oil cooler to the new tank as described in this chapter.

7. Dip a new tank gasket in coolant and install in the core header grooves. Make sure the gasket does not twist when the tank is reinstalled.

8. Fit the tank to the core header with the top and bottom of the new tank aligned with the other tank.

9. Install 2 Barbee No. 200 crimp clamps or equivalent on the header as shown in **Figure 25** and tighten just enough to compress the new gasket.

10. Using a pair of pliers as shown in **Figure 26**, crimp the 4 cinch tabs shown in **Figure 27** to secure the tank to the core header.

11. Clamp the remaining tabs using the same procedure as in Step 10 while following the sequence shown in **Figure 28**. Some tabs will be blocked by the clamps.

12. Remove the crimp clamps and squeeze the tabs that were behind the clamps down into place with the other tabs.

13. Leak test the radiator at 20 psi (138 kPa). Minor seal leaks can usually be corrected by recrimping the header tabs on both sides of the apparent leak.

7

Oil Cooler Replacement

1. Remove the radiator and separate the outlet tank from the core header as described in this chapter.

2. Remove the nuts and washers from the oil cooler inlet and outlet connections. Lift the oil cooler from the outlet tank.

3. If the cooler is damaged or defective, discard it. If the cooler is to be reused, remove and discard the neoprene gaskets from the inlet/outlet connections.

4. Installation is the reverse of removal. Install new gaskets on the cooler to be used. Start the cooler retaining nuts by hand, then apply water-resistant sealer to the exposed threads. Tighten the cooler nuts to 15 ft.-lb. (20 N•m); excessive torque can cut the cooler gaskets.

Drain Valve Replacement

1. Remove the radiator as described in this chapter.

2. Turn the drain valve until fully open and pull the stem and sea from the radiator tank and drain valve body. See **Figure 29**.

3. Squeeze the sides of the drain valve body together with pliers and remove from the inlet tank opening.

4. To reinstall, squeeze the sides of the drain valve body together with pliers and insert in the inlet tank opening until it locks in place.

5. Fit the stem into the body opening and push until the stem tabs engage with the drain valve body. Turn the drain valve stem until it is fully closed.

6. Reinstall the radiator as described in this chapter.

Radiator and Heater Hose Replacement

Hose life is rated by manufacturers at 2 years. It is a good idea to replace *all* cooling system hoses at this interval, even if they appear to be good. This

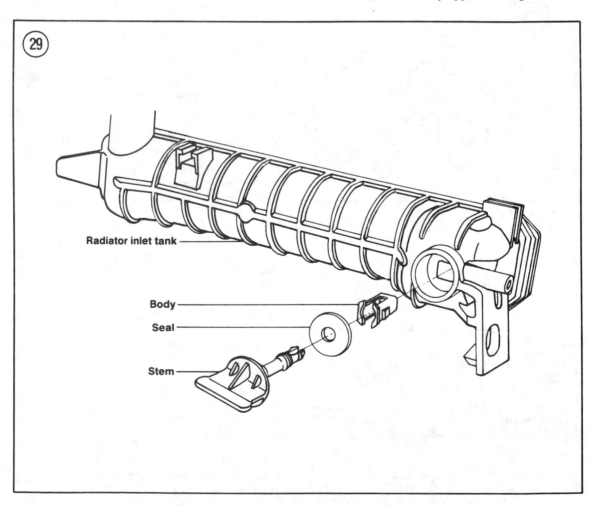

(29)

Radiator inlet tank

Body

Seal

Stem

will prevent an unnecessary and inconvenient roadside breakdown and possible engine damage resulting from a ruptured hose and subsequent overheating. If your vehicle is equipped with the optional rear overhead heater, do not overlook the short lengths of hose used to connect the rear heater unit piping to the engine compartment when servicing the heater hoses.

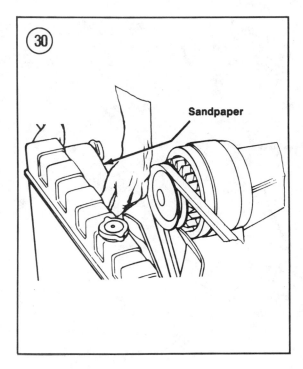

Sandpaper

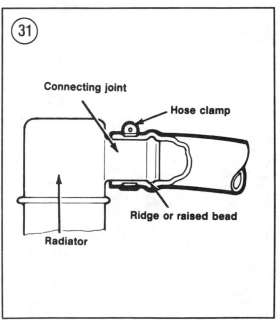

Connecting joint

Hose clamp

Ridge or raised bead

Radiator

Replace any hoses that are cracked, brittle, mildewed or very soft or spongy. If a hose is in doubtful condition, but not definitely bad, replace it to be on the safe side. Even though the hoses are easily accessible, this will avoid the inconvenience of a roadside repair.

Always replace a cooling system or radiator hose with the same type as removed. Plain or pleated rubber hoses do not have the same strength as reinforced molded hoses. Check the hose clamp condition and, if necessary, install new clamps with a new hose.

1. Place a clean container under the radiator drain valve (**Figure 5**). Remove the radiator cap and open the drain valve. Drain about one quart of coolant when replacing an upper hose. Completely drain the coolant to replace a lower hose. If the coolant is clean, save it for reuse.

2. Loosen the clamp at each end of the hose to be removed. Grasp the hose and twist it off the connection with a pulling motion.

3. If the hose is corroded to the fitting, cut it off with a sharp knife about one inch beyond the end of the fitting. Remove the clamp and slit the remaining piece of hose lengthwise, then peel it off the fitting.

4. Clean all corrosion from the fitting with sandpaper (**Figure 30**), then rinse the fitting to remove any particles.

5. Position the new clamps at least 1/4 in. from each end of the new hose. Wipe the inside diameter of the hose and the outside of the fitting with dishwashing liquid.

Install the hose end on the fitting with a twisting motion.

6. Position the clamps for easy access as shown in **Figure 31**. Tighten each clamp snugly with a screwdriver or nut driver. Recheck them for tightness after operating the vehicle for a few days.

7. Fill the radiator with the coolant removed in Step 1. Start the engine and operate it for a few minutes, checking for signs of leakage around the connection. Recheck the coolant level and top up, if necessary.

COOLING FAN

A fixed drive fan which mates directly to the water pump hub is used on I4 engines without air conditioning. See A, **Figure 32**. Vehicles equipped with air conditioning, a V6 engine or a heavy-duty cooling system use a fan drive clutch. See B or C, **Figure 32**.

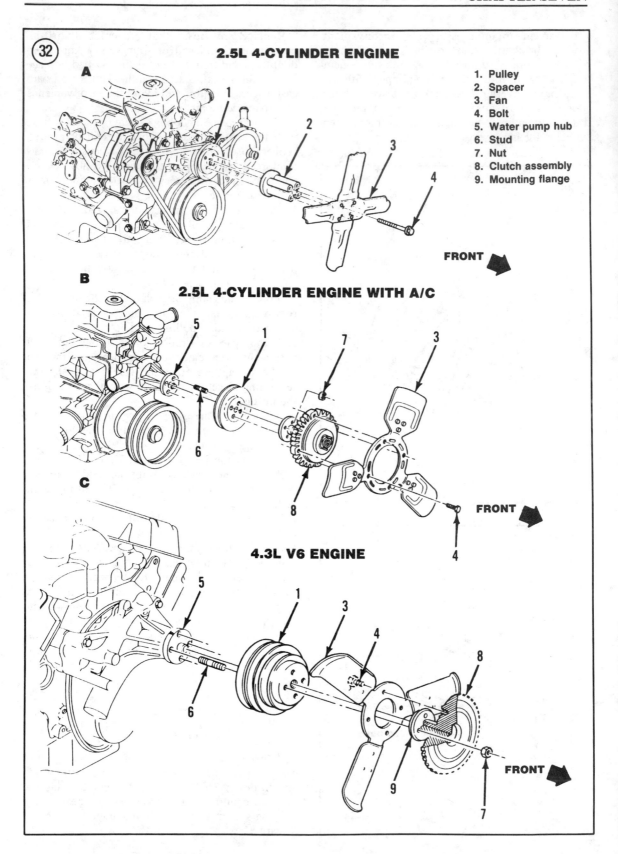

2.5L 4-CYLINDER ENGINE

A

1. Pulley
2. Spacer
3. Fan
4. Bolt
5. Water pump hub
6. Stud
7. Nut
8. Clutch assembly
9. Mounting flange

FRONT

2.5L 4-CYLINDER ENGINE WITH A/C

B

C

4.3L V6 ENGINE

FRONT

FRONT

The fan drive clutch incorporates a temperature-controlled fluid coupling that permits use of a powerful fan without great power loss or noise. In this design, the fan blade assembly is attached to a clutch housing or fluid coupling containing a silicone-base oil. A temperature-sensitive bi-metallic coil on the clutch opens and closes a valve inside the clutch to control fluid flow according to engine temperature. As the temperature rises, the flow of fluid causes a resistance between the drive and driven plate in the clutch, engaging the fan. This automatically controls fan speed to provide proper engine cooling under all conditions according to the temperature of the air passing through the radiator core.

Fan Clutch Diagnosis

A fan drive clutch may make noise whenever it is engaged for maximum cooling or during the initial few minutes of operation after sitting overnight when the silicone fluid in the assembly has settled and must be redistributed. In either case, the noise is normal and will cease after a few minutes. If an excessive noise persists under high speed engine operation, an internal failure has locked up the clutch assembly.

The fan drive clutch can fail due to fluid loss, control valve failure or bi-metallic coil malfunction. When overheating occurs with little or no coolant loss, try rotating the fan on a hot engine (engine OFF). There should be some resistance when the fan is rotated manually. If the fan rotates freely without drag more than 5 times, the clutch assembly has failed and should be replaced.

Removal/Installation

On some installations, the fan is more easily removed from underneath the vehicle. The following generalized procedures can be used with any fan installation. Before attempting the procedure, however, it is a good idea to follow it visually while looking at the engine compartment.

> *CAUTION*
> *When correctly installed, lateral movement of up to 1/4 in. measured at the fan tip is normal and results from the type of bearing used. Excessively loose, bent or damaged fans should not be reused, as any distortion will affect fan balance and operation. Damaged fans cannot be properly repaired and should be discarded.*

Rigid Fan Removal/Installation

Refer to A, **Figure 32** (typical) for this procedure.
1. Disconnect the negative battery cable.
2. Remove the radiator shroud and/or raise the front of the vehicle with a jack and place it on jackstands. If vehicle must be raised, be sure to block the rear wheels to prevent it from rolling in either direction.
3. Check the fan mounting system to see if the drive belt tension should be relieved. If so, loosen the alternator adjusting and pivot bolts to relieve the drive belt tension.
4. Remove the fan blade retaining fasteners from the water pump hub. Remove the fan blade and spacer.
5. Check the fan blade carefully for cracks, breaks, loose rivets or broken welds. Replace the fan if any defect is noted.
6. Installation is the reverse of removal. Tighten the fan blade fasteners to specifications (**Table 1**). Adjust the fan belt as described in this chapter, if necessary.

7

Fan Drive Clutch Removal/Installation

Refer to B, **Figure 32** (typical) for this procedure.
1. Disconnect the negative battery cable.
2. Remove the radiator shroud and/or raise the front of the vehicle with a jack and place it on jackstands. If vehicle must be raised, be sure to block the rear wheels to prevent it from rolling in either direction.
3. Check the fan mounting system to see if the drive belt tension should be relieved. If so, loosen the alternator adjusting and pivot bolts to relieve the drive belt tension.
4. Scribe balance marks on the fan clutch and water pump hub for proper alignment during installation.
5. Remove the attaching fasteners holding the fan clutch hub to the water pump hub. Remove the fan clutch assembly from the vehicle.
6. Remove the fasteners holding the fan to the drive coupling. Separate the fan and coupling.
7. Place clutch assembly on workbench in an upright position to prevent silicone from draining into the fan drive bearing. If clutch is not going to be reinstalled immediately, store in an upright position.
8. Check the fan blade carefully for cracks, breaks, loose rivets or broken welds. Replace the fan if any defect is noted.

9. Installation is the reverse of removal. Check fan drive clutch flange-to-water pump hub for proper mating. Align balance marks made in Step 4. Tighten attaching fasteners to specifications (**Table 1**). Adjust drive belts as described in this chapter.

WATER PUMP

A water pump may warn of impending failure by making noise. If the pump seal is defective, coolant may leak from behind the pump pulley. The water pump can be replaced on all models without discharging the air conditioning system. The pump is serviced as an assembly.

Removal/Installation
(I4 Engine)

1. Disconnect the negative battery cable.
2. Drain the cooling system as described in this chapter.
3. Loosen accessory units and remove the drive belts.
4. Remove the fan or fan clutch assembly as described in this chapter.
5. Disconnect the lower radiator hose and heater hose from the water pump.
6. If alternator adjusting brace is attached to one of the water pump mounting bolts, loosen the alternator adjusting bolt.
7. Remove the water pump mounting bolts (**Figure 33**). Remove the water pump and discard the gaskets.
8. Clean the water pump and engine block mounting surfaces to remove all gasket residue.
9. Installation is the reverse of removal. Coat new water pump gaskets with water-resistant sealer. Coat fastener threads with pipe sealant part No. 1052080 or equivalent and tighten to specifications (**Table 1**). Refill the cooling system as described in this chapter and check for leaks. Adjust the drive belts as described in this chapter.

Removal/Installation
(V6)

Refer to **Figure 33** for this procedure.
1. Disconnect the negative battery cable.
2. Drain the cooling system as described in this chapter.
3. Loosen all accessory units and remove their drive belts.
4. Remove the fan clutch assembly as described in this chapter.

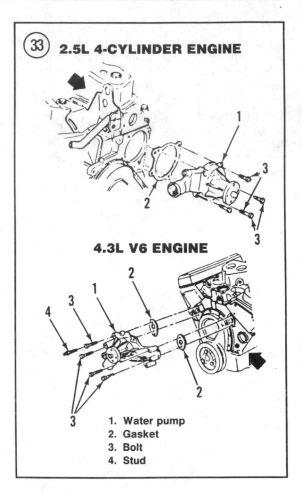

33 **2.5L 4-CYLINDER ENGINE**

4.3L V6 ENGINE

1. Water pump
2. Gasket
3. Bolt
4. Stud

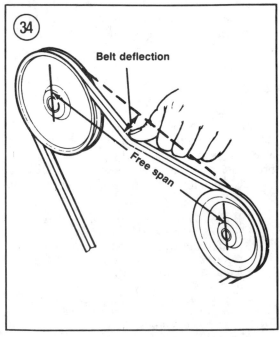

34

Belt deflection

Free span

5. Remove the bolts holding the lower alternator brace to the water pump. Pivot the brace downward and out of the way.

6. Remove the bolts holding the upper alternator brace to the water pump.

7. Disconnect the lower radiator hose and heater hose from the water pump.

8. Unbolt and remove the water pump. Discard the gasket.

9. Clean the water pump and engine block mounting surfaces to remove all gasket residue.

10. Installation is the reverse of removal. Install a new gasket. If a gasket is not available, run a 3 mm (1/8 in.) bead of RTV sealant (part No. 1052289 or equivalent) on the pump sealing surface. Coat fastener threads with pipe sealant part No. 1052080 or equivalent and tighten to specifications (**Table 1**). Refill the cooling system and check for leaks. Adjust drive belt tension as described in this chapter.

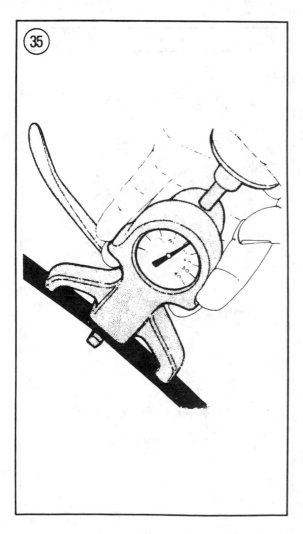

DRIVE BELTS

The water pump/fan drive belt, as well as the belts which drive the alternator and other accessory units, should be inspected at regular intervals (Chapter Three) to make sure they are in good condition and are properly tensioned.

Worn, frayed, cracked or glazed belts should be replaced immediately. The components to which they direct power are essential to the safe and reliable operation of the vehicle. If correct adjustment is maintained on all belts, they will usually all give the same service life. For this reason and because of the cost involved in replacing an inner belt (requiring the removal of all outer belts), it is a good idea to replace all belts as a set. The added expense is small compared to the cost of replacing the belts individually and eliminates the possibility of a breakdown on the road which could cost far more in time and money.

A V-belt should be correctly tensioned at all times. If loose, the belt will not permit the driven components to operate at maximum efficiency. The belt will also wear rapidly because of the increased friction caused by slipping. Belts that are too tight will be overstressed and prone to premature failure. An excessively tight belt will also overstress the accessory unit's bearings, resulting in their premature failure.

A single serpentine drive belt is used on 1987 models. A spring-loaded belt tensioner automatically maintains tension.

Tension Adjustment

The tension of standard drive belts can be checked according to belt deflection (**Figure 34**), but GM recommends the use of a belt tension gauge (**Figure 35**) (part No. J-23600 or equivalent) whenever possible as the most accurate means of setting belt tension. If access to the drive belt is limited, tension may be established by the deflection method. Drive belt specifications are provided in **Table 2**.

1A. To check tension by deflection, depress the belt at a point midway between the 2 pulleys (**Figure 34**). If the free span between the pulleys is less than 12 inches, the belt should deflect 1/8-1/4 in. when approximately 10 lb. pressure is applied. Drive belts with a greater span should deflect 1/8-3/8 in.

1B. To check belt tension with a tension gauge, install the gauge on the drive belt (**Figure 35**) and check tension according to the gauge manufacturer's instructions. Compare to the specifications in **Table 2**.

2. If adjustment is required, loosen the accessory pivot and adjustment bolts. See **Figure 36** (I4) or **Figure 37** (V6) for typical alternator installations.
3. Move the accessory unit toward or away from the engine as required until correct tension is obtained.

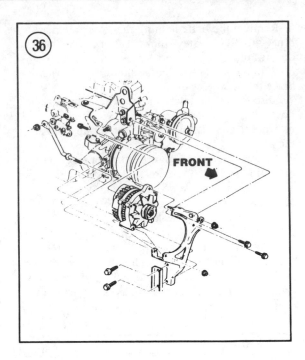

> *CAUTION*
> *Do not pry on the accessory unit to reposition it. Most adjustment brackets have a slot provided for use of a breaker bar as a pry tool. To move the accessory, insert a suitable breaker bar in the bracket slot and reposition the unit as required.*

4. Tighten the adjustment bolt, release pressure on the accessory unit, then tighten the pivot bolt.
5. Recheck belt tension. If necessary, repeat the procedure to obtain the correct tension.

Removal (Standard Drive Belt)

Vehicles equipped with power steering, air conditioning or an air pump may require removal of accessory drive belts before the fan drive belt can be removed. Depending upon the positioning of the accessory unit, some steps of this procedure may have to be performed from underneath the vehicle. With some installations, it may be more convenient to remove the fan assembly before proceeding. Refer to **Figure 38** (I4) or **Figure 39** (V6) as required for this procedure.
1. Determine which accessory belts must be removed and in what order.
2. Loosen the accessory pivot and adjustment bolts.
3. Move the accessory unit toward the engine until there is enough slack in the belt to permit its removal from the pulleys. Remove the belt from the pulleys and lift it over the fan.
4. If replacing an inner belt, repeat Step 2 and Step 3 as necessary to remove the required belt(s).
5. Install the new belt(s) over the fan and fit in the grooves of the appropriate pulleys.
6. Pry the accessory unit away from the engine until its belt appears to be properly tensioned.

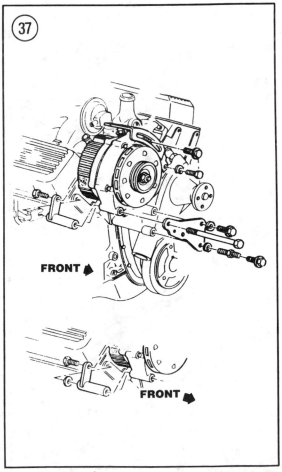

> *CAUTION*
> *Do not pry on the accessory unit to reposition it. Most adjustment brackets have a slot provided for use of a breaker bar as a pry tool. To move the accessory, insert a suitable breaker bar in the bracket slot and reposition the unit as required.*

7. Tighten the adjustment bolt, release pressure on the accessory unit, then tighten the pivot bolt.

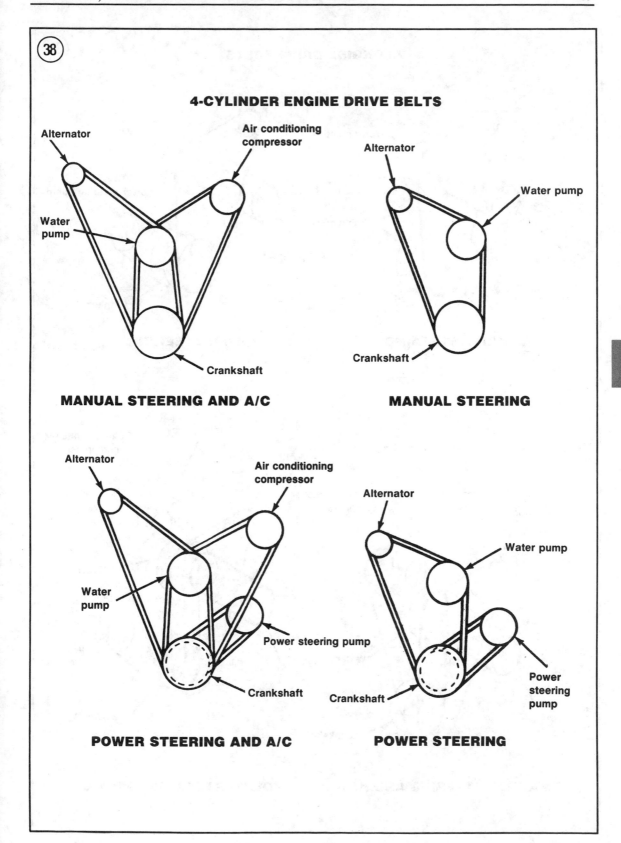

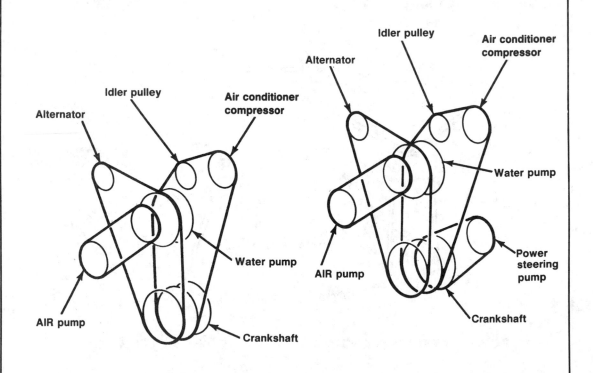

V6 ENGINE DRIVE BELTS

MANUAL STEERING

POWER STEERING

MANUAL STEERING AND A/C

POWER STEERING AND A/C

8. If outer belts were removed, repeat Step 6 and Step 7 to tension each remaining drive belt.

9. Recheck belt tension with the tension gauge. If necessary, repeat the procedure to obtain the correct tension.

Removal (Serpentine Belt)

Rotate the tensioner counterclockwise and slip the belt off the drive pulleys. Hold the tensioner in that position while slipping the new belt around the pulleys. When belt is installed, check tension with a gauge. If it is not 100-140 ft.-lb., make sure the dowel pin on the bracket engages the tensioner hole. If it does, replace the tensioner. If it does not, reposition the tensioner and recheck the belt tension. If it is still out of specifications, replace the tensioner.

HEATER SYSTEM

Front Heater

The base heater system consists of a blower air inlet and a heater/defroster assembly to provide heating, ventilation and windshield defogging. An optional heater system provides heating, power upper/lower ventilation, ram lower ventilation and windshield/side window defogging. All functions are controlled by the heater/defroster module, which is secured to the rear of the dash in the passenger compartment. Function operation is controlled by 2 (base) or 3 (optional) indexed snap-in cables connected between the instrument panel control assembly and the heater/modular ducting. Access to the blower motor and resistor block for testing and service is provided in the engine compartment. Mounting gaskets on all components prevent air, water and noise from entering the passenger compartment.

Rear Heater

An optional auxiliary rear heater functions independently of the front heater and is operated by a separate set of controls on the instrument panel. The heater core and blower assembly is installed on the rear floor panel near the rear wheelwell on the driver's side of the vehicle and protected by a heater cover (**Figure 40**).

7

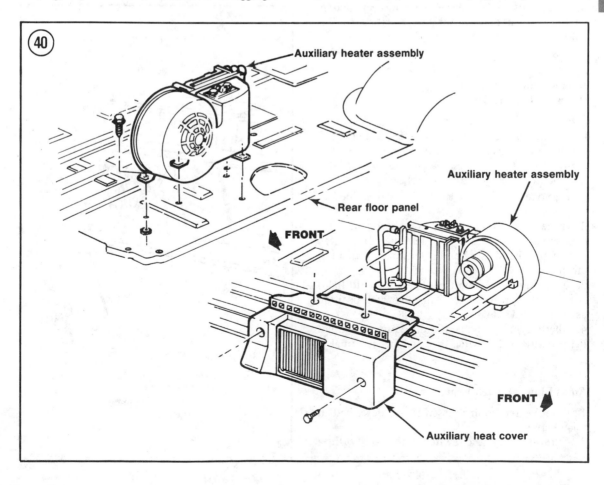

40
Auxiliary heater assembly
Auxiliary heater assembly
Rear floor panel
FRONT
FRONT
Auxiliary heat cover

The rear heater unit is connected into the front heater system by pipes which are teed into the heater inlet/outlet hoses in the engine compartment. A vacuum-operated water valve installed in the heater inlet hose shuts off coolant flow to the auxiliary heater core and eliminates any radiant heat during warm weather.

Troubleshooting
(Front or Rear Heater)

1. If the heater does not produce heat, make sure the engine will warm up in a reasonable amount of time. If the thermostat sticks in the open position, the engine will not completely warm up. Since hot engine coolant provides heat for the heater, a defective thermostat may be the problem.
2. If equipped with the optional auxiliary rear heater, make sure the vacuum-operated water valve functions properly. See Step 13, *Cooling System Flushing,* in this chapter.
3. If the heater blower does not work, check the fuse in the H-AC cavity of the fuse panel.
4. If the fuse is good, test the blower switch, resistor block and motor as described in this chapter.

Blower Motor Switch Testing
(Front or Rear Heater)

Power to the blower motor is provided through the ignition switch and a 25-amp fuse in the H-AC cavity of the fuse panel. Blower motor speed is controlled in all modes by the switch on the instrument panel control assembly.

1. Remove the control assembly as described in this chapter.
2. If the problem is in the blower speed, check for continuity between the B+ terminal of the fan switch and the M1, M2 and H terminals with a test lamp.
3. There should be continuity (lamp should light) between the terminals according to switch position as shown in **Table 3**.
4. There should be no continuity (lamp should not light) between the switch case and any terminal.

Front Blower Switch Replacement

1. Remove the control assembly as described in this chapter.
2. Carefully pry the switch knob off with a screwdriver.

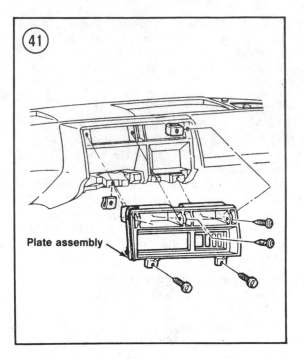

Plate assembly

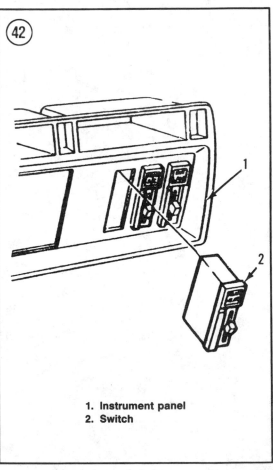

1. **Instrument panel**
2. **Switch**

3. Remove the fasteners holding the switch to the control assembly.

4. Align the pin on the new switch with the hole in the mounting bracket and install the fasteners securely.

5. Push the knob on the switch shaft as far as it will go. Reinstall the control assembly.

Rear Blower Switch Replacement

1. Disconnect the negative battery cable.

2. Remove the accessory trim plate from the instrument panel. See **Figure 41**.

3. Reach behind the instrument panel and unplug the electrical connector at the switch.

4. Carefully pry or pop the press-fit switch from the instrument panel. See **Figure 42**.

5. Installation is the reverse of removal.

Resistor Block Test

The front heater resistor block is mounted on the heater housing in the engine compartment. See **Figure 43** (typical). The rear heater resistor block is mounted on the auxiliary heater assembly (**Figure 44**) inside the vehicle.

1A. Front heater—Unplug the resistor block electrical connector.

1B. Rear heater—Remove the auxiliary heater cover (**Figure 40**) and unplug the resistor block electrical connector.

2. Remove the resistor block retaining screws. Remove the resistor block.

3. Test the resistors for an open circuit with a self-powered test lamp. Replace resistor block if an open circuit is found.

4. Reinstall the resistor block and reconnect the electrical connector. On rear heater installations, reinstall the cover.

7

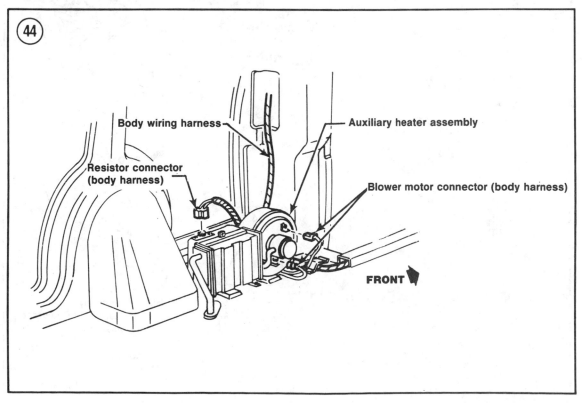

Control Assembly
Removal/Installation

Refer to **Figure 45** (typical) for this procedure.
1. Disconnect the negative battery cable.
2. Remove the lower trim plate from the steering column.
3. Remove the 5 screws holding the instrument cluster trim plate. Let the trim plate hang by its wiring at the left side of the cluster.
4. Remove the control assembly attaching screws. Pull the assembly out far enough to unplug the electrical and vacuum connectors and disconnect the cables. See **Figure 45** and **Figure 46**.
5. Remove the control assembly from the instrument panel.
6. Installation is the reverse of removal.

Control Cables

The control cables connect to the control assembly and heater crank arms by snap-on retaining tabs. See **Figure 47** (typical).

Cable Adjustment

The temperature cable has a slider-type self-adjustment feature. As the temperature lever is moved through its full range of travel, the cable clip assumes a position to seat the temperature valve in both extreme positions. The vent/defrost cable requires no adjustment.

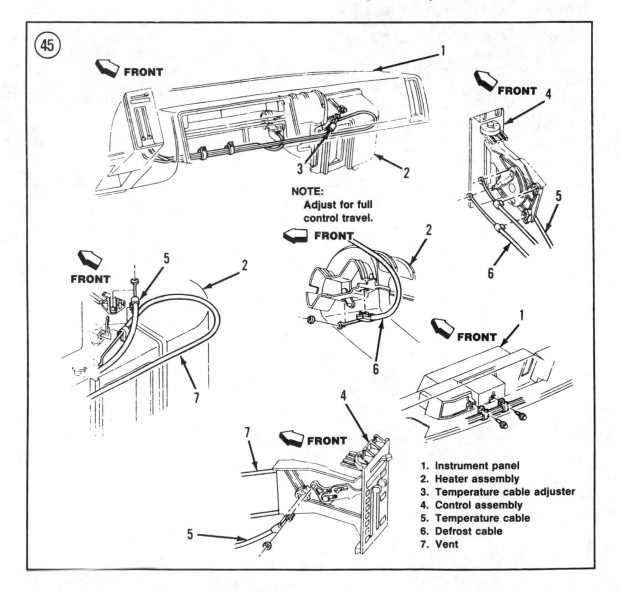

NOTE:
Adjust for full control travel.

1. Instrument panel
2. Heater assembly
3. Temperature cable adjuster
4. Control assembly
5. Temperature cable
6. Defrost cable
7. Vent

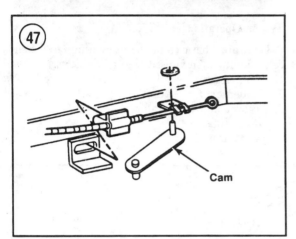

Cam

Front Blower Motor Assembly
Removal/Installation

Refer to **Figure 48** (typical) for this procedure.
1. Disconnect the negative battery cable.
2. Unplug the wiring connectors at the blower motor (**Figure 49**) and resistor block (**Figure 43**).
3. Disconnect the ground strap.
4. Remove the coolant recovery tank. See **Figure 3**.
5. Unbolt and reposition the windshield washer reservoir.
6. Remove the blower motor housing attaching fasteners. If necessary, pry gently on the flange, then remove the blower motor assembly from the engine compartment dash panel.

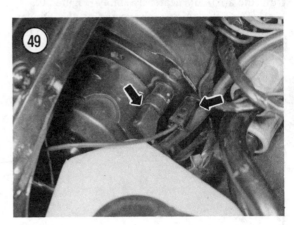

7

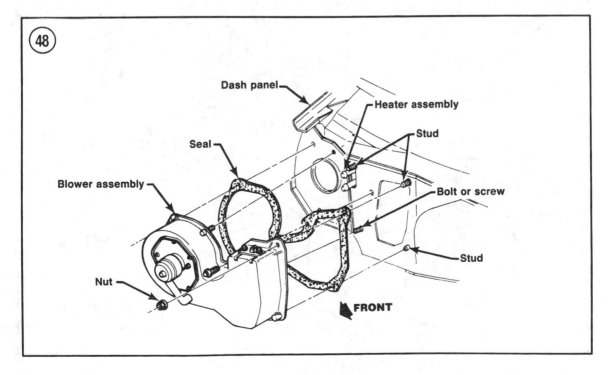

Dash panel

Heater assembly

Stud

Seal

Blower assembly

Bolt or screw

Stud

Nut

FRONT

7. To remove the blower motor from the assembly, hold the blower motor cage and remove the nut holding the cage to the motor shaft. Remove the cage, then unbolt and remove the blower motor from the assembly.

8. Installation is the reverse of removal. Check the condition of the seal between the blower motor assembly and dash panel. Replace seal as required.

Rear Blower Motor Assembly
Removal/Installation

Refer to **Figure 50** and **Figure 44** for this procedure.

1. Disconnect the negative battery cable.

2. Unbolt and remove the auxiliary heater cover from the auxiliary heater assembly (**Figure 50**).

3. Unplug the wiring connector at the blower motor (the resistor wiring connector plugs into the heater core, which does not have to be removed for blower removal). See **Figure 44**.

4. Remove the blower motor attaching fasteners. If necessary, pry gently on the flange, then remove the blower motor from the blower motor assembly. See **Figure 51**.

5. To remove the cage from the blower motor, hold the blower motor cage and remove the nut holding the cage to the motor shaft. Remove the cage from the blower motor.

6. Installation is the reverse of removal.

AIR CONDITIONING

This section covers the maintenance and minor repairs that can prevent or correct common air conditioning problems. Major repairs require special training and equipment and should be left to a dealer or air conditioning expert.

System Operation

There are 5 basic components common to the air conditioning system used with all vehicles.

1. Compressor.
2. Condenser.
3. Accumulator/dehydrator.
4. Orifice tube.
5. Evaporator.

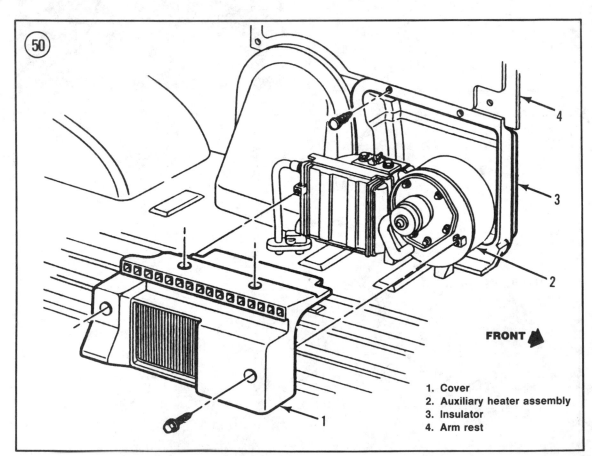

1. Cover
2. Auxiliary heater assembly
3. Insulator
4. Arm rest

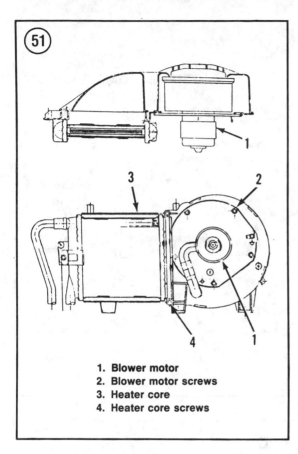

1. Blower motor
2. Blower motor screws
3. Heater core
4. Heater core screws

For practical purposes, the cycle begins at the compressor. See **Figure 52**. The refrigerant enters the low-pressure side of the compressor in a warm low-pressure vapor state. It is compressed to a high-pressure hot vapor and pumped out of the high-pressure side to the condenser.

Air flow through the condenser removes heat from the refrigerant and transfers the heat to the outside air. As the heat is removed, the refrigerant condenses to a warm high-pressure liquid.

The refrigerant then flows through the plastic expansion tube, which includes a mesh screen and orifice to the evaporator. As the refrigerant leaves the expansion tube, it changes from a warm high-pressure liquid to a cold, low-pressure liquid. In the evaporator, the refrigerant removes heat from the passenger compartment air that is blown across the evaporator's fins and tubes. This changes the refrigerant from a cold, low-pressure liquid back to a warm, low-pressure vapor. The vapor passes into the accumulator/dehydrator, where moisture is removed and impurities are filtered out. The refrigerant is stored in the accumulator/dehydrator until it is needed. From the accumulator/dehydrator, the refrigerant then returns to the compressor as a warm low-pressure vapor with a small amount of low-pressure liquid that did not boil off completely and the cycle begins again.

7

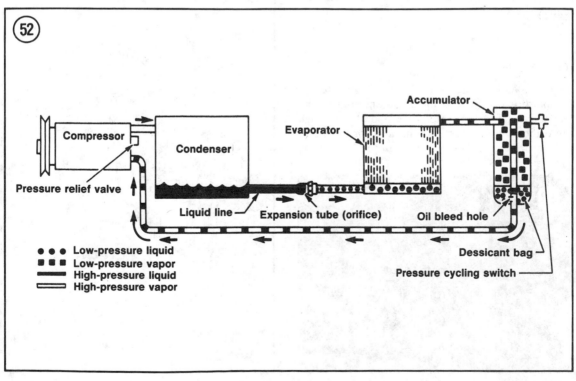

Low-pressure liquid
Low-pressure vapor
High-pressure liquid
High-pressure vapor

Compressor

The compressor is located on the drive belt end of the engine, like the alternator, and is driven by a V-belt. The large pulley on the front of the compressor contains an electromagnetic clutch (**Figure 53**). This activates and operates the compressor when the air conditioning is switched on. A pressure relief valve opens to discharge refrigerant if operating pressure exceeds 440 psi (3036 kPa).

Condenser

The condenser is mounted in front of the radiator. Air passing through the condenser tubes and fins removes heat from the refrigerant in the same manner it removes heat from the engine coolant as it passes through the radiator. The cooling fan also pulls air through the condenser.

Accumulator/dehydrator

The accumulator/dehydrator is a small tank-like unit, usually mounted near one of the wheel wells. It functions as a storage container for refrigerant. The bottom of the accumulator/dehydrator contains desiccant, which dries any moisture that enters the system.

Orifice Tube

The plastic orifice tube is located inside the evaporator inlet pipe at the liquid line connection. It meters refrigerant into the evaporator through an orifice. Filter screens are installed on each side of the orifice tube to prevent the tube from being

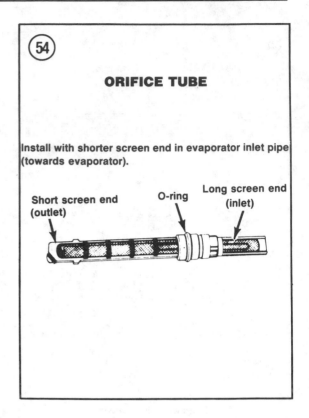

ORIFICE TUBE

Install with shorter screen end in evaporator inlet pipe (towards evaporator).

Short screen end (outlet)   O-ring   Long screen end (inlet)

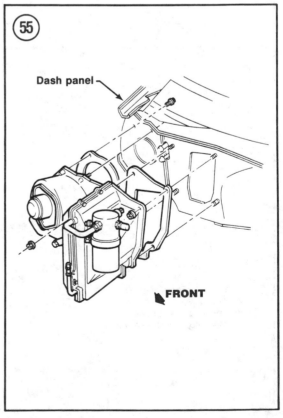

Dash panel

FRONT

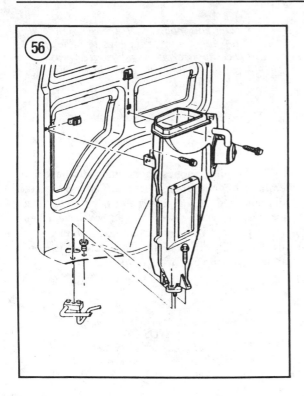

plugged by contamination (**Figure 54**). The tube can be removed and the filters cleaned, but the tube is serviced only by replacement.

Evaporator

The evaporator for the front air conditioning unit is mounted inside the heater case assembly in the engine compartment cooling unit attached to the dash panel (**Figure 55**).

The evaporator for the optional rear overhead air conditioning unit is installed in the blower motor assembly at the rear of the wheelwell on the driver's side of the vehicle (**Figure 56**).

Warm air is blown across the evaporator fins and tubes, where it is cooled and dried, then ducted into the passenger compartment.

Vacuum Tank

The air conditioning system incorporates a vacuum supply tank (**Figure 57**) to store vacuum for use whenever manifold vacuum decreases, as

7

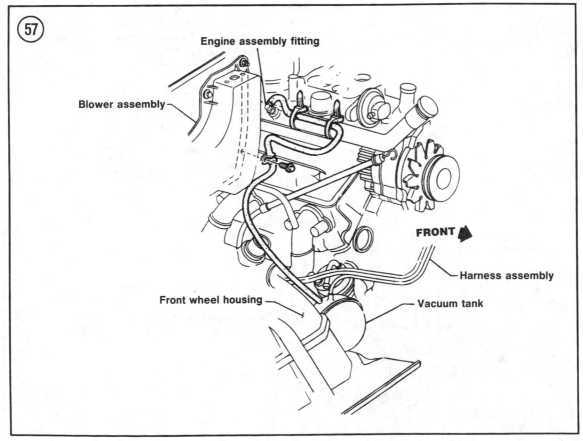

Engine assembly fitting

Blower assembly

FRONT

Harness assembly

Front wheel housing

Vacuum tank

during heavy acceleration. This assures a steady supply of vacuum for continuous use, regardless of engine operating condition.

Pressure Sensing Switch

This switch, located at the accumulator/dehydrator, cycles on and off to prevent an evaporator freeze-up. Cycling of the compressor will cause occasional slight changes in engine speed and power under certain operating conditions; this should be considered normal.

REFRIGERANT

The air conditioning system uses a refrigerant called dichlorodifluoromethane, or R-12.

WARNING
Refrigerant creates freezing temperatures when it evaporates. This can cause frostbite if it touches the skin, and blindness if it touches the eyes. If discharged near an open flame, R-12

creates poisonous gas. If the refrigerant can is hooked up to the pressure side of the compressor, it may explode. Always wear safety goggles and gloves when working with R-12.

Charging

This section applies to partially discharged or empty air conditioning systems. If a hose has been disconnected or any internal part of the system exposed to air, the system should be evacuated and recharged by a dealer or air conditioning shop. Recharge kits are available from auto parts stores. Refer to **Figure 58** for this procedure.

NOTE
The following procedure is for use with manifold gauge set part No. J-23575 and adapter part No. J-5420. If a

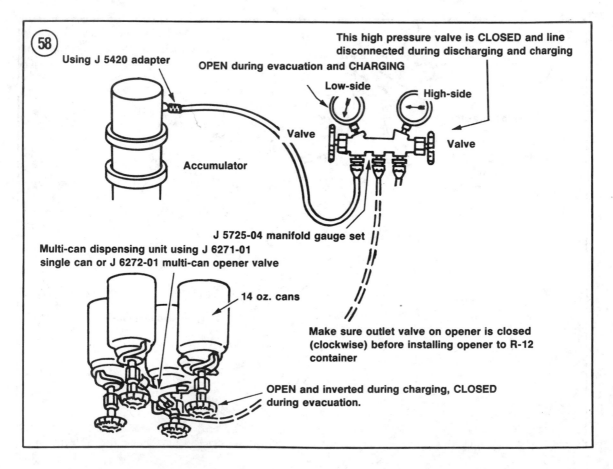

different gauge set is used, follow the instructions provided by the manufacturer.

1. Carefully read and understand the gauge manufacturer's instructions before charging the system.

2. Connect the low-pressure gauge of manifold gauge set J-5725-04 to the accumulator fitting.

3. Connect the center gauge set hose to the R-12 can.

4. Make sure the high-pressure gauge valve is closed.

5. Start the engine and run at normal idle.

6. Turn the air conditioning control lever OFF.

7. Open the R-12 source valve. Let one 14-ounce can of R-12 flow into the system through the accumulator fitting.

8. As soon as the can is empty, engage the compressor by returning the A/C control lever to NORM and turning the blower on HI. This will draw the remaining R-12 charge into the system.

9. Shut the R-12 source valve OFF. Run the engine for 30 seconds to clear the lines and gauges.

WARNING
Never remove a gauge line from its adapter with the line connected to the air conditioning system. Disconnect the line at the service fitting. Removing the charging hose at the gauge set while still connected to the accumulator can cause serious personal injury.

10. Remove the hose adapter at the accumulator quickly to prevent excessive R-12 loss. Install the protective cap on the accumulator fitting.

11. Check the system for leaks. Shut the engine off.

Routine Maintenance

Basic maintenance of the air conditioning system is easy. At least once a month, even in cold weather, start your engine, turn on the air conditioner and operate it at each of the control settings. Operate the air conditioner for about 10 minutes, with the engine running at about 1,500 rpm. This will ensure that the compressor seal does not deform from sitting in the same position for a long period of time. If deformation occurs, the seal is likely to leak.

The efficiency of the air conditioning system also depends in great part on the efficiency of the cooling system. If the cooling system is dirty or low on coolant, it may be impossible to operate the air conditioner without the engine overheating.

Inspect the coolant. If necessary, flush and refill the cooling system as described in this chapter.

NOTE
Do not install a bug screen on vehicles with air conditioning. The screen reduces air flow and thus affects air conditioner efficiency. During hot weather, a bug screen can cause the engine to overheat.

Use an air hose and a soft brush to clean the radiator and condenser fins and tubes. Remove any bugs, leaves or other embedded debris.

Check drive belt tension as described in this chapter.

If the condition of the cooling system thermostat is in doubt, test it as described in this chapter.

Once you are sure the cooling system is in good condition, the air conditioning system can be inspected.

Inspection

1. Clean all lines, fittings and system components with solvent and a clean rag. Pay particular attention to the fittings; oily dirt around connections almost certainly indicates a leak. Oil from the compressor will migrate through the system to the leak. Carefully tighten threaded connections, but do not overtighten and strip the threads. If the leak persists, it will soon be apparent as oily dirt will continue to accumulate.

2. Clean the condenser fins and tubes with a soft brush and an air hose or with a high-pressure stream of water from a garden hose. Remove any bugs, leaves or other embedded debris. Carefully straighten any bent fins with a screwdriver, taking care not to puncture or dent the tubes.

3. Start the engine and check the operation of the blower motor and the compressor clutch by turning the controls on and off. If either the blower or clutch fails to operate, shut off the engine and check the air conditioner fuse. See *Fuses and Fusible Links,* Chapter Eight. If it is blown, replace it. If not, remove and clean the fuse holder contacts. Then check the clutch and blower operation again. If they still will not operate, take the vehicle to a dealer or air conditioning specialist.

Troubleshooting

If the air conditioner fails to blow cold air, the following steps can help locate the problem.

1. First, stop the vehicle and look at the control settings. One of the most common air conditioning problems occurs when the temperature is set for maximum cold and the blower is set on LOW. This promotes ice buildup on the evaporator fins and tubes, particularly in humid weather. Eventually, the evaporator may have iced over. Turn the blower on HI and place a hand over an air outlet. If the blower is running but there is little or no air flowing through the outlet, the evaporator will ice over completely and restrict air flow. Leave the blower on HI and turn the temperature control off or to its warmest setting and wait. It will take 10-15 minutes for the ice to start melting.

2. If the blower is not running, the fuse may be blown, there may be a loose wiring connection or the blower motor may be burned out. First, check the fuse block for a blown or incorrectly seated fuse, then check the wiring for loose connections.

3. If the blower runs but not on high speed, check for a blown fusible link in the electrical wiring between the junction terminal and air conditioner relay.

4. Shut off the engine and inspect the compressor drive belt. If worn or loose, replace or tighten as required. See *Drive Belts* in this chapter.

5. Start the engine. Check the compressor clutch by turning the air conditioner on and off. If the clutch does not activate, its fuse may be blown or the evaporator temperature-limiting switches may be defective. If the fuse is defective, replace it. If the fuse is not the problem, have the system checked by a dealer or an air conditioning specialist.

6. If the system appears to be operating as it should, but air flow into the passenger compartment is not cold, check the condenser for debris that could block air flow. Recheck the cooling system as described in this chapter. If the preceding steps have not solved the problem, take the vehicle to a dealer or air conditioning shop for service.

Table 1 TIGHTENING TORQUES

Fastener	ft.-lb.	N·m
Alternator		
I4		
Top bolt	20	27
Lower bolt	37	50
V6		
Top bolt	18.4	25
Lower bolt	35	47
Back brace nut	30	42
Coolant reservoir fastener		
Upper	6.3	8.5
Lower	4.4	6.0
Cooling fan		
I4 w/o A/C	20	27
I4 with A/C		
Nuts	18.4	25
Studs	9.2	12.5
Bolts	7.3	10
V6		
Nuts	20	27
Studs	6	8
Bolts	20	27
Fan shroud screws	18	25
Radiator		
Attaching fasteners	18	25
Oil cooler nuts	15	20
Thermostat housing bolts	21	28
Water pump		
I4	17	23
V6	22	30

Table 2 STANDARD DRIVE BELT TENSION

Belt	Tension (in lbs.) New	Used*
I4		
Air conditioning	169	90
Power steering	146	67
V6		
Alternator	135	67
Air conditioning	169	90
AIR pump	146	67
Power steering	146	67

A belt is considered used after one complete revolution on the engine pulleys.

Table 3 BLOWER MOTOR CONTINUITY

Switch position	Terminals
Off	No continuity
M1	B + to M1
M2	B + to M2
HI	B + to H

7

CHAPTER EIGHT

ELECTRICAL SYSTEM

All vehicles covered in this manual are equipped with a 12- volt, negative-ground electrical system. Many electrical problems can be traced to a simple cause such as a blown fuse, a loose or corroded connection, a loose alternator drive belt or a frayed wire. While these are easily corrected problems which may not appear important, they can quickly lead to serious difficulty if allowed to go uncorrected.

Complete overhaul of electrical components such as the alternator, distributor or starter motor is neither practical nor economical. In many cases, the necessary bushings, bearings or other worn parts are not available for individual replacement. If tests indicate a unit with problems other than those discussed in this chapter, replace it with a new or rebuilt unit. Make certain, however, that the new or rebuilt part to be installed is an exact replacement for the defective one removed. Also make sure to isolate and correct the cause of the failure before installing a replacement. For example, an uncorrected short in an alternator circuit will most likely burn out a new alternator as quickly as it damaged the old one. If in doubt, always consult an expert.

This chapter provides service procedures for the battery, charging system, starter, ignition system, lights, switches, turn indicators, horn, windshield wipers and washers, fuses and fusible links.

BATTERY

The battery is the single most important component in the automotive electrical system. It is also the one most frequently neglected. In addition to checking and correcting the battery electrolyte level in unsealed batteries on a weekly basis (Chapter Three), the battery should be cleaned and inspected at periodic intervals.

New vehicles are equipped with a sealed Delco Freedom II battery (side terminal type) which requires no maintenance. See **Figure 1**. A test indicator (built-in hydrometer) is installed in one cell. It provides visual information of battery condition for testing only and should not be used to determine whether the battery is properly charged or discharged, good or bad.

When a standard vent cap battery is used as a replacement, it should be checked periodically for electrolyte level, state of charge and corrosion. During hot weather periods, frequent checks are recommended. If the electrolyte level is below the bottom of the vent well in one or more cells, add distilled water as required. To assure proper mixing of the water and acid, operate the engine immediately after adding water. *Never* add battery acid instead of water—this will shorten the battery's life.

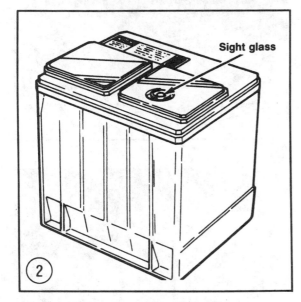

Delco Freedom II and other maintenance-free batteries do not permit or require the addition of water. The battery case is completely sealed except for small vent holes in the top. The vent holes are provided to allow battery gases to escape. This type of battery should be kept in an upright position, as tipping the case more than 45° in any direction may allow electrolyte to escape through the vent holes.

Using the Test Indicator

This procedure applies to the test indicator on original equipment batteries. Other brands may differ.

Make sure the battery is level and the test indicator sight glass (**Figure 2**) is clean. If necessary, wipe the sight glass with a paper towel moistened with water. A penlight is often useful under dim lighting conditions to determine the indicator color. Look down into the sight glass and refer to **Figure 3**. If the dot appears green in color, the battery has a sufficient charge for testing. If it appears dark or black, charge the battery before testing. A clear or light yellow appearance indicates that the battery should be replaced and the charging system checked. Do not charge, test or jump start the battery when the sight glass appears light yellow in color.

Care and Inspection

1. Disconnect both battery cables (negative first, then positive) and remove the battery hold-down or retainer clamp (**Figure 4**).

8

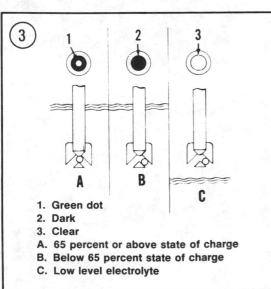

1. Green dot
2. Dark
3. Clear
A. 65 percent or above state of charge
B. Below 65 percent state of charge
C. Low level electrolyte

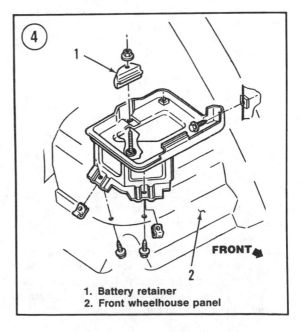

1. Battery retainer
2. Front wheelhouse panel

2. Attach a battery carrier or carrier strap and lift the battery from the engine compartment.

3. Check the entire battery case for cracks or other damage.

4. If the battery has removable vent caps, cover the vent holes in each cap with small pieces of masking tape.

> *NOTE*
> *Keep cleaning solution out of the battery cells in Step 5 or the electrolyte will be seriously weakened.*

5. Scrub the top of the battery with a stiff bristle brush, using a baking soda and water solution (**Figure 5**). Rinse the battery case with clear water and wipe dry with a clean cloth or paper towels. Remove the masking tape from the filler cap vent holes, if so equipped.

6. Inspect the battery tray in the engine compartment for corrosion. Remove and clean if necessary with the baking soda and water solution. See **Figure 4**. Rinse with clear water and wipe dry, then reinstall.

7. Clean the battery cable clamps with a stiff wire brush or one of the many tools made for this purpose (**Figure 6**). The same tool is used for cleaning the threaded battery posts (**Figure 7**).

8. Reposition the battery on the battery tray and remove the carrier or strap. Engage the hold-down block lip in the slot on the battery case and tighten the bolt enough to hold the battery from moving; overtightening it can crack the battery case.

9. Reinstall the positive battery cable, then the negative battery cable. Some models use a ground connection at the air conditioning bracket (**Figure 8**). If so equipped, be sure the connection is clean and tight.

> *CAUTION*
> *Be sure the battery cables are connected to their proper terminals. Connecting the battery backwards will reverse the polarity and can damage the alternator.*

10. Tighten the battery cable connections to 9 ft.-lb. (12 Nm). Tightening the connections more than this can cause damage to the battery case. Coat the connections with a petroleum jelly such as Vaseline or a light mineral grease.

11. If the battery has removable filler caps, check the electrolyte level. The electrolyte should cover the battery plates by at least 1/4 in. (6 mm). See **Figure 9**. Top up with distilled water to the bottom of the fill ring in each cell, if necessary.

Open Circuit Voltage Test (Maintenance-free Batteries)

This procedure applies to sealed batteries without removable filler caps. The use of a digital voltmeter capable of reading to 1/100 volt is recommended to read open circuit voltage accurately. The relationship between open circuit voltage (OCV) and battery specific gravity is a

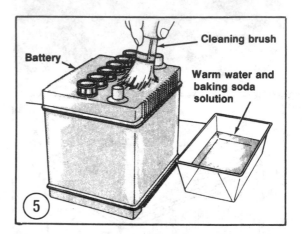

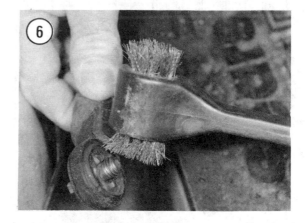

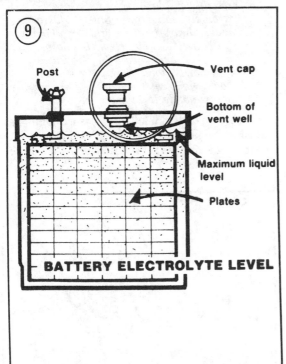

direct one. To determine the state of charge or specific gravity of a maintenance-free battery, perform the test below.

1. The battery surface charge must be removed if the vehicle has just been driven. Turn the headlights on for 20 seconds.

2. Turn the headlights off and wait a minimum of 5 minutes to allow battery voltage to stabilize.

3. Connect a digital voltmeter across the negative and positive battery terminals to determine open circuit voltage.

4. Check the voltmeter and interpret the reading as follows:

    a. 12.60 volts—full charge.
    b. 12.45 volts—75 percent charge.
    c. 12.30 volts—50 percent charge.
    d. 12.15 volts—25 percent charge.

5. If the battery open circuit voltage is below 12.45 volts at an approximate outside temperature of 70° F (21° C), charge the battery for 20 minutes at 35 amps and repeat the test. If the battery again fails the test, replace it.

Load Test (Maintenance-free Batteries)

1. Disconnect the negative battery cable, then the positive battery cable.

2. Install a pair of screw-in battery charging posts (**Figure 10**) or a charging strap adapter (**Figure 11**) to provide an adequate conductive surface.

8

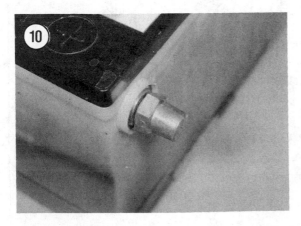

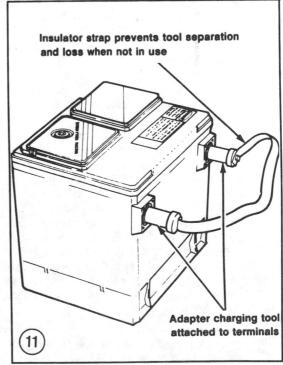

3. Connect a voltmeter and battery load tester to the charging posts or strap adapter.

4. Apply a 300 amp load for 15 seconds to remove any surface charge from the battery (this is unnecessary if the battery has been in storage).

5. Wait 15 seconds after turning the load off to allow the battery to recover, then refer to **Table 1** and apply the specified load according to the battery in your vehicle for 15 seconds while watching the voltmeter.

6. Turn the load off and interpret the voltmeter reading as follows:

   a. Above 70° F—9.6 volts.
   b. 50-70° F—9.4 volts.
   c. 30-50° F—9.1 volts.
   d. 15-30° F—8.8 volts.
   e. 0-15° F—8.5 volts.
   f. Below 0° F—8.0 volts.

If the voltmeter reading is at or above the specified minimum voltage according to the ambient temperature, the battery is good. If battery voltage is less than the minimum voltage, the battery should be discarded and a new one installed.

Unsealed Battery Testing

This procedure applies to batteries with removable filler caps.

Hydrometer testing is the best way to check battery condition. Use a hydrometer with numbered gradations from 1.100-1.300 rather than one with just color-coded bands. To use the hydrometer, squeeze the rubber ball, insert the tip in a cell and release the ball (**Figure 12**).

Draw enough electrolyte to float the weighted float inside the hydrometer. When using a temperature-compensated hydrometer, release the electrolyte and repeat this process several times to make sure the thermometer has adjusted to the electrolyte temperature before taking the reading.

Hold the hydrometer vertically and note the number in line with the surface of the electrolyte. This is the specific gravity for the cell. Return the electrolyte to the cell from which it came.

The specific gravity of the electrolyte in each battery cell is an excellent indicator of that cell's condition. A fully charged cell will read 1.260 or more at 80° F (27° C). If the cells test below 1.220, the battery must be recharged. Charging is also necessary if the specific gravity varies more than 0.050 from cell to cell.

NOTE
If a temperature-compensated hydro-meter is not used, add 0.004 to the specific gravity reading for every 10° above 80° F (27°degrees C). For every 10° below 80° F (27° C), subtract 0.004.

Safety Precautions

When working with batteries, use extreme care to avoid spilling or splashing the electrolyte. This solution contains sulfuric acid, which can ruin clothing and cause serious chemical burns. If any electrolyte is spilled or splashed on clothing or skin, immediately neutralize with a solution of baking soda and water, then flush with an abundance of clean water.

WARNING
Electrolyte splashed into the eyes is extremely dangerous. Safety glasses should always be worn while working with batteries. If electrolyte is splashed into the eyes, call a physician immediately, force the eyes open and flood with cool, clean water for approximately 15 minutes.

If electrolyte is spilled or splashed onto any surface, it should be immediately neutralized with baking soda and water solution and then rinsed with clean water.

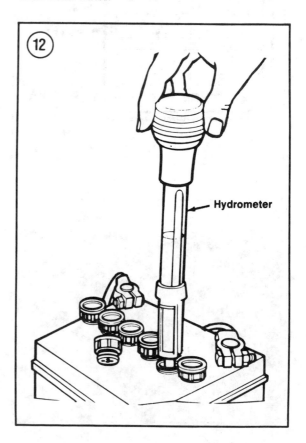

Hydrometer

While batteries are being charged, highly explosive hydrogen gas forms in each cell. Some of this gas escapes through filler cap openings (unsealed battery) or vent openings (sealed battery) and may form an explosive atmosphere in and around the battery. This condition can persist for several hours. Sparks, an open flame or a lighted cigarette can ignite this gas, causing an internal battery explosion and possible serious personal injury.

Take the following precautions to prevent an explosion:

1. Do not smoke or permit any open flame near any battery being charged or which has been recently charged.

2. Do not disconnect live circuits at battery terminals, since a spark usually occurs when a live circuit is broken.

3. Take care when connecting or disconnecting any battery charger. Be sure its power switch is off or it is unplugged before making or breaking any connection. Poor connections are a common cause of electrical arcs which cause explosions.

Charging

A good state of charge should be maintained in batteries used for starting. Check the battery with a voltmeter as shown in **Figure 13**. Any battery that cannot deliver at least 9.6 volts under a starting load should be recharged. If recharging does not bring it up to strength or if it does not hold the charge, replace the battery.

A cold battery will not accept a charge readily. If the temperature is below 40° F (5° C), the battery should be allowed to warm up to room temperature before charging. The battery does not have to be removed from the vehicle for charging. Just make certain that the area is well-ventilated, the battery cables are disconnected and there is no chance of sparks or flames occurring near the battery.

WARNING
Charging batteries give off highly explosive hydrogen gas. If this explodes, it may spray battery acid over a wide area.

Disconnect the negative battery cable first, then the positive cable. Install a pair of screw-in battery charging posts (**Figure 10**) or a charging strap adapter (**Figure 11**) to provide an adequate conductive surface for the charger leads. On unsealed batteries, make sure the electrolyte is fully topped up. Remove the vent caps and place a folded paper towel over the vent openings to absorb any electrolyte that may spew as the battery charges.

Connect the charger to the battery—negative to negative, positive to positive. If the charger output is variable, select a high setting (30-40 amps), set the voltage selector to 12 volts and plug the charger in. Let the battery charge for 30 minutes, then reduce the charge rate to 5-10 amps.

8

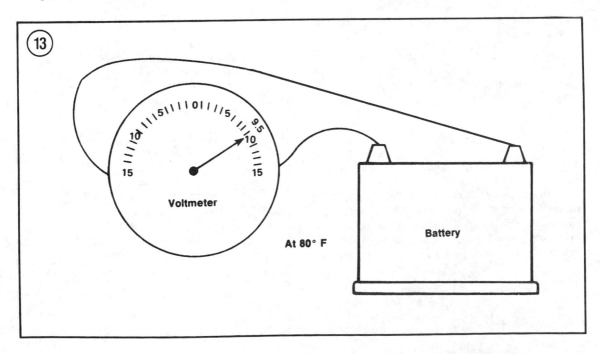

Voltmeter

At 80° F

Battery

Once the battery starts to accept a charge, the charge rate should be reduced to a level that will prevent excessive gassing and electrolyte spewing. This is especially important with sealed batteries, as excessive gassing will reduce the amount of electrolyte (which cannot be replaced) in the battery cells.

The length of time required to recharge a battery depends upon its size, state of charge and temperature. Generally speaking, the current input time should equal the battery amp-hour rating. For example, a 45 AH battery will require a 9-amp charging rate for 5 hours ($9 \times 5 = 45$) or a 15-amp charging rate for 3 hours ($15 \times 3 = 45$). On unsealed batteries, check charging progress with the hydrometer.

Jump Starting

If the battery becomes severely discharged on the road, it is possible to start and run a vehicle by jump starting it from another battery. If the proper procedure is not followed, however, jump starting can be dangerous.

Before jump starting an unsealed battery when temperatures are 32° F (0° C) or lower, check the condition of the electrolyte. If it is not visible or if it appears to be frozen, do *not* attempt to jump start the battery, as the battery may explode or rupture. Do *not* jump start sealed batteries when the temperature is 32° F (0° C) or lower.

WARNING
Use extreme caution when connecting a booster battery to one that is discharged to avoid personal injury or damage to the vehicle.

1. Position the 2 vehicles so that the jumper cables will reach between batteries, but the vehicles do not touch. Set the parking brake on each vehicle.

CAUTION
Do not disconnect the battery of the vehicle to be started. This could damage the electronic ignition module or vehicle electrical system.

2. Turn the heater blower on in the vehicle to be started to remove any transient voltage. Make sure all other switches and lights are turned off.
3. Connect the jumper cables in the order and sequence shown in **Figure 14**.

WARNING
An electrical arc may occur when the final connection is made. This could cause an explosion if it occurs near the battery. For this reason, the final

connection should be made to the alternator mounting bracket or another good engine ground and not the battery itself.

4. Check that all jumper cables are out of the way of moving parts on both engines.
5. Start the vehicle with the good battery and run the engine at a moderate speed.
6. Start the vehicle with the discharged battery. Once the engine starts, run it at a moderate speed.

CAUTION
Racing the engine may damage the electrical system.

7. Remove the jumper cables in the exact reverse order shown in **Figure 14**. Begin at point No. 4, then 3, 2 and 1.

Replacement Batteries

When replacing a battery, be sure to install one with sufficient power to handle the engine's cranking requirements. As a general rule, the battery's cold cranking capacity should equal the engine displacement in cubic inches. For example, a 350 cid V8 requires a battery with a minimum of 350 cold cranking amps. In winter climates, the battery's cold cranking specification should exceed the engine displacement by 50 percent, as battery efficiency can be reduced during cold weather.

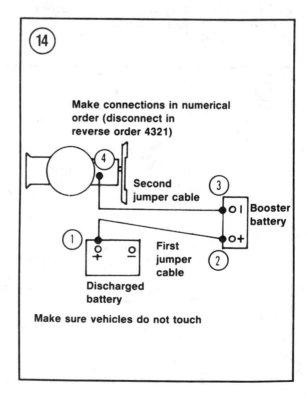

(14)

Make connections in numerical order (disconnect in reverse order 4321)

Second jumper cable

Booster battery

First jumper cable

Discharged battery

Make sure vehicles do not touch

Battery Cables

Poor terminal connections will cause excessive resistance. Defective cable insulation can cause partial short circuits. Both conditions may result in an abnormal voltage drop in the starter motor cable. When this happens, the resulting hard-start condition will place further strain on the battery. Cable condition and terminal connections should be checked periodically. **Figure 15** (I4) and **Figure 16** (V6) show proper cable routing and cable clip location.

CHARGING SYSTEM

The charging system consists of the alternator, voltage regulator, battery, ignition switch, ammeter or charge indicator light, fusible link and connecting wiring.

A drive belt driven by the engine crankshaft pulley turns the alternator, which produces electrical energy to charge the battery. As engine speed varies, the voltage output of the alternator varies. The regulator maintains the voltage to the electrical system within safe limits. The ammeter or charge indicator light signals when charging is not taking place.

All models use an SI or CS Delcotron with an internal solid-state regulator. The output rating is stamped on the alternator frame.

Complete troubleshooting of the charging system requires test equipment and skills which the average home mechanic does not possess. However, there are basic tests which can be done to pinpoint most problems.

Charging system troubles are generally caused by a defective alternator, voltage regulator, battery or a blown fuse. They may also be caused by something as simple as incorrect drive belt tension.

The following are symptoms of problems you may encounter:

1. *Battery dies frequently, even though the ammeter indicates no discharge*—This can be caused by a drive belt that is slightly loose. With the engine off, grasp the alternator pulley with both

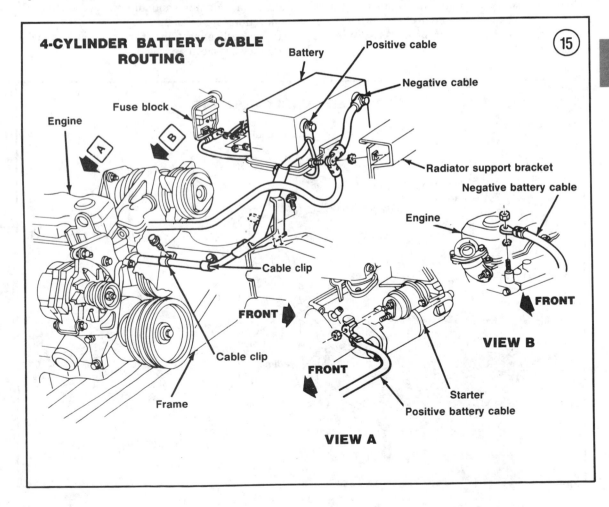

4-CYLINDER BATTERY CABLE ROUTING (15)

Battery
Positive cable
Negative cable
Fuse block
Engine
A
B
Radiator support bracket
Negative battery cable
Engine
Cable clip
FRONT
VIEW B
FRONT
Cable clip
Frame
FRONT
Starter
Positive battery cable
VIEW A

8

hands and try to turn it. If the pulley can be turned without moving the belt, the drive belt is too loose. As a rule, keep the belt tight enough so that it can be deflected only about 1/2 in. under moderate thumb pressure applied between the pulleys. The battery may also be at fault; test the battery condition as described in this chapter.

2. *Ammeter needle does not move or indicator bulb does not light when ignition switch is turned on*—This may indicate a defective ignition switch, battery, voltage regulator or ammeter. Try to start the engine. If it doesn't start, check the ignition switch and battery.

   a. If equipped with an ammeter and the engine starts, remove and test the ammeter.

   b. If equipped with an indicator light and the engine starts, check for a blown bulb.

   c. If the problem persists, the alternator brushes may not be making contact. Perform the *Charging System Test* in this section.

3. *Ammeter needle fluctuates between "Charge" and "Discharge"*—This usually indicates that the charging system is working intermittently. Check drive belt tension first, then check all electrical connections in the charging circuit. As a last resort, check the alternator.

4. *Battery requires frequent addition of water or lamps require frequent replacement*—The alternator is probably overcharging the battery.

5. *Excessive noise from the alternator*—Check for loose mounting brackets and bolts. The problem may also be worn bearings or (in some cases) lack of lubrication. If an alternator whines, a shorted diode may be the problem.

Preliminary Testing

The first indication of charging system trouble is usually a slow engine cranking speed during starting or headlights that dim as engine speed decreases. This will often occur long before the charge warning light or ammeter indicates that there is a potential problem. When charging system trouble is first suspected, perform the following checks.

1. Check the alternator drive belt for correct tension (Chapter Seven).

2. Check the battery to make sure it is in satisfactory condition and fully charged and that all connections are clean and tight.

3. Check all connections at the alternator to make sure they are clean and tight.

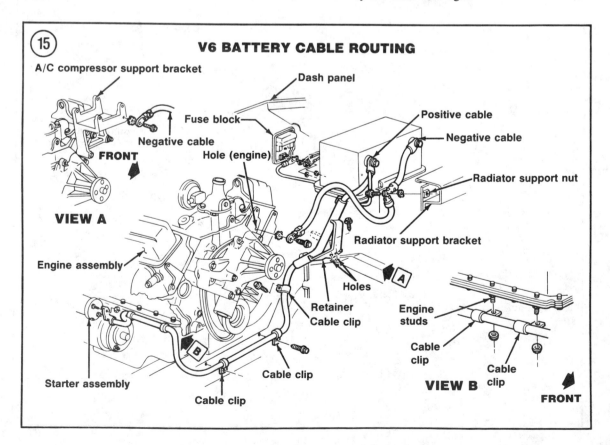

(15) V6 BATTERY CABLE ROUTING

NOTE
If locating the fusible link in Step 4 proves difficult, connect a voltmeter between a good engine ground and the alternator BAT terminal. If the meter shows no voltage reading, the fusible link is probably burned out and should be replaced. But if a voltage reading is present, the link is probably good and you can stop looking.

4. Check the fusible link located in the line between the starter solenoid and the alternator. If burned, determine the cause and correct it, then install a new fusible link.

If there are still indications that the charging system is not performing as it should after each of the above points has been carefully checked and any unsatisfactory conditions corrected, perform a *Charging System Test* as described in this chapter.

SI Charging System

The SI charging system with integral regulator is used on 1985 and some 1986 models. This consists of the battery, alternator with integral voltage regulator, ignition switch, charge indicator light or ammeter gauge, fusible link and connecting wiring. The various Delcotron alternators used on the vehicles covered in this manual differ primarily in output rating. The output rating is stamped on the Delcotron frame.

The integral solid-state voltage regulator is serviced by replacement only.

SI Alternator

The SI alternator is a 3-phase current generator consisting of stationary conductors (stator), a rotating field (rotor) and a rectifying bridge of silicon diodes. See **Figure 17**. The alternator generates alternating current which is converted to direct current by the silicon diodes for use in the vehicle's electrical system. Alternator output is regulated by a voltage regulator to keep the battery charged. The alternator is mounted on the front of the engine and is belt-driven by the crankshaft pulley.

Make sure the connections are not reversed when working on the alternator. Current flow in the wrong direction will damage the diodes and render the alternator unserviceable. The alternator BAT or B terminal (**Figure 17**) must be connected to battery voltage. When charging the battery in the vehicle, disconnect the battery leads before connecting the charger. This is a precaution against incorrect current bias and heat reaching the alternator.

8

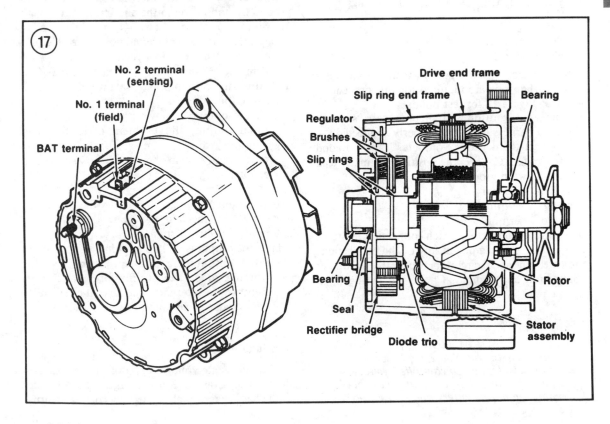

(17)

No. 2 terminal (sensing)
No. 1 terminal (field)
BAT terminal
Drive end frame
Slip ring end frame
Bearing
Regulator
Brushes
Slip rings
Bearing
Seal
Rectifier bridge
Diode trio
Rotor
Stator assembly

SI Charging System Test

A voltmeter with a 0-20 volt scale and an engine tachometer are required for an accurate charging system test.

1. Check the alternator drive belt tension. See Chapter Seven.
2. Check the battery terminals and cables for corrosion and/or loose connections. Clean and tighten as necessary.
3. Check all wiring connections between the alternator and engine.
4. Connect the positive voltmeter lead to the positive battery cable clamp. Connect the negative voltmeter lead to the negative battery cable clamp. Make sure the ignition and all accessories are off.
5. Record the voltage displayed on the voltmeter scale. This is the battery or base voltage.
6. Connect a tachometer to the engine according to manufacturer's instructions.
7. Start the engine and bring its speed up to about 1,500 rpm. The voltmeter reading should increase from that recorded in Step 5, but not by more than 2 volts.
8. If the voltage does not increase, perform the *Undercharge Test*. If the voltage increase is greater than 2 volts, remove the alternator and have it checked by a dealer or an automotive electrical shop for grounded or shorted field windings.

Undercharge Test

A voltmeter with a 0-20 volt scale, an ammeter and a carbon pile are required for this procedure. Refer to **Figure 17** for test points.

1. Turn the ignition switch on. Make sure all electrical harness leads are properly connected.
2. Connect the negative voltmeter lead to a good engine ground. Connect the positive voltmeter lead in turn between ground and:
   a. BAT terminal.
   b. No. 1 terminal.
   c. No. 2 terminal.
3. Read the voltmeter as each connection in Step 2 is made. A zero reading at any of the connections indicates an open circuit between the voltmeter connection and ground. Check the wiring if an open circuit is indicated.

CAUTION
An open in the No. 2 lead (sensing) circuit will cause uncontrolled voltage, battery overcharge and possible damage to the battery and accessories.

Late-model alternators have a built-in feature to prevent these problems by not allowing the unit to turn on if there is an open in the No. 2 lead circuit. Such an open could occur between terminals, at the crimp between the harness wire or terminal, or in the wire itself.

4. Disconnect the voltmeter. Disconnect the negative battery cable.
5. Disconnect the alternator wiring connector at the BAT terminal. Connect an ammeter between the BAT terminal and the wiring connector.
6. Reconnect the negative battery cable. Turn on all accessories.
7. Connect a carbon pile across the battery posts.
8. Start the engine and run at approximately 2,000 rpm. Adjust the carbon pile to obtain the maximum current output.
9. If the ammeter reading is within 10 amps of the alternator's rated output, the unit is satisfactory.
10. If the ammeter reading is not within 10 amps of the rated output, locate the test hole in the end frame. If test hole is accessible, continue testing. If it is not accessible, remove the alternator and have it checked by your dealer or an automotive electrical shop.
11. Insert a thin screwdriver in the test hole and touch its blade to the alternator end frame to ground the tab inside to the end frame. See **Figure 18**. Since the tab is within 3/4 in. of the casting surface, the screwdriver should not be inserted into the end frame more than 1 inch.
12. Run the engine at approximately 2,000 rpm and adjust the carbon pile to obtain the maximum current output.
   a. If the output is now within 10 amps of the rated output, the problem is in the field winding, diode trio, rectifier bridge or regulator. Perform the *Regulator Test* in this chapter.

If the regulator is good, remove the alternator and have it checked by your dealer or an automotive electrical shop.
   b. If the output is still not within 10 amps of the rated output, the problem is in the field winding, diode trio, rectifier bridge or stator. Remove the alternator and have it checked by your dealer or an automotive electrical shop.

Regulator Test

The solid-state voltage regulator can be tested on the vehicle. Connect a fast charger and voltmeter to the battery terminals, observing correct polarity.

Turn the ignition on and slowly increase the charge rate. When the indicator lamp on the instrument panel starts to dim, read the voltmeter scale. The lamp should dim at a reading between 13.5-16 volts. If it dims at a voltage setting outside this range, the regulator is defective.

Charge Indicator Lamp

If the alternator and voltage regulator are operating satisfactorily and the charge indicator warning lamp remains on, the charge indicator relay located inside the voltage regulator may be defective. To determine the cause of the problem, perform the following procedure.

1. *Switch off, lamp on*—Disconnect the leads from the alternator No. 1 and No. 2 terminals. If the lamp remains on, there is a short circuit between the 2 leads. If the lamp goes out, the rectifier bridge is faulty and must be replaced, as this condition will result in an undercharged battery.

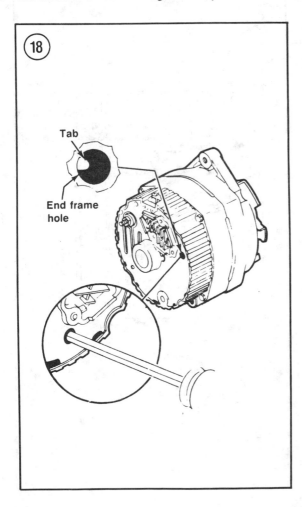

2. *Switch on, lamp off, engine stopped*—This defect can be caused by the conditions listed in Step 1, by reversal of the No. 1 and No. 2 leads at these 2 terminals or by an open circuit. To determine where the open exists, proceed as follows:

a. Connect a voltmeter between the No. 2 alternator terminal and ground. If a reading is obtained, proceed to the next step. If the reading is zero, repair the open circuit between the No. 2 alternator terminal and the battery. If the lamp comes on, no further check is required.

CAUTION
Do not ground the No. 2 lead or terminal in Step b.

b. Disconnect the No. 1 and No. 2 terminal leads at the alternator. Turn the ignition switch on and momentarily ground the No. 1 terminal.

c. If the lamp does not come on, check for a blown fuse or fusible link, burned-out lamp bulb, defective lamp socket or an open in the No. 1 lead circuit between the alternator and ignition switch.

d. If the lamp lights, remove the ground at the No. 1 terminal and reconnect the No. 1 and No. 2 wires to the alternator. Insert a screwdriver in the test hole (**Figure 18**) to ground the wiring.

e. If the lamp does not light, check the connection between the wiring harness and No. 1 alternator terminal. If the wiring is good, have the alternator brushes, slip rings and field winding checked.

f. If the lamp lights, repeat the voltmeter check in the previous step. If a reading is now obtained, replace the regulator.

3. *Switch on, lamp on, engine running*—Possible causes are improper drive belt tension, a defective or discharged battery, faulty wiring or an open circuit between the alternator and battery.

CS Charging System

The CS charging system with integral regulator is used on some 1986 and later models. This consists of the battery, a CS-130 alternator with integral voltage regulator, digital charge indicator display and wiring. CS stands for "charging system;" the number after it indicates the outer diameter of the stator laminations in millimeters. Although similar in design to the SI model, the CS alternator contains a new digital integral regulator and has no test hole to ground the regulator for full-field testing. The CS alternator is smaller, lighter in weight and does not use a diode trio. **Figure 19** shows the location of the BAT and regulator terminals.

The regulator limits system voltage by cycling the rotor field current on/off about 400 times per second. This "duty cycle" changes according to engine operation and temperature. At lower speeds, the field may be on 90 percent of the time and off 10 percent of the time. As engine speed increases, less field current is required to generate the necessary system voltage. Thus, the field may be on 10 percent of the time and off 90 percent of the time at higher engine speeds. The regulator cannot be tested with an ohmmeter; a special tester is required.

The indicator lamp in a CS charging system functions differently than in an SI system. Any defect causes it to light at full illumination, and the lamp will also light when charging voltage is too high or too low.

CS Charging System Test

The following general test procedure is recommended by Delco-Remy for the CS Delcotron system. If the vehicle does not have an indicator lamp, omit Steps 3-5. Refer to **Figure 19** and **Figure 20** for this procedure.
1. Test the battery and charge it, if necessary, before testing the charging system.
2. Inspect the drive belt and all circuit wiring. Correct any problems noted.
3. Turn the ignition on, but do not start the engine. The indicator lamp should light. If it does, proceed with Step 5.
4. If the indicator lamp does not light in Step 3, disconnect the harness connector at the regulator terminals and ground the "L" terminal in the harness with a jumper wire.
   a. If the lamp now lights, remove the Delcotron for service.
   b. If the lamp does not light, there is an open circuit between the ignition switch and the grounded "L" terminal in the harness.
5. Start and run the engine at approximately 2,000 rpm. If the lamp does not turn off, disconnect the Delcotron harness connector.
   a. If the lamp then stays off, remove the Delcotron for service.
   b. If the lamp remains on, there is a grounded "L" wire in the harness.
6. If the indicator lamp lights during normal operation, or if the battery is consistently under- or overcharged, proceed as follows:
   a. Disconnect the harness at the Delcotron.

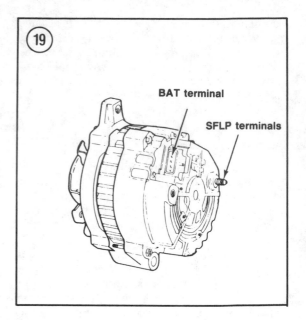

⑲

BAT terminal

SFLP terminals

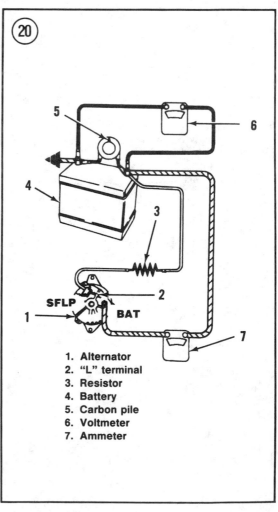

⑳

5

6

4

3

SFLP

1

2

BAT

7

1. **Alternator**
2. **"L" terminal**
3. **Resistor**
4. **Battery**
5. **Carbon pile**
6. **Voltmeter**
7. **Ammeter**

b. Connect a voltmeter between the "L" terminal in the harness connector and ground. If the regulator has an "I" terminal, connect it to the positive voltmeter lead with a jumper wire.

c. Turn the ignition ON, but do not start the engine. If the voltmeter shows no voltage, look for an open circuit in the harness.

d. Reconnect the Delcotron harness and run the engine at approximately 2,000 rpm with all accessories off.

e. Connect the voltmeter across the battery terminals and measure battery voltage. If the reading exceeds 16 volts, the regulator is defective.

7. Connect an ammeter in the Delcotron output circuit (BAT terminal) and use a carbon pile to load the battery for maximum charging current at approximately 13 volts. If charging current is not within 15 amps of the Delcotron's rated output, repair or replace the Delcotron.

Alternator Removal/Installation

This procedure is generalized to cover all applications. Access to the alternator is quite limited in some engine compartments and care should be taken to avoid personal injury. Refer to **Figure 21** (I4) or **Figure 22** (V6) for this procedure.

1. Disconnect the negative battery cable.

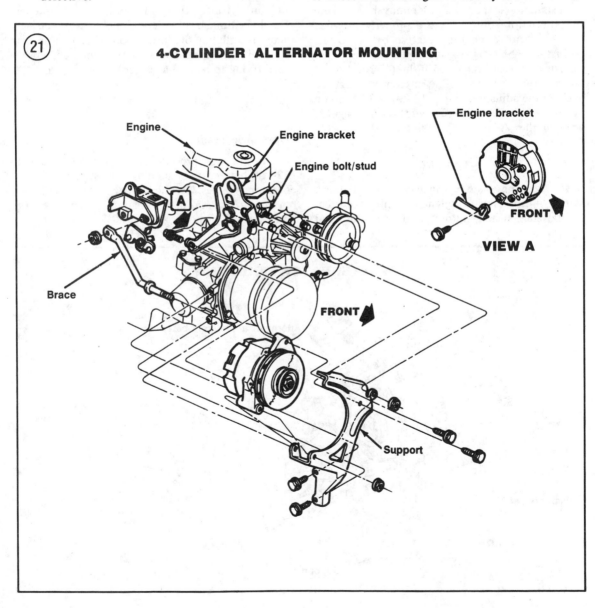

(21) **4-CYLINDER ALTERNATOR MOUNTING**

Engine

Engine bracket

Engine bolt/stud

Engine bracket

A

FRONT

VIEW A

Brace

FRONT

Support

8

2. Disconnect the upper radiator hose from the fan shroud. See **Figure 23**.

3. Unclamp the wiring harness from the radiator core support.

4. Unbolt the upper fan shroud from the radiator core support. Remove the upper fan shroud.

5. Unplug the electrical connectors at the rear of the alternator.

6. Loosen the alternator adjusting and pivot bolts. See **Figure 24**.

7. Move the alternator toward the engine and remove the drive belt from the alternator pulley.

8. Support the alternator with one hand and remove the adjustment and pivot bolts. Remove the alternator.

9. Installation is the reverse of removal. Make sure the alternator connectors are properly installed before reconnecting the negative battery cable. Adjust the belt tension (Chapter Seven), then tighten the pivot bolt to 35 ft.-lb. (47 N•m) on I4 engines or 37 ft.-lb. (50 N•m) on V6 engines. Tighten the adjusting bolt to 18 ft.-lb. (25 N•m) on I4 engines or 20 ft.-lb. (27 N•m) on V6 engines. Tighten the V6 back brace nut to 30 ft.-lb. (42 N•m).

STARTER

The starting system consists of the battery, starter motor, starter solenoid, ignition switch, neutral start switch (automatic transmission) and connecting wiring. Vehicles equipped with a manual transmission have a clutch interlock switch which requires that the clutch pedal be fully depressed before the starting circuit will operate. A Delco-Remy 5MT or 10MT starter is used on all models.

When the ignition switch is turned to START with the transmission in PARK or NEUTRAL (automatic) or the clutch pedal fully depressed, it transmits current from the battery to the starter solenoid, which mechanically engages the starter with the engine flywheel.

Starting system problems are relatively easy to find. In most cases, the trouble is a loose or dirty electrical connection. However, any repairs inside the unit itself (other than brush replacement) should be done by a dealer or automotive electrical shop. Installation of a professionally rebuilt unit is generally less expensive and thus more practical than trying to rebuild a starter motor at home.

On-vehicle Testing

Three of these procedures require a fully charged 12-volt battery, to be used as a booster, and a pair of jumper cables. Use the jumper cables as outlined in *Jump Starting* in this chapter, following all of the precautions noted.

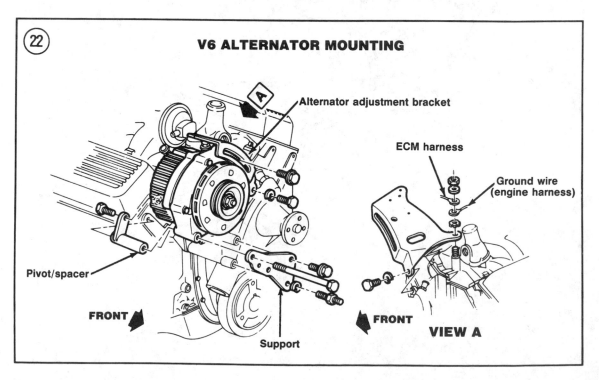

22 **V6 ALTERNATOR MOUNTING**

A — Alternator adjustment bracket

ECM harness

Ground wire (engine harness)

Pivot/spacer

FRONT

FRONT

Support

VIEW A

Engine cranks very slowly or not at all

1. Turn on the headlights. If the lights are very dim, the battery or connecting wires are most likely at fault. Check unsealed batteries with a hydrometer. Check wiring for breaks, shorts and dirty connections. If the battery and wires are satisfactory, turn the headlights on and crank the engine. If the lights dim drastically, the starter is probably shorted to ground.

2. If the lights remain bright or dim only slightly when cranking, the trouble may be in the starter, starter solenoid, or wiring. If the starter spins, check the solenoid and wiring to the ignition switch.

3. Note whether the solenoid plunger is pulled into the solenoid when the starter circuit is closed (it should make a loud click).

    a. If the plunger is pulled in, the trouble is in the solenoid switch, starter motor or starter motor circuit. Remove the starter motor for repairs to either motor or switch.

    b. If the plunger is not pulled in, connect a jumper lead between the solenoid battery terminal and the terminal on the solenoid to

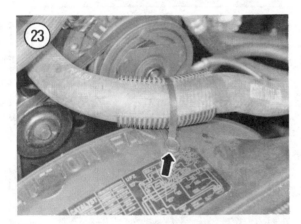

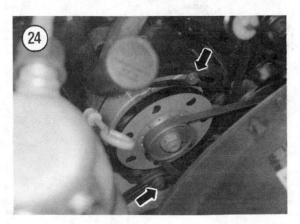

which the purple lead is attached. If the starter now works, the solenoid is good. The problem is in the neutral start or clutch interlock switch, ignition switch or in the wires or connections between the switches.

4. If the starter still will not crank properly, refer the problem to a dealer or automotive electrical specialist.

Slow cranking starter

1. Connect the jumper cables. Listen to the starter cranking speed as the engine is started. If the cranking speed sounds normal, check the battery for loose or corroded connections or a low charge. Clean and tighten the connections as required. Recharge the battery if necessary.

2. If cranking speed does not sound normal, clean and tighten all starter solenoid connections and the battery ground on the frame and/or engine.

3. Repeat Step 1. If the cranking speed is still too slow, replace the starter.

Starter solenoid clicks, starter does not crank

1. Clean and tighten all starter and solenoid connections. Make sure the terminal eyelets are securely fastened to the wire strands and are not corroded.

2. Remove the battery terminal clamps. Clean the clamps and battery posts. Reinstall the clamps and tighten securely.

3. If the starter does not crank, connect the 12-volt booster battery to the vehicle's battery with the jumper cables. If the starter still does not crank, replace it.

Starter solenoid chatters (no click), starter does not crank

1. Check the purple wire connection at the starter solenoid. Clean and tighten if necessary.

2. Place the transmission in PARK (automatic) or NEUTRAL (manual).

3. Disconnect the purple wire at the starter solenoid. Connect a jumper wire between this solenoid connector and the positive battery terminal.

4. Connect the 12-volt booster battery to the vehicle's battery with the jumper cables. Try starting the engine (depress the clutch on manual transmission vehicles with a clutch interlock switch).

5. If the engine starts, check the ignition switch, neutral start switch or clutch interlock switch and the system wiring for an open circuit or a loose connection. If the engine does not start, replace the starter solenoid.

8

Starter spins but does not crank

1. Remove the starter as described in this chapter.
2. Check the starter pinion gear. If the teeth are chipped or worn, inspect the flywheel ring gear for the same problem. Replace the starter and/or ring gear as required.
3. If the pinion gear is in good condition, disassemble the starter and check the armature shaft for corrosion. See *Brush Replacement* in this chapter for disassembly procedure.
4. If there is no corrosion, the starter drive assembly is slipping. Replace the starter with a new or rebuilt unit.

Starter will not disengage when ignition switch is released

This problem is usually caused by a sticking solenoid but the pinion may jam on the flywheel ring gear of high-mileage vehicles. If equipped with a manual transmission, the pinion can often be temporarily freed by rocking the vehicle in high gear.

Loud grinding noises when starter runs

This can be caused by improper meshing of the starter pinion and flywheel ring gear or by a broken overrunning clutch mechanism.
1. Remove the starter as described in this chapter.
2. Check the starter pinion gear. If the teeth are chipped or worn, inspect the flywheel ring gear for the same problem. Replace the starter and/or ring gear as required.
3. If the pinion gear is in good condition, disassemble the starter and check the overrunning clutch mechanism. See *Brush Replacement* in this chapter for disassembly procedure.

Starter Solenoid Replacement

1. Disconnect the negative battery cable.
2. Remove the plastic protective cover from the solenoid electrical connectors, if installed.
3. Disconnect the field strap at the starter from the motor terminal.
4. Remove the solenoid-to-drive housing screws and the motor terminal bolt.
5. Rotate the solenoid 90° and remove from the drive housing with the plunger return or torsion spring.
6. Installation is the reverse of removal.

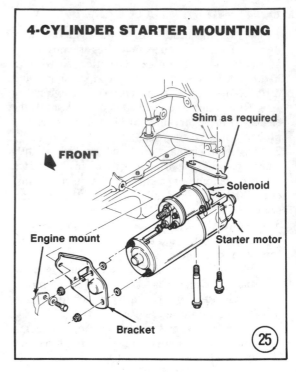

4-CYLINDER STARTER MOUNTING

Shim as required

FRONT

Solenoid

Engine mount

Starter motor

Bracket

25

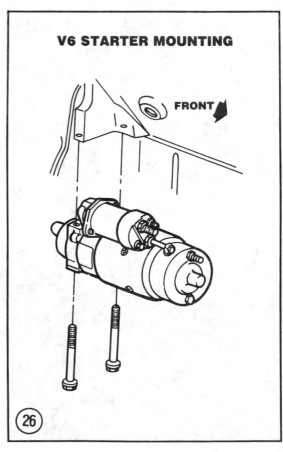

V6 STARTER MOUNTING

FRONT

26

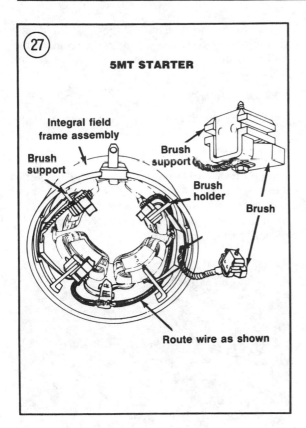

5MT STARTER

Integral field
frame assembly

Brush
support

Brush
support

Brush
holder

Brush

Brush

Route wire as shown

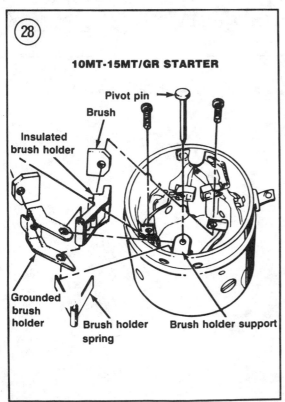

10MT-15MT/GR STARTER

Pivot pin

Brush

Insulated
brush holder

Grounded
brush
holder

Brush holder
spring

Brush holder support

Starter Removal/Installation (All Engines)

Refer to **Figure 25** (I4) or **Figure 26** (V6) for this procedure.
1. Disconnect the negative battery cable.
2. Set the parking brake and place the transmission in PARK or 1st gear.
3. Securely block the rear wheels so the vehicle will not roll in either direction.
4. Raise the front of the vehicle with a jack and place it on jackstands.
5. Remove any starter motor brace or heat shield that will interfere with starter motor removal.
6. Remove the starter motor mounting bolts and let the starter drop down out of position. Retrieve any mounting shims that may fall out.
7. Disconnect the starter cable and solenoid wires. Remove the starter motor.
8. Installation is the reverse of removal. Reinstall any shims that were removed to assure proper pinion-to-flywheel mesh. Tighten the mounting bolts to 31 ft.-lb. (41 N•m) on I4 engines or 28 ft.-lb. (38 N•m) on V6 engines.

Starter Brush Replacement (Delco 5MT Starter)

Brush replacement requires partial disassembly of the starter. Always replace brushes in complete sets. Refer to **Figure 27** for this procedure.
1. Remove the 2 through-bolts, commutator end frame and insulator washer.
2. Separate the field frame from the drive housing. Remove the armature and washer.
3. Remove the brush holder from the brush support.
4. Remove the brush holder screw. Separate the brush and holder.
5. Inspect the plastic brush holder for cracks or broken mounting pads.
6. Check the brushes for length and condition. Replace all if any are worn to 1/4 in. or less in length.
7. Reverse Steps 1-4 to assemble the starter.

Starter Brush Replacement (Delco 10MT Starter)

Brush replacement requires partial disassembly of the starter. Always replace brushes in complete sets. Refer to **Figure 28** for this procedure.
1. Remove the terminal nut and disconnect the field lead from the solenoid terminal.
2. Remove the 2 through-bolts and separate the end frame and field frame assembly from the drive end housing.

8

3. Remove the brush and lead attaching screws.

4. Remove the brush holder pivot pins.

5. Remove the brush holder and spring assemblies from the field housing.

6. Check the brushes for length and condition. Replace all if any are worn to 1/4 in. or less in length.

7. Make sure the brush holders are clean and that the brushes do not bind in their holders.

8. Check the brush springs. Replace if distorted or discolored.

9. Reverse Steps 1-5 to complete brush installation. Hold brushes against field frame when reinstalling armature. Tighten through-bolts to 55-85 in.-lb. (6-9 N•m).

HIGH ENERGY IGNITION (HEI) SYSTEM

The High Energy Ignition (HEI) system with Electronic Spark Timing (EST) is used on all engines. The HEI/EST system consists of the battery, a breakerless distributor (with integral ignition module), ignition coil, ignition switch, spark plugs and connecting primary and secondary wiring.

The HEI-EST system differs from the standard HEI system in that the distributor has no vacuum or centrifugal advance mechanisms. Spark timing is controlled directly by the electronic control module or ECM.

Electronic Spark Control (ESC) is used on fuel-injected V6 engines to control detonation by automatically retarding ignition timing when necessary.

HEI Distributor

The HEI distributor uses a magnetic pick-up assembly. Some models also incorporate a Hall-effect switch.

The magnetic pickup assembly contains a permanent magnet, a pole piece with internal teeth and a pickup coil. A timer core with external teeth rotates inside the pole piece. When the timer core teeth align with the pole piece teeth, a voltage is induced in the pickup coil.

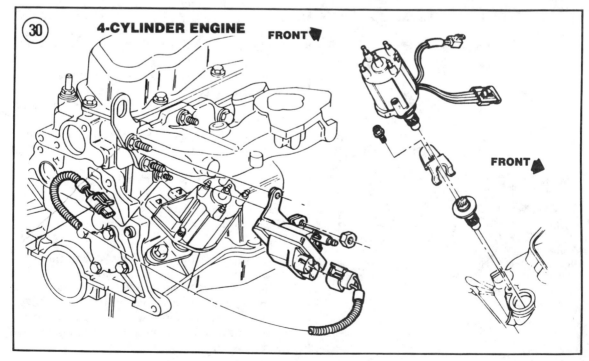

The Hall-effect switch consists of a plastic cup which contains 4 openings or windows and 4 vanes or solid portions (one for each cylinder). A permanent magnet is positioned on one side of the cup, with a Hall sensor on the other. As the cup rotates, the magnetic field varies according to the position of the window or vane between the sensor and magnet. When a vane passes between the sensor and magnet, a voltage signal is produced.

In both systems, this voltage signal is sent to an electronic module in the distributor. The module breaks the coil primary circuit, inducing a high voltage in the ignition coil secondary windings. This high voltage is sent to the distributor where it is directed to the appropriate spark plug by the rotor.

On engines with the HEI-EST ignition system, the ECM evaluates data from various engine sensors to calculate the required spark timing and directs the distributor accordingly. No vacuum or centrifugal advance mechanisms are used with the HEI-EST distributor and no changes can be made in the advance curve.

The ignition coil is an integral part of some 1985 V6 distributor caps. All other distributors use a remote coil.

A radio noise suppression capacitor is located in the distributor.

Distributor Removal/Installation

The V6 distributor is mounted vertically at the rear of the engine block. See A, **Figure 29**. The I4 distributor is mounted underneath the intake manifold and below the coil on the passenger side of the engine at the rear. See **Figure 30**. A hexagon shaft installed in the end of the distributor shaft drives the oil pump on V6 engines.

1. Disconnect the negative battery cable.
2. Remove the engine cover and console. See Chapter Four (I4) or Chapter Five (V6).

3. Remove the air cleaner assembly. See Chapter Six.
4. 1985 V6—Disconnect all wiring connectors from the distributor cap (B, **Figure 29**).
5. Disconnect the distributor-to-wiring harness connector. On distributors using a remote coil, disconnect the primary and secondary leads at the ignition coil.
6. Rotate the distributor cap lug hooks counterclockwise with a screwdriver. Late-model distributor caps are retained with 2 capscrews. Remove the distributor cap.
7. Turn the engine over by hand until the No. 1 cylinder is at top dead center on its compression stroke. The 0 degree mark on the timing tab will align with the notch inscribed on the pulley and the distributor rotor will point to the No. 1 terminal in the distributor cap.

> *NOTE*
> *If the distributor rotor does not point to No 1 terminal, No. 1 cylinder is on its exhaust stroke, not its compression stroke. Rotate the crankshaft one full turn so the marks align as described in Step 6.*

8. Disconnect and plug the vacuum advance line if so equipped, or at the distributer.
9. Scribe an alignment mark on the distributor housing in line with the rotor tip. Scribe a corresponding mark on the engine block. The marks are for reinstallation reference.
10. Remove the distributor hold-down nut or bolt and clamp. See **Figure 30** (I4) or **Figure 31** (V6). An offset distributor wrench will be useful in reaching the clamp nut/bolt. It may also be necessary to retrieve the nut/bolt and clamp with a magnetic tool.

> *NOTE*
> *The oil pump drive shaft may come out with the V6 distributor. If so, be sure to reinstall it when you reinstall the distributor.*

11. Pull upward on the distributor with a rotating motion. As the drive gear disengages from the camshaft drive gear, the rotor will move slightly.

> *NOTE*
> *Do not rotate engine while distributor is out of the block or it will be necessary to retime the engine.*

12. If the crankshaft was accidentally rotated while the distributor was out of the block, proceed as follows:

8

a. Remove the No. 1 spark plug. Hold a finger over the plug hole and rotate the crankshaft pulley until compression pressure is felt.

b. Continue to rotate the engine slowly until the timing mark on the crankshaft damper aligns with the TDC mark on the timing pointer.

NOTE
Always rotate the engine in the direction of normal rotation. Do not back engine up to align timing marks.

c. Install the distributor in the engine block with the rotor tip pointing in the direction of the No. 1 terminal in the distributor cap.

NOTE
It may be necessary to crank the engine with the starter after the distributor drive gear is partially engaged in order to engage the oil pump intermediate shaft. If this is required, return the crankshaft to the initial timing alignment. Install but do not tighten the retaining clamp and screw/bolt. Rotate the distributor to advance the timing to a point where the pickup coil is properly aligned.

13. If the crankshaft has not been moved since the distributor was removed, simply align the rotor tip with the housing mark and the housing mark with the block mark, then install the distributor in the block.

14. Reverse Steps 1-8 to complete installation.

15. Check ignition timing with a timing light and adjust to specifications. See Chapter Three. When timing is correctly adjusted, tighten the distributor hold-down clamp nut/bolt securely.

Ignition Coil

The HEI ignition uses an "E-core" coil. Unlike a standard oil-filled coil, it is potted in plastic and the iron core is laminated around the windings much like a small transformer. The HEI remote coil is externally mounted on the engine. Its secondary lead connector looks like the top of a spark plug. Positive and negative primary leads are housed in a single snap-in connector. The coil has very low primary resistance and is used without a ballast resistor. All other HEI coils are mounted in the distributor cap. **Figure 32** shows the external HEI coil (A) and the cap-mounted HEI coil (B).

Ignition Coil Replacement (External HEI)

1. Disconnect the negative battery cable.

2. Disconnect the secondary lead from the center tower.

3. Remove the primary wire connector.

4. Remove the 4 screws holding the coil and bracket to the engine or fender apron. Remove the coil and bracket.

5. Installation is the reverse of removal.

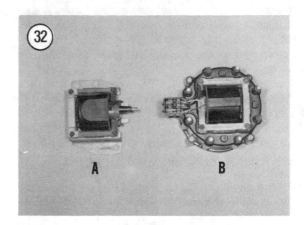

A   B

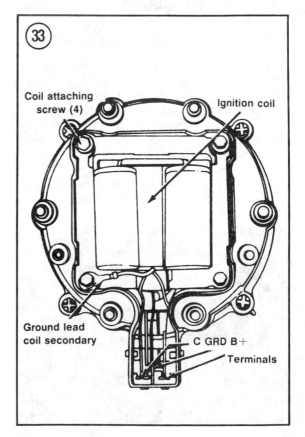

Coil attaching screw (4)

Ignition coil

Ground lead coil secondary

C GRD B+
Terminals

Ignition Coil Replacement (Integral Cap Coil)

Although integral coils are physically interchangeable, they differ in construction according to application. Always replace an integral coil with one bearing the same coil number (located on top of the coil). Refer to **Figure 33** for this procedure.

1. Remove the distributor cap.

2. Remove the coil cover attaching screws and cover.

3. Remove the coil attaching screws. Note that the coil ground lead is installed under one of the attaching screws.

4. Push the tach and battery lead clips from the cap connector with a small screwdriver. It is not necessary to remove the ground lead from the connector.

5. Lift the coil from the cap.

6. Remove, clean and inspect the coil arc seal. This rubber insulating seal absorbs moisture to prevent shorting and should be replaced if it has lost its flexibility.

7. Remove and inspect the carbon button and spring. Replace if button is excessively worn or damaged, or if spring has lost its tension.

8. Installation is the reverse of removal.

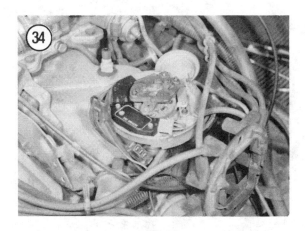

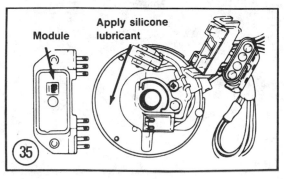

Ignition Module

The ignition amplifier module used with the HEI ignition is a solid-state, moisture-resistant unit which has its components permanently sealed to resist vibration and outside contaminants. The module is located inside the distributor. See **Figure 34** (typical). All connections are waterproof. The module has built-in reverse polarity and transient voltage protection. The primary (low voltage) coil current is regulated by the magnetic pick-up or Hall-effect switch.

Replacement can be made with the distributor in the engine, but it will be far easier to remove the distributor for module replacement. The standard HEI and HEI-ESC module has 4 terminals; the HEI-EST modules have 7 terminals. Although the HEI and HEI-ESC modules are identical in appearance, they are not electrically interchangeable between systems. Modules cannot be repaired and must be replaced if defective. Whenever a module is replaced, always install one bearing the same number stamped on top of the old module.

Ignition Module Replacement

Replacement can be made with the V6 distributor in the engine but I4 module service is far easier if the distributor is removed from the engine. Refer to **Figure 35** for this procedure.

1. Disconnect the negative battery cable.

2A. I4—Remove the distributor as described in this chapter.

2B. V6—Remove the distributor cap as described in this chapter.

3. Remove the distributor rotor attaching screws. Remove the rotor.

4. Carefully disconnect the wiring connector at each end of the module with needlenose pliers or a thin screwdriver blade.

5. Remove the 2 module screws. Remove the module.

NOTE
The module base which mates against the distributor body is covered with silicone grease to protect the module from heat. Do not remove the grease if the same module is to be reinstalled. If a new module is installed, apply the packet of grease included with it on the module base before installation.

6. Wipe the distributor base and the module with a clean, dry cloth. Apply silicone grease to the

distributor and module base before installing the new module.

7. Installation is the reverse of removal.

LIGHTING SYSTEM

Sealed Beam Headlights

Rectangular combination high/low sealed beam lamps are standard equipment on all models. Halogen lamps are optional. Always replace a burned-out headlight with another of the same type. While halogen and ordinary sealed beam lamps are physically interchangeable, the wiring circuitry is different and the lamps should not be interchanged.

> *CAUTION*
> *Torx head fasteners are used extensively in the lighting assemblies of late-model vehicles. Do not try to remove such fasteners with a Phillips head screwdriver—use an appropriate Torx head driver to prevent damage to the fastener head.*

A good ground is necessary for proper exterior light operation. Always check for an unsatisfactory ground first when troubleshooting a dim lamp or one that fails to light. Do not overlook a loose ground strap between the engine and body dash panel—this can affect headlight as well as instrument gauge operation. Failure of one circuit in the bulb requires replacement of the entire sealed beam unit.

If both filaments in the lamp fail at the same time, the problem is generally a short in the wiring to that particular lamp. Check the fuse to make sure it is the correct amperage rating and replace it if it is not. Carefully inspect the wiring and connector for deterioration, chafing or other damage and correct as required. **Figure 36** and **Figure 37** show the wiring harnesses for the front and rear lights respectively.

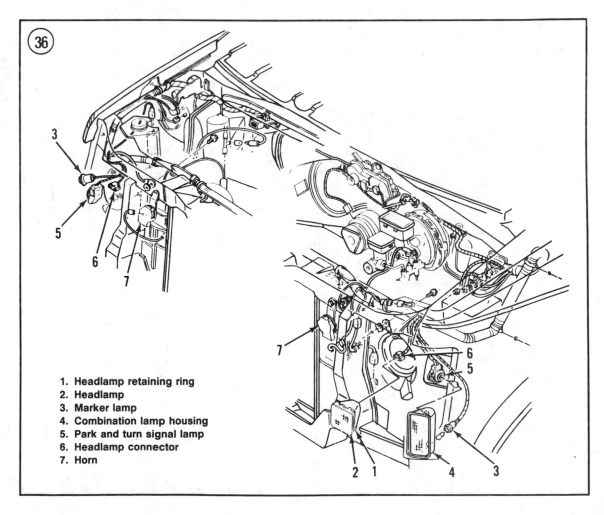

1. Headlamp retaining ring
2. Headlamp
3. Marker lamp
4. Combination lamp housing
5. Park and turn signal lamp
6. Headlamp connector
7. Horn

Sealed Beam Headlight Replacement

Refer to **Figure 38** (typical) for this procedure.
1. Open and support the hood.
2. Disconnect the negative battery cable.
3. Remove the screws holding the headlight bezel in place. Remove the bezel.

4. Use a hooked tool such as a cotter pin remover to disengage the retaining spring from the headlamp assembly retaining ring.

NOTE
Do not turn the headlight adjustment screws by mistake in Step 5. This will

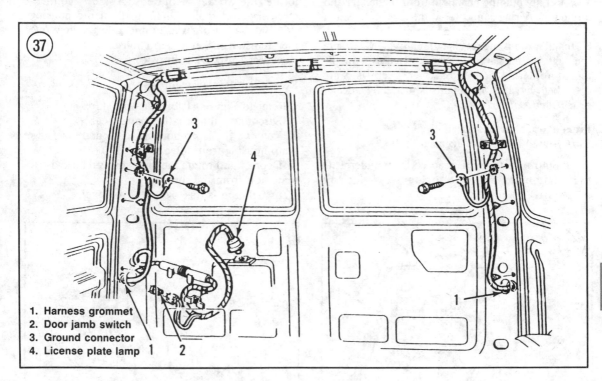

1. Harness grommet
2. Door jamb switch
3. Ground connector
4. License plate lamp

8

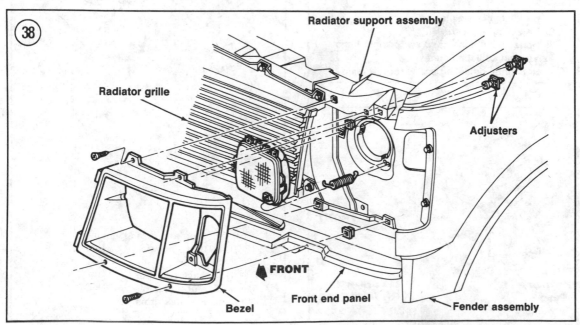

Radiator support assembly

Radiator grille

Adjusters

FRONT

Bezel

Front end panel

Fender assembly

disturb the aim of the headlight beam and require readjustment by a dealer or certified station.

5. Remove the screws holding the retaining ring (**Figure 39**). Remove retaining ring from vehicle.
6. Rotate headlight as required to disengage it from the adjustment screws.
7. Carefully pull the headlight from the fender and unplug the wiring connector at the rear of the lamp. Remove the headlight from the vehicle.
8. Installation is the reverse of removal. Make sure the lugs on the lamp engage the recesses in the lamp holder. If the adjustment screws were disturbed, have the headlights adjusted by a dealer or certified station.

Front Park, Side Marker and Turn Signal Lamp Replacement

All bulb sockets can be reached from underneath the front bumper. Refer to **Figure 40** for this procedure.

To replace a bulb, reach behind the bumper and locate the socket. Rotate socket 90° counterclockwise and remove it from the lamp housing. Pull old bulb from socket and insert a new one, then reinstall socket in lamp housing and rotate 90° clockwise to secure it in place.

To replace a bulb, reach behind the bumper and locate the socket. Rotate socket 90° counterclockwise and remove it from the lamp housing. Pull old bulb from socket and insert a new one, then reinstall socket in lamp housing and rotate 90° clockwise to secure it in place.

Rear Lamp Replacement

Refer to **Figure 41** for this procedure.
1. Disconnect the negative battery cable.
2. Remove the lamp housing screw and disengage lamp housing from filler panel.
3. Depress and rotate the bulb counterclockwise to remove it from the socket.
4. Installation is the reverse of removal.

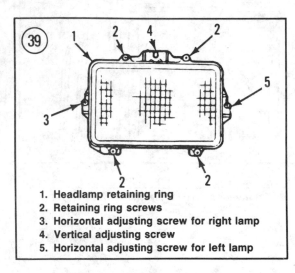

1. Headlamp retaining ring
2. Retaining ring screws
3. Horizontal adjusting screw for right lamp
4. Vertical adjusting screw
5. Horizontal adjusting screw for left lamp

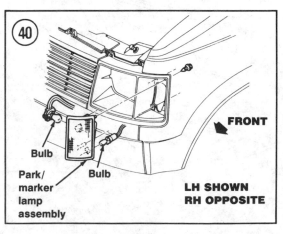

Bulb

Park/ marker lamp assembly

Bulb

FRONT

LH SHOWN RH OPPOSITE

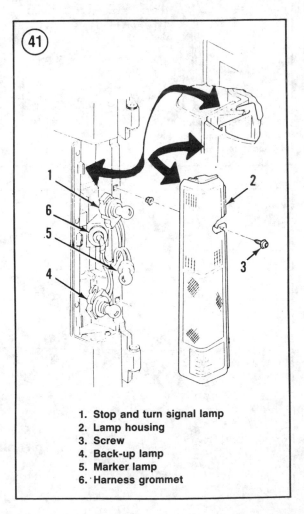

1. Stop and turn signal lamp
2. Lamp housing
3. Screw
4. Back-up lamp
5. Marker lamp
6. Harness grommet

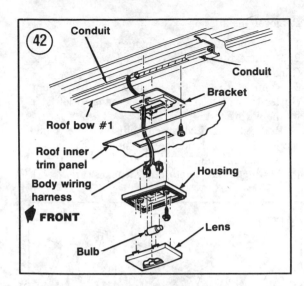

(42)

Conduit

Conduit

Bracket

Roof bow #1

Roof inner
trim panel

Body wiring
harness

Housing

▲ **FRONT**

Lens

Bulb

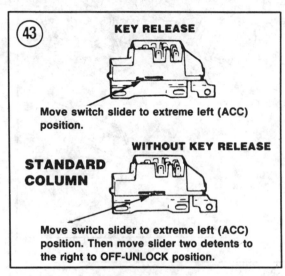

(43)

KEY RELEASE

Move switch slider to extreme left (ACC)
position.

WITHOUT KEY RELEASE

**STANDARD
COLUMN**

Move switch slider to extreme left (ACC)
position. Then move slider two detents to
the right to OFF-UNLOCK position.

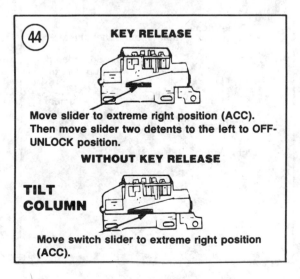

(44)

KEY RELEASE

Move slider to extreme right position (ACC).
Then move slider two detents to the left to OFF-
UNLOCK position.

WITHOUT KEY RELEASE

**TILT
COLUMN**

Move switch slider to extreme right position
(ACC).

Dome Lamp Bulb Replacement

Refer to **Figure 42** for this procedure.
1. Disconnect the negative battery cable.
2. Carefully pry the lens from the dome lamp assembly.
3. Remove the bulb from the wiring harness clips.
4. Installation is the reverse of removal.

Instrument Lights

The instrument cluster bezel must be removed to replace any lamp. See *Instruments* in this chapter.

IGNITION SWITCH

A blade-type terminal switch with one multiple connector is used. The switch is attached to the steering column with a stud and screw. The switch is separate from the key/lock cylinder but the 2 assemblies are synchronized through an actuator rod. The column-mounted dimmer light switch is attached in such a way that it must be removed in order to remove the ignition switch.

Removal

1. Disconnect the negative battery cable.
2. Insert the ignition key in the lock cylinder and turn it to LOCK.
3. Remove the steering column shroud or protective shields.
4. Remove the 3 support bracket bolts. Lower the steering column.
5. Depress the locking tab on the switch multiple connector and unplug the connector from the switch.
6. Remove the dimmer switch fasteners. Disengage the switch from its actuator rod and remove from the steering column.
7. Remove the ignition switch fasteners. Disengage the switch from its actuator rod and remove from the steering column.

Installation

1. Standard column—If equipped with key release feature, position the ignition switch slider to the extreme left as shown in **Figure 43**. If not equipped with key release feature, position the switch slider to the extreme left, then move it 2 detents to the right to the OFF-UNLOCK position (**Figure 43**).
2. Tilt column—If equipped with key release feature, position the switch slider to the extreme right, then move it 2 detents to the left to the OFF-UNLOCK position (**Figure 44**). If not

8

equipped with key release feature, position the ignition switch slider to the extreme right (**Figure 44**).

3. Install the actuator rod in the switch slider hole.

4. Install the switch to the steering column and tighten the lower stud to 35 in.-lb. (3.9 N•m).

5. Install the dimmer switch and depress it sufficiently to insert a 3/32 in. drill bit as shown in **Figure 45**.

6. Move the dimmer switch upward to remove all lash, then tighten the attaching screws and nuts to 35 in.-lb. (3.9 N•m).

7. Reverse Steps 1-5 of *Removal* to complete installation.

Testing

1. Perform Steps 1-5 of *Ignition Switch Removal* in this chapter.

2. Identify the switch terminals according to **Figure 46**.

3. Test the switch with an ohmmeter or a self-powered test lamp. There should be continuity as indicated in **Figure 46**.

HEADLIGHT SWITCH

The combination 3-position headlight switch is mounted in the lower left of the instrument panel. It controls circuits to the headlights, parking/marker and taillights, license plate, interior and instrument panel lights. Removal of the switch is recommended for ease in continuity testing.

Removal/Installation

1. Disconnect the negative battery cable.

2. Remove the steering column lower trim plate (**Figure 47**).

3. Remove the screws holding the instrument cluster trim plate. Let trim plate hang to left side by the wiring.

4. Remove the instrument cluster trim panel screws. Reach behind the left side of the cluster trim panel and unplug the electrical connectors at the headlight and panel/dome switches (**Figure 48**).

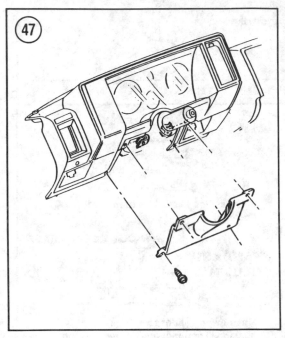

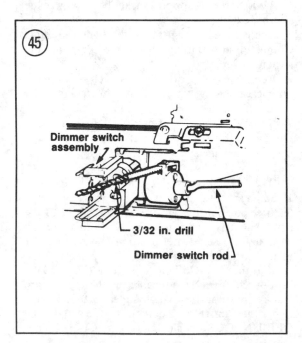

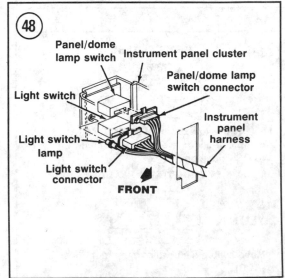

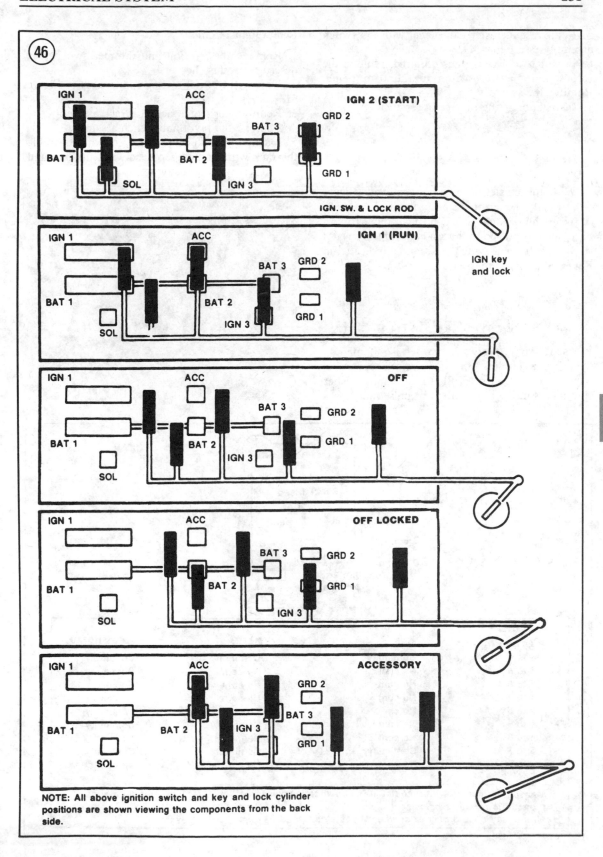

NOTE: All above ignition switch and key and lock cylinder
positions are shown viewing the components from the back
side.

5. Remove the cluster trim panel with the switch assembly. See **Figure 49**.

6. If switch replacement is required, remove the screws holding the switch to the trim panel. Remove the switch.

7. Installation is the reverse of removal.

Testing

1. With the cluster trim panel removed (**Figure 49**), identify the terminals according to **Figure 50**.

2. Test the switch at each position with an ohmmeter or self-powered test lamp. If there is not continuity in each switch position as indicated in **Figure 50**, replace the switch.

WIPER/WASHER SWITCH

A stalk-type wiper/washer switch is mounted on the steering column. A printed circuit board in the wiper motor controls all timing and washer commands in the intermittent or pulse mode.

Removal/Installation

1. Remove the ignition and dimmer switches as described in this chapter.

2. Unplug the switch wiring connector. See **Figure 51**.

3. Remove the switch actuator rack assembly.

4. Remove the pivot and switch assembly.

5. Installation is the reverse of removal. Assemble the rack with its first tooth between the first and second teeth of the sector.

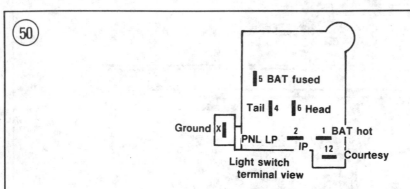

SWITCH POSITIONS

SWITCH TERMINALS	OFF	PARK	HEADLAMP
1 to X	Continuity	Continuity	Continuity
1 to 6	No cont.	No cont.	Continuity
1 to 5	No cont.	No cont.	No cont.
1 to 4	No cont.	No cont.	No cont.
2 to 5*	No cont.	Continuity	Continuity
4 to 5	No cont.	Continuity	Continuity
4 to 6	No cont.	No cont.	No cont.
5 to X	Continuity	Continuity	Continuity
5 to 6	No cont.	No cont.	No cont.
5 to 12	**	**	**

*Measure continuity with rheostat in full counterclockwise position. Test lamp should dim as rheostat is rotated clockwise.

**Continuity should only exist when rheostat is turned beyond detent in switch.

Testing

To test the wiper switch, unplug the connector at the wiper motor and probe the connector terminals with a voltmeter connected to ground (**Figure 52**), referring to **Table 2** for terminal and switch position. If the switch does not function as specified in **Figure 52** and **Table 2**, make sure the switch is OFF and probe the terminals and switch positions for continuity with an ohmmeter or self-powered test lamp. If each switch position reads continuity, the switch is defective. If one or more switch positions do not read continuity, look for an open or short in the wiring harness between the motor and switch.

COOLANT TEMPERATURE SWITCH

Vehicles with a standard cluster use a temperature warning lamp in the instrument panel. Those equipped with the optional gauge cluster have a temperature gauge. Both types are controlled by a thermal switch in the cylinder head which senses coolant temperature.

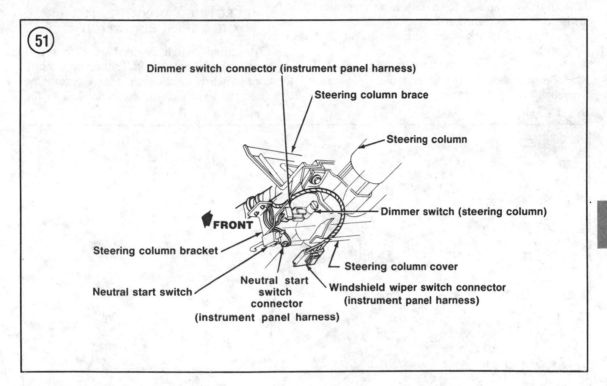

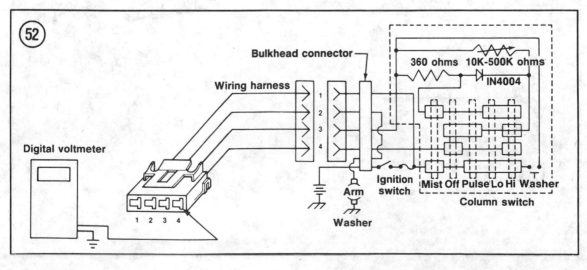

Testing

Refer to **Figure 53** for location of I4 and V6 engine switches.

1. Remove the temperature switch as described in this chapter.

2. Measure the resistance across the terminals with an ohmmeter. The resistance should be between approximately 4,000 ohms at a temperature of 59° F (15° C).

Replacement

1. Remove the radiator cap to relieve any pressure in the cooling system. Partially drain the cooling system below the level of the cylinder head(s). See Chapter Seven.

2. Unplug the electrical lead at the switch. Remove the switch with a suitable open-end wrench.

3. Wrap a piece of Teflon tape around the threads of the new switch. Teflon paste or other electrically conductive water-resistant sealers can also be used.

4. Install the new switch and torque to 72 in.-lb. (7 N•m).

5. Reconnect the electrical lead to the switch terminal.

6. Refill the radiator and reinstall the radiator cap.

ELECTRIC CHOKE HEATER/ OIL PRESSURE SWITCH

A 2-terminal switch is used on carburetted engines with an oil pressure indicator light; a single terminal switch is used on all other engines. One circuit in the switch controls current flow to the

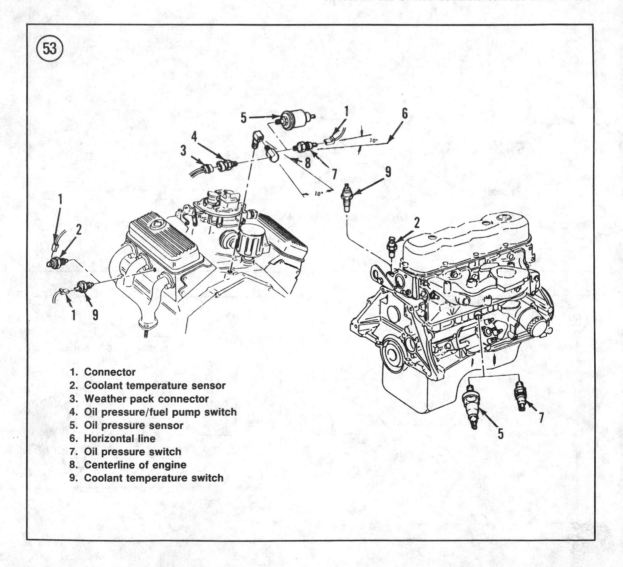

1. Connector
2. Coolant temperature sensor
3. Weather pack connector
4. Oil pressure/fuel pump switch
5. Oil pressure sensor
6. Horizontal line
7. Oil pressure switch
8. Centerline of engine
9. Coolant temperature switch

electric choke heater; the other circuit operates the oil pressure warning light on the instrument panel in case of oil pressure loss. **Figure 54** is a schematic of the switch wiring.

Vehicles equipped with an oil pressure gauge use a variable resistance sender unit.

The I4 switch or sender unit is installed in the engine block near the oil filter or filter adapter housing. The V6 switch or sender unit is installed in the intake manifold near the distributor. See **Figure 53** for location. Note that the fuel-injected V6 engine also uses a separate oil pressure/fuel pump switch. This serves a separate circuit which is a back-up for the fuel pump relay. If the relay fails, the fuel pump is activated by engine oil pressure.

Testing

The oil pressure sending unit fitted to engines with an oil pressure gauge requires special equipment not commonly available to the home mechanic. Have the sending unit on such vehicles tested by a Chevrolet or GMC dealer.

To test the switch used on engines with an indicator light, turn the ignition switch ON but do not start the engine. The indicator light should come on. If it does not, disconnect the wire at the switch terminal and ground it with a jumper lead. If the indicator light comes on, replace the switch. If the light does not come on, check for a burned-out indicator bulb or an open circuit between the bulb and switch.

INSTRUMENTS

Current is supplied to the instrument cluster gauges and lamps by a printed circuit. This is made of copper foil bonded to a polyester base such as Mylar. There is no approved procedure for in-vehicle testing of the printed circuit. Using a probe may pierce the printed circuit or burn the copper conductor. If no damage seems apparent, check each circuit with a test light or ohmmeter. If an open or short circuit is found, replace the printed circuit board.

Instrument cluster bulbs can be replaced by removing the cluster assembly.

Instrument Cluster
Removal/Installation

Refer to **Figure 55** for this procedure.
1. Disconnect the negative battery cable.
2. Remove the lower steering column trim plate.
3. Remove the screws holding the instrument panel cluster trim plate. Remove the trim plate.
4. Remove the screws holding the instrument panel cluster.
5. Disconnect the transmission shift indicator cable from the steering column, if equipped with an automatic transmission.
6. Unplug all electrical connectors and disconnect the speedometer cable.
7. Remove the cluster.
8. Installation is the reverse of removal.

8

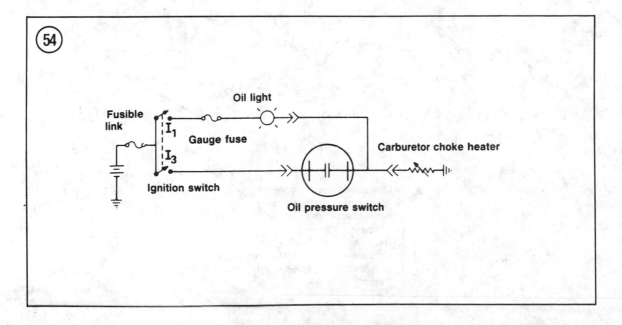

Printed Circuit Board Replacement

1. Remove the instrument cluster as described in this chapter.
2. Remove all bulbs and retaining nuts from the cluster housing. See **Figure 56**.
3. Remove the printed circuit.
4. Installation is the reverse of removal.

HORN

A single horn is standard equipment. Dual horns are optional. The horn is bracket-mounted at the front of the engine compartment on the radiator support (**Figure 57**). Voltage is applied to the horn relay at all times. Depressing the horn pad grounds the relay coil and closes its contacts, transmitting

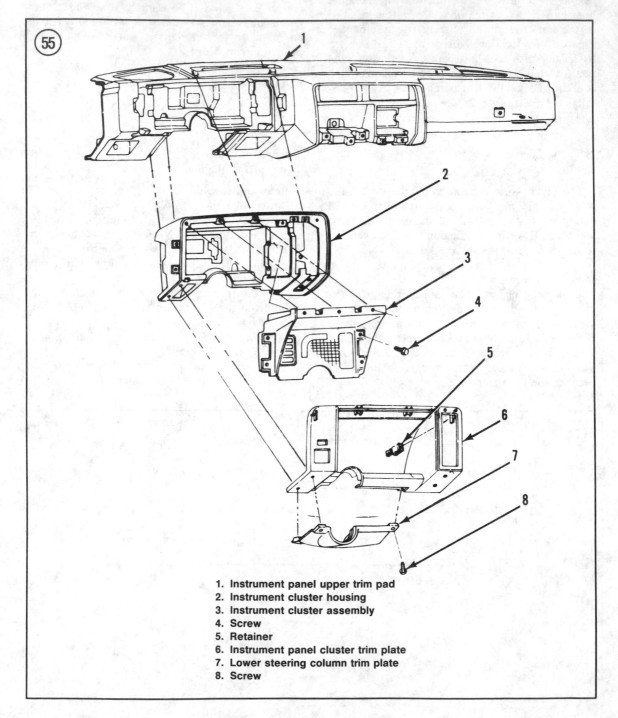

1. Instrument panel upper trim pad
2. Instrument cluster housing
3. Instrument cluster assembly
4. Screw
5. Retainer
6. Instrument panel cluster trim plate
7. Lower steering column trim plate
8. Screw

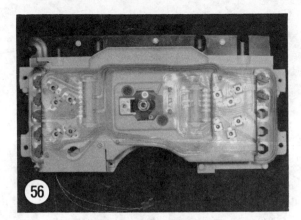

56

voltage from the relay to the horn. If the horn does not sound, check the fuse in the fuse block cavity marked HORN, then check the horn mounting screw. The screw provides a ground for the horn circuit. If corroded or loose, clean or tighten as required.

Testing

1. Ground the horn relay coil. The relay is located in the swing-down convenience center on the left-hand side of the instrument panel near the fuse block. See **Figure 58**.

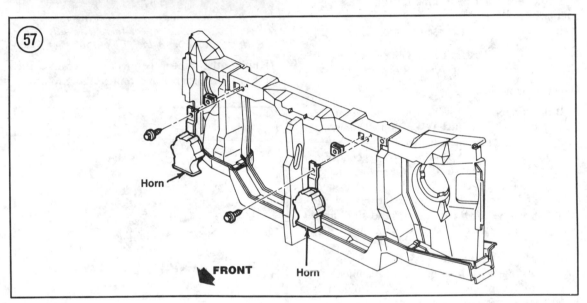

57

Horn

FRONT

Horn

8

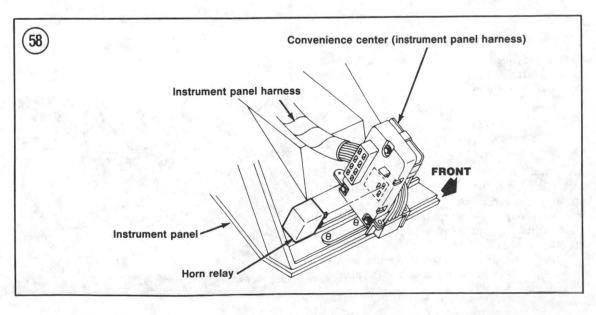

58

Convenience center (instrument panel harness)

Instrument panel harness

FRONT

Instrument panel

Horn relay

2. If the horn sounds, disconnect the black relay lead. If the horn stops sounding with the lead disconnected, the horn switch is faulty. If the horn continues to sound, isolate the relay from the circuit.

3. Use a self-powered test lamp and check to see if the black wire relay contacts are open. If they are, look for a short in the black wire. If they are not open, replace the relay.

Replacement

1. Disconnect the horn wire from the horn terminal.
2. Remove the horn bracket bolt.
3. Remove the horn and bracket from the engine compartment.
4. Installation is the reverse of removal.

WINDSHIELD WIPERS AND WASHERS

Wiper Troubleshooting

1. If the wipers do not work, check the fuse in the fuse block cavity marked WIPERS. See *Electrical Circuit Protection* in this chapter.
2. If the wipers do not work with a good fuse, connect a jumper lead from the wiper motor housing to the vehicle body and test for ground. Ground is supplied by a ground strap and the attaching screws. Check the screws and strap for a loose connection or corrosion. Clean or tighten as necessary.
3. If the wipers still do not work, check wiper switch continuity as described in this chapter.
4. If switch continuity is good, the problem is either a defective motor or an open circuit in the wiring.

Wiper Motor Current Draw Test

1. Remove the fuse from the fuse block cavity marked WIPERS. Connect an ammeter across the fuse cavity terminals.

CAUTION
Cover the windshield with newspaper before the next step so the glass will not be scratched.

2. Turn the ignition switch ON. Run the wiper in high speed with the windshield dry. The normal current draw is 5 amps.
  a. A current draw of less than 5 amps indicates that the internal circuit breaker is weak or that the brushes are bad.
  b. A current draw in excess of 5 amps indicates a shorted or grounded armature. Replace the motor.

Wiper Motor Removal/Installation

CAUTION
The wiper motor contains ceramic permanent magnets. Handle the motor carefully and do not tap with a hammer or the magnets may be damaged.

Refer to **Figure 59** for this procedure.
1. Disconnect the negative battery cable.
2. Remove the cowl vent grille, if necessary to provide access.
3. Loosen but do not remove the drive link to the motor crank arm nuts. Separate the drive link from the crank arm.

NOTE
The wiper motor uses locking-type connectors. Disconnect these carefully when testing or replacing the motor.

4. Unplug the motor connector. Remove the motor attaching screws and remove the motor.

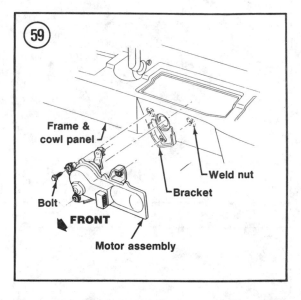

5. Installation is the reverse of removal. Tighten the attaching screws to 51-73 in.-lb. (4.5-6.5 N•m).

ELECTRICAL CIRCUIT PROTECTION

Electrical circuits are protected by fuses, circuit breakers and fusible links. In addition, a swing-down convenience center located near the fuse block contains the headlight warning buzzer, horn relay and hazard flasher.

Fuses

A fuse is a "safety valve" installed in an electrical circuit which "blows" (opens the circuit) when excessive current flows through the circuit. This protects the circuit and electrical components such as the alternator from damage.

The fuse block is a swing-down assembly located under the instrument panel to the left of the steering column (**Figure 60**). Fuse and circuit breaker identification is provided on the fuse block.

To test for blown mini fuse:

1. **Pull fuse out and check visually.**
2. **With the circuit activated, use a test light across the points shown.**

MINI FUSE COLOR CODE	
Rating	Color
5 amp	Tan
10 amp	Red
20 amp	Yellow
25 amp	White

All models use mini-fuses. The mini-fuse is a flat design with 2 blades connected by a metal link encapsulated in plastic. When the fuse is installed, the end of each metal blade is exposed, allowing the fuse condition to be checked with test probes. The plastic is color-coded according to amperage value. Some colors make it difficult to determine whether the fuse is good or bad. **Figure 61** shows a blown mini-fuse, test points and color codes.

Whenever a failure occurs in any part of the electrical system, always check the fuse first to see if it is blown. Usually, the trouble is a short circuit in the wiring. This may be caused by worn-through insulation or by a wire that has worked its way loose and shorted to ground. Occasionally, the electrical overload which causes a fuse to blow may occur in a switch or motor.

A blown fuse should be treated as more than a minor annoyance; it should serve as a warning that something is wrong in the electrical system. Before replacing a fuse, determine what caused it to blow and correct the problem. Always carry several spare fuses of the proper amperage values in the glovebox. Never replace a fuse with one of higher amperage rating than that specified for use. Failure to follow these basic rules could result in heat or fire damage to major parts or loss of the entire vehicle.

Fuse Replacement

To replace a mini-fuse, grasp the plastic covered top and pull the fuse from the fuse block. Insert a new one of the same amperage value (color) in its place.

Circuit Breakers

Some circuits are protected by circuit breakers. These may be mounted in the fuse block, installed in the circuit itself or located within the switch assembly. A circuit breaker conducts current through an arm made of 2 different types of metal connected together. If too much current passes through this bimetal arm, it heats up and expands. One metal expands faster than the other, causing the arm to move and open the contacts to break the current flow. As the arm cools down, the metal contracts and the arm closes the contacts, allowing current to pass. Cycling inline circuit breakers will repeat this sequence as long as power is applied or until the condition is corrected. Non-cycling circuit breakers use a coil around the bimetal arm to hold it in an open position until power is shut off or the condition is corrected.

8

Fusible Links

Fusible links are different than fuses. A fusible link is a short length of wire several gauges smaller than the circuit it protects. It is covered with a thick non-flammable insulation and is intended to burn out if an overload occurs, thus protecting the wiring harness and circuit components.

> *CAUTION*
> *Always replace a burned fusible link with a replacement bearing the same color code or wire gauge. Never use ordinary wire, as this can cause an overload, an electrical fire and complete loss of the vehicle.*

Burned-out fusible links can usually be detected by melted or burned insulation. When the link appears to be good but the starter does not work, check the circuit for continuity with an ohmmeter or self-powered test lamp.

Fusible Link Replacement

Refer to **Figure 62** for this procedure.
1. Obtain the proper service fusible link. Make sure the replacement link is a duplicate of the one removed in terms of wire gauge, length and insulation. Do not substitute any other type or gauge of wire.
2. Disconnect the negative battery cable.
3. Disconnect the damaged fusible link and/or eyelet terminal from the component to which it is attached.
4. Cut the harness behind the connector to remove the damaged fusible link.
5. Strip approximately 1/2 inch from the harness wire insulation.
6. Install a connector on the end of the new fusible link. Fit the other end of the connector on the harness wire and crimp so that both wires are securely fastened.
7. Solder the connection with rosin core solder. Use enough heat to obtain a good joint, but do not overheat.

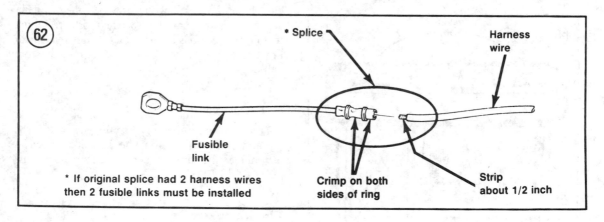

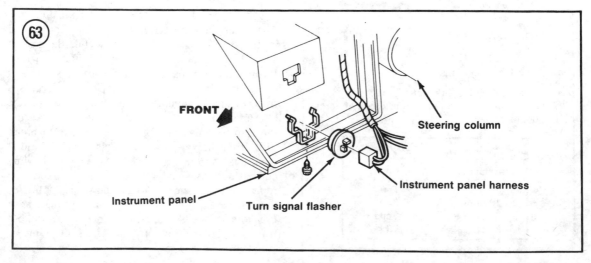

8. Wrap all exposed wires with insulating tape.
9. Connect the fusible link to the component from which it was removed.
10. Reconnect the negative battery cable.

TURN SIGNALS

The turn signal flasher is located behind the instrument panel near the steering column lower panel support. See **Figure 63**.

Testing

1. *One side flashes later than the other, or only one side operates*—Check for a burned-out bulb. Clean socket of any corrosion. Check for a badly grounded bulb. Check for breaks in the wiring.
2. *Turn signals do not work at all*—Check the fuse in the fuse block cavity marked "T/LPS" by operating the back-up lights. If the fuse is good, check the wiring for a break or poor connection. If the wiring is good, install a new turn signal flasher unit.

3. *Lights flash slowly or stay on*—Make sure the battery is fully charged. Check the fuse in the "T/LPS" cavity for a poor contact. Check for a break or poor connection in the wiring. If none of these problems are found, replace the turn signal flasher.
4. *Lights flash too quickly*—Check for a burned-out bulb or disconnected wire. If none are found, replace the turn signal flasher.

HAZARD FLASHER

The hazard flasher is identical in appearance to the turn signal flasher. It is located in the convenience center near the fuse block. See **Figure 64**.

Testing

1. Check the fuse in the fuse block cavity marked STOP/HAZ by operating the stop lights.
2. If the fuse is good and the turn signals operate on both sides, replace the hazard flasher.

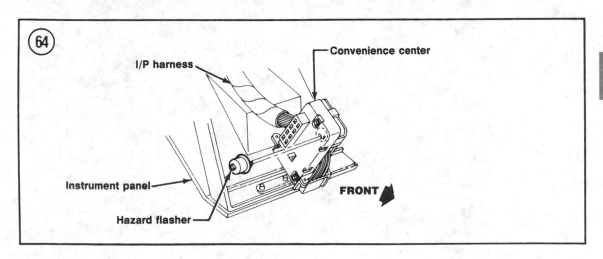

Table 1 BATTERY LOAD SPECIFICATIONS

Battery type	Load test (amperes)
Delco 099	150
Delco 102	170
Delco 103	200
Delco 104 and 105	250
Delco 108	370

Table 2 WIPER/WASHER SWITCH CHECK

Switch mode	Battery voltage @ terminals
Mist	1 and 3
Off	1
Pulse/delay	1 and 3
Low	1 and 3
High	1, 3 and 4
Wash (in Off)	1 and 3
Mist	

CLUTCH AND TRANSMISSION

The vehicles covered in this manual may be equipped with a 4-speed or 5-speed manual transmission. A 4-speed automatic transmission is standard on some models and optional on others.

Power is transmitted from the engine to the transmission, then by the drive shaft to the differential where it is sent to the axle shafts which turn the wheel hubs. Manual transmissions are connected to the engine by the clutch; automatic transmissions are connected to the engine by a torque converter.

This chapter provides inspection, linkage adjustment, removal, installation and overhaul procedures for the clutch and manual transmission, as well as inspection and replacement procedures for the automatic transmission.

Repair of an automatic transmission requires special skills and tools and should be left to a dealer or other qualified shop. The inspection procedures will tell you if professional service is necessary. **Table 1** is at the end of the chapter.

CLUTCH

Components

A hydraulic clutch system is used on all models. The major components of the clutch system are the flywheel, driven plate or disc, pressure plate/cover assembly, clutch fork and clutch release bearing (**Figure 1**). The clutch operating system consists of the pedal/bracket assembly, clutch hydraulic system and clutch release lever.

A clutch master cylinder furnishes hydraulic fluid to operate a slave cylinder mounted on the clutch housing. The slave cylinder in turn actuates the clutch release lever.

The hydraulic system transmits pedal pressure to the clutch release lever, which moves the release bearing into contact with the pressure plate release fingers to control engagement and disengagement of the clutch. The hydraulic clutch is self-adjusting.

Parts Identification

Some clutch parts have 2 or more names. To prevent confusion, the following list gives part names used in this chapter and common synonyms.

    a. Bellhousing—flywheel housing.
    b. Clutch disc—driven plate, friction disc.
    c. Clutch fork—release fork or arm, throw-out lever or arm, withdrawal lever.
    d. Pressure plate—clutch plate, clutch cover.
    e. Release bearing—throw-out bearing.

Hydraulic Clutch System

The hydraulic clutch system consists of a clutch master cylinder with reservoir, slave cylinder and nylon connecting hose (**Figure 2**). The clutch master cylinder is attached to the firewall at one side of the brake vacuum booster. The slave cylinder is attacted to the clutch housing.

The hydraulic clutch system automatically keeps the clutch adjusted. No clutch linkage or pedal position adjustment is required.

If the clutch master cylinder or slave cylinder is defective, it is safer and more economical to replace it with a new or professionally rebuilt unit than to attempt rebuilding it.

Clutch Inspection

1. Start the engine and run at idle. Apply the footbrake and hold the clutch pedal approximately 1/2 in. (12 mm) from the floor mat. Shift the transmission from 1st to REVERSE several times.
   a. If this can be done smoothly, the clutch is releasing fully.

b. If the shift is not smooth, the clutch requires service.
2. Shut the engine off and check the clutch pedal bushings for excessive wear or sticking.
3. Securely block the wheels that remain on the ground. Raise the vehicle with a jack and place it on jackstands. Check the clutch fork for proper

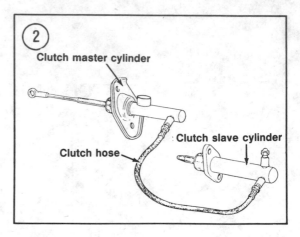

② Clutch master cylinder

Clutch slave cylinder

Clutch hose

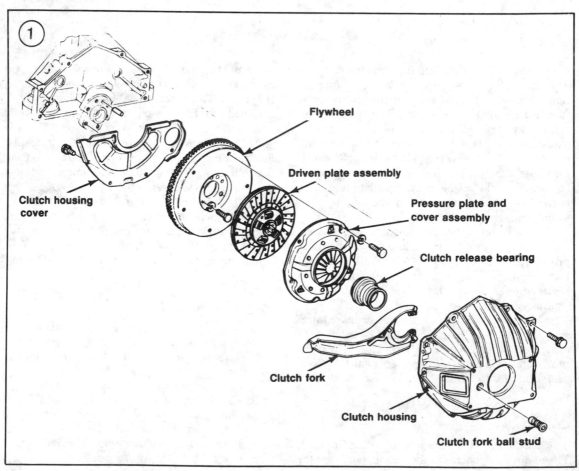

① Flywheel

Driven plate assembly

Clutch housing cover

Pressure plate and cover assembly

Clutch release bearing

Clutch fork

Clutch housing

Clutch fork ball stud

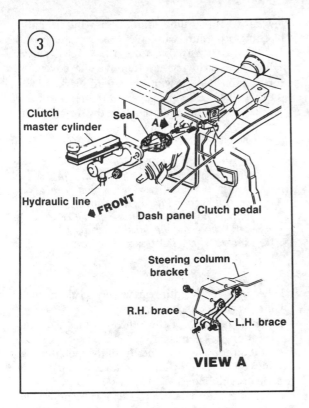

VIEW A

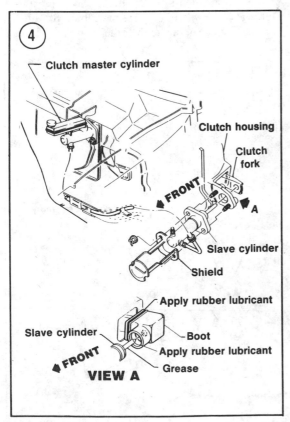

VIEW A

installation on the ball stud. Insufficient fork lubrication can cause the fork to separate from the ball.

4. Check engine mounts (Chapter Four or Chapter Five). If loose or damaged, they can let the engine shift its position.

5. Have an assistant fully depress and hold the clutch pedal while you measure slave cylinder pushrod travel. The pushrod should extend at least 1.03 in. (26 mm) against the release lever.

Clutch Master Cylinder
Removal/Installation

Refer to **Figure 3** for this procedure.

1. Disconnect the negative battery cable.
2. Remove the hush panel inside the cab.
3. Remove the retaining clip and disconnect the clutch master cylinder pushrod at the clutch pedal.
4. Use a flare nut wrench and disconnect the slave cylinder hydraulic line at the master cylinder. Plug the line and cap the fitting to prevent leakage and the entry of contamination.
5. Remove the nuts holding the master cylinder to the firewall. Remove the master cylinder from the engine compartment.
6. Installation is the reverse of removal. Tighten the master cylinder attaching nuts to specifications (**Table 1**). Fill the master cylinder reservoir with new DOT 3 brake fluid and bleed the hydraulic system as described in this chapter.

Slave Cylinder
Removal/Installation

Refer to **Figure 4** for this procedure.

1. Securely block both rear wheels so the vehicle will not roll in either direction.
2. Raise the front of the vehicle with a jack and place it on jackstands.
3. Disconnect the master cylinder hydraulic line at the slave cylinder. Plug the line and cap the fitting to prevent leakage or the entry of contamination.
4. Remove the nuts holding the slave cylinder to the bell housing. Remove the slave cylinder.
5. To install the slave cylinder, reconnect the master cylinder hydraulic line to the slave cylinder housing.
6. Fill the master cylinder reservoir with new DOT 3 brake fluid and bleed the hydraulic system as described in this chapter.
7. Position the slave cylinder on the bell housing and install the retaining nuts. Tighten nuts to specifications (**Table 1.**).
8. Remove the jackstands and lower the vehicle to the ground. Remove the wheel chocks.

9

Hydraulic Clutch Bleeding

The clutch hydraulic system uses the same type of fluid as the brake hydraulic system.

After long usage, brake fluid absorbs enough atmospheric moisture to significantly reduce its boiling point and make it prone to vapor lock under certain condition. While no hard and fast rule exists for changing the fluid in the clutch hydraulic system, it should be checked at least annually by bleeding fluid from the slave cylinder and inspecting it for moisture. If moisture is present, the system should be drained, refilled and bled.

The hydraulic clutch system must also be bled whenever air enters it. This occurs when the clutch hydraulic line has been disconnected, when the fluid level in the master cylinder is low or when the master/slave cylinder is defective. Air in the system will compress, rather than transmit pedal pressure to the clutch operating parts, making shifting gears very difficult.

This procedure requires handling brake fluid. Be careful not to get any brake fluid on painted surfaces. Two people are needed: one to operate the clutch pedal and the other to open and close the bleeding valve.

Periodically check the brake fluid level in the clutch master cylinder during bleeding and top up as required. If the fluid level is allowed to drop too low, air will enter the hydraulic lines and the entire bleeding procedure will have to be repeated.

1. Clean away any dirt around the clutch master cylinder reservoir cover. Remove the cover and top up the reservoir with brake fluid marked DOT 3 or DOT 4. Leave the cover off the reservoir and place a clean shop cloth over the reservoir to prevent the entry of contamination.

NOTE
DOT 3 means that the brake fluid meets current Department of Transportation quality standards. If the fluid container does not say DOT 3 somewhere on the label, buy a brand that does. DOT 4 brake fluid can also be safely used.

2. Securely block both rear wheels so the vehicle will not roll in either direction.
3. Raise the front of the vehicle with a jack and place it on jackstands.
4. Unbolt the slave cylinder from the bell housing. Remove the slave cylinder without disconnecting the hydraulic line.
5. Fit an appropriate size box-end wrench over the bleed valve and attach a length of plastic or rubber tubing to the valve. Be sure the tubing fits snugly on the valve. Submerge the other end of the tubing

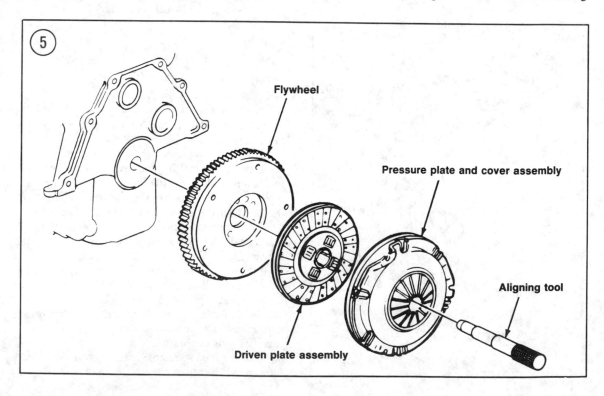

(5)

Flywheel

Pressure plate and cover assembly

Aligning tool

Driven plate assembly

in a jar containing several inches of clean DOT 3 or DOT 4 brake fluid.

NOTE
Do not allow the end of the tubing to come out of the brake fluid during bleeding or the fluid level in the master cylinder reservoir to run dry. This could allow air into the system and the bleeding procedure would have to be repeated.

6. Hold the slave cylinder at 45 degree angle with the bleed valve at the highest point.
7. Have an assistant pump the clutch pedal 2-3 times, then depress and hold the pedal to the floor.
8. While the pedal is held down, open the slave cylinder bleed valve 1/3-1/2 turn. Let the fluid and air escape. Close the bleed valve while the pedal is still down, then have the assistant release the pedal and allow it to return to its normal position.
9. Repeat Step 7 and Step 8 until the fluid entering the jar contains no air bubbles.
10. Remove the tubing from the bleed valve and close the valve tightly with the wrench.
11. Reinstall the slave cylinder to the bell housing. Tighten the fasteners to specifications (**Table 1**).
12. Remove the jackstands and lower the vehicle to the ground. Remove the wheel chocks.
13. Remove the cloth over the master cylinder resevoir and top up the reservoir as required, then reinstall the cap.
14. Road test the vehicle to make sure the clutch releases and engages satisfactorily. If the clutch won't release properly after the hydraulic system is bled, the master or slave cylinder may be defective.

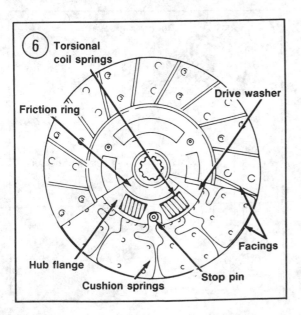

6 Torsional coil springs

Drive washer

Friction ring

Hub flange

Cushion springs

Stop pin

Facings

Clutch Removal

Refer to **Figure 1** and **Figure 5** for this procedure.
1. Support the engine and remove the transmission as described in this chapter.
2. Remove the slave cylinder from the bell housing as described in this chapter.
3. Remove the bell housing. Slide the clutch fork off the ball stud and remove fork from dust boot.

NOTE
If clutch cover and flywheel are marked with a visible "X," omit Step 4.

4. Make alignment marks on the clutch cover and flywheel for reference during reassembly.
5. Insert a dummy shaft or alignment tool through the clutch disc hub.

NOTE
An input shaft from a junk transmission can be used as a dummy shaft. Inexpensive aligning bars can also be purchased from some auto parts stores. Some tool rental dealers and parts stores rent universal aligning bars which can be adapted.

6. Unbolt the clutch cover from the flywheel. Loosen the bolts in several stages using a diagonal pattern to prevent warping the cover.
7. Remove the pressure plate and disc from the flywheel.

Clutch Disc Inspection

Refer to **Figure 6** for this procedure.
1. Check the clutch disc for the following:
   a. Oil or grease on the facings.
   b. Glazed or warped facings.
   c. Loose or missing rivets.
   d. Facings worn to within 1/16 in. (2 mm) of any rivet.
   e. Broken torsional coil or cushion springs (loose springs are considered normal).
   f. Warped or distorted hub flange.
   g. Missing stop pins.
   h. Loose fit or rough movement on the transmission input shaft splines.
2. Remove small amounts of oil or grease with aerosol brake cleaner and dress the facings with a wire brush, if necessary. However, if the facings are soaked with oil or grease, replace the disc. The disc must also be replaced if any of the other defects is present or if the facings are partially worn and a new pressure plate is being installed.

Pressure Plate Inspection

Refer to **Figure 7** for this procedure.

1. Check the pressure plate for:
   a. Scoring.
   b. Overheating (blue-tinted areas).
   c. Burn marks.
   d. Cracks.
   e. Uneven mating surfaces.
2. Clean the mating surfaces with a cloth moistened in solvent to remove any oil film.
3. Check the diaphragm springs for wear or damage at the release bearing contact surface. Check for bent, excessively worn or broken spring fingers. Replace the pressure plate and cover assembly if any defects are found.
4. If the clutch trouble is still not apparent, take the pressure plate and disc to a competent machine shop. Have the disc and pressure plate checked for runout and the diaphragm springs checked for correct finger height. Do not attempt to dismantle the pressure plate or readjust the fingers yourself. This requires the proper tools and experience.

Release Bearing Inspection

Never reuse a release bearing unless necessary. When other clutch parts are worn, the bearing is probably worn. If it is necessary to reinstall the old bearing, do not wash it in solvent.

1. Wipe all dirt or oil from the bearing with a clean cloth.
2. Hold the inner race from moving and rotate the outer race while applying a slight amount of pressure. Replace the bearing if rotation is noisy or rough.
3. Check the bearing for wear signs at the point where the fork and fingers contact it. Replace the bearing if one side is worn more than the other and check for a bent or off-center fork.
4. Check the bearing assembly for burrs. If present, clean with fine crocus cloth, then check the transmission input shaft for scoring and polish out with crocus cloth.
5. Install bearing assembly to clutch fork and check for snug fit. Replace the bearing as required.

Clutch Installation

Refer to **Figure 1** and **Figure 5** for this procedure.

1. Be sure your hands are clean and free of oil or grease.
2. Make sure the disc facings, pressure plate and flywheel are free of oil, grease and other foreign material.

3. If installing a new clutch disc, lightly sand the friction surface of the flywheel and pressure plate with medium-fine emery cloth. Sand accross (not around) the surfaces until they are covered with fine scratches. This breaks the glaze and helps in seating a new clutch disc.
4. Place the clutch disc and pressure plate in position on the flywheel. The side of the disc stamped "FLYWHEEL" should face the flywheel with the torsional springs facing the transmission when assembled.
5. Position the clutch cover on the flywheel, aligning the clutch cover and flywheel "X" or alignment marks.

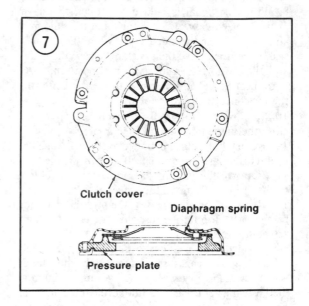

Clutch cover
Diaphragm spring
Pressure plate

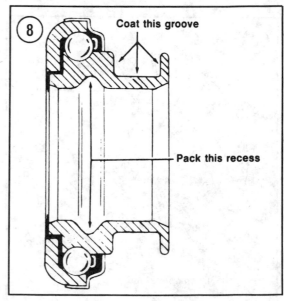

Coat this groove
Pack this recess

6. Start but do not tighten the cover bolts. Center the disc and pressure plate with a dummy shaft or alignment tool.

7. Gradually tighten the cover bolts in a diagonal pattern to specification (**Table 1**). Remove the alignment tool.

8. Lubricate the outer diameter of the release bearing with extreme pressure (E.P.) multipurpose grease as shown in **Figure 8**. Pack the inner diameter recess of the bearing with E.P. multipurpose grease.

9. Lubricate the ball stud and clutch fork fingers with graphite grease. Install fork on ball stud.

10. Install release bearing on clutch fork, Install bell housing over clutch fork. Tighten bolts to specifications (**Table 1**).

11. Install the dust boot.

12. Install transmission as described in this chapter.

13. Install the clutch slave cylinder as described in this chapter.

Clutch Pedal
Removal/Installation

Refer to **Figure 9** for this procedure.

1. Disconnect the negative battery cable.

2. Remove the hush panel from inside the vehicle.

3. Disconnect the clutch interlock switch from the clutch pedal and bracket assembly.

4. Remove the retaining clip holding the master cylinder pushrod to the clutch pedal, then disconnect the pushrod from the pedal.

5. Remove the pivot retainer clip from the clutch pedal. Remove the clutch pedal from the bracket.

6. Remove the bushings from the steering column support bracket. Remove the spring from the pedal.

7. Installation is the reverse of removal. Lightly lubricate the retaining pin and bushings with graphite grease before installation. Adjust the clutch interlock switch as described in this chapter.

Clutch Interlock Switch

Vehicles equipped with a manual transmission have a clutch interlock switch. The engine will not start unless the clutch pedal is fully depressed. Refer to **Figure 10** for this procedure.

1. Disconnect the negative battery cable.

2. Remove the hush panel from inside the vehicle.

3. Unplug the electrical connector at the interlock switch.

4. Remove the screw holding the switch to the bracket. Remove the switch.

5. Installation is the reverse of removal. Adjust the switch as follows:

    a. Move slider A forward on shaft B.

    b. Manually push the clutch pedal all the way to the floor. This will automatically adjust the switch.

---

(9)

Steering column bracket

Bushing

Bushing

Spring

FRONT

Retainer

Washer

Pin

Clutch master cylinder rod

NOTE—Lightly lubricate the pin and bushings before installing.

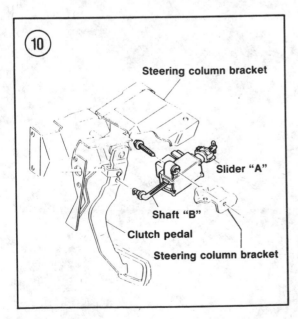

(10)

Steering column bracket

Slider "A"

Shaft "B"

Clutch pedal

Steering column bracket

9

Pilot Bearing
Removal/Installation

The transmission input shaft rides on a solid oil-inpregnated bearing pressed into the crankshaft bore. A glazed, worn or improperly lubricated pilot bearing will produce an objectionable squeal or chirping noise when the clutch is activated. The pilot bearing is pressed in place and should not be loose. A bearing that has been removed should never be reinstalled. If removed for any reason, install a new bearing.

Check the bearing for a varnished or glazed appearance or heat discoloration. Replace the bearing if any of these conditions are noted. Check the bearing inner surface for excessive wear resulting in a bell-mouthed condition. Replace the bearing if worn or damaged and check the input shaft for corresponding damage; replace input shaft as required.

New bearings have lubricant pressed into them during manufacture and should not be lubricated with any type of grease. Under certain storage conditions, however, some of this lubricant protection can be lost. For this reason, it is a good idea to soak a new bearing for at least 30 minutes in non-detergent, 30W engine oil prior to installation.

1. Remove the clutch as described in this chapter.
2. Remove the bearing from the crankshaft with tool part No. J-1448 or equivalent. See **Figure 11** (typical). A hook type puller and slide hammer can also be used to remove the bearing.
3. Clean the crankshaft bearing bore.

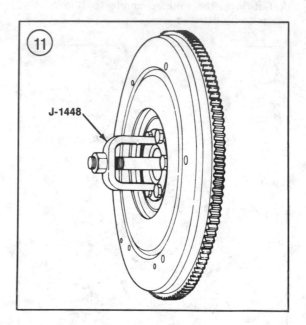

J-1448

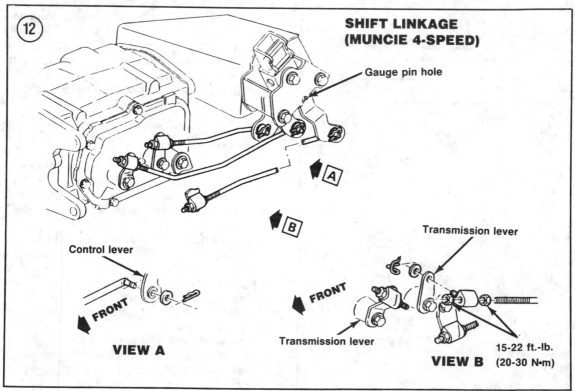

SHIFT LINKAGE (MUNCIE 4-SPEED)

Gauge pin hole

Control lever

FRONT

VIEW A

Transmission lever

Transmission lever

FRONT

15-22 ft.-lb. (20-30 N•m)

VIEW B

4. Fit the new bearing on the pilot of tool part No. J-1552 or another suitable installer. The radius in the bearing bore should face the tool shoulder.

5. Lubricate the outer diameter of the bearing with several drops of machine oil. Install the bearing in the crankshaft.

6. Reinstall the clutch as described in this chapter.

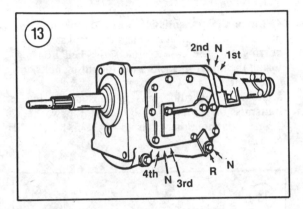

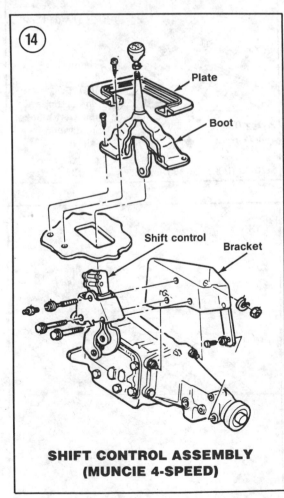

**SHIFT CONTROL ASSEMBLY
(MUNCIE 4-SPEED)**

MANUAL TRANSMISSION

The vehicles covered in this manual may be equipped with a Muncie 4-speed or Warner T5 5-speed manual transmission. The Muncie 4-speed uses external shift linkage which can be adjusted as required. The shift mechanism on the T5 is located within the shift control housing and does not require adjustment. It can be serviced independently of the transmission, if necessary.

MUNCIE 4-SPEED TRANSMISSION

Shift Linkage Adjustment

Refer to **Figure 12** for this procedure.

1. Make sure the ignition is off. Securely block both rear wheels so the vehicle will not roll in either direction.

2. Raise the front of the vehicle with a jack and place it on jackstands.

3. Loosen the shift rod swivel locknuts so that the rods can move freely through the swivels.

4. Place all transmission levers in the NEUTRAL position. See **Figure 13**.

5. Move the shift control lever to the neutral detent and install 1/4 in. gauge pin in the lever alignment slot.

6. Tighten the shift rod swivel locknuts to 15-22 ft.-lb. (20-30 N•m) and remove the gauge pin.

7. Check the linkage to make sure that it operates properly and smoothly through all gear changes. Readjust, if required.

**Shift Control Assembly
Removal/Installation**

Refer to **Figure 14** for this procedure.

1. Securely block both rear wheels so the vehicle will not roll in either direction.

2. Raise the front of the vehicle with a jack and place it on jackstands.

3. Disconnect the shift rods from the transmission control levers.

4. Unbolt and remove the shift control assembly from the transmission.

5. Remove the jackstands and lower the vehicle to the ground. Remove the wheel chocks.

6. Working inside wth passenger compartment, remove the screws holding the plate to the floorboard.

7. Remove the screws holding the boot to the floorboard.

8. Remove the shift lever and boot assembly.

9. Installation is the reverse of removal. Tighten shift control assembly bolts to 30-36 ft.-lb. (40-50 N•m).

9

Transmission Removal

This procedure requires three guide pins. These can be made by cutting the heads off extra transmission-to-bellhousing bolts, grinding a taper on the cut ends, then cutting a screwdriver slot in the ends.

1. Securely block both rear wheels so the vehicle will not roll in either direction.
2. Raise the front of the vehicle with a jack and place it on jackstands.
3. Drain the transmission lubricant into a clean container. See Chapter Three.
4. Remove the drive shaft. See Chapter Eleven.
5. Disconnect the speedometer cable at the extension housing.
6. Unplug all electrical connectors at the transmission.
7. Remove the shift control assembly as described in this chapter.
8. Unbolt the transmission mount. See **Figure 15** (typical).
9. Support the transmission with a transmission jack. Raise the jack enough to take the transmission weight off the crossmember. Unbolt and remove the crossmember from the vehicle.
10. Support the engine with a hydraulic jack. Use a block of wood between the jack and engine to protect the oil pan.
11. Remove the upper bolts holding the transmission to the bellhousing. Install guide pins in the holes, then remove the lower bolts. See **Figure 16**.

NOTE
Once the transmission is out of the vehicle, do not depress the clutch pedal or the clutch disc will fall out of position.

12. Pull the transmission to the rear until the input shaft clears the bellhousing, then lower the tranmission to the floor with the jack and remove it from under the vehicle.
13. Remove the guide pins from the bellhousing.

Transmission Installation

1. Lightly lubricate the input shaft bearing retainer and the splined part of the transmission input shaft with high-temperature grease. Do not apply too much grease or the clutch disc can become contaminated during operation.
2. Raise the transmission on a jack until the input shaft splines are aligned with the clutch disc splines. The clutch release bearing and hub must be properly positioned in the release lever fork.

3. Install a guide pin in each lower bellhousing-to-transmission case bolt hole.

NOTE
If the front bearing retainer hangs up on the release bearing hub during Step 4, work the release lever back and forth until the hub properly engages the retainer.

4. Move the transmission forward on the guide pins until the input shaft enters the crankshaft pilot bearing and the case contacts the bell housing. Install the upper treansmission mounting bolts and lockwashers.
5. Remove the guide pins and install the lower transmission mounting bolts and lockwashers. Tighten all mounting bolts to 40-51 ft.-lb. (55-70 N•m).

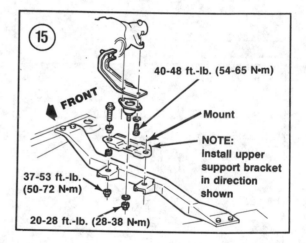

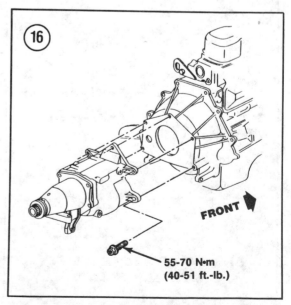

6. Slip the shift lever into the rubber boot, then position the shift control to the support. Install and tighten control assembly-to-support bolts.

7. Reinstall shift levers to transmission.

8. Reinstall the transmission support cross-member to the frame side rails.

9. Raise the transmission slightly and install the rear support.

10. Connect the drive shaft. See Chapter Eleven.

11. Remove the transmission and engine support jacks.

12. Connect the speedometer cable and any electrical connectors.

13. Connect each shift rod to its respective transmission shift lever and adjust the linkage as described in this chapter.

14. Reinstall any other components (support brackets, exhaust pipe, etc.) removed to provide working clearance.

15. Fill the transmission with 1.3 qt. of SAE 80W-90 lubricant. See Chapter Three.

16. Remove the jackstands and lower the vehicle to the ground. Remove the wheel chocks.

WARNER T5 5-SPEED TRANSMISSION

Shift Lever Removal/Installation

Refer to **Figure 17** for this procedure.

1. Remove the screws holding the shift lever boot retainer.

2. Pull the retainer up enough to remove the screws holding the shift lever boot.

3. Carefully slide boot up the lever.

4. Hold shift lever at wrench slot with an appropriate tool and unscrew the control lever nut.

5. Unscrew and remove the shift lever.

6. Installation is the reverse of removal.

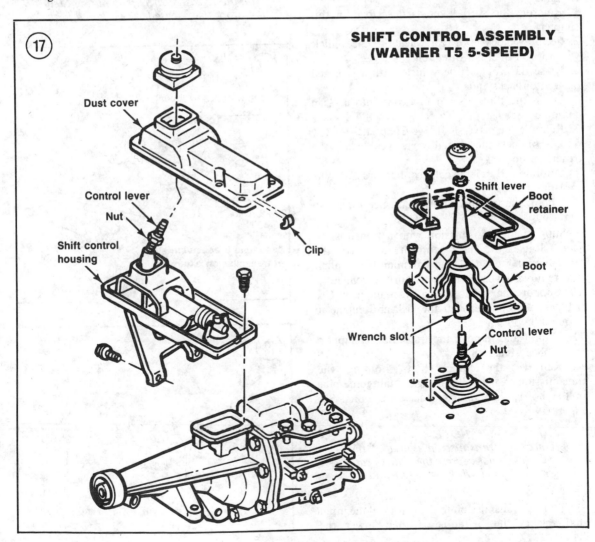

SHIFT CONTROL ASSEMBLY (WARNER T5 5-SPEED)

(17)

Dust cover

Control lever

Nut

Shift control housing

Clip

Shift lever

Boot retainer

Boot

Wrench slot

Control lever

Nut

Control Lever Removal/Installation

Refer to **Figure 17** for this procedure.

1. Remove the shift lever as described in this chapter.
2. Remove the transmission as described in this chapter.
3. Remove the dust cover hold-down clips, then remove the dust cover.
4. Unbolt the control lever assembly.
5. Installation is the reverse of removal. Tighten side bolts to 35 ft.-lb. (47 N•m) and top bolts to 13 ft.-lb. (17 N•m).

Transmission Removal

This procedure requires a pair of guide pins. These can be made by cutting the heads off extra transmission-to-bellhousing bolts, grinding a taper on the cut ends, then cutting a screwdriver slot in the ends.

1. Remove the shift lever as described in this chapter.
2. Securely block both rear wheels so the vehicle will not roll in either direction.
3. Raise the front of the vehicle with a jack and place it on jackstands.
4. Drain the transmission lubricant into a clean container. See Chapter Three.
5. Remove the drive shaft. See Chapter Eleven.
6. Disconnect the speedometer cable at the extension housing.
7. Unplug all electrical connectors at the transmission.
8. Unbolt the transmission mount. See **Figure 15** (typical).
9. Support the transmission with a transmission jack. Raise the jack enough to take the transmission weight off the crossmember. Unbolt and remove the crossmember from the vehicle.
10. Support the engine with a hydraulic jack. Use a block of wood between the jack and engine to protect the oil pan.
11. Unbolt and remove the transmission support braces. See **Figure 18**.
12. Remove the upper bolts holding the transmission to the bellhousing. Install guide pins in the holes, then remove the lower bolts. See **Figure 19**.

NOTE
Once the transmission is out of the vehicle, do not depress the clutch pedal or the clutch disc will fall out of position.

13. Pull the transmission to the rear until the input shaft clears the bellhousing, then lower the

transmission to the floor with the jack and remove it from under the vehicle.
14. Remove the guide pins from the bellhousing.

Transmission Installation

1. Lightly lubricate the input shaft bearing retainer and the splined part of the transmission input shaft with high-temperature grease. Do not apply too much grease or the clutch disc can become contaminated during operation.
2. Raise the transmission on a jack until the input shaft splines are aligned with the clutch disc splines. The clutch release bearing and hub must be properly postioned in the release lever fork.
3. Install a guide pin in each lower bellhousing-to-transmission case bolt hole.

NOTE
If the front bearing retainer hangs up on the release bearing hub during Step 4, work the release lever back and forth

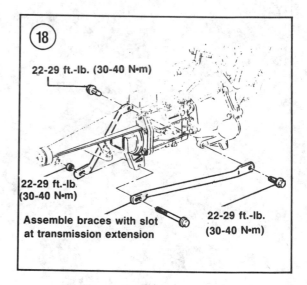

18

22-29 ft.-lb. (30-40 N•m)

22-29 ft.-lb. (30-40 N•m)

Assemble braces with slot at transmission extension

22-29 ft.-lb. (30-40 N•m)

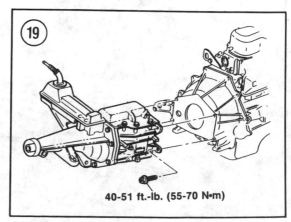

19

40-51 ft.-lb. (55-70 N•m)

until the hub properly engages the retainer.

4. Move the transmission forward on the guide pin until the input shaft enters the crankshaft pilot bearing and the case contancts the bell housing. Install the upper transmission mounting bolts and lockwashers.

5. Remove the guide studs and install the lower transmission mounting bolts and lockwashers. Tighten all mounting bolts to 40-51 ft.-lb. (55-70 N•m).

6. Reinstall the support braces and tighten fasteners to 22-29 ft.-lb. (30-40 N•m).

7. Reinstall the transmission support cross-member to the frame side rails.

8. Raise the transmission slightly and install the rear support.

9. Connect the drive shaft. See Chapter Eleven.

10. Remove the transmission and engine support jacks.

11. Connect the speedometer cable and any electrical connectors.

12. Fill the transmission with 2.2 qt. of DEXRON automatic transmission fluid. See Chapter Three.

13. Remove the jackstand and lower the vehicle to the ground. Remove the wheel chocks.

14. Reinstall the shift lever as described in this chapter.

AUTOMATIC TRANSMISSION

Optional equipment on vehicles covered in this manual is a Turbo-Hydramatic 700-R4 automatic transmission. The 700-R4 is a hydraulically operated 4-speed overdrive unit with a compound planetary gear system and torque converter.

To determine the exact transmission application, check the nameplate attached or stamped on the transmission case. This nameplate contains the transmission model, model year and serial number. This information is required for ordering replacement parts.

The torque converter contains a converter clutch mechanism to provide a direct mechanical connection between the engine and transmission at predetermined speed/load conditions. A solenoid-operated valve in the transmission valve body is controlled by the Computer Command Control ECM. Based on sensor data, the ECM applies or releases the converter clutch. When applied, this feature reduces slippage losses in the converter, which translates into better fuel economy.

The THM 700-R4 uses an external throttle valve (TV) control cable to control shift points and quality.

The 700-R4 uses DEXRON II automatic transmission fluid. Use of a transmission fluid other than that specified can result in a transmission malfunction and/or premature failure. Fluid checking and changing procedures are described in Chapter Three.

This section includes checks and adjustment procedures to be performed with the transmission in the vehicle. Many problems can be corrected with the adjustment procedures provided here. Automatic transmission overhaul, however, requires professional skills, many special tools and extremely high standards of cleanliness. Although procedures for removal and installation are included in this chapter, disassembly and overhaul should be left to a Chevrolet or GMC dealer, or a competent automatic transmission repair shop.

Neutral Start/Backup Light Switch Testing

The switch is mounted on the steering column mast jacket (**Figure 20**).

9

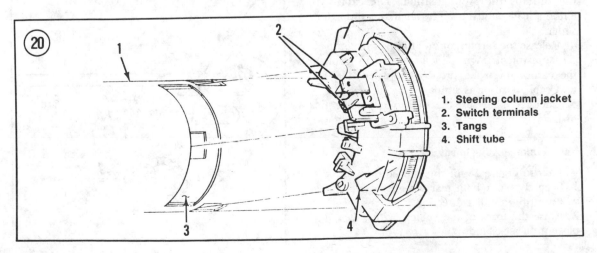

20

1. Steering column jacket
2. Switch terminals
3. Tangs
4. Shift tube

1. Unplug the wiring connector from the switch.
2. Connect a self-powered test lamp between the connector and switch terminals.
3. Turn the ignition switch ON, but do not start the engine.
4. Move the gearshift lever through the gear range and check for continuity in each position. There should be continuity only when the lever is in PARK or NEUTRAL. If the test lamp lights in any other position, adjust the switch as described in this chapter.

Neutral Start/Backup Light Switch Adjustment

Refer to **Figure 20** (typical) for this procedure.
1. Move the switch housing as far toward the low gear detent as possible.
2. Move the shift lever into PARK. The switch housing and housing back should ratchet into place, automatically adjusting the switch.

Throttle Valve (TV) Cable System

The TV cable system (**Figure 21**) controls transmission line pressure, shift points, shift feel, part throttle and detent downshifts.

TV Cable Adjustment

Refer to **Figure 21** (typical) for this procedure.
1. Remove the air cleaner to provide access to the slider. See Chapter Six.
2. Depress the readjust tab (**Figure 22**). Move the slider back through the fitting (away from the carburetor or TBI lever) until the slider stops against the fitting. Release the readjust tab.
3. Manually open the carburetor or TBI lever to the full throttle stop position. The cable will automatically adjust itself by ratcheting through its slider.
4. Release the carburetor or TBI lever to complete the adjustment. **Figure 23** shows the TV cable at the carburetor when properly adjusted; the TBI unit cable position is similar.
5. Check to make sure the TV cable does not stick or bind.

Shift Linkage Adjustment

Refer to **Figure 24** for this procedure.
1. Securely block both rear wheels so the vehicle will not roll in either direction.
2. Raise the front of the vehicle with a jack and place it on jackstands.

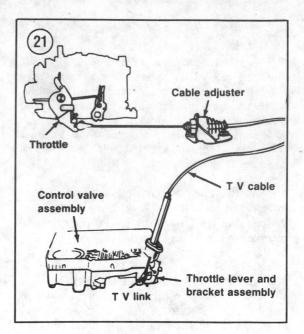

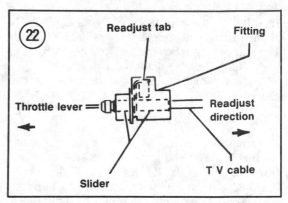

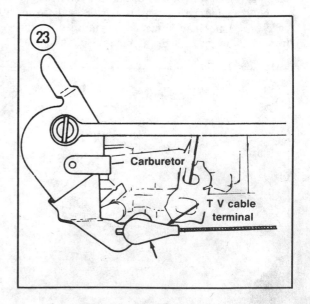

3. Loosen the equalizer nut shown in **Figure 24**.

4. Place column selector lever in its NEUTRAL position.

5. Move the shift lever as far forward as possible, then back 2 detents to the NEUTRAL position. See **Figure 25**.

6. Hold the rod shown in **Figure 24** tightly in its swivel and tighten the nut loosened in Step 3 to 11 ft.-lb. (15 N•m).

7. Place the column selector lever in the PARK position and check linkage adjustment.

   a. The selector lever should engage in all positions.

   b. The engine should start only in the PARK or NEUTRAL positions. If it starts in any other position, or does not start in PARK and NEUTRAL, readjust the neutral start switch as described in this chapter.

Transmission Removal

1. Disconnect the negative battery cable.

2. Remove the engine cover. See Chapter Four (I4) or Chapter Five (V6).

3. Remove the air cleaner assembly. (Chapter Six).

4. Disconnect the TV cable at the carburetor or TBI unit.

5. Securely block both rear wheels so the vehicle will not roll in either direction.

6. Raise the vehicle with a jack and place it on jackstands.

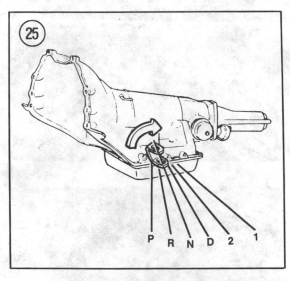

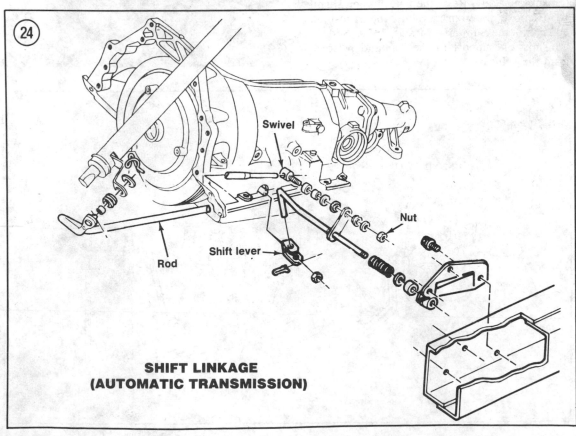

**SHIFT LINKAGE
(AUTOMATIC TRANSMISSION)**

7. Place a suitable container under the transmission and drain the fluid. See Chapter Three. Temporarily reinstall the oil pan.

8. Disconnect and remove the drive shaft (Chapter Eleven).

9. Disconnect the speedometer cable at the transmission. See **Figure 26** (typical).

9. Disconnect the shift linkage at the transmission (**Figure 27**).

10. Disconnect all electrical leads at the transmission. Remove any clips retaining leads to the transmission case.

11. Remove the support brace bolts at the converter. See **Figure 28**.

12. Disconnect the exhaust pipe (I4) or exhaust crossover pipe (V6) at the exhaust manifold(s).

13. Remove the converter cover. Mark the flywheel and torque converter for reassembly reference.

14. Install a wrench on the crankshaft pulley bolt to rotate the crankshaft and gain access to a converter attaching bolt/nut. Remove the fastener, then rotate the crankshaft a partial turn to align another bolt/nut for removal. Continue this procedure until all fasteners are removed.

15. Place a transmission jack under the transmission case. Raise the transmission slightly.

16. Remove the transmission support-to-mount bolts and the support-to-frame bolts. Slide the transmission support to the rear and remove it from the vehicle.

17. Lower the transmission slightly with the jack to provide access to the oil cooler lines and TV cables. Disconnect the oil cooler lines (**Figure 29**) and TV cable at the transmisssion. Plug the oil lines and cap the fittings to prevent leakage or entry of contamination.

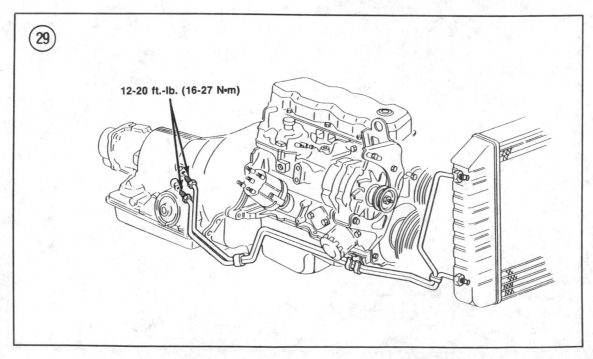

12-20 ft.-lb. (16-27 N•m)

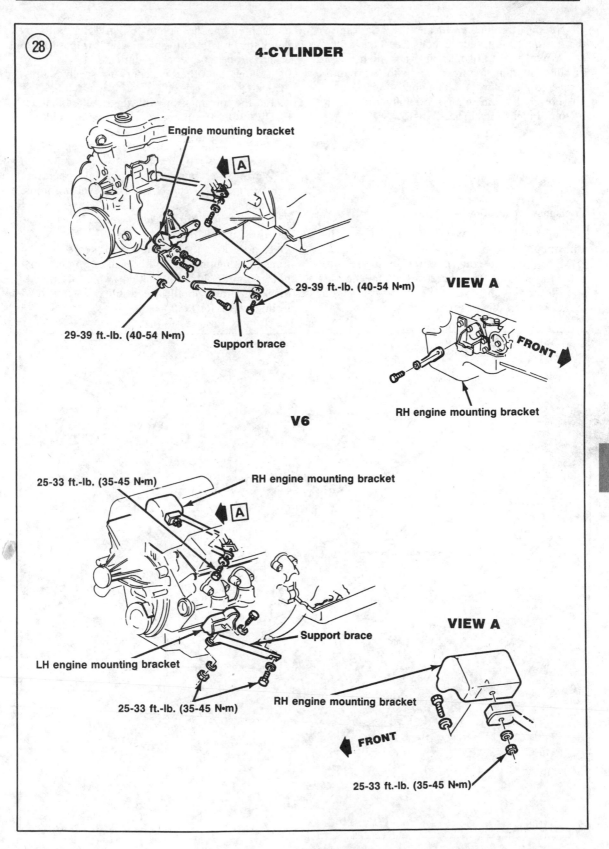

(28)

4-CYLINDER

Engine mounting bracket

A

29-39 ft.-lb. (40-54 N•m)

29-39 ft.-lb. (40-54 N•m)

Support brace

VIEW A

FRONT

RH engine mounting bracket

V6

25-33 ft.-lb. (35-45 N•m)

RH engine mounting bracket

A

Support brace

LH engine mounting bracket

25-33 ft.-lb. (35-45 N•m)

RH engine mounting bracket

VIEW A

FRONT

25-33 ft.-lb. (35-45 N•m)

9

18. Support the engine with another jack. Remove the transmission-to-engine bolts. See **Figure 30**.

19. Move the transmission back slightly and install a holding fixture or strap to prevent the torque converter from falling out.

20. Lower the transmission carefully and remove it from under the vehicle.

Transmission Installation

Installation is the reverse of removal, plus the following:

1. Make sure the converter weld nuts are flush with the flex plate before installing the flex plate-to-converter bolts. The converter should rotate freely in this position.

2. Tighten the flex plate-to-converter bolts by hand, then retighten to specifications (**Figure 30**) to ensure proper converter alignment.

3. Tighten all other fasteners to specifications (**Table 1**).

4. Fill the transmission with the required amount of DEXRON II automatic transmission fluid. See Chapter Three.

5. Check the fluid level (Chapter Three). Add or remove fluid as required.

6. Warm the engine to normal operating temperature, then recheck the fluid level and adjust as required.

7. Adjust the shift linkage and TV cable as described in this chapter.

8. Road test the vehicle. Make sure the transmission shifts smoothly, makes no abnormal noises and holds the vehicle when in PARK (parking brake should be applied). After road testing, check for fluid leaks.

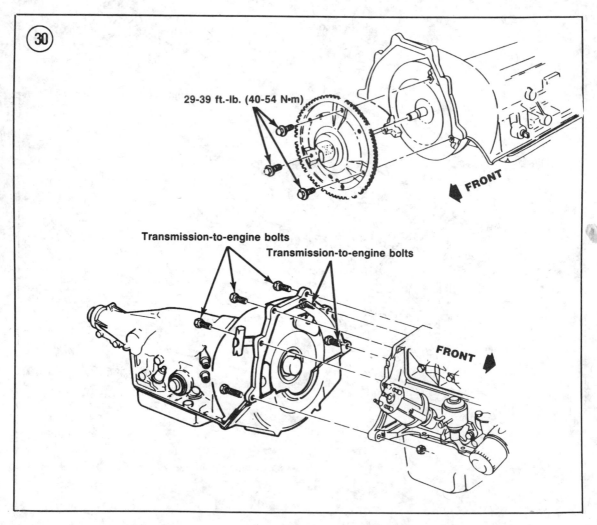

(30)

29-39 ft.-lb. (40-54 N•m)

FRONT

Transmission-to-engine bolts

Transmission-to-engine bolts

FRONT

Table 1 TIGHTENING TORQUES

Fastener	ft.-lb.	N·m
CLUTCH		
Bellhousing-to-engine		
I4	46	62
V6 carburetted	46	62
V6 fuel injected	55	75
Cover-to-bellhousing	12.5	17
Master cylinder		
Attaching fasteners	12.5	17
Braces-to-steering column bracket	8.5	11.5
Pressure plate-to-flywheel		
I4	18	25
V6	29.5	40
Slave cylinder-to-bellhousing	12.5	17
MANUAL TRANSMISSION		
Crossmember-to-mount		
4-speed	26	35
5-speed	18	25
Crossmember-to-frame	37	50
Drain & fill plugs	17	23
Transmission		
To bell housing	50	65
To mount		
I4	40	60
V6	33	45
AUTOMATIC TRANSMISSION		
Oil cooler lines	12-20	16-27
Oil pan screws	8	11
Support braces		
I4	29-39	40-54
V6	25-33	35-45
Transmission-to-engine		
I4	47-62	65-85
V6	29-39	40-54

9

FRONT SUSPENSION, WHEEL BEARINGS AND STEERING

All models use an independent front suspension with unequal upper and lower control arms, ball-joint assemblies and cast steering knuckles. Front wheel relationship is maintained by 2 tie rods connected to an intermediate or relay rod and steering arms on the knuckles.

Coil springs are mounted between the lower control arms and spring housings on the frame/front end sheet metal. Tubular shock absorbers mounted inside the coil springs provide ride control. The upper end of each shock absorber extends through the upper control arm frame brackets and is retained with rubber bushings and a nut. The lower shock absorber end is attached to the lower control arm. A spring steel stabilizer shaft controls front suspension side roll. The stabilizer ends are connected to the lower control arms by link bolts isolated by rubber grommets.

The upper control arm is connected to a cross shaft, which is bolted in turn to frame brackets. A ball-joint is riveted to the outer end of the control arm and pre-loaded by a rubber spring for proper ball seating in the socket. The upper ball-joint connects to the steering knuckle with a prevailing torque nut.

The inner ends of the lower control arm contain pressed-in bushings and are attached to the frame with bolts. The lower ball-joint is pressed into the lower control arm and connects to the steering knuckle with a prevailing torque nut. **Figure 1** shows the major components of the front suspension, including the brake caliper, rotor and wheel bearings.

Tightening torques (**Table 1**) are provided at the end of the chapter.

FRONT SUSPENSION

Shock Absorber Operational Check

Shock absorbers can be routinely checked while installed on the vehicle. Bounce the front of the vehicle up and down several times and release. Repeat this action with the rear of the vehicle. In either case, the vehicle should not continue to bounce more than twice. Excessive bouncing is an indication of worn shock absorbers. This test is not conclusive, since the spring stiffness of the vehicle makes it difficult to detect marginal shock absorbers.

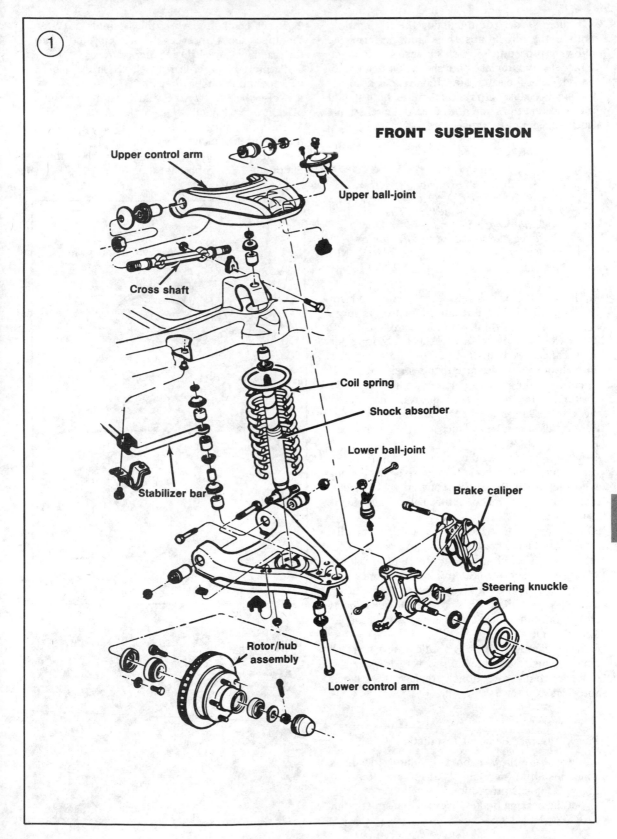

FRONT SUSPENSION

Upper control arm

Upper ball-joint

Cross shaft

Coil spring

Shock absorber

Lower ball-joint

Brake caliper

Stabilizer bar

Steering knuckle

Rotor/hub assembly

Lower control arm

10

If there is any doubt about their condition, remove the shock absorbers and perform the following procedure. If a shock absorber is found to be defective, replace both shocks on that end of the vehicle at the same time. If one shock absorber has failed because of physical damage, both should be replaced at the same time, even if the remaining shock appears to be satisfactory.

NOTE
Comparison of a used shock absorber believed to be good with a new shock absorber is not a valid test. The new shock absorber will tend to offer more resistance due to the greater friction of the new rod seal.

1. Inspect the shock absorber piston rod for bending, galling and abrasions. Discard the shock absorber if any of these conditions are noted.
2. Check the outside of the shock absorber for fluid leakage. A light film of fluid on the rod is normal, but severe leakage requires replacement.
3. Holding the shock absorber in the installed position, completely extend the rod, then invert the shock and completely compress the rod. Repeat this step several times to expel any trapped air.
4. Secure the lower end of the shock absorber in a vise with protective jaws. If protective jaws are not available, place the shock between soft wooden blocks or wrap it in shop cloths before clamping it in the vise.
5. Compress and extend the piston rod as rapidly as possible and check the damping action. The resistance should be smooth and uniform throughout each stroke, and the resistance felt during extension should be greater than during compression. Repeat this step with the other shock absorber. Both shock absorbers in a pair should feel the same.
6. If the damping action is erratic or resistance to rapid extension/compression is very low (or the same in both directions), replace the shock absorbers as a set.

Shock Absorber Removal/Installation

Always use new rubber insulators/bushings when installing new shock absorbers. Refer to **Figure 2** for this procedure.
1. Set the parking brake. Place the transmission in PARK or NEUTRAL.

2. Reach behind the wheel/tire assembly and clean the upper shock absorber threads. Oil the threads for ease in removal during Step 4.
3. Securely block both rear wheels so the vehicle will not roll in either direction.
4. Raise the front of the vehicle with a jack and place it on jackstands.
5. Hold the upper end of the shock absorber from turning with an open-end wrench. Remove the upper retaining nut with a second wrench. Remove the retainer and rubber bushing.

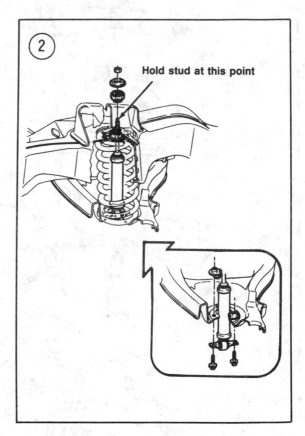

Hold stud at this point

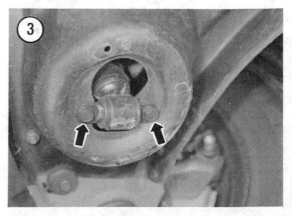

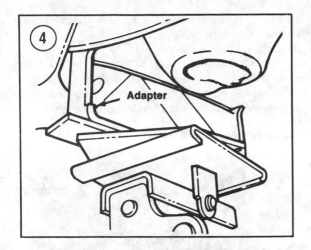

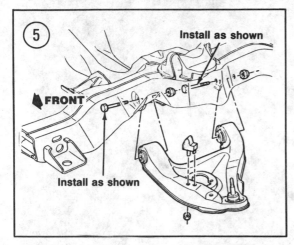

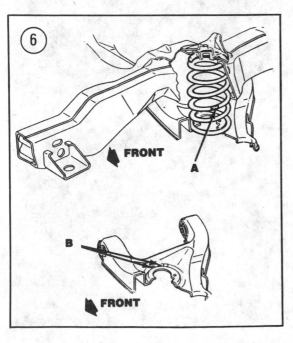

6. Remove the 2 bolts holding the lower pivot to the control arm (**Figure 3**). Pull the shock absorber out from the bottom.

7. Installation is the reverse of removal. Tighten the upper nut and lower bolts to specifications (**Table 1**). Remove the jackstands, lower the vehicle to the ground and remove the wheel chocks.

Coil Spring Removal/Installation

The use of adapter part No. J-23028 is recommended to protect the inner bushings during this procedure.

1. Remove the wheel cover or hub cap and loosen the front wheel lug nuts.

2. Place the transmission in NEUTRAL to prevent the steering wheel from locking.

3. Securely block both rear wheels so the vehicle will not roll in either direction.

4. Raise the front of the vehicle with a jack and place it on jackstands.

5. Remove the wheel/tire assembly.

6. Remove the lower shock absorber mounting bolts. See **Figure 3**. Push the shock absorber upward to compress it.

7. Install tool part No. J-23028 to the hydraulic jack and position it as shown in **Figure 4**.

8. Remove the stabilizer bar from the lower control arm as described in this chapter to provide sufficient working clearance.

9. Raise the jack to relieve any tension on the control arm pivot bolts.

> *WARNING*
> *Install a chain through the spring and control arm as a safety precaution. The chain is not meant to hold the spring in a compressed position, but to keep the spring from flying out if compression is released suddenly. Secure the chain with a bolt, nut and washers.*

10. Remove the rear pivot bolt, then the front pivot bolt. See **Figure 5**.

11. Lower the jack slowly to lower the control arm and relieve the spring compression. Remove the safety chain and spring from the control arm.

12. Installation is the reverse of removal. Install the spring with the tape at the lowest position (A, **Figure 6**). The end of the spring must cover all or part of one inspection drain hole (B, **Figure 6**) when properly installed.

10

Stabilizer Bar Removal/Installation

Refer to **Figure 7** (typical) for this procedure.
1. Securely block both rear wheels so the vehicle will not roll in either direction.
2. Raise the front of the vehicle with a jack and place it on jackstands.
3. Remove the link bolt holding each end of the stabilizer bar to the lower control arm (**Figure 8**). Remove the retainer, grommet, spacer and rubber bushings.
4. Remove the bracket mounting bolts at each side of the frame. See **Figure 9**. Remove the brackets, rubber bushings and stabilizer bar.
5. Installation is the reverse of removal. Align the rubber bushings in their brackets with the bushing slit facing the front of the vehicle. Tighten the link nuts and bracket bolts to specifications (**Table 1**).

Lower Control Arm
Removal/Installation

This procedure requires the use of ball-joint remover part No. J-23742 or part No. J-8806. Refer to **Figure 5**.
1. Remove the wheel cover or hub cap and loosen the front wheel lug nuts.
2. Securely block both rear wheels so the vehicle will not roll in either direction.
3. Raise the front of the vehicle with a jack and place it on jackstands. Position the jackstands under the frame jack pads to the rear of the front wheels.
4. Remove the front wheel/tire assembly.
5. Remove the coil spring as described in this chapter.
6. Remove the cotter pin from the ball-joint castellated nut. See **Figure 10**. Loosen the nut 2-3 turns.
7. Break the ball-joint loose from the steering knuckle with tool part No. J-23742 or part No. J-8806. See **Figure 11**. Remove the ball-joint nut.
8. Guide the lower control arm past the splash shield with a putty knife or screwdriver (**Figure

12**). Remove the control arm. Use a wooden block between the frame and upper control arm to keep the knuckle out of the way.
9. Installation is the reverse of removal. Install the front leg of the arm into the crossmember before installing the rear leg in the frame bracket. Install both pivot bolts with their heads facing the front of the vehicle (**Figure 5**) and tighten to specifications (**Table 1**). Install cotter pin from rear of nut.

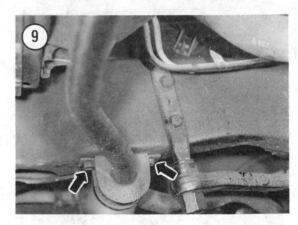

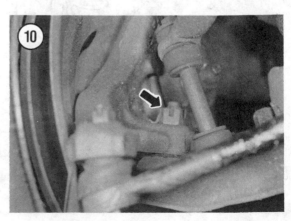

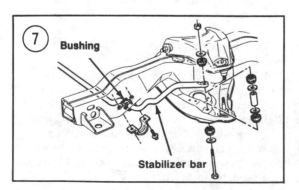

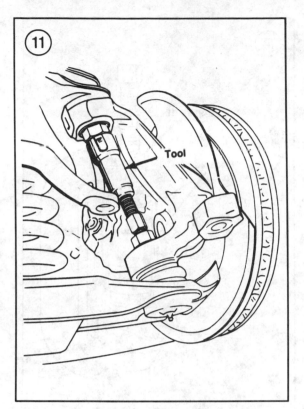

Lower Ball-joint Inspection

The lower front suspension ball-joint is pressed into the lower control arm. The ball-joint contains a visual wear indicator (**Figure 13**). Ball-joint inspection is done with the vehicle on the ground so that its weight will load the ball-joints properly.

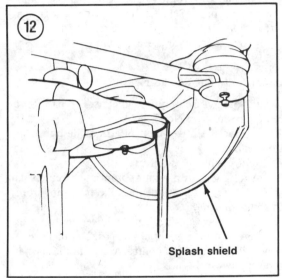

Splash shield

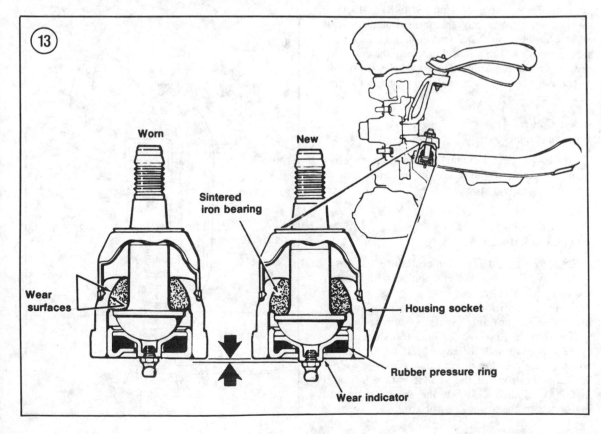

Ball-joint wear is indicated by the position of the grease fitting nipple. On a new ball-joint, this nipple will project 0.050 in. (1.27 mm) below the surface of the ball-joint cover. As normal wear occurs, the nipple will gradually move up into the cover.

To inspect the ball-joint, clean the grease fitting and nipple to remove all dirt, grease and contamination. Scrape the cover with a screwdriver. If the nipple is flush with or inside the cover surface, replace the ball-joint.

Lower Ball-joint Replacement

This procedure requires the use of ball-joint remover tool part No. J-23742.
1. Remove the lower control arm as described in this chapter.
2. Remove the grease fitting.
3. Install a C-clamp with appropriate receivers as shown in **Figure 14** and press the ball-joint from the control arm.
4. Place a new ball-joint in the lower control arm with the seal grease purge facing inboard. Press a new ball-joint into the control arm with the special tools shown in **Figure 15**.
5. Install the control arm as described in this chapter. Tighten the ball stud nut to 81 ft.-lb. (110 N•m), then tighten enough more to align the nut slot with the stud hole. Install a new cotter pin from the rear of the nut and lubricate the ball-joint grease fitting (Chapter Three). Have front end alignment checked by a dealer or front end shop.

Lower Control Arm Bushing Replacement

Front and rear bushing replacement requires many special tools and should be referred to a dealer or qualified specialist.

Upper Control Arm Removal/Installation

Refer to **Figure 16** for this procedure.
1. Remove the wheel cover or hub cap and loosen the front wheel lug nuts.
2. Note the position of the shims; they must be reinstalled in the same position from which they were removed. Remove the nuts and shims.
3. Securely block both rear wheels so the vehicle will not roll in either direction.
4. Raise the front of the vehicle with a jack and install jackstands between the spring seats and ball-joints of the lower control arms.

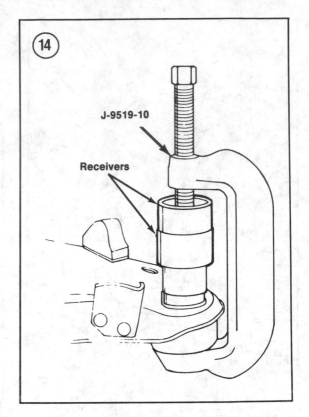

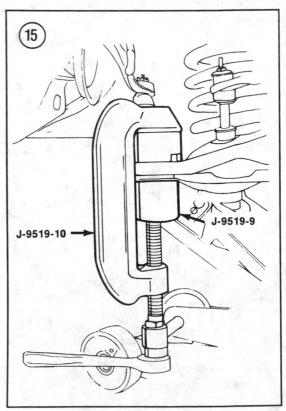

5. Remove the wheel/tire assembly.

6. Remove and discard the upper ball-joint cotter pin. Remove the castellated nut (**Figure 17**).

7. Separate the ball-joint stud from the steering knuckle with tool part No. J-23742, J-8806 or equivalent. See **Figure 18**.

8. Support the hub to prevent damage to the brake hose.

9. Remove the upper control arm bolts. Remove the control arm.

10. Installation is the reverse of removal. Tighten the upper control arm bolts to 66 ft.-lb. (90 N•m) after installing alignment shims in their original position. Remove support from hub assembly and connect ball stud to steering knuckle. Tighten fasteners to specifications (**Table 1**). Install a new cotter pin from the rear of the nut. Have front end alignment checked by a dealer or front end shop.

Upper Ball-joint Inspection

Refer to **Figure 19** for this procedure.

1. Securely block both rear wheels so the vehicle will not roll in either direction.

2. Raise the front of the vehicle with a jack. Install jackstands under each control arm as close as possible to the lower ball-joint.

NOTE
*The control arm bumper (**Figure 16**) must not touch the frame.*

3. Install a dial indicator against the wheel rim at the point shown in **Figure 19**.

4. Grasp the front wheel and push in on the bottom of the tire while pulling out on the top. Read the dial indicator. Reverse the push-pull procedure and reread the dial indicator.

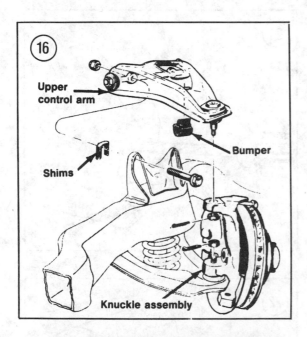

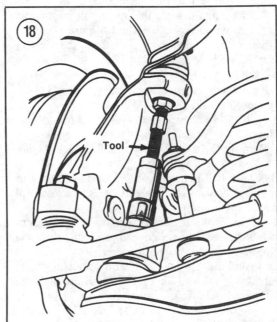

10

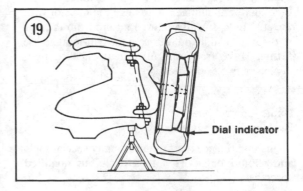

5. Replace the ball-joint as described in this chapter if any of the following are noted:
  a. The indicator reading exceeds 0.125 in. (3.18 mm).
  b. Looseness can be felt with the ball stud disconnected from the knuckle.
  c. The ball stud can be twisted in its socket by hand.

Upper Ball-joint Replacement

1. Remove the wheel cover or hub cap and loosen the front wheel lug nuts.
2. Securely block both rear wheels so the vehicle will not roll in either direction.
3. Raise the front of the vehicle. Install jackstands between the spring seats and lower control arm ball-joints to relieve spring tension on the upper control arm.
4. Remove the wheel/tire assembly.
5. Remove and discard the upper ball-joint cotter pin. Remove the castellated nut (**Figure 17**).
6. Separate the ball-joint stud from the steering knuckle with tool part No. J-23742, J-8806 or equivalent. See **Figure 18**.
7. Drill the 4 rivets 1/4 in. deep with a 1/8 in. diameter drill bit (**Figure 20**).
8. Drill the rivet heads off with a 1/2 in. drill bit (**Figure 21**).
9. Remove the rivets with a suitable punch (**Figure 22**). Remove the ball-joint.
10. Check ball-joint mounting area on control arm for cracks or signs of metal fatigue. Replace control arm, if any are noted.
11. If rivet holes in control arm differ in size from bolts supplied in service ball-joint kit, drill the rivet holes to the proper diameter.
12. Install the new ball-joint with 4 attaching bolts and nuts as shown in **Figure 23**. Bolts must be inserted from bottom with nuts on top. Tighten the nuts to specifications (**Table 1**).
13. Reverse Steps 1-6 to complete installation. Tighten the castellated nut to 52 ft.-lb. (70 N•m), then tighten it sufficiently to align the nut slot with the stud hole. Install a new cotter pin from the rear of the nut. Install and lubricate the ball-joint grease fitting. Have front end alignment checked by a dealer or front end shop.

**Upper Control Arm
Bushing Replacement**

Bushing replacement requires many special tools and should be referred to a dealer or qualified specialist.

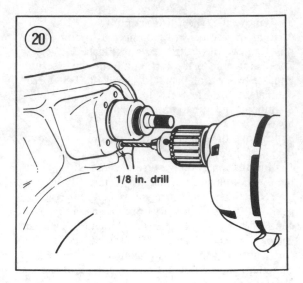

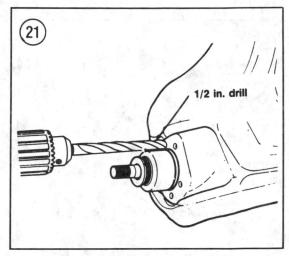

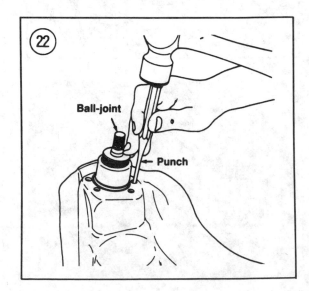

WHEEL ALIGNMENT

Several suspension angle affect the running and steering of the front wheels. These angles must be properly aligned to prevent excessive wear, as well as to maintain directional stability and ease of steering. The angles are:

a. Caster.
b. Camber.
c. Toe.
d. Steering axis inclination.
e. Steering lock angles.

Steering axis inclination and steering lock angles are built in and cannot be adjusted. These angles are measured to check for bent suspension parts. Caster and camber should not be adjusted without the use of an alignment rack. Toe can be adjusted at home as described in this section. However, the procedure given should be used only as a temporary measure to allow you to drive the vehicle to a dealer or alignment shop where accurate measurements can be made and set.

WARNING
Do not attempt to adjust alignment angles by bending or twisting suspension or steering linkage components.

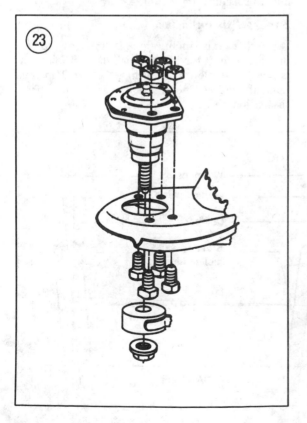

Pre-alignment Check

Adjustment of the steering and various suspension angles is affected by several factors. For this reason, steering and handling problems which may seem to be caused by misalignment can result from other factors which are easily corrected without expensive equipment. The following procedure should be carried out whenever steering, handling or tire wear problems exist. It should also be performed before having the alignment checked or prior to adjusting the toe setting.

1. Check tire pressure (with tires cold) and adjust to the specified pressure, if necessary. Both front tires should be the same size, ply rating and load range.
2. Check tire condition. See *Tire Wear Analysis*, Chapter Two.
3. Check the radial and lateral runout of both front tires with a dial indicator. Place the indicator plunger against the tire tread and slowly rotate the wheel. Then position the indicator against the outer sidewall of the tire and slowly rotate the wheel. If either the radial or lateral runout exceeds 0.080 inch:

   a. Deflate the tire.
   b. Rotate the tire 90° on the rim.
   c. Lubricate the rim with liquid soap.
   d. Reinflate the tire to the specified pressure.
   e. Recheck runout. If still excessive, check for foreign material between the wheel and hub. Clean as required and recheck.
   f. If runout is still too high, check for a bent wheel. If the wheel is not bent, the tire is defective.

4. Check all suspension components, steering components and linkage for wear, damage or improper adjustment. Replace if required as described in this chapter.
5. Check the steering gearbox mounting bolt torque. Retighten as required.
6. Make sure the suspension is properly lubricated. See Chapter Three.
7. Check brakes for proper operation. See Chapter Twelve.
8. Check the shock absorbers for proper operation as described in this section.
9. Check wheels and balance as required.
10. Check rear suspension for looseness.

Front tire wear problems can indicate alignment problems. These are covered under *Tire Wear Analysis*, Chapter Two.

10

Caster and Camber

Caster is the inclination from vertical of the line through the ball-joints (**Figure 24**). Positive caster shifts the wheel forward; negative caster shifts the wheel rearward. Caster causes the wheels to return to a straight-ahead position after a turn. It also prevents the wheels from wandering due to wind, potholes or uneven road surfaces.

Camber is the inclination of the wheel from vertical (**Figure 24**). With positive camber, the top of the tire leans outward. With negative camber, the top of the tire leans inward. Excessive camber causes tire wear. Negative camber wears the inside of the tire; positive camber wears the outside.

Toe

Since the front wheels tend to point outward when the vehicle is moving in a forward direction, the distance between the front edges of the tire (A, **Figure 25**) is generally slightly less than the distance between the rear edges (B, **Figure 25**) when the vehicle is at rest.

Toe Adjustment

Although toe adjustment requires only a simple homemade tool, it usually is not worth the trouble for home mechanics. Alignment shops include toe adjustment as part of the alignment procedure, so you probably will not save any money by doing it yourself. The procedure described here can be used for an initial toe setting after spindle or ball-joint replacement and allow you to drive the vehicle to a dealer or alignment shop.

1. With the steering wheel centered, roll the vehicle forward about 15 ft. on a smooth, level surface.
2. Mark the center of the tread at the front and rear of each tire.
3. Measure the distance between the forward chalk marks (A, **Figure 25**). Use 2 pieces of telescoping aluminum tubing. Telescope the tubing so each end contacts a chalk mark. Using a sharp center scribe, mark the small diameter tubing where it enters the large diameter tubing.
4. Measure between the rear chalk marks with the telescoping tubes. Make another mark on the small tube where it enters the large one. The distance between the 2 scribe marks is the toe-in and must be divided in half to determine the amount of toe at each wheel.
5. If toe-in is incorrect, loosen the clamp nuts on each end of the tie rod adjusting sleeve (**Figure 26**) at each wheel.
6. Rotate each adjusting sleeve as required until correct toe alignment is obtained.
7. Reposition the clamps if necessary. They should be located 3/16 in. from the end of the sleeve with the nut end of the bolt facing the front of the vehicle.
8. When the toe is correctly set, tighten the clamp nuts to specifications (**Table 1**).

Steering Axis Inclination

Steering axis inclination is the inward or outward lean of the line through the ball-joints. It is not adjustable on the vehicles covered in this manual but is measured to check for bent suspension parts.

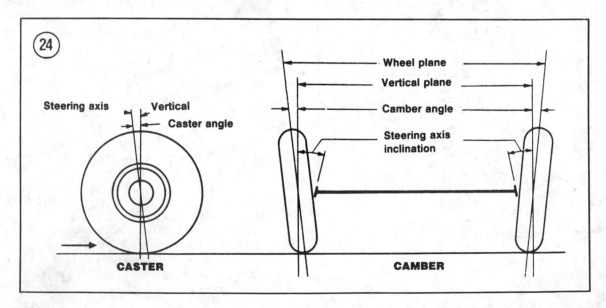

Steering Lock Angles

When a vehicle turns, the inside wheel makes a smaller circle than the outside wheel. Because of this, the inside wheel turns at a greater angle than the outside wheel. These angles are not adjustable on the vehicles covered in this manual.

WHEEL BEARINGS

The front wheels use adjustable tapered roller bearings which must be cleaned, repacked with grease and adjusted at periodic intervals. A grease

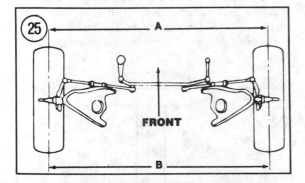

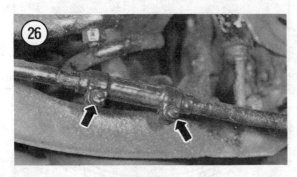

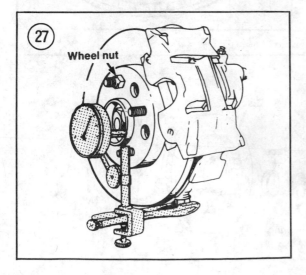

retainer at the inner end of the hub prevents lubricant from leaking onto the brake rotor. A retainer locknut and cotter pin hold the entire assembly on the spindle.

The rear wheel bearings are sealed and receive their lubrication from the oil carried in the rear differential. There is no adjustment required for the rear bearings.

Front Wheel Bearing Adjustment

1. Securely block both rear wheels so the vehicle will not roll in either direction.
2. Raise the front of the vehicle with a jack and place it on jackstands.
3. Remove the wheel cover or hub cap.
4. Carefully pry the grease cap from the hub and wipe the grease from the end of the spindle.
5. Remove and discard the spindle nut cotter pin.
6. Rotate the wheel in a forward direction while tightening the spindle nut to 12 ft.-lb. (16 N•m).
7. Back the spindle nut off until it reaches the "just loose" position, then tighten the nut finger-tight.
8. Loosen the spindle nut enough to align a slot in the nut with either spindle hole (but not more than 1/2 flat) and install a new cotter pin without bending the ends of the pin over. This should provide a bearing end clearance of 0.001-0.005 in. (0.03-0.13 mm).
9. Install a dial indicator as shown in **Figure 27** and measure the hub assembly end play. If properly adjusted, the indicator gauge should read within the specification provided in Step 8. If the wheel is still loose, its rotation is noisy or rough or the indicator reading is not within specifications, remove the bearings and cups to check for dirt, damage or excessive wear.
10. When bearing adjustment is satisfactory, bend the ends of the cotter pin over to lock it in place, then reinstall the grease cap.
11. Lower the vehicle to the ground and install the wheel covers or hub caps, if so equipped. Remove the wheel chocks.

Front Wheel Bearing Replacement

If rough and noisy operation or looseness is not eliminated by adjustment, the wheel bearings should be removed, cleaned, inspected and repacked with the specified lubricant or replaced as required. A lithium-based grease such as GM Lubricant part No. 1051344 or equivalent should be used. Do not use other types of grease, as they are not compatible and can result in premature bearing failure.

10

Refer to **Figure 28** for this procedure.

1. Remove the wheel cover or hub cap and loosen the front wheel lug nuts.

2. Securely block both rear wheels so the vehicle will not roll in either direction.

3. Raise the front of the vehicle with a jack and place it on jackstands.

4. Remove the wheel/tire assemblies.

5. Remove the brake caliper. See Chapter Twelve.

6. Carefully pry the grease cap from the hub and wipe the grease from the end of the spindle.

7. Remove and discard the spindle nut cotter pin.

8. Remove the spindle nut and washer from the spindle.

9. Grasp the brake disc/hub assembly and pull it outward enough to loosen the outer wheel bearing. Remove the outer wheel bearing from the spindle.

10. Pull the brake disc/hub assembly straight off the spindle to prevent damage to the inner bearings or spindle.

11. Remove and discard the grease seal. Remove the inner bearing assembly from the hub.

12. Insert tool part No. J-29117 or equivalent behind the bearing races in the hub assembly (**Figure 29**) and drive the races out.

> *WARNING*
> *Do not spin bearings with compressed air in Step 13; it is capable of rotating the bearings at speeds far in excess of those for which they were designed. The bearing could disintegrate, causing damage and injury.*

13. Thoroughly clean the bearings, races and inside of the hub with solvent. Blow dry with compressed air.

14. Check the bearing rollers and cups for scoring, pitting, cracking, scratching or excessive wear. If any of these defects are found, replace the bearings and cups as an assembly.

15. Install new races in the hub assembly with an appropriate driver.

16. Carefully clean the spindle with a cloth moistened in solvent.

17. Lightly grease the spindle at the outer and inner bearing seats, the shoulder and seal seat with a good quality, high-temperature wheel bearing grease, such as GM Lubricant part No. 1051344.

18. Pack the inside of the hub with GM Lubricant part No. 1051344 or equivalent until it is level with the inside diameter of the outer bearing cups. See **Figure 30**.

19. If installing the original bearings, thoroughly pack the bearing assemblies with GM Lubricant part No. 1051344 or equivalent. If a bearing packer is not available, work the lubricant in carefully by hand.

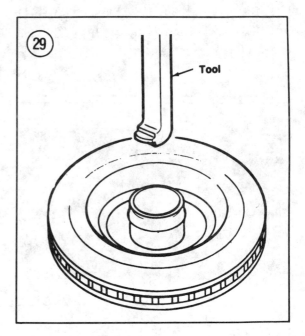

(29)
Tool

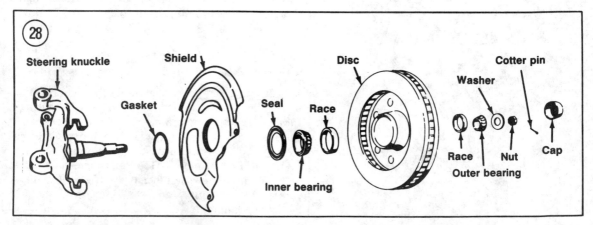

(28)
Steering knuckle   Shield   Disc   Cotter pin
Gasket   Seal   Race   Washer
Inner bearing   Race   Nut   Cap
Outer bearing

20. Lightly coat the inner cone with the same lubricant and install the inner bearing assembly in the inner cup.

21. Place a new seal in the hub. Cover with a flat plate or a block of wood and tap into place until the seal is flush with the hub. Wipe a thin coat of grease across the seal lip.

22. Install the disc/hub assembly on the spindle, keeping the hub centered to prevent damage to the seal.

23. Install the outer wheel bearing assembly and thread the spindle nut in place.

24. Adjust the wheel bearings as described in this chapter. Reinstall the brake caliper.

STEERING SYSTEM

Vehicles covered in this manual may be equipped with manual (non-power) or integral power steering. The steering system on all models is a parallelogram type which connects both front wheels to the steering gear by a Pitman arm and idler arm. The 2 tie rods are connected to the steering arms and relay rods by ball studs. The left end of the relay rod is supported by the Pitman arm, which is driven by the steering gearbox sector shaft. The right end of the relay rod is supported by an idler arm, which pivots on a support connected to the frame rail. A steering damper is incorporated in the steering linkage to dampen road shock. **Figure 31** (typical) shows the major steering linkage components.

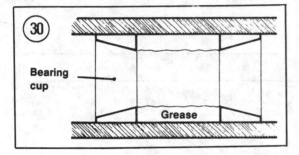

Bearing cup

Grease

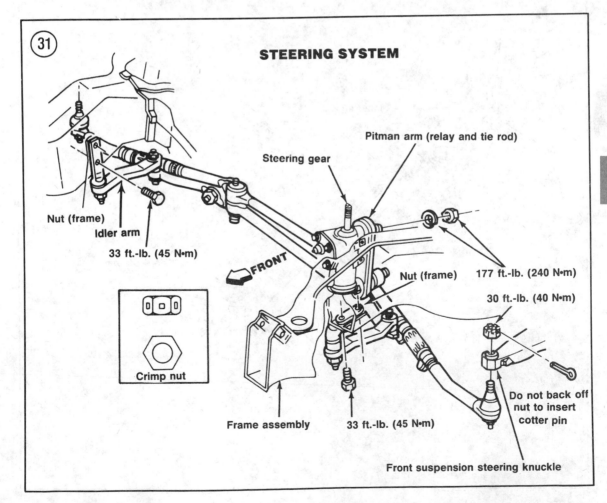

STEERING SYSTEM

Pitman arm (relay and tie rod)

Steering gear

Nut (frame)

Idler arm

33 ft.-lb. (45 N•m)

FRONT

Nut (frame)

177 ft.-lb. (240 N•m)

30 ft.-lb. (40 N•m)

Crimp nut

Frame assembly

33 ft.-lb. (45 N•m)

Do not back off nut to insert cotter pin

Front suspension steering knuckle

10

Bent, distorted or otherwise damaged steering linkage should never be straightened and reused. Such components should be replaced with new ones. Any linkage with excessively loose ball-joints should also be replaced.

Steering Linkage/Suspension Check

1. Raise the vehicle on one side with a jack until the tire is about one inch off the ground.
2. Install a dial indicator as shown in **Figure 32**.
3. Place the steering wheel in the locked position.
4. Grasp the front wheel at each side and move the wheel in and out at the back.
5. The dial indicator should read 0.108 in. (2.74 mm) or less. If the reading exceeds this

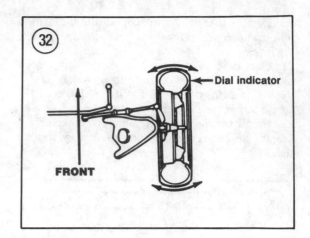

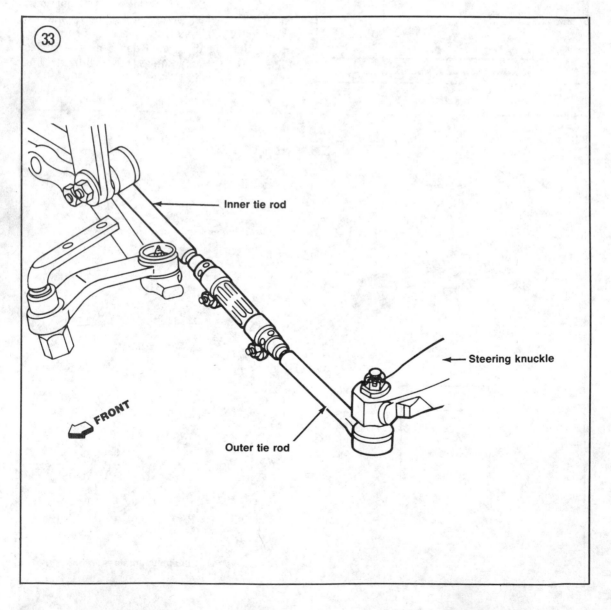

specification, inspect all linkage pivots and ball studs for looseness. Replace as necessary.

Tie Rod, Relay Rod and Idler Arm Removal/Installation

Refer to **Figure 31** for this procedure.
1. Securely block both rear wheels so the vehicle will not roll in either direction.
2. Raise the front of the vehicle with a jack and place it on jackstands.
3. Make sure the steering wheel and front wheels are in the straight-ahead position.
4. Remove and discard the cotter pins from the appropriate linkage ball studs. Remove the ball stud nuts.
5. Separate the linkage by tapping on the ball stud bosses with a hammer while supporting the linkage with another heavy hammer.
6A. Tie rod or relay rod—Remove the linkage components from the vehicle. See **Figure 33**.
6B. Idler arm—Unbolt the idler arm from the frame and remove from the vehicle. See **Figure 34**.

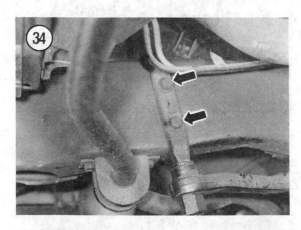

7. If further service is necessary, clamp the tie rod in a vise with protective jaws. If protective jaws are not available, wrap the tie rod with shop cloths.

NOTE
If the tie rod adjusting sleeve fasteners are rusted and require a breakaway torque of more than 7 ft.-lb. (9 N•m) to loosen the fasteners in Step 8, discard the nuts and bolts and use a penetrating oil to loosen the clamps. Install new nuts and bolts during reassembly.

8. Loosen the adjusting sleeve clamps and unscrew the defective part. Note and record the number of turns required for removal.
9. If the components are to be reused, clean all threads. Lubricate the threads of all components to be reassembled with a good quality extreme pressure (E.P.) chassis grease.
10. Installation is the reverse of removal, plus the following:
   a. Install new ball stud seals with tool part No. J-24434 as appropriate.
   b. Reassemble components with the same number of turns required to disassemble them. This will provide an approximate toe-in adjustment.
   c. Tighten each ball stud nut to 40 ft.-lb. (54 N•m), then remove and discard nuts. Install a new prevailing torque nut (Part No. 351249) on each ball stud and tighten to specifications (**Table 1**). If the nut and ball stud holes do not align, further tighten the nut, then install a new cotter pin through the nut and stud holes.
   d. Lubricate all linkage grease fittings.
   e. Check and adjust tire pressures as required.
   f. Remove the jackstands and lower the vehicle to the ground. Remove the wheel chocks.
   g. Have a dealer or wheel alignment shop check and adjust toe-in to specifications.

Pitman Arm Removal/Installation

1. Securely block both rear wheels so the vehicle will not roll in either direction.
2. Raise the front of the vehicle with a jack and place it on jackstands.
3. Remove the nut from the Pitman arm ball stud (**Figure 35**).
4. Separate the relay rod from the Pitman arm with puller part No. J-24319-01 or equivalent. Pull down on the relay rod to remove it from the stud.

10

5. Remove the Pitman arm nut from the sector shaft (**Figure 36**).

> *CAUTION*
> *Do not hammer on the puller in Step 6 to separate the Pitman arm from the sector shaft. This can cause internal damage to the steering gearbox.*

6. Mark the Pitman arm-to-sector shaft relationship. Separate the Pitman arm from the sector shaft with puller part No. J-6632 or equivalent as shown in **Figure 37**.

7. Installation is the reverse of removal. Tighten all fasteners to specifications (**Table 1**).

Steering Damper Removal/Installation

Refer to **Figure 36** for this procedure.

1. Securely block both rear wheels so the vehicle will not roll in either direction.

2. Raise the front of the vehicle with a jack and place it on jackstands.

3. Unbolt the steering damper from the frame attachment.

4. Unbolt the steering damper from the steering linkage. Remove the steering damper.

5. Installation is the reverse of removal. Tighten all fasteners to specifications (**Table 1**).

Steering Knuckle Replacement

1. Remove the wheel cover or hub cap, if so equipped. Loosen the wheel lug nuts.

2. Securely block both rear wheels so the vehicle will not roll in either direction.

3. Raise the front of the vehicle with a jack and place it on jackstands.

4. Remove the wheel/tire assembly.

5. Remove the brake caliper. See Chapter Twelve.

6. Remove the brake disc/hub assembly as described under *Front Wheel Bearing Replacement* in this chapter.

7. Remove the shield attaching bolts and shield (**Figure 38**).

8. Separate the tie rod end from the steering knuckle with puller part No. J-6627 or equivalent (**Figure 39**).

9. Remove the knuckle seal (**Figure 40**). Save it for reuse if the same steering knuckle is to be reinstalled; discard it if a new knuckle will be installed.

10. Remove the ball studs from the steering knuckle as described under *Ball-joint Replacement* in this chapter.

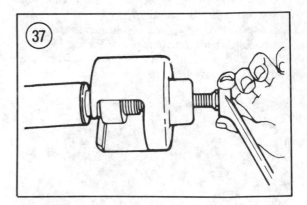

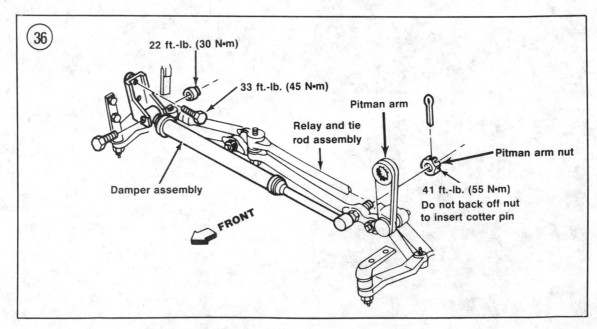

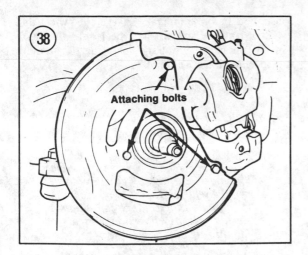

Attaching bolts

11. Place a hydraulic jack under the lower control arm near the spring seat. Raise the jack until it supports the control arm.

12. Raise the upper control arm to disconnect the ball-joint stud from the knuckle.

13. Raise the knuckle from the lower ball-joint stud. Remove the knuckle.

14. Installation is the reverse of removal. Tighten all fasteners to specifications (**Table 1**).

Steering Gearbox
Removal/Installation

Refer to **Figure 41** (typical) for this procedure.

1. Disconnect the negative battery cable.

2. Remove the steering coupling shield, if so equipped.

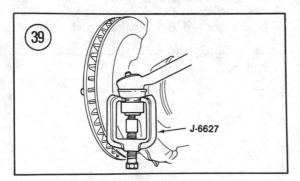

J-6627

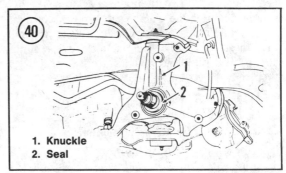

1. Knuckle
2. Seal

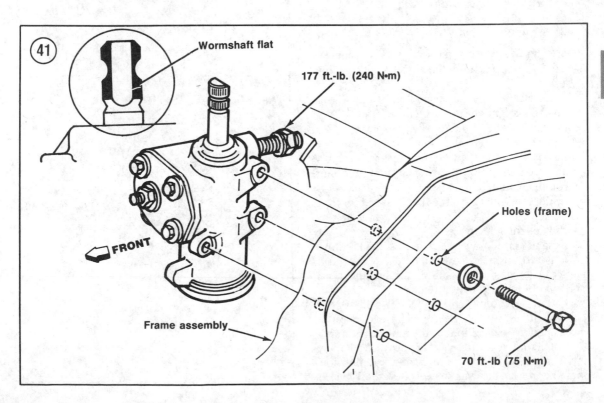

Wormshaft flat

177 ft.-lb. (240 N•m)

Holes (frame)

FRONT

Frame assembly

70 ft.-lb (75 N•m)

10

3. Power steering—Disconnect the pressure and return lines at the gearbox. Plug the lines and cap the fittings to prevent leakage.

4. Loosen and remove the intermediate shaft pinch bolt.

5. Remove the Pitman arm as described in this chapter.

6. Remove the bolts holding the steering gearbox to the frame. Remove the gearbox.

7. Installation is the reverse of removal. Make sure the frame mounting surface is clean and flat. Position flat on stub shaft to index with intermediate shaft flat. Tighten all fasteners to specifications (**Table 1**).

8. Power steering—Fill the power steering pump reservoir with power steering fluid. Start the engine and run for several seconds, then recheck the fluid level and top up if necessary. Repeat this procedure until the fluid level remains constant after running the engine. With the engine running, turn the steering wheel lock-to-lock several times and recheck the fluid level. Top up if necessary, then shut the engine off.

Steering Wheel Removal/Installation

> *WARNING*
> *Use of a puller other than part No. J-1859-03 or equivalent can shear or loosen the plastic fasteners used to maintain steering wheel rigidity.*

Refer to **Figure 42** (typical) for this procedure.

1. Tilt wheel—Position the wheel in its full-up position.

2. Make sure the steering wheel and front wheels are in the straight-ahead position.

3. Disconnect the negative battery cable.

4A. Standard wheel—Remove 2 screws from the underside of the pad assembly. Lift pad assembly up and disconnect the horn wire bayonet connector by rotating counterclockwise.

4B. Sport wheel—Pry the pad assembly free. Disconnect the horn wire bayonet connector by rotating counterclockwise.

5. Expand and remove the snap ring, then remove and discard the steering wheel nut.

6. Scribe an alignment mark on the steering wheel and shaft for reinstallation reference.

7. Install wheel puller part No. J-1859-03 or equivalent and remove the steering wheel. Steering wheel pullers are available from auto parts stores.

8. Installation is the reverse of removal. Make sure the front wheels are in the straight-ahead position, then align the steering wheel and shaft marks

inscribed before removal. Engage the wheel and shaft serrations and fit the wheel onto the shaft. Install a new wheel nut and snap ring. Tighten nut to specifications (**Table 1**).

Steering Column Removal

> *WARNING*
> *The steering column is very susceptible to damage during and after removal from the vehicle. Hammering, dropping or leaning on the column can damage internal plastic injections used to maintain rigidity.*

This procedure applies to both standard and tilt-wheel columns. Refer to **Figure 43**.

1. Disconnect the negative battery cable.

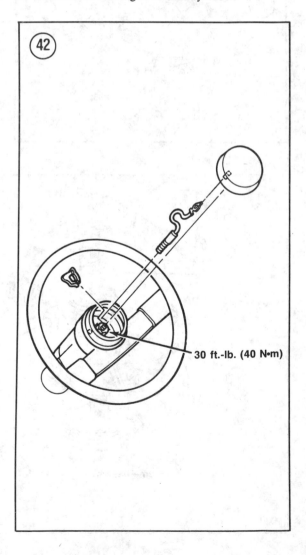

30 ft.-lb. (40 N•m)

2. Unplug the wiring connectors at the steering column jacket.

3. Remove the steering wheel as described in this chapter.

4. Remove the steering column bracket attaching nuts.

5. Remove the cover and seal at the base of the column against the firewall.

6. Remove the protective cap from the steering column/intermediate shaft coupling in the engine compartment, if so equipped.

7. Remove the upper intermediate shaft pinch bolt/screw.

8. Grasp the steering column assembly and pull it rearward to disconnect the lower stub shaft from the flexible coupling.

9. Remove the steering column from the vehicle.

Steering Column Installation

Refer to **Figure 43** for this procedure.

1. Install bracket A to the steering column jacket. Tighten fasteners E, F, G and H in that order to 30 ft.-lb. (40 N•m).

2. Fit steering column in place and loosely install the capsule nuts on their studs.

3. Fit cover and seal on front of dash panel, then install and tighten bolt B to 7 ft.-lb. (9 N•m).

4. Install cover fasteners C and D and tighten to 7 ft.-lb. (9 N•m).

5. Tighten capsule nuts to 25 ft.-lb. (34 N•m).

6. Fit intermediate shaft joint over steering column stub shaft. Install and tighten pinch bolt to 30 ft.-lb. (40 N•m) maximum.

7. If intermediate shaft was removed, connect to steering gear splined shaft, making sure that the 2 flats align, then install and tighten pinch bolt to 30 ft.-lb. (40 N•m).

8. Install the steering wheel as described in this chapter.

9. Reconnect all electrical connectors.

10. Reconnect the negative battery cable.

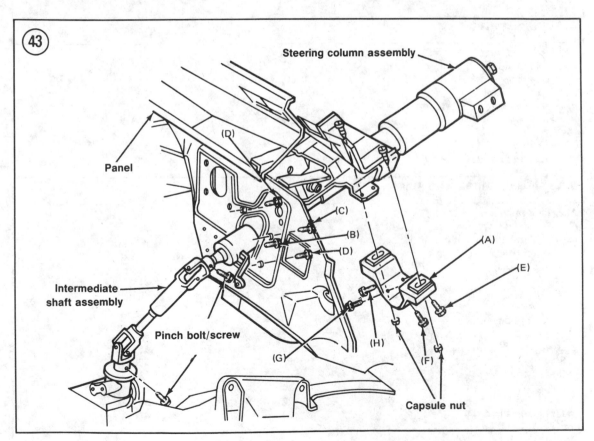

Table 1 is on the following page.

Table 1 TIGHTENING TORQUES

Fastener	ft.-lb.	N·m
SUSPENSION		
Ball-joint stud nuts		
Lower	81	110
Upper	52	70
Lower control arm		
Bumper	22	30
To frame	96*	130*
Stabilizer bar		
Bracket-to-frame	22	30
Link nut	13	17
Steering knuckle splash shield	10	14
Shock absorber		
Upper nut	15	20
Lower bolts	18	25
Upper ball-joint-to-control arm	8	11
Upper control arm		
Pivot shaft nuts	85	115
To frame	66	90
Wheel lug nuts	90	122
STEERING LINKAGE		
Ball-joint stud nuts	66	90
Hydraulic damper		
To relay rod	41	55
To frame bracket	22	30
Idler arm-to-frame	33	45
Pitman arm nut	177	240
Tie rod		
Clamp nuts	13	18
To steering knuckle	30	40
STEERING GEARBOX AND PUMP		
Attaching fasteners	70	95
Fluid line fittings @ gearbox	25	35
Intermediate shaft pinch bolt	30	40
Power steering pump		
V6 bracket bolts		
Upper	18	25
Lower	30	40
Side	59	80
I4 bracket bolts		
Upper	37	50
Lower	18	25
Side	37	50
V6 stud nuts		
Large	30	40
Small	22	30
Steering wheel nut	30	40

* Tighten with vehicle weight on wheels.

REAR SUSPENSION, DIFFERENTIAL AND DRIVE SHAFT

This chapter provides service procedures for the rear suspension, the rear axle assembly, drive shaft and differential. Tightening torques are provided in **Table 1** at the end of the chapter.

REAR SUSPENSION

Variable rate, single leaf composite springs are used for the rear suspension. The eye at the front of each spring is bolted to the unibody side rail front hanger; the rear eye is shackled to the unibody rear body hanger. This method of attachment allows the spring to change its length while the vehicle is in motion.

Two U-bolts are used to attach the center of each spring to the semi-floating rear axle housing. Ride control is provided by tubular shock absorbers which are angle-mounted between the frame and lower U-bolt anchor plate. **Figure 1** shows the major components of the rear suspension.

Shock Absorber Inspection

Shock absorbers in doubtful condition can be inspected as described under *Front Suspension,* Chapter Ten.

Shock Absorber Removal/Installation

Always use new rubber insulators/bushings when installing new shock absorbers. Refer to **Figure 2** (typical) for this procedure.

1. Securely block the front wheels. Raise the rear of the vehicle with a jack and place it on jackstands.
2. Place a hydraulic jack underneath the axle housing. Raise the axle to remove its weight from the springs.
3. Remove the nut and bolt holding the shock absorber to its upper mounting bracket (**Figure 3**).
4. Remove the nut and bolt holding the shock absorber to its lower mounting bracket (**Figure 4**). If removing the right shock absorber, disengage the parking brake bracket from the shock mounting bolt and move to one side.
5. Remove the shock absorber from the vehicle.
6. Position the upper end of the shock absorber on the mounting bracket with the insulator/bushing and washer. Install the attaching bolt and nut. Finger-tighten the nut on the bolt.
7. Repeat Step 6 to attach the lower end of the shock absorber. If installing the right shock absorber, reinstall the parking brake bracket once the bolt is installed. Finger-tighten the nut on the bolt.

11

①

REAR SUSPENSION

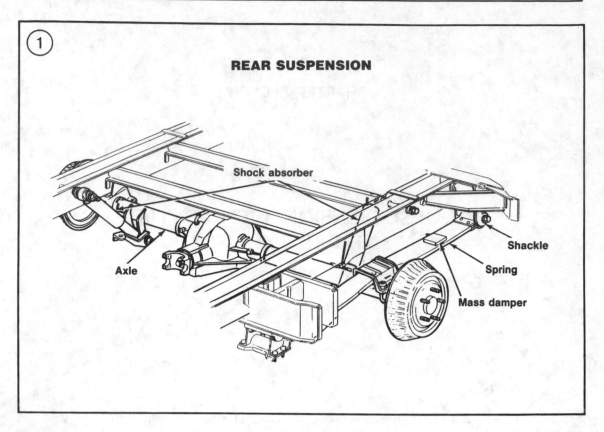

②

1. Shock absorber
2. Nut
3. Washer
4. Bolt
5. Bolt

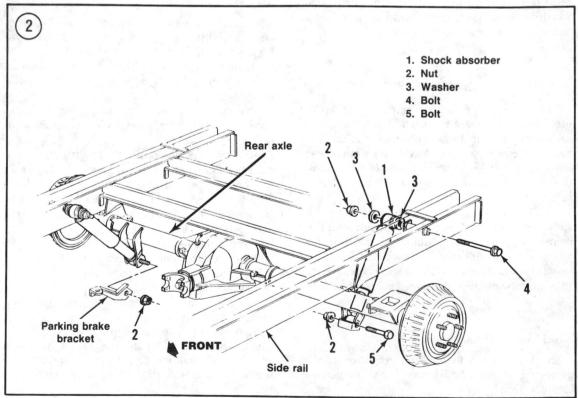

8. Tighten the upper and lower shock absorber fasteners to specifications (**Table 1**).

9. Remove the jackstands and lower the vehicle to the ground. Remove the wheel chocks.

Leaf Spring Removal/Installation

Remove and install springs one at a time. Refer to **Figure 5** and **Figure 6** for this procedure.

1. Loosen the rear wheel lug nuts.

2. Securely block the front wheels so the vehicle will not roll in either direction.

3. Raise the rear of the vehicle with a jack and place it on jackstands. Support the body/chassis and axle separately to relieve the load on the springs.

4. Remove the wheel/tire assembly.

5. Loosen (do not remove) the shackle-to-spring and shackle-to-body retaining nuts.

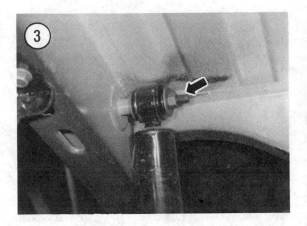

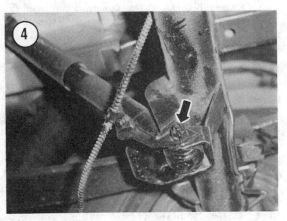

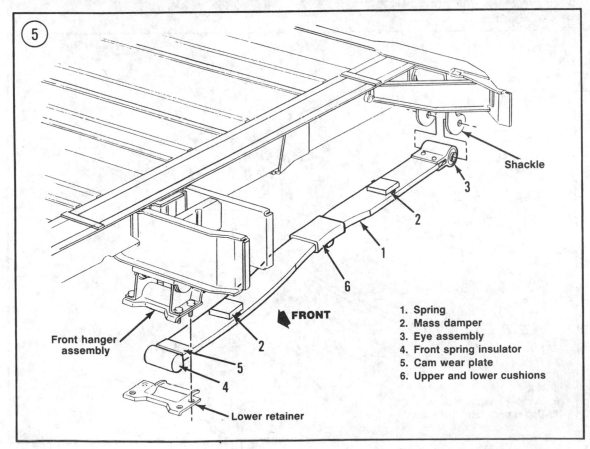

1. Spring
2. Mass damper
3. Eye assembly
4. Front spring insulator
5. Cam wear plate
6. Upper and lower cushions

Shackle

Front hanger assembly

FRONT

Lower retainer

11

6. Disconnect the lower end of the shock absorber from the axle shock mount.

7. Remove the U-bolt retaining nuts. Drive the U-bolts from the anchor plate. Remove the anchor plate.

> ### WARNING
> *Use caution in Step 8 and restrain the spring to prevent it from rotating on the front hanger bolt.*

8. Remove the nuts, washers and retainer from the front spring hanger.

9. Slide the spring assembly forward until the spring-to-shackle bolt can be reached through the rear bumper bracket. Remove the nut, washer and bolt.

10. Remove the spring from the vehicle.

11. Installation is the reverse of removal. Tighten all fasteners to specifications (**Table 1**).

Leaf Spring Eye Replacement

1. Remove the leaf spring as described in this chapter.

2. Remove the rivets holding the eye assembly to the spring by first center-punching and then drilling them out with a suitable size bit.

3. Remove eye assembly from spring.

4. Position a new eye assembly on spring. Install the 10 mm bolts and nuts provided with eye assembly. Tighten fasteners to specifications (**Table 1**).

5. Reinstall the leaf spring as described in this chapter.

DRIVE SHAFT

A drive shaft assembly is used to transmit torque from the transmission to the rear axle. See **Figure 7** (typical). The drive shaft connects to the transmission with a single cardan universal joint.

All vehicles covered in this manual use a 1-piece drive shaft. A universal joint and splined slip yoke with damper assembly are located on the transmission end of the shaft (**Figure 8**). A universal joint on the other end of the shaft connects to the differential companion flange with retainer straps.

All drive shafts are tubular and use needle bearing type universal joints. The universal joints are factory-lubricated and cannot be lubricated while on the vehicle.

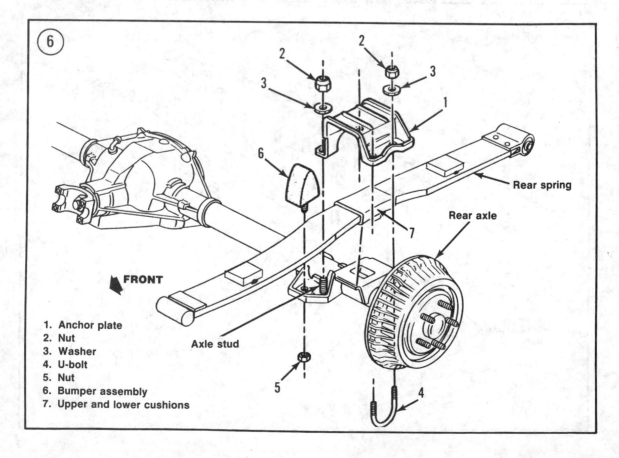

1. Anchor plate
2. Nut
3. Washer
4. U-bolt
5. Nut
6. Bumper assembly
7. Upper and lower cushions

Rear spring

Rear axle

Axle stud

FRONT

A repair kit is available containing a new spider with bearing assemblies and snap rings to overhaul worn universal joints.

The relationship of the front/rear universal joint angle is very important. The angle between the drive and driven yokes of the universal joint must be approximately the same in order for the alternating acceleration/deceleration of one joint to offset the alternating acceleration/deceleration of the other joint. If these angles are not almost identical, rough operation and vibration will result.

Drive shafts and coupling shafts are balanced assemblies and must not be painted or undercoated. Correct alignment is required when a drive shaft is removed and reinstalled to prevent drive line vibrations. Correct phasing is also required. This means that the U-joints must be installed on the shafts in the same plane.

Removal/Installation

If the drive shaft must be disconnected but need not be removed from the vehicle, perform Steps 1-3 and wire the end of the shaft to the underbody for support. Do not pound on the yoke ears while removing or installing the drive shaft, as this can fracture the nylon injection rings used in some factory-installed universal joints.

Refer to **Figure 7** for this procedure.

1. Securely block the wheels that remain on the ground. Raise the vehicle with a jack and place it on jackstands.
2. Scribe or chalk alignment marks on the shaft and case or differential pinion flange for reassembly reference.
3. Remove the nuts holding the retainer straps at the pinion flange. Remove the retainer straps and

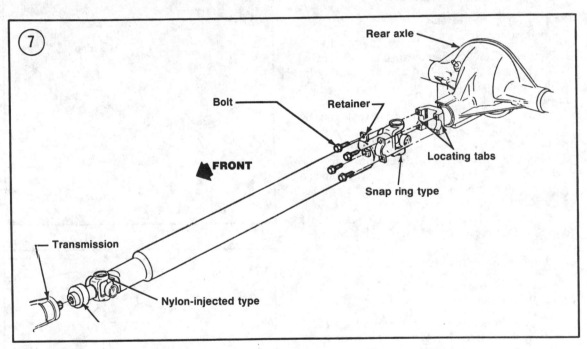

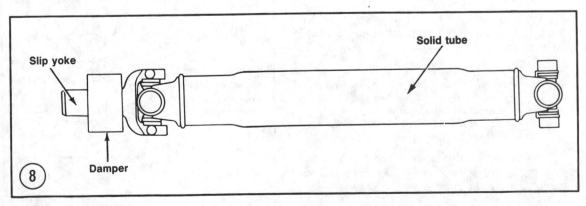

tape the bearing cups to the trunnion to prevent their loss.

4. Slide the drive shaft forward to disconnect the trunnion from the axle flange.

5. Move the drive shaft to the rear and pass it under the axle housing to disengage it from the transmission.

6. Remove the drive shaft from underneath the vehicle.

7. Installation is the reverse of removal. Tighten the retainer strap bolts to specifications (**Table 1**).

DRIVE SHAFT UNIVERSAL JOINTS

The single cardan joint consists of a single spider and 4 sets of needle bearings, bearing seals, caps and cap retainers. Replacement universal joint kits may be of the internal snap ring type (**Figure 9**) or external snap ring type (**Figure 10**).

Factory Installed Universal Joint Disassembly

Production universal joints are retained by nylon injected rings. Removal of the universal joint destroys the nylon ring and the universal joint must be discarded.

1. Support the lower ear of the drive shaft yoke on a 1 1/8 in. socket on the base plate of a hydraulic press.

2. Install a cross press such as tool part No. J-9522-3 over the open horizontal bearing cup and press the lower bearing cup from the yoke ears. See **Figure 11**.

3. Rotate the drive shaft 180° and repeat Step 1 and Step 2 to press the opposite bearing cup from the yoke.

4. Remove the spider from the yoke.

Service Replacement Universal Joint Disassembly

1. Paint alignment marks on the drive shaft and slip yoke for reassembly reference. Remove the slip yoke from the drive shaft.

2. Remove the loose bearing caps from the spider. Apply liberal quantities of penetrating oil to the bearing caps in the shaft yoke.

CAUTION
Clamp only the forged portion of the slip yoke or drive shaft yoke in the vise in Step 3. Clamping the drive shaft tube in a vise can distort the tube and result in drive line vibration after installation.

3. Clamp the drive shaft yoke or slip yoke in a vise with protective jaws. If protective jaws are not available, wrap the yoke in shop cloths.

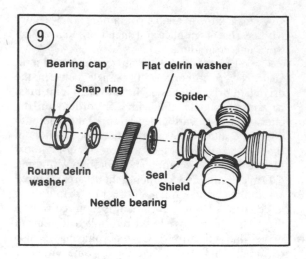

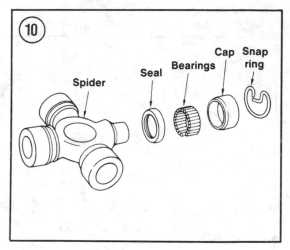

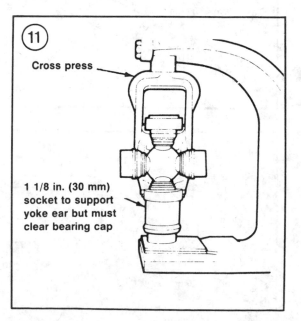

4. Remove the snap rings or retaining rings from the opposite bearing caps with pliers. If necessary, tap the ends of the bearing caps with a hammer to relieve any pressure on the snap rings.

5. Tap the end of one bearing cap with a hammer and drive the opposite cap from the yoke. Remove the bearing cap.

6. Repeat Step 5 to remove the other bearing cap.

7. Remove the drive shaft yoke or slip yoke from the spider.

8. Unclamp and reposition the yoke in the vise. Repeat Steps 4-6 to remove the remaining bearing caps. Remove the spider from the yoke.

Cleaning and Inspection

1. If replacing original universal joints that used nylon injected retaining rings, remove any remaining sheared plastic from the yoke grooves.

2. Clean the yoke bearing cap bores with solvent and a wire brush.

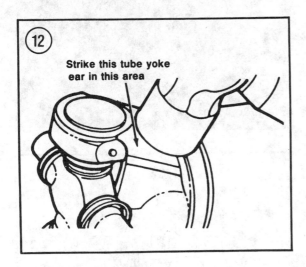

3. Wash the bearing caps, bearings and spider in solvent. Wipe dry with a clean shop cloth.

4. Check the caps, bearings and spider for brinneling, flat spots, scoring, cracks or excessive wear. Replace the entire assembly if any part(s) show such conditions.

Assembly

1. Lubricate all components with chassis grease. Wipe the outside of the bearing caps with a thin film of chassis grease.

2. Install the bearing cap seals on the spider.

3. Partially install a bearing cap and needle bearing assembly in the shaft yoke.

4. Place the spider in the shaft yoke. Install the opposite bearing cap and needle bearing assembly in the yoke bore.

5. Support the yoke on the vise jaws. Seat both caps in the yoke by tapping lightly with a hammer. See **Figure 12**.

6. Install the bearing cap snap rings or retaining rings (**Figure 13**). If retaining rings are used, tape the caps on the spider to hold them in place until the drive shaft is reinstalled.

7. Reposition the shaft yoke in the vise and install the 2 remaining bearing cap and needle bearing assemblies. Install the bearing cap snap rings or retaining rings. If retaining rings are used, tape the caps on the spider to hold them in place until the drive shaft is reinstalled.

> *CAUTION*
> *Do not reinstall the drive shaft if the universal joints show any signs of binding when checked in Step 8 or drive line vibration and possible damage may result.*

8. Check the assembled joint for free movement. If misalignment during installation has caused a bind, tap the drive shaft ears sharply with a hammer (**Figure 12**). If this does not relieve the binding condition, disassemble the joint as described in this chapter and locate the cause of the problem.

REAR AXLE AND AXLE SHAFTS

This section includes removal, installation and inspection procedures for the standard rear axle, which uses semi-floating axle shafts. Rear axle repair requires special skills and many expensive special tools. The inspection procedures will tell you if repairs are necessary. Refer service on locking rear axles to your dealer.

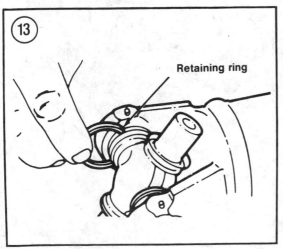

Carrier Gasket Replacement

1. Securely block both front wheels so the vehicle will not roll in either direction.
2. Raise the vehicle with a jack and place it on jackstands.
3. Place a clean container underneath the carrier housing.
4. Remove the cover bolts (**Figure 14**).

> *CAUTION*
> *Two carrier cover bolts attach brake line holders to the cover. Lift the lines up and place them on top of the axle housing to prevent any possible damage.*

4. Pry the cover loose with a screwdriver and let the lubricant drain into the container.
5. Remove the cover. Remove and discard the gasket.
6. Clean the gasket sealing surfaces on the cover and carrier.
7. Install the cover with a new gasket.
8. Install the cover bolts and tighten to specifications (**Table 1**) in a crosswise pattern to assure a uniform draw on the gasket.
9. Remove the fill plug (A, **Figure 15**) and fill the carrier with the recommended type and quantity of lubricant (Chapter Three) to within 3/8 in. of the fill plug hole. Reinstall the fill plug and tighten to specifications (**Table 1**).
10. Remove the jackstands and lower the vehicle to the ground. Remove the wheel chocks.

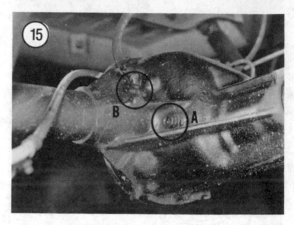

Axle Shaft Removal/Installation

1. Remove the wheel cover or hub cap. Loosen the rear wheel lug nuts.
2. Securely block both rear wheels so the vehicle will not roll in either direction.
3. Raise the rear of the vehicle with a jack and place it on jackstands.
4. Remove the wheel/tire assembly and brake drum (Chapter Twelve).
5. Remove the carrier cover and drain the lubricant as described in this chapter.
6. Remove the rear axle pinion shaft lock screw and pinion shaft (**Figure 16**). Discard the lock screw.
7. Push the flanged end of the axle shaft in toward the center of the vehicle. Remove the C-lock from the shaft (**Figure 17**).
8. Carefully withdraw the axle shaft from the carrier housing to prevent damage to the oil seal.
9. Installation is the reverse of removal. Install a new pinion shaft lock screw and tighten to specifications (**Table 1**).

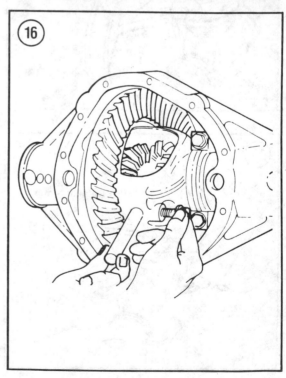

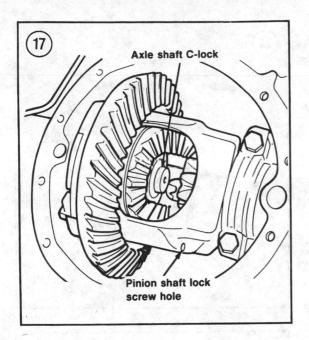

Axle shaft C-lock

Pinion shaft lock screw hole

Axle Shaft Oil Seal/Bearing Replacement

1. Remove the axle shaft as described in this chapter.
2. Pry the seal from the housing with a suitable tool.
3. Install a bearing removal tool to a slide hammer, as shown in **Figure 18**.
4. Insert the tool in the bore and engage its tangs with the bearing outer race. Remove the bearing.
5. Lubricate a new bearing with gear lubricant.
6. Install the bearing with an installer tool as shown in **Figure 19**. The tool must bottom against the housing shoulder to properly seat the seal.
7. Lubricate the seal lips with gear lubricant.
8. Fit the seal in the housing bore and tap in place with a seal installer until it is flush with the axle tube.
9. Reinstall the axle shaft as described in this chapter.

Pinion Oil Seal Replacement

1. Disconnect the drive shaft from the rear axle pinion flange as described under *Drive Shaft Removal/Installation* in this chapter. Wire the drive shaft up and out of the way.
2. Scribe a mark on the pinion flange, pinion shaft and pinion nut for reassembly reference. Using the marks will allow pinion bearing preload to be properly maintained.
3. Using a holding tool such as part No. J-8614-01 or equivalent, remove the pinion nut and washer. See **Figure 20**.

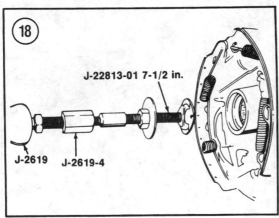

J-22813-01 7-1/2 in.

J-2619   J-2619-4

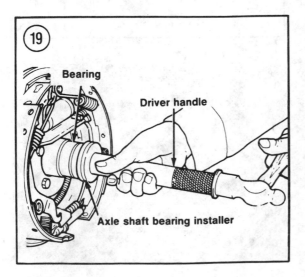

Bearing

Driver handle

Axle shaft bearing installer

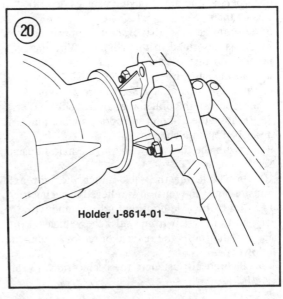

Holder J-8614-01

11

4. Place a suitable container under the pinion flange to catch any leaking fluid, then remove the flange with holding tool part No. J-8614-01 or equivalent and suitable puller as shown in **Figure 21**.

5. Carefully drive the old seal from the carrier with a blunt chisel.

6. Check pinion flange seal surface for signs of excessive wear, damage or grooving. Replace flange if necessary.

7. Check carrier seal bore for similar wear, damage or burring. If burrs are found, remove with a suitable file.

8. Fit a new pinion seal on installer part No. J-23911 or equivalent. See **Figure 22**.

9. Wipe outer diameter of pinion flange and lip of new seal with special seal lubricant part No. 1050169. Install seal in carrier seal bore.

10. Reinstall pinion flange. Use holding tool part No. J-8614-01 or equivalent and tighten flange nut 1/16 in. (1.59 mm) beyond the alignment marks made in Step 2.

11. Reconnect drive shaft to pinion flange.

Rear Axle Removal/Installation

1. Remove the wheel covers or hub caps. Loosen the rear wheel lug nuts.

2. Securely block both front wheels so the vehicle will not roll in either direction.

3. Raise the rear of the vehicle with a jack. Support the vehicle with jackstands placed at the frame. Install the jack under the rear axle housing.

4. Disconnect the lower ends of the shock absorbers at the axle housing pads as described in this chapter.

5. Disconnect the drive shaft from the pinion flange as described in this chapter. Wire the shaft up and out of the way.

6. Carefully pry open the axle housing clips used to route the brake lines. See **Figure 23** (typical).

7. Disconnect the brake lines at the backing plates.

8. Remove the U-bolts and spring anchor plates as described in this chapter.

9. Disconnect the vent hose at the axle housing. See B, **Figure 15**.

10. Slowly lower the jack under the rear axle housing until the tension is relieved at each spring.

11. Lower the axle housing to the ground with the jack and remove it from under the vehicle.

12. Installation is the reverse of removal, plus the following:

   a. Tighten all fasteners to specifications (**Table 1**).

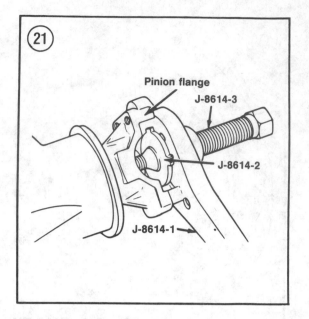

(21)

Pinion flange

J-8614-3

J-8614-2

J-8614-1

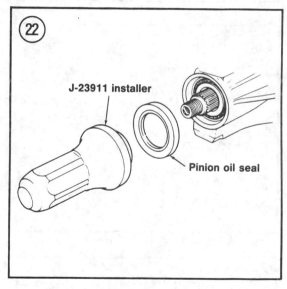

(22)

J-23911 installer

Pinion oil seal

(23)

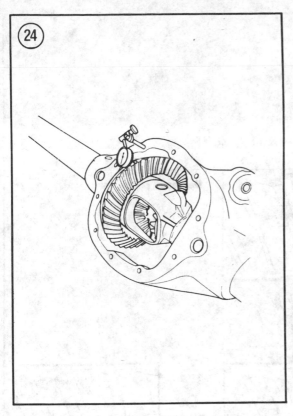

b. Fill the axle with the specified lubricant (Chapter Three).

c. Bleed the brakes (Chapter Twelve).

d. Adjust the parking brake (Chapter Twelve).

Differential Inspection

Inspection of the differential case and drive pinion assembly before removal from the carrier housing can be helpful in determining the cause of a differential problem.

1. Wipe as much lubricant as possible from the internal components. Use paper towels or clean lint-free cloths.

2. Mount a dial indicator as shown in **Figure 24** to measure ring gear backlash. The indicator plunger should touch the drive side of a ring gear tooth at right angles to the tooth. Hold the pinion from turning with one hand and rotate the ring gear against the dial indicator with the other. Backlash should be 0.005-0.009 in. (0.13-0.23 mm). If not, have the differential disassembled and adjusted.

3. Measure ring gear runout. It should not exceed 0.002 in. (0.05 mm). If it does, have the differential repaired.

4. Rotate the ring gear and check for broken, chipped or worn teeth. Check the differential for rough movement. Have the differential repaired if these conditions are found.

5. Inspect all bearings and cups for pitting, galling, flat spots or cracks. Repair as required.

6. Check the differential case for an elongated or enlarged pinion mate shaft bore.

7. Inspect the machined thrust washer surface area for nicks, gouges, cracks or burrs.

8. Check the case for cracks or other damage. Replace the case if any of these conditions are found.

Tooth Contact Pattern Test

1. Wipe all oil from the axle housing. Clean each ring gear tooth carefully.

2. Apply a light coat of gear marking compound to the drive side of the ring gear teeth (**Figure 25**).

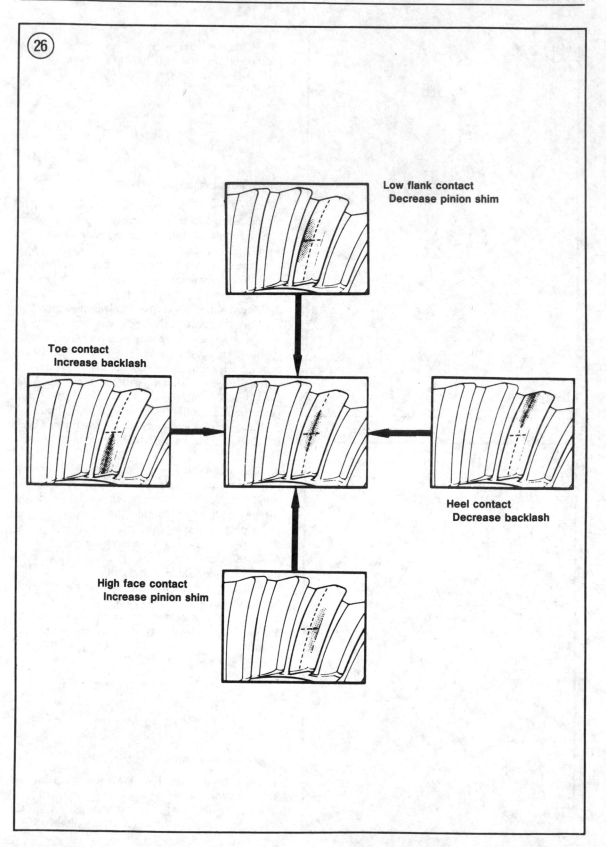

㉖

Low flank contact
Decrease pinion shim

Toe contact
Increase backlash

Heel contact
Decrease backlash

High face contact
Increase pinion shim

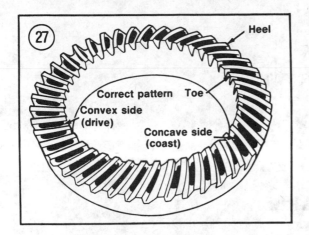

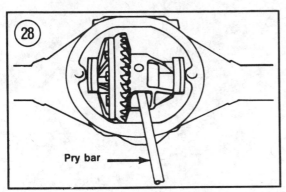

3. Rotate the ring gear slowly in both directions. Compare the contact pattern pressed into the marking compound with those shown in **Figure 26**.

The desired tooth contact pattern under a light load is shown in **Figure 27**. If the pattern is not correct, have the differential disassembled and adjusted.

Differential Removal/Installation

1. Inspect the differential housing as described in this chapter.
2. Remove the axle housing as described in this chapter.
3. Mark the differential bearing caps with a centerpunch for reassembly alignment reference.
4. Remove the differential bearing cap bolts.
5. Pry the rear axle case from the carrier as shown in **Figure 28**. Work carefully to prevent damage to the gasket sealing surface.
6. Tie the left and right bearing shims and outer races in sets for proper reinstallation.
7. Installation is the reverse of removal. Tighten all fasteners to specifications (**Table 1**).

Table 1 TIGHTENING TORQUES

Fastener	ft.-lb.	N•m
Bumper-to-axle nut	18	25
Cam-to-hanger assembly nut	16	22
Carrier cover bolts	20	27
Differential bearing cap	55	75
Fill plug	25-35	34-48
Hanger assembly nuts	81	110
Lower plate-to-anchor plate nut	40	55
Pinion shaft lockscrew	25	34
Retainer-to-hanger assembly nut	26	36
Retainer strap bolts	12-17	16-23
Shackle-to-frame or spring	81	110
Shock absorber		
To frame nut	75	102
To frame bolt	82	112
To axle nut	75	102
U-bolt-to-anchor plate nut	48	65
Wheel lug nuts	90	122

11

CHAPTER TWELVE

BRAKES

Front disc brakes and self-adjusting rear drum brakes are standard on all models. All vehicles use a dual hydraulic brake system with 2 independent circuits. See **Figure 1** (typical). A failure in one circuit leaves the other circuit intact and functional. One circuit operates the front brakes and the other circuit operates the rear brakes. Failure of one of the brake circuits will normally be indicated by the instrument panel brake warning light turning on. However, if the light is burned out or the wiring faulty, the first indication of a brake failure may occur when the brakes are applied, requiring much more pedal pressure than normal.

Rear drum brakes are a single anchor, duo-servo design. A dual reservoir master cylinder (**Figure 2**) is used, with the smaller front reservoir connected to the rear drum brakes. The larger rear reservoir is connected to the front disc brakes. A combination valve is bracket-mounted with the master cylinder to the dash panel (manual brakes) or vacuum booster (power brakes). See **Figure 3** (power brakes). The pressure differential warning switch in the combination valve compares front and rear brake pressure. If a pressure loss occurs in either brake system, the instrument panel warning light comes on to alert the driver. The light shuts off when the system is serviced, bled and the brake pedal depressed to center the piston. The proportioning section of the valve balances braking pressure between the front and rear brakes to minimize rear wheel skidding during hard braking.

Vehicles equipped with power brakes utilize a booster unit which utilizes engine intake manifold vacuum and atmospheric pressure for its power. See **Figure 4**.

A ratchet-type foot-operated parking brake lever is mounted under the left side of the instrument panel (**Figure 5**) and is connected to the rear wheel brakes through a series of cables underneath the floor pan.

Tightening torques are provided in **Table 1** at the end of the chapter.

FRONT DISC BRAKES

The front disc brake assembly uses a low drag, single piston Delco pin slider caliper. The caliper is located on abutment surfaces machined on the leading and trailing edges of the caliper anchor bracket. No return spring is used in the caliper piston bore. Lining wear is compensated for by increased piston extension and the lateral sliding motion of the caliper.

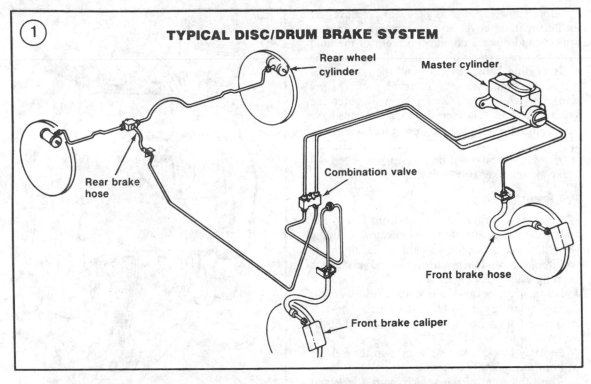

TYPICAL DISC/DRUM BRAKE SYSTEM

① Rear wheel cylinder

Master cylinder

Rear brake hose

Combination valve

Front brake hose

Front brake caliper

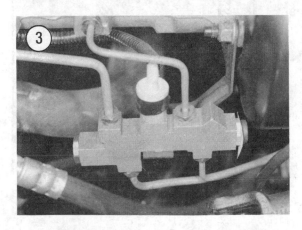

12

Before replacing disc brake pads, remove the master cylinder cover and use a large syringe to remove and discard about 50 percent of the fluid from the rear reservoir. This will prevent the master cylinder from overflowing when the caliper piston is compressed for reinstallation. *Do not drain the entire reservoir* or air will enter the system. Recheck the reservoir when the pads have been reinstalled and top up as required with fresh DOT 3 or DOT 4 brake fluid. If no hydraulic line is opened, it should not be necessary to bleed the brake system after pad replacement.

Pad Inspection

An integral spring clip on the front disc brake pads serves as an audible wear indicator. As lining wear reaches the point where replacement is required, the clip touches the rotor and produces a warning sound. See **Figure 6**.

1. Set the parking brake. Place the transmission in 1st gear (manual) or PARK (automatic).
2. Remove the wheel covers or hub caps. Loosen the front wheel lug nuts.
3. Securely block both rear wheels so the vehicle will not roll in either direction.
4. Raise the front of the vehicle with a jack and place it on jackstands.
5. Remove the front wheel/tire assemblies.
6. Visually check the thickness of the inboard lining through the inspection hole in the center of the caliper. Check the thickness of the lining at both ends of the outboard pads. See **Figure 7**.
7. If the lining is worn to within 1/32 in. of the pad on bonded linings or to within 1/32 in. of the rivet

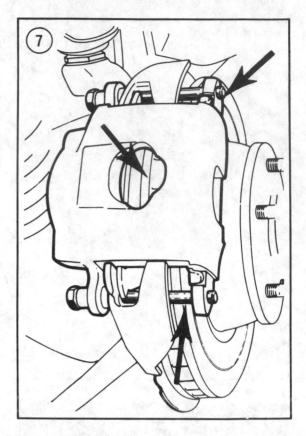

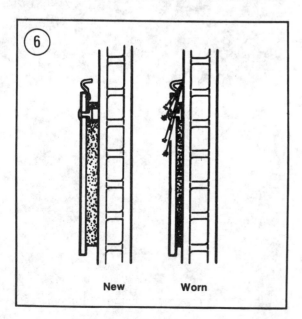

New   Worn

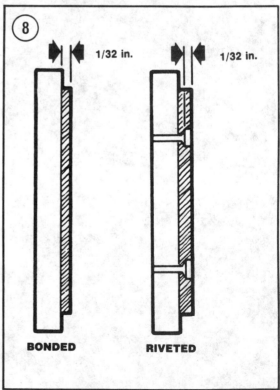

1/32 in.   1/32 in.

BONDED   RIVETED

heads on riveted linings, replace the pads as a set on both front wheels. See **Figure 8**.

8. Install the wheel/tire assemblies. Install the lug nuts finger-tight, then remove the jackstands and lower the vehicle to the ground. Remove the wheel chocks.

9. Tighten the wheel lug nuts to specifications (**Table 1**) in an alternating pattern. Reinstall the wheel covers or hub caps.

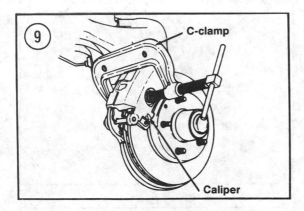

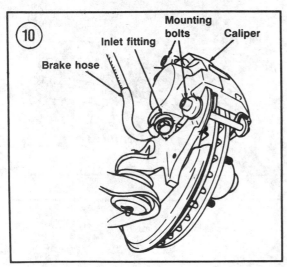

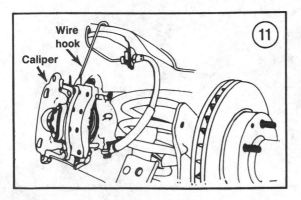

Pad Replacement

1. Set the parking brake. Place the transmission in 1st gear (manual) or PARK (automatic).

2. Remove the wheel covers or hub caps. Loosen the front wheel lug nuts.

3. Remove the rear master cylinder cover and use a large syringe to remove about half the brake fluid in the rear reservoir.

NOTE
Discard this brake fluid. Do not reuse.

4. Securely block both rear wheels so the vehicle will not roll in either direction.

5. Raise the front of the vehicle with a jack and place it on jackstands.

6. Remove the front wheel/tire assemblies.

7. Install a C-clamp as shown in **Figure 9** and tighten until the piston bottoms in the bore.

8. Remove the C-clamp. Remove the 2 Allen head mounting bolts (**Figure 10**).

WARNING
If the bolts are corroded, discard and install new ones when the caliper is reinstalled.

9. Remove the caliper with an upward rotating motion. Suspend it from the coil spring with a wire hook to prevent stressing the brake hose. See **Figure 11**.

10. Remove the pads from the caliper.

11. Remove the sleeves from the caliper bolt holes. Remove the bushings from the bolt hole grooves. See **Figure 12** (typical).

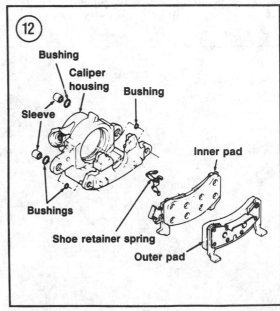

12

12. Inspect the pads. Light surface dirt, oil or grease stains may be sanded off. If oil or grease has penetrated the surface, replace the pads. Since brake fluid will ruin the friction material, pads must be replaced if any brake fluid has touched them.

13. Check the caliper piston seal and boot area for brake fluid leaks. If brake fluid has leaked from the caliper housing, replace the caliper. If the leak appears to come from the seal area, rebuild the caliper as described in this chapter.

14. Inspect the brake rotor as described in this chapter.

15. Lubricate new sleeves and rubber bushings, the caliper bushing grooves and the end of the mounting bolts with Delco Moraine Silicone Lubricant or equivalent. See **Figure 13**.

16. Install the bushings in the caliper bolt hole grooves. Install the sleeves in the bolt holes until their ends are flush with the inside machined surface of the lugs.

17. Install the retainer spring on the inner pad (**Figure 14**) with a rotating motion.

18. Install the inner pad carefully (**Figure 15**). If the inner pad retainer clip is bent during installation, the brakes may rattle.

19. Install the outer pad in the caliper.

20. Install the caliper over the brake rotor with a rotating motion, holding the outer pad against the rotor braking surface to prevent pinching the piston boot. Align the holes in the caliper lugs with the holes in the caliper mounting bracket.

21. Insert the mounting bolts through the sleeves in the inboard mounting lugs and make sure the bolts pass under the ears on the inboard brake pad (**Figure 16**). Guide the bolts through to engage the

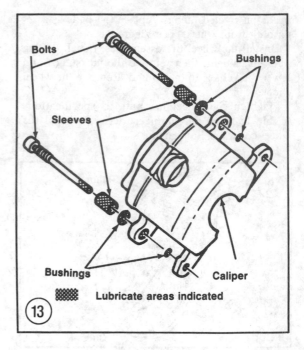

Bolts

Bushings

Sleeves

Bushings   Caliper

▓ Lubricate areas indicated

(13)

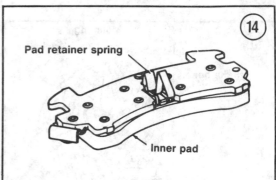

(14)

Pad retainer spring

Inner pad

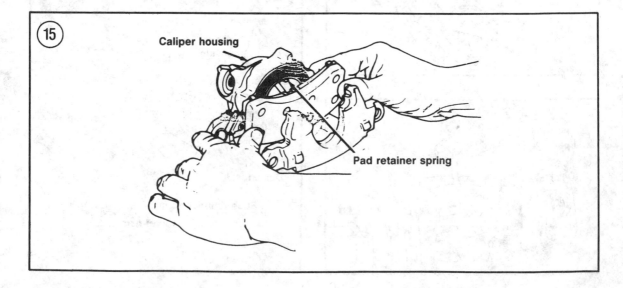

(15)

Caliper housing

Pad retainer spring

holes in the outboard shoe and the outboard lugs on the caliper. Tighten bolts to specifications (**Table 1**).

> *NOTE*
> *The following step is necessary to dampen out any pad vibrations that might cause the brake pads to squeal. Pressure on the brake pedal is required to hold the pads firmly in place while the pad ears are cinched to the caliper.*

22. Have an assistant depress and hold the brake pedal in an applied position while you use a pair of channel lock pliers to tightly cinch the outer pad ears to the caliper. See **Figure 17**. If channel lock pliers are not available, you can accomplish the same thing by peening the outer pad ears with a suitable hammer and punch.

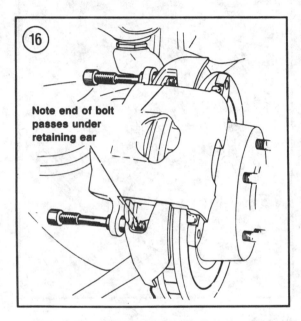

Note end of bolt passes under retaining ear

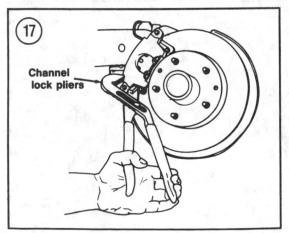

Channel lock pliers

23. Install the wheel/tire assemblies. Install the lug nuts finger-tight, then remove the jackstands and lower the vehicle to the ground. Remove the wheel chocks.

24. Tighten the wheel lug nuts to specifications (**Table 1**) in an alternating pattern. Reinstall the wheel covers or hub caps.

> *WARNING*
> *Do not use brake fluid from a previously opened container in Step 25. Brake fluid absorbs moisture from the air and moisture in the hydraulic lines can result in erratic or slow braking.*

25. Fill the master cylinder to within 1/4 in. of the reservoir side wall with fresh DOT 3 or DOT 4 brake fluid from an unopened container.

26. Install the reservoir cover and check for leaks around the caliper and hoses.

27. Depress the brake pedal several times to position the caliper and pads.

28. Check for firm pedal pressure. Road test the vehicle to make sure the brakes operate properly.

Caliper Removal

1. Perform Steps 1-8 of *Pad Replacement* in this chapter.

2. Have an assistant carefully depress the brake pedal. This should hydraulically push the piston from the caliper bore. Remove the piston.

3. Disconnect the brake hose from the caliper at the inlet fitting (**Figure 10**) and discard the copper washers. Plug the caliper inlet port and hose outlet to prevent dirt from entering.

4. Mark the left and right calipers for identification if both are removed.

Caliper Installation

1. Install the caliper over the brake rotor with a rotating motion, holding the outer pad against the rotor braking surface to prevent pinching the piston boot. Align the holes in the caliper lugs with the holes in the caliper mounting bracket.

2. Insert the mounting bolts through the sleeves in the inboard mounting lugs and make sure the bolts pass under the ears on the inboard brake pad (**Figure 16**). Guide the bolts through to engage the holes in the outboard shoe and the outboard lugs on the caliper. Tighten bolts to specifications (**Table 1**).

3. Install the brake hose to the inlet fitting with new copper washers.

4. Bleed the brakes as described in this chapter.

5. Perform Steps 22-28 of *Pad Replacement* in this chapter to complete installation.

12

Rotor Inspection

1. Loosen the front wheel lug nuts.
2. Securely block both rear wheels so the vehicle will not roll in either direction.
3. Raise the front of the vehicle with a jack and place it on jackstands.
4. Remove the wheel/tire assemblies.
5. Tighten the wheel bearings just enough to remove all bearing free play.
6. Attach a dial indicator to some part of the suspension so that the indicator stylus touches the rotor surface approximately one inch from the outer edge of the rotor. See **Figure 18**.
7. Set the dial indicator to zero, then slowly turn the brake rotor one complete revolution to check runout. Note the high and low readings on the indicator gauge. If the total between the two readings exceeds 0.004 in. (0.102 mm), have the rotor resurfaced by a dealer or replace it if the wear is excessive.

> *NOTE*
> *If the rotor is resurfaced, its finished thickness should not be less than the minimum dimension cast on the rotor.*

8. Check the rotor for parallelism (thickness variation) with a micrometer at 12 equal points on the rotor. Take each reading with the micrometer positioned one inch from the edge of the rotor. If measurements vary more than 0.0005 in. (0.013 mm), resurface or replace the rotor.
9. Use the micrometer to measure the thickness of the rotor at several points around the circumference and at varying distances from the center. If the rotor measures less at any point than the minimum stamped on the rotor, replace it.
10. Inspect the rotor for cracks, rust or scratches. Replace the rotor if cracked. Light rust can be removed with crocus cloth or medium emery paper. Light scoring of the rotor which does not exceed 0.015 in. (0.38 mm) results from normal operation and does not affect brake operation. Heavy rust or deep scratches should be removed by resurfacing the rotor. This can be done by a dealer or machine shop. However, the rotor must not be machined more than 0.020 in. (0.508 mm) on each side. Replace the rotor if resurfacing will reduce its thickness below the minimum stamped on the rotor.
11. Adjust the wheel bearings (Chapter Ten) and reverse Steps 1-4 to return the vehicle to service.

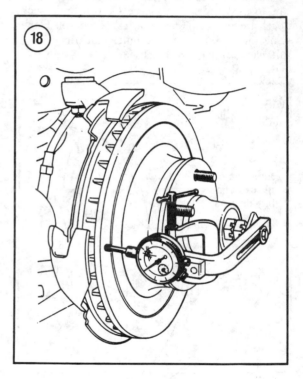

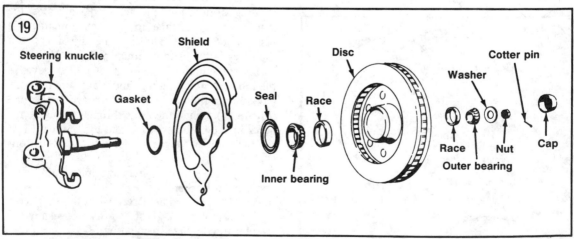

Steering knuckle — Shield — Gasket — Seal — Inner bearing — Race — Disc — Washer — Cotter pin — Race — Outer bearing — Nut — Cap

Rotor Removal/Installation

1. Remove the wheel covers or hub caps. Loosen the front wheel lug nuts.
2. Securely block both rear wheels so the vehicle will not roll in either direction.
3. Raise the front of the vehicle with a jack and place it on jackstands.
4. Remove the wheel/tire assemblies.
5. Remove the brake caliper as described in this chapter but do not disconnect the brake hose. Suspend the caliper from the suspension with a length of wire to prevent stressing the brake hose (**Figure 11**).

CAUTION
Do not damage or deform the hub grease cap by removing it with pliers in Step 6. Work carefully with a screwdriver and pry the cap off.

6. Remove the hub grease cap. Remove and discard the cotter pin.
7. Remove the wheel bearing nut. Grasp the hub and rotor assembly in both hands and pull it off the spindle. The outer wheel bearing and washer will slide out when the hub is removed. The inner wheel bearing and grease seal will remain in the hub. See **Figure 19**.
8. Mark rotor-to-hub position, then unbolt the rotor and hub assembly.

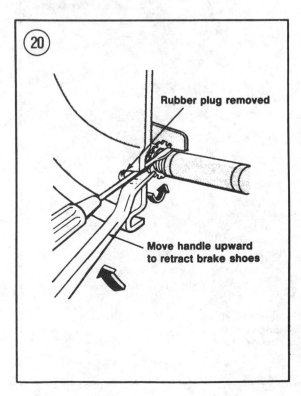

Rubber plug removed

Move handle upward to retract brake shoes

9. Remove and discard the hub grease seal.
10. Installation is the reverse of removal, plus the following:
    a. If a new rotor is being installed, remove the protective coating with carburetor degreaser.
    b. Adjust the wheel bearings as described in Chapter Ten.

REAR DRUM BRAKES

The rear drum brakes are a self-adjusting duo-servo design. The drums fit over the rear wheel hub studs and are retained by the wheel/tire lug nuts.

Brake Drum Removal/Installation

If the drum and lining on one side require cleaning and dressing, this service should be carried out on the opposite side also.

WARNING
Do not inhale brake dust. It may contain asbestos, which can cause lung cancer.

1. Set the parking brake and block the front wheels.
2. Remove the wheel covers or hub caps. Loosen the rear wheel lug nuts.
3. Raise the rear of the vehicle with a jack and place it on jackstands.
4. Remove the wheel/tire assembly. Remove the drum.
5. If the brake drum will not come off easily, remove the access hole plug from the support plate. Insert a narrow screwdriver through the adjusting hole, disengage and hold the adjusting lever away from the adjusting screw. Back off the screw with a brake adjusting tool. See **Figure 20**. Be careful not to damage the adjusting screw notches; otherwise, the self-adjusting mechanism will not function properly. If adjustment is backed off, make sure adjuster lever seats properly in the shoe web.
6. If a new drum is being installed, remove the protective coating with carburetor degreaser.
7. Install the brake drum. Install the wheel/tire assembly. Install the wheel lug nuts finger-tight.
8. Lower the vehicle to the ground and tighten the lug nuts to specifications (**Table 1**) in an alternating pattern. Reinstall the wheel cover or hub cap and remove the wheel chocks.
9. If brake adjustment was backed off to remove the drum, adjust the brakes as described in this chapter.

12

Drum and Shoe Inspection

> *WARNING*
> *Do not clean brake drum or shoe assembly with compressed air in Step 1. Brake linings contain asbestos and the dust can be hazardous to your health. If the drum or shoe assembly is extremely dirty, clean with a vacuum cleaner or use an old paint brush and wear a painter's mask over your nose and mouth.*

1. Wipe the inside of the drum with a clean dry cloth to remove any sand, dirt or other foreign matter. Clean all other parts (except the linings) with aerosol brake cleaner or new brake fluid. Do not use gasoline, kerosene or solvent as a cleaning agent.

> *CAUTION*
> *If cleaning with brake fluid, keep it off the lining surfaces. Brake fluid will ruin the linings and they will have to be replaced.*

2. Check drum for visible scoring, excessive or uneven wear, corrosion or glazed heat spots. Any scoring sufficiently deep to snag a fingernail is reason enough for having the drums turned and the linings replaced. Minor scratches or scoring can be removed with fine emery cloth. If this is done, clean thoroughly with compressed air to remove any abrasive. If heat spots (blue-tinted areas) are noted, replace the drum.

3. If you have precision measuring equipment, measure the drum for wear and out-of-roundness. If you do not have the equipment, this can be done by a dealer or machine shop. If the drum has surface damage or out-of-round exceeds 0.006 in. (0.152 mm), have it resurfaced on a lathe by a dealer or machine shop. However, the inside diameter after resurfacing must not exceed the maximum wear specification cast in the drum. If the drum would have to be cut larger than this to correct it, it must be replaced.

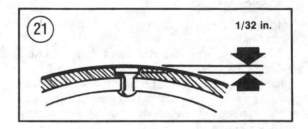

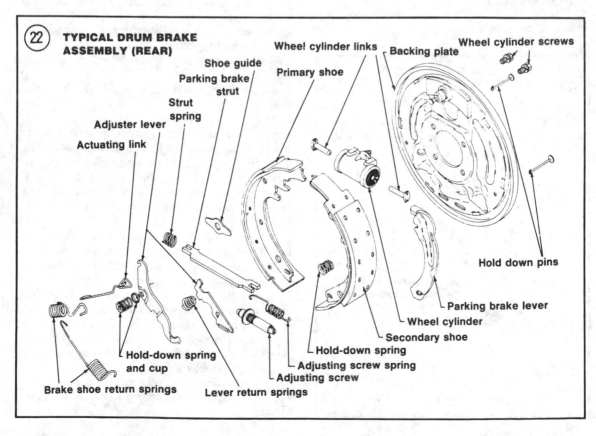

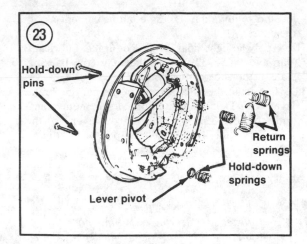

Hold-down pins

Return springs

Hold-down springs

Lever pivot

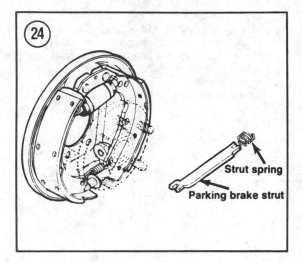

Strut spring

Parking brake strut

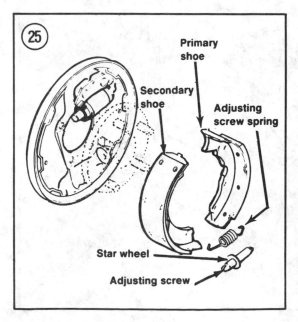

Primary shoe

Secondary shoe

Adjusting screw spring

Star wheel

Adjusting screw

4. Inspect the lining material on the brake shoes. Make sure it is not cracked, unevenly worn or separated from the shoes. Dirt and foreign particles that are embedded in the lining can often be removed with a wire brush, but lining replacement is recommended instead. Light surface oil or grease stains may be sanded off. If oil or grease has soaked beneath the surface, replace the shoes. Since brake fluid will ruin the linings, the shoes must be replaced if brake fluid has touched them. Shoes must also be replaced if the lining material has worn to within 1/32 in. of a rivet (riveted lining) or the shoe (bonded lining). **Figure 21** shows the wear dimension on riveted shoes.

5. Check all springs for signs of overheating, weakness or deformation (paint discoloration or distorted end coils indicate overheating). Replace as required.

6. Inspect the wheel cylinders for signs of leakage or boot damage. If wet areas are found near the cylinder boots, the wheel cylinder should be overhauled or replaced with a rebuilt unit.

Brake Disassembly

Brakes should be reconditioned at least in pairs—both front or both rear—or all 4 wheels at the same time. In addition, new linings should be arced to the contour of the drums. This is a job for a dealer or automotive brake specialist.

Refer to **Figure 22** (typical) for this procedure.

1. Remove the brake drum as described in this chapter.

2. Unhook the primary and secondary shoe return springs with a brake tool. Large pliers can also be used, but a brake tool will make the job much easier.

3. Depress the shoe hold-down spring cups and rotate 90°, then remove the hold-down springs and lever pivot from the hold-down pins. See **Figure 23**.

4. Lift up on the actuator and disconnect the actuating link from the anchor pin. Remove the link, lever, pawl and return spring.

5. Spread the shoes enough to clear the wheel cylinder connecting links. Disconnect and remove the parking brake strut and spring (**Figure 24**).

6. Expand the shoes until they clear the axle flange. Disconnect the parking brake cable at the parking brake lever and remove the shoe assembly from the backing plate.

7. Note the adjuster spring position, then remove the spring and adjuster screw (**Figure 25**).

8. Remove the circlip holding the parking brake lever to the secondary shoe. Separate the parking brake lever from the secondary shoe.

12

Brake Inspection

1. Carefully pry back the lower edge of each wheel cylinder boot and check for leakage. A slight film of brake fluid on the piston rods is normal, but if there is an excessive amount of fluid in the boots or wet stains outside the cylinder, it should be rebuilt or replaced as described in this chapter.

2. Inspect the backing plate for signs of oil that may have leaked past the axle seal. If oil is present, replace the seals. See Chapter Eleven.

3. Check and tighten the backing plate fasteners. Thoroughly clean the backing plate and all brake components. Use only rubbing alcohol or brake fluid as a cleaner—do not use mineral-based detergents. Clean the shoe contact surfaces to the bare metal with emery cloth. Make certain all loose dirt, rust, corrosion and abrasives are removed.

4. Check the adjuster screw operation. If it does not turn smoothly, disassemble, clean and lubricate it.

Brake Assembly

Refer to **Figure 26** for this procedure.

1. Check the new linings to make sure they are not nicked or burred. If they are bonded linings, check for and remove any excess bonding cement along the edges.

2. Apply a light coat of Delco Brake Lubricant (part No. 5450032) or equivalent to the backing plate at the shoe contact points.

3. Lubricate the fulcrum end of the parking brake lever with Delco Brake Lubricant (or equivalent) and connect the parking brake lever to the secondary shoe. Install the circlip retainer (**Figure 27**).

4. Lubricate the adjuster screw threads with clean brake fluid.

NOTE
Adjuster screw spring coils must not be positioned over the starwheel in Step 5. Left- and right-hand adjuster springs differ and should not be interchanged. The right-hand thread adjusting screw must go on the left support plate and the left-hand thread screw on the right support plate. The adjuster starwheel must face the secondary shoe and align with the access hole in the support plate.

5. Reassemble the adjuster (if disassembled for cleaning). See **Figure 28**. Turn the adjuster screw

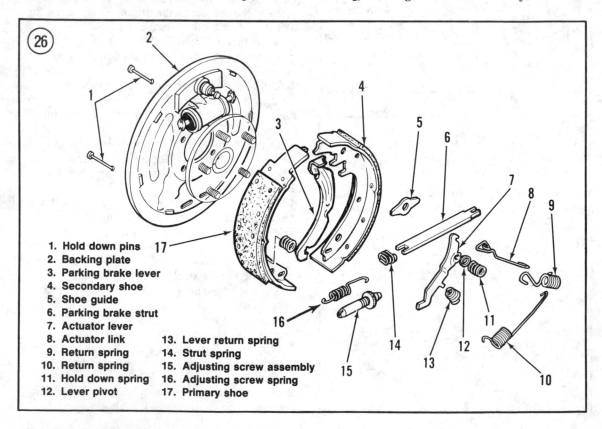

26

1. Hold down pins
2. Backing plate
3. Parking brake lever
4. Secondary shoe
5. Shoe guide
6. Parking brake strut
7. Actuator lever
8. Actuator link
9. Return spring
10. Return spring
11. Hold down spring
12. Lever pivot
13. Lever return spring
14. Strut spring
15. Adjusting screw assembly
16. Adjusting screw spring
17. Primary shoe

into the adjusting pivot nut to the limit of the threads, then back off 1/2 turn.

6. Position the brake shoes to the backing plate. Install the adjuster screw and spring as shown in **Figure 28**.

7. Spread the shoes enough to install the parking brake strut and spring. The spring end of the strut should engage the primary shoe.

8. Install the actuator pivot, lever and return spring.

9. Install the actuator link in the shoe retainer. Lift up on the lever and connect the link and lever.

10. Insert the hold-down pins through the backing plate and shoes. Install the lever pivot on the secondary shoe. Install the hold-down spring and cup assemblies over the pins. Depress each cup with the brake tool and rotate 90°.

11. Install and connect the primary and secondary return springs.

12. Make sure that all components connected to the anchor pin are stacked flat on the pin.

13. Once both brakes on the axle have been assembled, make a preliminary adjustment. Pull the adjuster lever away from the adjusting screw starwheel just far enough to disengage it. Rotate the starwheel to expand the brakes far enough so the drum can be installed with a slight drag, then back the starwheel off 1 1/4 turns to slightly retract the shoes.

14. If the adjuster does not operate properly, check the following points:

    a. Make sure the cable ends are not pulled out of their crimped collars. If they are, replace the cable.

    b. Make sure the lever hook is square and parallel with the lever. If it is not, it may be possible to bend it slightly to correct the condition. If not, replace the lever.

    c. Make sure the adjusting screw socket is seated in the secondary shoe notch.

15. Install the drums and wheel/tire assemblies as described in this chapter.

16. Adjust the parking brake as described in this chapter.

17. Make a final brake adjustment by repeatedly driving the vehicle backward and forward and stopping with firm pedal pressure until the pedal height and resistance are satisfactory.

Wheel Cylinder Removal/Installation

1. Remove the brake drum and shoes as described in this chapter.

> *CAUTION*
> *Do not bend the brake line away from the wheel cylinder after unscrewing the nut in Step 2. Bending the brake line will make it difficult to reconnect and may cause it to crack. The wheel cylinder will separate from the brake line when it is removed from the backing plate.*

2. Clean all dirt and contamination from the brake line fitting at the rear of the support plate.

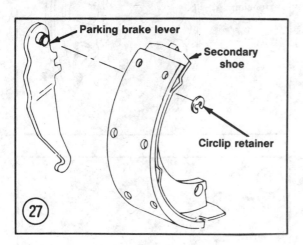

(27)

Parking brake lever

Secondary shoe

Circlip retainer

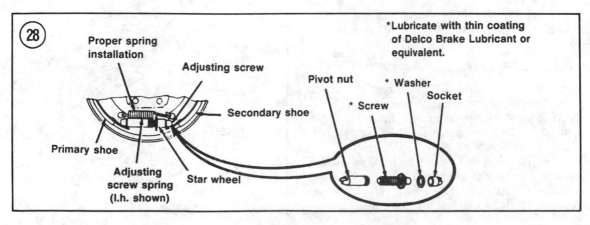

(28)

Proper spring installation

Adjusting screw

Secondary shoe

Primary shoe

Adjusting screw spring (l.h. shown)

Star wheel

*Lubricate with thin coating of Delco Brake Lubricant or equivalent.

Pivot nut

* Screw

* Washer

Socket

12

Disconnect the brake line and cover the end of the line with a clean, lint-free cloth to prevent contamination from entering the hydraulic system.

3. Remove the screws holding the wheel cylinder to the support plate. If attached with a clip retainer, pry the retainer from the support plate with 2 awls as shown in **Figure 29**. Remove the wheel cylinder.

4. Install the wheel cylinder to the support plate. If retained by screws, tighten to specifications in **Table 1**. If retained by a clip, position a new one over the wheel cylinder stud and press in place with a 1 1/8 in. 12-point socket and extension (**Figure 30**).

5. Connect the brake inlet tube to the wheel cylinder and tighten the tube nut to specifications (**Table 1**).

BRAKE ADJUSTMENT

Disc Brakes

Disc brakes are automatically adjusted. No adjustment procedure is necessary or provided.

Drum Brakes

Drum brakes are self-adjusting. Adjustment occurs when the vehicle is driven in reverse and the brakes are applied. If the brake pedal can be pushed within a few inches of the floor, the brakes should be adjusted by backing the vehicle up several times and sharply applying the brakes. Test the adjustment by driving the vehicle at about 20 mph and braking to a smooth stop. If the pedal travel is still excessive, repeat the procedure as required.

> *NOTE*
> *Brake drums should be cold when adjusting the shoes. If the shoes are adjusted when the drums are hot and expanded, they may drag when the drums cool and contract.*

Manual adjustment is unnecessary unless the brakes have been serviced. If so, proceed as follows:

Recommended procedure

1. With the brake drum off, disengage the actuator lever from the starwheel.
2. Measure the inner diameter of the brake drum with clearance gauge part No. J-21177 or part No. J-22364. See **Figure 31**.
3. Using the opposite side of the tool, position it against the linings (**Figure 32**) and rotate the starwheel with a small screwdriver blade as required until the tool just fits over the linings.

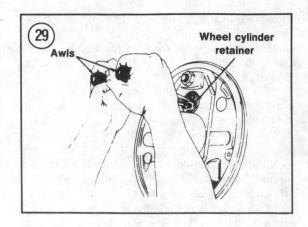

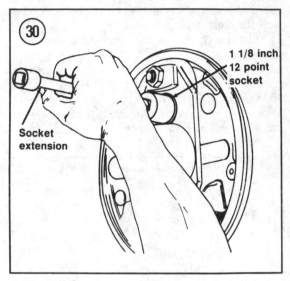

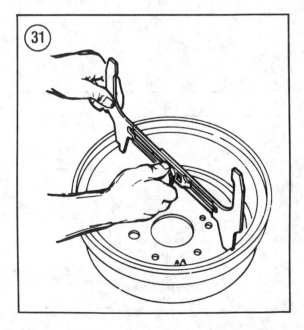

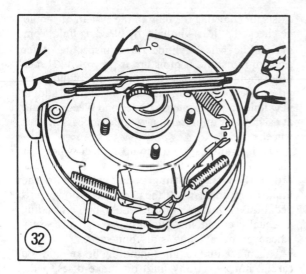

(32)

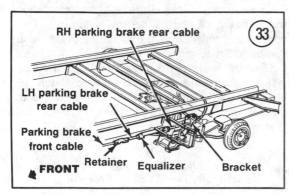

RH parking brake rear cable

(33)

LH parking brake
rear cable

Parking brake
front cable

FRONT   Retainer   Equalizer   Bracket

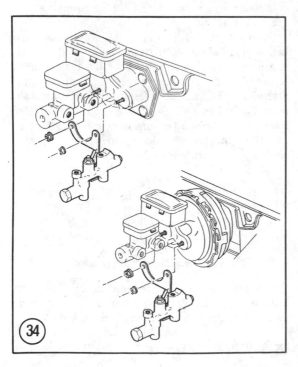

(34)

4. Install the brake drum as described in this chapter.

Alternate procedure

If the brake clearance gauge is not available, the brake drum can be used as an adjustment tool.

1. Rotate the starwheel with a small screwdriver blade as required until the drum slides over the linings with a slight drag.

2. Rotate the starwheel another 1 1/4 turns to retract the shoes. This will give enough clearance for final adjustment by driving the vehicle as described in this chapter.

3. Install the brake drum as described in this chapter.

4. Repeat the procedure on the opposite wheel.

5. Install the wheel/tire assemblies.

6. Remove the jackstands and lower the vehicle to the ground.

7. Make a final brake adjustment by repeatedly driving the vehicle backward and forward and stopping with firm pedal pressure until the pedal height and resistance are satisfactory.

Parking Brake

All vehicles use a foot-operated ratchet-type parking brake pedal, mounted to the left of the brake pedal (and clutch on manual transmission models). See **Figure 5** (typical). The parking brake should be adjusted whenever the parking brake cables have been disconnected or replaced, or when pedal travel is less than 9 or more than 16 ratchet clicks under heavy foot pressure.

1. Depress the parking brake pedal 2 ratchet clicks.

2. Securely block both front wheels so the vehicle will not roll in either direction.

3. Raise the rear of the vehicle with a jack and place it on jackstands.

4. Clean the equalizer connector nut and threads with a wire brush, then lubricate the threads with clean brake fluid.

5. Tighten the equalizer nut until a moderate amount of drag can be felt when the rear wheels are rotated forward.

6. Remove the jackstands and lower the vehicle to the ground. Remove the wheel chocks.

MASTER CYLINDER

The aluminum master cylinder uses dual plastic reservoirs with individual reservoir covers. The master cylinder is attached to the cowl (non-power brakes) or the vacuum booster (power brakes). See **Figure 34**.

12

A quick take-up feature is incorporated in the aluminum housing to provide a large volume of fluid to the disc brakes as soon as the pedal is applied. This allows the calipers to be designed so the pistons (and brake pads) retract farther than in previous designs when the brakes are not in use. This reduces brake drag and increases fuel mileage.

If the master cylinder is defective, it is safer and more economical to replace it with a new or professionally rebuilt unit than to attempt overhaul.

Removal/Installation

Refer to **Figure 34** (typical) for this procedure.
1. Power brakes—With the engine stopped, depress the brake pedal to expel any vacuum remaining in the brake booster system.
2. Disconnect the negative battery cable.

CAUTION
Brake fluid will damage paint. Wipe up any spilled fluid immediately, then wash the area with soap and water.

3. Disconnect the electrical leads and hydraulic lines at the master cylinder. Use a flare nut wrench to avoid rounding the fitting nuts. Cap the lines and plug the master cylinder ports to prevent leakage and entry of contamination.
4. Manual brakes—Working inside the passenger compartment under the instrument panel, disconnect the master cylinder pushrod from the brake pedal.
5. Remove the 2 attaching nuts from the cowl studs (non-power brakes) or vacuum booster unit studs (power brakes). Carefully remove the master cylinder and combination valve bracket. Temporarily reinstall the combination valve bracket on the attaching studs.
6. Installation is the reverse of removal. Tighten all fasteners to specifications (**Table 1**). Fill the master cylinder reservoirs to within 1/4 in. of the top of the side walls with clean DOT 3 or DOT 4 brake fluid. Bleed the brakes as described in this chapter.
7. Start the engine and depress the brake pedal to set the warning light in position. Check for external leaks.

BRAKE BLEEDING

After long usage, brake fluid absorbs enough atmospheric moisture to significantly reduce its boiling point and make it prone to vapor lock during repeated hard braking applications, such as mountain driving. While no hard and fast rule

exists for changing the fluid in the system, it should be checked at least annually by bleeding fluid from one of the wheel cylinders and inspecting it for signs of moisture. If moisture is present, the brake fluid should be replaced. To do this, follow the procedure for bleeding the brakes. Continue adding new fluid to the master cylinder and bleeding fluid at each wheel until fresh, new fluid appears at each wheel.

The hydraulic system should be bled whenever air enters it. Air in the brake lines will compress, rather than transmitting pedal pressure to the brake operating parts. If the pedal feels spongy or if pedal travel increases considerably, brake bleeding is usually called for. Bleeding is also necessary whenever a brake line is disconnected.

This procedure requires handling brake fluid. Be careful not to get any fluid on brake discs, pads, shoes or drums. Clean all dirt and contamination from the bleed valves before beginning. Two people are needed: one to operate the brake pedal and the other to open and close the bleed valves.

Since the brake system consists of 2 individual systems (front and rear), each system should be bled separately. Bleeding should be conducted in the following order: master cylinder, right rear, left rear, right front, left front.

NOTE
Do not allow the master cylinder reservoirs to run dry during bleeding.

Exhaust the vacuum reserve by applying the brakes several times.

Omit Steps 2-4 if the master cylinder was bench-bled before installation.
1. Clean away all dirt around the master cylinder. Remove the reservoir cover and diaphragm assemblies. Top up the reservoirs with brake fluid rated DOT 3 or DOT 4. Leave the covers off the reservoirs and place a clean shop cloth over the top of the master cylinder to prevent any contamination from entering the fluid.

NOTE
DOT 3 means that the brake fluid meets current Department of Transportation quality standards. If the fluid does not say DOT 3 somewhere on the label, buy a brand that does. DOT 4 brake fluid can also be safely used.

2. Loosen the master cylinder hydraulic line nuts with a flare nut wrench and place a shop cloth under the fittings to catch any leaking fluid.
3. Have an assistant slowly depress the brake pedal until it reaches the floorboard and hold it

there while you tighten the master cylinder hydraulic line nuts loosened in Step 2.

4. Repeat Step 2 and Step 3 as required until no air escapes from the fittings.

5. Fit an appropriate size box-end wrench over the bleed screw on the right rear wheel and attach a length of plastic or rubber tubing to the bleed screw. Be sure the tubing fits snugly on the screw. Submerge the other end of the tubing in a container partially filled with clean DOT 3 or DOT 4 brake fluid. See **Figure 35** (typical).

NOTE
Do not allow the end of the tubing to come out of the brake fluid during bleeding or the fluid level in the reservoirs to run dry. Either could allow air to enter the system and require that the bleeding procedure be repeated.

6. Open the bleed screw about 3/4 turn and have the assistant slowly depress the brake pedal to the floorboard. When the pedal reaches the floorboard, close the bleed screw. After the screw is closed, have the assistant slowly release the pedal.

7. Wait 15 seconds and repeat Step 6 until the fluid entering the jar from the tubing is free of air bubbles.

8. Repeat this procedure at each of the remaining bleed screws. Top up the master cylinder

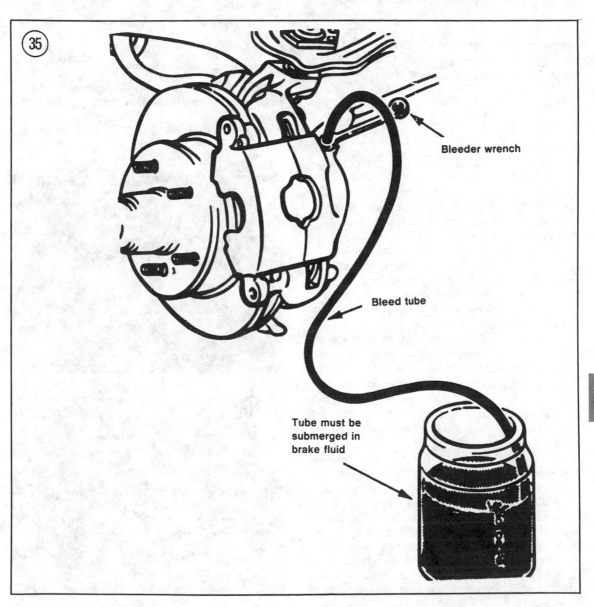

Bleeder wrench

Bleed tube

Tube must be submerged in brake fluid

12

frequently to prevent the reservoirs from running dry.

9. Road test the vehicle to make sure the brakes operate correctly. If the brake warning light remains on after the system has been bled and the braking action is satisfactory, center the combination valve as described in this chapter.

POWER BRAKE VACUUM BOOSTER

The vehicles covered in this manual equipped with power brakes use either a single or tandem diaphragm Bendix vacuum booster unit mounted to the engine compartment cowl. The booster unit uses intake manifold vacuum and atmospheric pressure to reduce braking effort. The power booster can be serviced if defective. Since the procedure is complex and requires the use of many special tools, it is best left to a dealer.

Testing

1. Check the brake system for signs of a hydraulic leak. Make sure the master cylinder reservoirs are filled to within 1/4 in. of the top of the side walls.
2. Start the engine and let it idle for about 2 minutes, then shut it off. Place the transmission in NEUTRAL and set the parking brake.
3. Depress the brake pedal several times to exhaust any vacuum remaining in the system.
4. When the vacuum is exhausted, depress and hold the pedal. Start the engine. If the pedal does not start to fall away under foot pressure (requiring less pressure to hold it in place), the vacuum booster unit is not working properly.
5. Disconnect the vacuum line at the booster check valve (**Figure 36**) and connect a vacuum gauge with a tee fitting. Start the engine and check the gauge reading at idle. If the gauge does not read at least 18-21 in. Hg (at sea level), tune the engine. See Chapter Three. If tuning the engine does not solve the problem, there is a vacuum leak in the system.
6. Shut the engine off and watch the vacuum gauge. If the reading drops by more than one inch in one minute, replace the check valve.
7. With the engine off, the vacuum gauge connected and the system holding vacuum as specified in Step 5, depress and hold the brake pedal for several seconds, then release it. If the vacuum reading drops to zero, replace the booster.
8. Run the engine for at least 10 minutes at fast idle. Shut the engine off and let it stand for 10 minutes. Depress the brake pedal with about 20 lb. of force. If the pedal feel is not the same as it was with the engine running, replace the vacuum unit.

Vacuum Hose, Check Valve and Charcoal Filter Inspection

1. Check the vacuum hose between the booster unit and the charcoal filter (**Figure 36**) for leaks or a loose connection. Replace or tighten as required.
2. Disconnect the hose and remove the check valve from the booster unit (**Figure 36**). It should be possible to blow air into the brake booster end of the valve, but not into the intake manifold end. If air flows both ways or neither way, replace the check valve.
3. Repeat Step 2 to test the charcoal filter. See **Figure 37**.

Booster Removal/Installation

1. With the engine stopped, depress the brake pedal to expel any vacuum remaining in the brake booster system.
2. Install a prop under the master cylinder for support.

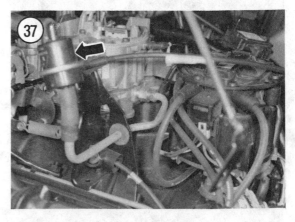

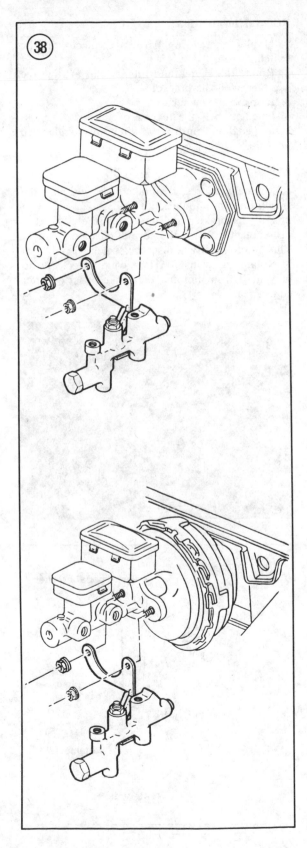

3. Loosen the clamp holding the charcoal filter vacuum line to the booster check valve. Disconnect the line at the check valve. See **Figure 36**. Remove the valve from the booster unit.

CAUTION
Move the master cylinder carefully in Step 4 to prevent bending or stressing the hydraulic lines.

4. Remove the nuts and lockwashers holding the master cylinder to the booster unit. Carefully pull the master cylinder and combination valve bracket from the booster studs and move them to one side to provide room for booster removal. Make sure the prop supports the master cylinder.

5. Working inside the passenger compartment, disconnect the booster pushrod from the brake pedal. Remove the nuts holding the booster unit to the cowl.

6. Remove the booster unit from the engine compartment.

7. Installation is the reverse of removal. Since the master cylinder lines are not disconnected during this procedure, it is not necessary to bleed the brake system. Start the engine and check brake operation. Road test the vehicle to make sure the brakes operate properly.

COMBINATION VALVE AND WARNING LIGHT SWITCH

The combination valve and warning light switch are combined into a single unit bracket-mounted to the cowl (non-power brakes) or vacuum booster (power brakes). See **Figure 38**.

If hydraulic pressure drops severely in either the front or rear brake system, the valve operates the switch which in turn activates the instrument panel warning light. The combination valve is not serviceable and must be replaced if any of its 3 functions do not work properly.

12

Centering

The combination valve must be centered whenever the brakes are bled. To do so, turn the ignition switch to the ACC or ON position, but do not start the engine. Depress the brake pedal firmly until the warning light goes out (if it was illuminated). Turn the ignition switch OFF. Check brake operation to make sure a firm pedal is obtained.

Electrical Circuit Testing

1. Squeeze the plastic locking ring on the electrical connector at the combination valve and pull the connector off. See **Figure 39**.
2. Connect the electrical connector to ground with a jumper lead.
3. Turn the ignition ON; the warning lamp should light. If the lamp does not light, check for a burned-out bulb or a short in the circuit wiring. If these are satisfactory, replace the combination valve.

Warning Light Switch Test

1. Connect a suitable length of hose to a rear brake bleed screw. Place the other end of the hose in a container partially filled with clean brake fluid.
2. Remove the master cylinder cover and diaphragm. Make sure both reservoirs are full to within 1/4 in. of the top. If not, top up as required with clean DOT 3 or DOT 4 brake fluid.
3. Turn the ignition ON. Open the bleed screw while an assistant applies moderate pressure to the pedal. The warning lamp on the instrument panel light should light.
4. Close the bleed screw. Have the assistant apply moderate-to-heavy pressure on the pedal. The instrument panel light should go out.
5. Repeat Steps 1-4 with a front brake bleed screw and look for the same results.
6. If the warning lamp does not perform as described during Step 3 and Step 4 and during Step 5, connect the switch terminal to ground with a jumper lead. If the lamp lights, the warning light switch in the combination valve is defective. Replace the combination valve.

Removal/Installation

Refer to **Figure 38** for this procedure.
1. Unplug the electrical connector at the combination valve (**Figure 39**).
2. Disconnect and plug the hydraulic lines at the combination valve. Use a flare nut wrench to avoid rounding off the corner of the fitting nuts.
3. Remove the nuts holding the valve to the master cylinder attaching studs. Remove the valve and bracket assembly from the studs.
4. Installation is the reverse of removal. Tighten the mounting nuts to specifications (**Table 1**). Bleed the brakes as described in this chapter.

STOPLIGHT SWITCH

The stoplight switch is mounted on the brake pedal arm with a tubular clip retainer (**Figure 40**).

Removal/Installation

1. Unplug the wiring harness connector at the switch.
2. Rotate the switch and tubular clip to align the clip tang with the bracket slot.
3. Remove the switch.
4. Installation is the reverse of removal. Depress brake pedal and push new switch into tubular clip until the switch shoulder bottoms out.

Adjustment

1. Manually depress the brake pedal and push the switch into the tubular clip.
2. Pull the brake pedal up against the pedal stop just enough to reach the normal released position. This automatically adjusts the switch.
3. Rotate the switch 1/2 turn counterclockwise to prevent it from holding the brake pedal on after adjustment.

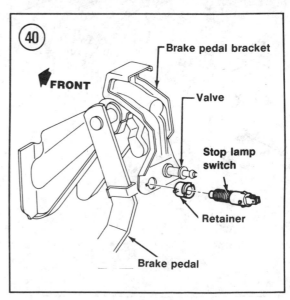

4. Check for free play between the pedal and switch by pulling the pedal upward. Electrical contact should be made when the pedal is depressed 0.53 in. (13.5 mm) from its fully released position.

5. If further adjustment is required, rotate or pull the switch in its clip until contact is made as specified in Step 4.

PARKING BRAKE

All models use a pedal-operated parking brake assembly. A cable connected to the parking brake pedal is routed to the equalizer. Separate cables connected to the equalizer are routed to each rear wheel. The parking brake cables on some vehicles are coated with a corrosion-resistant plastic. Such cables should be handled carefully to prevent damage to the plastic coating. If this coating is damaged, the corrosion resistance will be reduced and increased pedal effort will be required to activate the cables. Cable routing and retaining clip usage may differ according to model year but cables can be replaced using the following generalized procedures.

Parking Brake Pedal Removal/Installation

Refer to **Figure 41** for this procedure.
1. Make sure the parking brake is fully released.
2. Disconnect the negative battery cable.
3. Working underneath the instrument panel, disconnect the release rod.
4. Unplug the electrical connector from the parking brake switch.
5. Unbolt the parking brake assembly from the vehicle kick panel.
6. Disconnect the parking brake cable from the assembly. Remove the parking brake assembly.
7. Installation is the reverse of removal. Adjust the parking brake as described in this chapter.

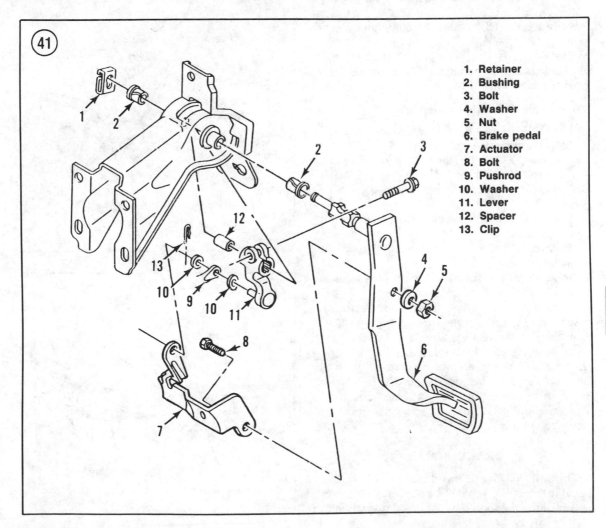

(41)

1. Retainer
2. Bushing
3. Bolt
4. Washer
5. Nut
6. Brake pedal
7. Actuator
8. Bolt
9. Pushrod
10. Washer
11. Lever
12. Spacer
13. Clip

Rear Cable Removal/Installation

The following steps can be used to replace either the right- or left-hand cable. Refer to **Figure 42** (right) or **Figure 43** (left) as required for this procedure.

1. Loosen the rear wheel lug nuts.
2. Securely block the front wheels. Raise the vehicle with a jack and place it on jackstands.
3. Mark the wheel/tire assembly relationship to the axle flange. Mark the brake drum relationship to the axle flange. Remove the wheel/tire assembly and brake drum.
4. Loosen the equalizer adjusting nut and disconnect the cable at the center retainer.
5. Squeeze the plastic retainer fingers and remove the retainer from the frame bracket.
6. Remove the rear brake shoes. Disconnect the cable from the secondary shoe.
7. Depress the cable retaining tangs at the backing plate. Remove the cable fitting from the backing plate.
8. Remove the cable from the frame attachment points.
9. Installation is the reverse of removal. Make sure the cable is properly routed and that the retainers hold the cable securely.

Front Cable Removal/Installation

Refer to **Figure 44** for this procedure.

1. Shift the transmission into NEUTRAL.
2. Securely block both rear wheels so the vehicle will not roll in either direction.
3. Raise the vehicle with a jack and place it on jackstands.
4. Loosen the equalizer nut. Disconnect the cable from the connector.
5. Compress the retainer tangs and loosen the cable at the frame.
6. Remove the jackstands and lower the vehicle to the ground.
7. Working in the passenger compartment, disconnect the cable at the parking brake pedal.
8. Compress the retainer tangs and withdraw the cable from the engine compartment.
9. Installation is the reverse of removal. It is advisable to tie a heavy cord to one end of the cable for use in guiding the new cable through the proper routing. Adjust the parking brake as described in this chapter.

BRAKE PEDAL

The pedal height and travel are fixed and cannot be adjusted. If the vehicle is equipped with power brakes, the pedal should be depressed several times

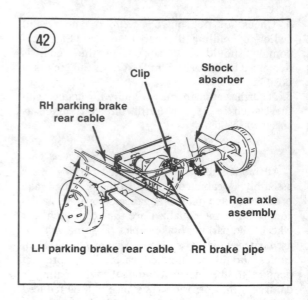
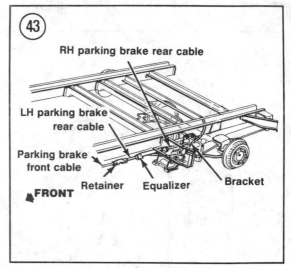
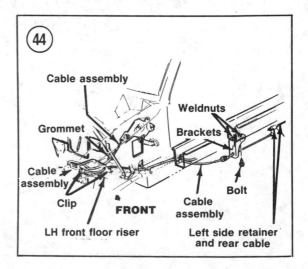

to exhaust any remaining vacuum before measuring pedal travel. If pedal travel exceeds 4 1/2 in. (114 mm) for non-power or 3.5 in. (89 mm) for power brakes, drive the vehicle backward and forward to activate the brake adjuster. If this does not bring pedal travel within specifications, bleed the brakes as described in this chapter. Adjust the parking brake as described in this chapter. Check for hydraulic fluid leaks and correct if found.

Inspect the front and rear brake linings and replace if excessively worn.

BRAKE HOSES AND TUBING

Figure 45 shows the front brake hose routing; **Figure 46** shows the rear brake hose routing. The condition of all flexible brake hoses and rigid tubing should be checked at least twice a year to

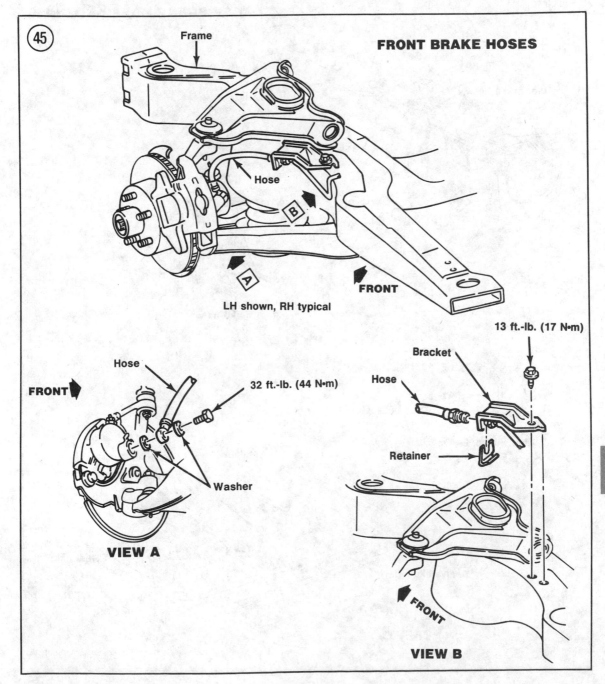

45 FRONT BRAKE HOSES

Frame

Hose

B

A

FRONT

LH shown, RH typical

Hose

FRONT

32 ft.-lb. (44 N•m)

Washer

VIEW A

13 ft.-lb. (17 N•m)

Bracket

Hose

Retainer

FRONT

VIEW B

12

make sure they are properly connected and are not leaking or deteriorated. Check hoses for leaks, blisters, cracking or chafing of the outer cover and road hazard damage.

Damaged or defective brake tubing should be replaced with double walled steel tubing. Do *not* use copper or aluminum tubing. These materials are affected by corrosion and fatigue cracks which can result in a dangerous brake failure. When replacing brake tubing, make sure to use a double flare connection; single flare connections will not withstand the required pressure. Replacement tubing should be installed with a minimum 0.75 in. clearance to all vibrating or moving components.

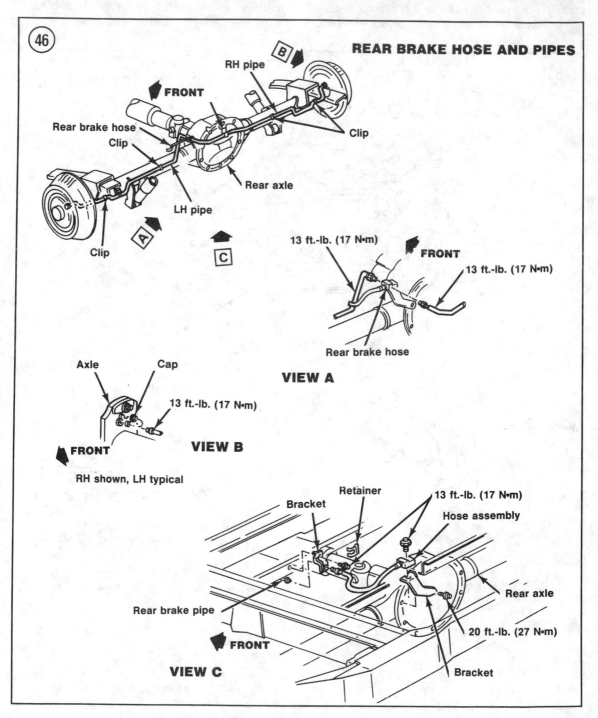

REAR BRAKE HOSE AND PIPES

46

RH pipe

FRONT

Rear brake hose
Clip

Clip

Rear axle

LH pipe

Clip

13 ft.-lb. (17 N•m)

FRONT

13 ft.-lb. (17 N•m)

Rear brake hose

VIEW A

Axle   Cap

13 ft.-lb. (17 N•m)

FRONT   **VIEW B**

RH shown, LH typical

Retainer

Bracket

13 ft.-lb. (17 N•m)

Hose assembly

Rear axle

Rear brake pipe

FRONT

20 ft.-lb. (27 N•m)

VIEW C   Bracket

Table 1 TIGHTENING TORQUES

Fastener	ft.-lb.	N•m
Brake pedal bolt	22-32	30-44
Brake tube fittings	13	17
Cable clip-to-frame bolt	9-12	11-16
Caliper		
Bleed screw	8-12	9-16
Inlet fitting	18-30	24-40
Mounting bolts	30-45	41-61
Combination valve nut	22-33	30-45
Master cylinder		
Attaching nuts	22-30	30-40
Hydraulic fittings	9-15	14-20
Power booster-to-cowl	22-33	30-45
Wheel cylinder screws	7-20	11-25
Wheel lug nuts	90	122

13

INDEX

13

13

NOTES